Ceremonies of the Sarum Missal

Ceremonies of the Sarum Missal

A Careful Conjecture

R. J. Urquhart

LONDON • NEW YORK • OXFORD • NEW DELHI • SYDNEY

T&T CLARK

Bloomsbury Publishing Plc

50 Bedford Square, London, WC1B 3DP, UK
1385 Broadway, New York, NY 10018, USA
29 Earlsfort Terrace, Dublin 2, Ireland

BLOOMSBURY, T&T CLARK and the T&T Clark logo are trademarks of
Bloomsbury Publishing Plc

First published in Great Britain 2021
This paperback edition published in 2022

Copyright © R. J. Urquhart, 2021

R. J. Urquhart has asserted his right under the Copyright, Designs and Patents Act, 1988,
to be identified as Author of this work.

Cover design: Charlotte James
Cover image © Artokoloro Quint Lox Limited / Alamy Stock Photo

All rights reserved. No part of this publication may be reproduced or
transmitted in any form or by any means, electronic or mechanical,
including photocopying, recording, or any information storage or retrieval
system, without prior permission in writing from the publishers.

Bloomsbury Publishing Plc does not have any control over, or responsibility for, any
third-party websites referred to or in this book. All internet addresses given in this
book were correct at the time of going to press. The author and publisher regret any
inconvenience caused if addresses have changed or sites have ceased to exist, but can
accept no responsibility for any such changes.

A catalogue record for this book is available from the British Library.

Library of Congress Cataloging-in-Publication Data
Names: Urquhart, R. J. (Richard), author.
Title: Ceremonies of the Sarum Missal : a careful conjecture / R.J. Urquhart.
Description: London ; New York : T&T Clark, 2020. |
Includes bibliographical references and index. |
Summary: "Richard Urquhart provides the first systematic attempt at describing the
ceremonial of the Sarum Mass in five hundred years. Using the sources available,
and tracing the Sarum rite and it's occasional use from the act of supremacy
through to modern times Urquhart has compiled a volume that offers the
best possible reconstruction and overview of these profoundly beautiful
rites from the liturgical treasury of the Church"– Provided by publisher.
Identifiers: LCCN 2020026891 (print) | LCCN 2020026892 (ebook) |
ISBN 9780567694263 (hb) | ISBN 9780567694270 (epdf) |
ISBN 9780567694294 (epub)
Subjects: LCSH: Catholic Church. Missal (Salisbury)
Classification: LCC BX5142 .U77 2020 (print) | LCC BX5142 (ebook) |
DDC 264/.020094231–dc23
LC record available at https://lccn.loc.gov/2020026891
LC ebook record available at https://lccn.loc.gov/2020026892

ISBN: HB: 978-0-5676-9426-3
PB: 978-0-5676-9667-0
ePDF: 978-0-5676-9427-0
ePUB: 978-0-5676-9429-4

Typeset by Newgen KnowledgeWorks Pvt. Ltd., Chennai, India

To find out more about our authors and books visit www.bloomsbury.com
and sign up for our newsletters.

Nihil obstat:
    R. D. Andreas Cole, *Censor deputatus*

Imprimatur:
    ✠Rmus. D. Patricius McKinney, *Ep. Nottingham.*

Nottingham, die 14 Januarii 2019

Contents

Preface	xiii
Note on authorities	xxi
List of abbreviations	xxiv
Key to the symbols used in the figures	xxvi

Book I The treasurer's purview		1
1	The church	3
2	Books, vessels and instruments	9
	§1. Books	9
	§2. Vessels	10
	§3. Instruments	12
3	The vestments	17
4	The colour of the vestments	21
Book II Liturgical gesture		31
5	Certain common ritual actions	33
	§1. Deportment and positions of the hands	33
	§2. Crossings	34
	§3. The different kinds of obeisance	34
	§4. Incensing	36
Book III Low Mass		39
6	Preparation	41
7	To the Gospel	45
8	From the Gospel to the preface	49
	§1. The Gospel to the creed	49
	§2. The offering of the sacrifice	50

	§3. The people's offertory	51
	§4. The bidding of the bedes and the sermon	52
	§5. The lavatory to the *Sanctus*	52
9	The Canon to the Communion	57
	§1. The first part of the Canon	57
	§2. The Sacring	58
	§3. The second part of the Canon	60
	§4. The Fraction and the priest's Communion	63
10	From the ablutions to the end of Mass	69
11	Administration of Holy Communion	75
12	The duties of the clerk at Low Mass	79

Book IV	High Mass	85
13	Preparation	87
14	From the entrance to the collects	91
15	From the collects to the sequence	99
16	The making of the chalice	103
17	From the Gospel to the offertory	107
18	From the offertory to the preface	117
	§1. The offering of the sacrifice	117
	§2. The first part of the incensations	118
	§3. The people's oblation, the bidding of the bedes and the sermon	123
	§4. The lavatory	124
	§5. The second part of the incensations	125
	§6. The conclusion of the offertory and the preface	126
19	The Canon to the Communion	129
	§1. The Canon	129
	§2. The Fraction and the *Preces in prostratione*	132
	§3. The Pax	133
20	From the ablutions to the end of Mass	137

21	The solemn administration of Holy Communion	141
22	The choir at High Mass	145
	§1. Preliminary notions	145
	§2. General directions for the deportment of the choir	146
	§3. The choir at Mass	147
	§4. Cantors	150
	§5. The ruling of the choir	152

Book V Special forms of Mass — 157

23	Mass for the dead	159
24	Weddings and the nuptial Mass	163
	§1. Preliminary notions and remote preparations	163
	§2. Proximate preparations	163
	§3. The sacrament of Matrimony	164
	§4. The nuptial Mass	167
25	Missa cantata	171
	§1. The solemn form	171
	§2. The simple form	174
	§3. Sung Mass with one or more ordained assistants	175

Book VI Processions and blessings — 185

26	Processions	187
	§1. The *Asperges* and the Sunday procession	187
	§2. Festal processions	191
	§3. The reception of major personages	192
27	The blessing of bread on Sundays	193

Book VII The ritual year — 195

28	Advent and Christmas	197
	§1. The season of Advent	197
	§2. The Ember Days	197
	§3. Christmas and Epiphany	198

29	Candlemas	201
	§1. Preparations	201
	§2. The blessing and distribution of candles	202
	§3. The procession and the Mass	203
	§4. The simple form of the rite	205
30	Septuagesima and Lent	207
	§1. Veils	207
	§2. The ferial procession	208
	§3. Ritual peculiarities	208
31	Ash Wednesday	211
32	Palm Sunday	215
	§1. Preparations	215
	§2. The blessing and distribution of the palms	216
	§3. The processions	217
	§4. The Mass	222
	§5. The simple form of the rite	224
33	Maundy Thursday	225
	§1. Mass and Vespers	225
	§2. The washing of the altars	228
34	Good Friday	231
	§1. Preparations	231
	§2. The lessons and the solemn collects	233
	§3. The worship of the Cross	234
	§4. Mass of the Presanctified and Vespers	237
	§5. The deposition in the Sepulchre	240
	§6. The simple form of the rite	242
35	Holy Saturday	245
	§1. Preparations	245
	§2. The new fire and the Paschal Candle	248
	§3. The lessons	252
	§4. The litanies and the blessing of the font with baptism	252
	§5. Mass with Vespers	256
	§6. The simple form of the rite	258

36	Eastertide		259
	§1.	The season of Easter	259
	§2.	Easter Day	260
	§3.	The Litanies	262
	§4.	Ascension	265
	§5.	Whitsun	266
37	Summer and Autumn		269
	§1.	Corpus Christi	269
	§2.	The weeks after Trinity	270
	§3.	All Souls	270

Appendix I: The laity in church	273
Appendix II: Form of bidding of the bedes	275
Appendix III: Ordo Missae with simple rubrics	277
Bibliokaiallography	291
Index	297

Preface

There is nothing that can mend completely the wilful destruction of our English Catholic rites in the sixteenth century. It is true that the work of the late Dr. Rock and of other, mostly Anglican, ecclesiologists in the nineteenth and twentieth centuries has rediscovered many details of those rites, but some of those authors wrote as antiquarians, and others sought but to dress the Protestant services of the Book of Common Prayer in Sarum attire. Even A. H. Pearson's *The Sarum Missal Done into English* did not go much beyond a compilation of rubrics. A systematic attempt at describing the ceremonial of the Sarum Mass, matching and surpassing the detail of the Customary, has not appeared in five hundred years, and this fact alone is sufficient to justify the existence of this book.

Two recent developments have turned such an endeavour from a merely speculative exercise into one which has the potential to acquire a degree of spiritual and pastoral relevance unsuspected since the passing of pre-Reformation English Catholicism.

Pope Benedict XVI's apostolic constitution, *Anglicanorum Coetibus*, has reopened the question of the catholicity of part of the Anglican patrimony. On one level, it is to be regretted that, of those Anglo-Catholics now reconciled, a dominant party is made up of those who favour the Roman books, whether Pian or Pauline, and that the inheritors of the older, Sarum-inspired, ecclesiologists, more purely Anglican by patrimony, have brought little influence with them. The new liturgical books of the Ordinariates make far more provision for 'Roman' and 'Prayer Book' elements than for those inherited or derived from Mary's Dowry. Anglicans have never lost interest in the forms of the old religion, from the internecine battles of the Elizabethan church, to the supposed popery of the Laudian interventions and through the controversy of the Non-Jurors' usagers to the Tractarians, the Ritualists and lastly the Anglo-Catholics of the twentieth century. In however debased a form, elements of the Sarum liturgy have survived in the Church of England, either mostly intact in the Book of Common Prayer or after piecemeal restoration, to our own day and have now been restored to the Catholic Church in the rites of the Anglican Ordinariates. Our fathers' worship was indeed Roman, more purely so than that of our immediate neighbours, but their Latin acquired a distinct and mellow English accent, now Anglo-Saxon and then Anglo-Norman, until with the turning of the years organically developed uses came into being. Of these, none was more resplendent or widespread than that of the church of Sarum. This liturgy, thoroughly Catholic in sentiment, thoroughly Roman in origin and thoroughly English in accent, should be seen at least as an extraordinary form of the Anglican rite, enriching the ceremonial, and eventually perhaps the texts themselves, of the Ordinariates' worship.

The same Pope's apostolic letter, *Summorum Pontificum*,[1] proposes that what was sacred for earlier generations remains sacred for us also.[2] This teaching seems to welcome all legitimate forms of worship, and not only the pre-conciliar Roman rite, back into the life of the Church. The undoubtedly increased (if still small) interest in Sarum's spirituality seems to call for a more profound and detailed study of the rite's nuts and bolts if the faithful are to benefit from this component of the Church's treasury of devotion.

The relevance of these two documents for a revival of Sarum Use as a living liturgy is unavoidably tied up with the rite's canonical status in the modern Church. This author can claim for himself neither canonical expertise nor authority of any kind. In the current uncertainty one does not have to be a probabiliorist to see that it would be a rash priest who attempted to celebrate the rite without a regular *celebret* from a legitimate superior. Nevertheless, the reader's indulgence is craved for the presentation of the following speculative paragraphs.

The legitimacy of the Use of Sarum within the majority of the metropolitical province of Canterbury until 1534 is beyond doubt. From 1534 to 1549, during the Anglican schism, most of those celebrating according to the Sarum books were at least in material, if not indeed in formal, schism. Schismatic priests celebrate the sacraments validly but illicitly. Most particular celebrations during those years, therefore, will have been illicit, but the rite itself lost none of its canonical legitimacy. In 1549, the rite was suppressed effectively by an authority that lacked the canonical competence to do so. Aschismatic priests who continued to use the Sarum books, whether at home or abroad, did so legitimately. The rite was restored upon the accession of Queen Mary and, from 1554, was undoubtedly used legitimately by the English clergy, who had been reconciled to the Church by the Cardinal Legate, Reginald Pole. In 1559, Parliament, again in canonical terms acting *ultra vires*, suppressed the rite anew, though its use was continued by the Catholic clergy, licitly (if illegally) at home and with no restrictions abroad.

In 1570, by the bull *Quo primum tempore*, a new Roman Missal was promulgated for the entire Latin Church which, however, contained important exemptions. Of these, the most relevant to our purpose was that which forbade the use of the new Missal to those churches which enjoyed customary use of at least two hundred years[3] without the fulfilment of certain conditions, all of which had to be met for celebrations according to the new Missal to be permitted.[4] These were: (1) that they should like the new Missal more than their traditional Missal (*magis placeret*); (2) that the church's

---

[1] *Acta Apostolicae Sedis*, Vol. XCIX, N.9, pages 777–81.

[2] 'Ciò che per le generazioni anteriori era sacro, anche per noi resta sacro e grande, e non può essere improvvisamente del tutto proibito o, addirittura, giudicato dannoso' (*Acta Apostolicae Sedis*, Vol. XCIX, N.9, page 798).

Benedict XVI's teaching is consonant with that of the most solemn expression of the Church's recent magisterium. The Fathers of the Second Vatican Council (1962–5) also express their solicitude for the preservation and fostering of all legitimately recognized rites, of which Sarum is undoubtedly one: *Traditioni denique fideliter obsequens, Sacrosanctum Concilium declarat Sanctam Matrem Ecclesiam omnes ritus legitime agnitos aequo iure atque honore habere* (Constitution 'Sacrosanctum Concilium', n. 4 in *Concilio Vaticano II*).

[3] Pope Gregory IX recognized the existence and influence of *instituta* of Sarum church in 1228 (Missal.v, referring to Wilkins I.562).

[4] The relevant paragraph is the following:

bishop or prelate should consent to the adoption of the new Missal; and (3) that the church's chapter should consent unanimously (*capitulique universi consensu*) to celebrations according to the new Missal. There is no mechanism in the bull to permit the suppression of the customary rite, only to permit celebrations according to the new Missal in those churches and by those clergy. Indeed, the bull explicitly states that it does not take away the traditional custom of celebrating (*nequaquam auferimus*). In other words, Pius V forbids absolutely the suppression of the traditional rites but permits (if and only if certain conditions are met) celebrations according to the new rite in addition to the old. *Quo primum tempore*, therefore, far from suppressing Sarum Use, preserved its canonical legitimacy intact and defended it against Romanizing reformers.

In fact, since Sarum Use is explicitly the use of the cathedral and diocese of Sarum (*Ecclesiae Sarum*), only the Bishop of Salisbury and the unanimous decision of the chapter of Salisbury acting together could permit the licit use of the new Roman Missal in that diocese, and even they could not canonically suppress the rite. It is also the case that they did not in fact suppress the rite, since in 1559,[5] after they subscribed the Act of Supremacy, they lost all legitimate canonical jurisdiction. The same can be said for the bishops and chapters of those other cathedrals in the province of Canterbury whose uses (Sarum or otherwise) had a history of two hundred years or more. In canonical terms, therefore, Sarum Use should remain the default rite for most of the old province of Canterbury.

Events can overtake the precautions of even the canniest canonist, however, and much liturgical chaos followed in the wake of the Elizabethan persecution. The English students at Douay were taught the new rite from 1576[6] and from then on the use of the Sarum books must have declined. Could, therefore, Sarum be dead, not through canonical suppression but through disuser, or has Sarum survived to our own day?

> Ut autem a sacrosancta Romana Ecclesia, ceterarum ecclesiarum matre et magistra, tradita ubique amplectantur omnes et observent, ne in posterum perpetuis futuris temporibus in omnibus Christiani orbis Provinciarum Patriarchalibus, Cathedralibus, Collegiatis et Parochialibus, saecularibus, et quorumvis Ordinum, monasteriorum, tam virorum, quam mulierum, etiam militiarum regularibus, ac sine cura Ecclesiis vel Capellis, in quibus Missa conventualis alta voce cum Choro, aut demissa, celebrari juxta Romanae Ecclesiae ritum consuevit vel debet alias quam juxta Missalis a nobis editi formulam decantetur, aut recitetur, etiamsi eaedem Ecclesiae quovis modo exemptae, Apostolicae Sedis indulto, consuetudine, privilegio, etiam juramento, confirmatione Apostolica, vel aliis quibusvis facultatibus munitae sint; nisi ab ipsa prima institutione a Sede Apostolica adprobata, vel consuetudine, quae, vel ipsa institutio super ducentos annos Missarum celebrandarum in eisdem Ecclesiis assidue observata sit: a quibus, ut praefatam celebrandi constitutionem vel consuetudinem nequaquam auferimus; sic si Missale hoc, quod nunc in lucem edi curavimus, iisdem magis placeret, de Episcopi, vel Praelati, Capitulique universi consensu, ut quibusvis non obstantibus, juxta illud Missas celebrare possint, permittimus; ex aliis vero omnibus Ecclesiis praefatis eorumdem Missalium usum tollendo, illaque penitus et omnino rejiciendo, ac huic Missali nostro nuper edito, nihil unquam addendum, detrahendum, aut immutandum esse decernendo, sub indignationis nostrae poena, hac nostra perpetuo valitura constitutione statuimus et ordinamus.

[5] The see had fallen vacant in 1557, with the death of John Capon. His nominated successor, Francis Mallet, was prevented by the death of Queen Mary from receiving the spiritualities of the see.
[6] Fortescue, *The Mass*, page 202.

A look at a list of dates will shew that Sarum, though undoubtedly moribund, has survived in at least occasional use as a Most Extraordinary Form of the Roman rite as used in England from the sixteenth century to the present, and that it has retained a place in the collective spirituality of English Catholicism.

1556	Last edition of the complete Sarum Manual for ordinary pastoral use[7]
1557	Last complete editions of the Sarum Missal[8] and Breviary[9]
1558	Last edition of the Sarum Processional[10]
1576	Last teaching of the Sarum Mass at Douay[11]
1604	A Sarum manual for the mission with a new title, *Sacra Institvtio Baptizandi, Matrimonium celebrandi, Infirmos ungendi, mortuos sepeliendi ac alii nonnulli ritus ecclesiastici juxta usum insignis Ecclesiae Sarisburiensis*, printed at Douay[12]
1610–32	Three editions of a *Manuale Sacerdotum … iuxta usum insignis Ecclesiae Sarisbiriensis*, a smaller version of the *Sacra Institutio* for the mission, printed at Douay[13]
1623 and 1626	*Missale Parvum pro Sacerdotibus in Anglia, Scotia, et Ibernia itinerantibus* published at St. Omer or Antwerp for the Jesuits (who follow the Roman rite), containing in an appendix (*Ordo etiam Baptizandi, aliaque Sacramenta ministrandi, et Officia quaedam Ecclesiastica rite peragenda, Ex Pontificali, et Rituali Romano, jussu Pauli PP. Quinti, extractum*) the marriage service with the trothplighting '*Ex Manual. Sarum*'[14]
1686	*Ordo Baptizandi … pro Anglia, Hibernia et Scotia*, printed in London by Henry Hills, containing Sarum elements[15]
1745	Recusants in Derbyshire alleged to be accustomed to a modified form of Sarum and surprised at French ritual[16]
1839	Ambrose Phillipps de Lisle urges the restoration of the Sarum rite and claims that the English bishops have the power to bring this about; *Veni Creator* sung 'in the old Salisbury Chant' at Mrs. Pugin's reception into the Church[17]

---

[7] M.viii.
[8] Dickinson, page lxxii.
[9] B III.li.
[10] *Processions*.330.
[11] Fortescue, *The Mass*, page 202.
[12] *Processions*.336.
[13] *Processions*.337; M.xxiv; Rock II.382.
[14] *Processions*.338; Morison, page 141.
[15] Reckoned by *Processions*.337 but not by Morison, page 141, among the Sarum books.
[16] Cox, page 311.
[17] Morison, page 144.

1842	Charles Seager's *Portiforii seu breviarii Sarisburiensis fasciculus primus*, the first Sarum Breviary for devotional use since 1557, published in London under the influence of Phillipps de Lisle and Dr. Rock[18]
1849	Dr. Daniel Rock publishes *Church of Our Fathers* hoping for and justifying restoration of Sarum Use[19]
1850–2009	The Archbishops of Westminster are enthroned using the form from Archbishop Chichele's pontifical with additional responds taken from the Sarum Processional[20]
1903	According to a persistent rumour, Sarum Use considered (but ultimately rejected) for ordinary public worship in the new Westminster Cathedral[21]
(ca. 1950)	The author recollects his late father telling him that he had known a Catholic priest who had permission from his bishop to celebrate according to Sarum Use *januis clausis*
1996–7	Annual Sarum Masses celebrated for the Oxford University Catholics[22]
2000	Mario Conti, bishop of Aberdeen, celebrated according to Sarum Use in the chapel of King's College, Aberdeen[23]
2009	Archbishop Nichols enthroned at Westminster 'according to the ancient Catholic rite used in similar circumstances for the Reception and Installation of the Archbishops of Canterbury prior to the Reformation ... adapted from the ancient rite taken from a Pontifical used at Canterbury in the time of Archbishop Chichele'[24]

The list is almost certainly incomplete. It may well omit documented instances of use. Other, textually undocumented, celebrations may safely be presumed to have taken place. It is also worth remembering that a book may continue in use for quite some time after its printing. Looking at this succession of dates and movements, we can see that, though Sarum is perhaps agonizing, it has never sunk to a state below consciousness: Sarum Use has given signs of life, however faint, in every generation.

To this list, which deals exclusively with Catholic publications and celebrations, or those carried out under Catholic influence, should be added consideration of the Anglicans' adoption, adaptation and reconstruction of Sarum forms, which are now to be considered part of the Anglican patrimony happily integrated into the Catholic Church's life.

---

[18] Morison, page 145.
[19] Rock I.283 and IV.294–7.
[20] Anon, 'An Archbishop's Enthronement', pages 66–7; Sweeney, pages 1032–3 (dating the practice to the 1902 enthronement only); *Installation of the Most Reverend Vincent Gerard Nichols*, page 3 (dating the practice to 1850 and the appointment of Cardinal Wiseman).
[21] Reid, page 119.
[22] Reid, page 118.
[23] Reid, page 118.
[24] *Installation of the Most Reverend Vincent Gerard Nichols*, page 3.

There can be no doubt that the Sarum Mass has not been celebrated habitually since the eighteenth century at least, but important events in the life of the faithful and the Church (weddings and the enthronements of archbishops, for instance) have been celebrated in Sarum Use (more or less) continually since the Elizabethan schism. The historical argument of complete disuser, in other words, is not strong enough to counter the postulated theoretical legitimacy of the rite in the canonical sphere.

An analogous case may be presented in that of the rite of Braga,[25] resuscitated from a moribund state (if not quite as bad as Sarum's) in the twentieth century, and there seems no reason why such a revival should not be possible for Sarum now. Canonically (for the reasons put forth above and, especially, after *Summorum Pontificum*), there seems to be no obstacle. Indeed, by analogy with the rites of the religious orders, it would be reasonable to interpret the Holy See's instruction on the application of *Summorum Pontificum* (*Universae Ecclesiae*) as permitting celebrations according to the Sarum books.[26] The modern student is reminded of the Roman Missal of 1970, in which the older form of the rite was not canonically suppressed, the difference being that Pius V explicitly protected the older rites whereas Paul VI merely neglected to suppress the Pian liturgy.[27]

Against this speculative argument, however, should be considered that the Roman Congregation for Divine Worship, in an administrative intervention that has not yet been tested in a canonical forum, has disallowed Sarum celebrations.[28] Neither the pious author nor the pious reader would wish to see this work used to put on celebrations that contradicted the mind of the Church, and official clarification of the rite's canonical status should be awaited.

The purpose of this work, then, is twofold. First, it is designed to remove many of the doubts that would assail the ceremonialist in the sanctuary were permission for the rite's revival to be obtained. Such restored clarity might itself strengthen the case for authorization and bring to fruition the hopes of those who would like to see in the cathedrals and parishes of the British Isles the celebration of the Mass according to the most traditional rite of the Catholic Church in the majority of England, Scotland and Ireland. Second, it is hortatory. Much is unknown about the ceremonial details of the Use of Sarum, and much more is unknown by the author, a rural schoolmaster with limited access to books and even more limited access to the society of true specialists. Nevertheless, even if he is to be numbered among those new writers who *semper aut*

---

[25] Reid, pages 118–19.
[26] *Acta Apostolicae Sedis*, Vol. CIII, N.6, pages 413–20.
[27] As Benedict XVI puts it in his letter accompanying the *motu proprio Summorum Pontificum*:

> Quanto all'uso del Messale del 1962, come *forma extraordinaria* della Liturgia della Messa, vorrei attirare l'attenzione sul fatto che questo Messale non fu mai giuridicamente abrogato e, di conseguenza, in linea di principio, restò sempre permesso. Al momento dell'introduzione del nuovo Messale, non è sembrato necessario di emanare norme proprie per l'uso possibile del Messale anteriore. Probabilmente si è supposto che si sarebbe trattato di pochi casi singoli che si sarebbero risolti, caso per caso, sul posto. (*Acta Apostolicae Sedis*, Vol. XCIX, N.9, page 795)

> In the case of the Sarum liturgy nowadays the words 'pochi casi singoli' are certainly applicable, but it would appear that it remains no less permitted in principle than the Roman books of 1962.

[28] Reid, page 118.

in rebus certius aliquid adlaturos se aut scribendi arte rudem vetustatem superaturos credunt,[29] he hopes earnestly that the publication of his work will encourage others to test his theories and correct his errors, so furthering the cause of the rite's revival. Indeed, if like a schoolboy mathematician he has shewn his workings in what may appear to be notes of excessive prolixity, he has done so precisely to enable his readers to criticize his work all the better. Insofar as he has brought together details from a plurality of sources and made inferences from the same in order to clarify points of ceremonial that have been obscure heretofore, he hopes that he has made some contribution, original yet free from fancy, to advancing knowledge in the field.

At the same time, it is not the author's purpose to produce a work of textual criticism or to reconstruct an imaginary 'authentic' liturgy through a collation of editions, disregarding the wide differences in practice between different churches. Nor is it the author's purpose to reconstruct exactly the daily round of prayer in the choir of Sarum, with the many features peculiar to the cathedral itself.[30] Accordingly, pontifical ceremonies are omitted, as is much of the intricate choral ceremonial.

It should go without saying that the author has not inherited the authority of the Chapter of Sarum in determining ceremonial or the interpretation of rubrics. His explanations and hypotheses are entirely devoid of any official standing. He has not produced an approved ceremonial manual such as those of Martinucci or Fortescue, and the book should be seen more as an essay or an exploration of Sarum ceremonial than a prescriptive textbook.

Nevertheless, the desired clarity concerning the ceremonial is obtained most conveniently by adopting the external form of those manuals whose presence in churches of the Roman rite was common until only yesterday, supplementing the often sparse rubrics of the Sarum books with ceremonial directions taken, after due examination, from other mediæval and early modern rites. At the same time, the work is not exhaustive. Knowledge of the Roman rite is presumed, and so much of the *ars celebrandi* recommended by the manualists is omitted. To do otherwise would have led more to creative invention of pseudo-Sarum ceremonies than to an exploration of genuine ritual. The result gives rather more explicit suggestions than would have been expected by a mediæval reader, accustomed to exact but less prescriptive rubrical norms and acting within the living tradition. Occasionally, where the rubrics are especially unclear, as in the cases of the incensations, the Pax and the ablutions, the title's 'A Careful Conjecture' is thoroughly appropriate. The notes aim to provide the student with some justification for the directions proposed. Thus, the work seeks to serve readers of two distinct, but, we may hope, overlapping, kinds: the *peritus* wishing to establish clear knowledge of the ceremonial when preparing a case for the rite's authorization, and the student in search of historical sources for the liturgy. It should be possible for the former to disregard the notes without missing information of value to him.

---

[29] Cf. Livy's *Praefatio*.
[30] For the distinction between general and ceremonial rubrics, these being those that obliged the choir of Sarum alone, see *Defensorium Directorii* [1].

Schoolmen will wish to know the efficient causes of the work. The remote cause is the writer's father, whose old notes the author first started studying early in his second decade and from whom he learnt an interest in mediæval liturgy. Without him, this study would never have been begun. The mediate cause are the many hours spent reading up on liturgy over the four years of a completely unrelated undergraduate course at the University of St. Andrews, whose libraries provided the author with much undiluted σχολή. The earliest draft of this work first took amorphous shape then. The proximate cause is Mr. Neil Mackenzie, author of *The Medieval Boy Bishops*, who, when the reinterment of Richard III was first mooted, asked for guidance with the celebration of a Requiem Mass according to Sarum Use, the rite followed in the late King's college at Fotheringhay. The author's reply that he had a few notes but that they would need to be written up properly has led directly to the work that the reader holds in his hands.

Late in the process of writing this book, it became possible for the author to acquire access to the Cambridge University Library. To that university and its librarians the author extends his gratitude.

Oakham Id. Feb. 2020

Note on authorities

The principal authority is the *Missale Sarum*, published by F. H. Dickinson in 1861–83. At present it may be considered the nearest thing to an *editio typica* that the Use of Sarum possesses. This represents the sixteenth-century rite and follows the Paris edition of 1526 while recording many rubrical variants of late books, both missals and graduals. Manuscript versions of the Missal are sometimes referred to, especially those edited by J. Wickham Legg in his *Sarum Missal* and dated by him to 1150–1325: the Crawford Missal (C), the Bologna Missal (B) and the Arsenal Missal (A). These, being earlier and sometimes contaminated by external influence, are used cautiously. Occasional appeal is made to W. H. Frere's *Graduale Sarisburiense*.[1] W. Maskell's *The Ancient Liturgy of the Church of England* has also been used sparingly. The incomplete and sometimes confusing instructions of the Missal are supplemented by the *Manuale* edited by A. J. Collins in 1960, which follows the edition of 1543 but also considers variant readings. For the processions, the *Processionale* edited by W. G. Henderson in 1882 and following the edition of 1508 collated with later variants is the primary authority, supplemented by W. H. Frere's *Use of Sarum II*.

Other than the liturgical books themselves, the chief guide to ceremonial followed is the Customary edited by W. H. Frere in *Use of Sarum I*.[2] This, a conflation of six manuscripts, follows for the most part a text of the late fourteenth century but includes details taken from four fifteenth-century manuscripts. Frere's Consuetudinary, presented in the same volume, is based on an early thirteenth-century text that records the liturgy of Sarum in the somewhat fluid period that encompasses the last days at Old Sarum and the early days of the new cathedral, probably before its construction and furnishing were complete, and serves to corroborate or elaborate upon details that are unclear in the Customary. Little use has been made of the customary found in Jones, which is no later than the Consuetudinary and may well reflect twelfth-century aspects of the rite.[3]

Other Sarum authorities have been consulted and are mentioned in the notes, most relevantly the miscellaneous collection of documents relating to Salisbury cathedral published by Chr. Wordsworth in *Salisbury Processions and Ceremonies* and Dr. D. Rock's monumental *The Church of our Fathers*, edited by G. W. Hart and W. H. Frere in 1905, the notes of which are a mine of authoritative information. Not to be despised are the writings of Clement Maydeston as edited by the same Chr. Wordsworth.

---

[1] For a brief and lucid review of these modern editions of the Missal and the Gradual, see Pfaff, pages 357–8.
[2] Frere's New Ordinal, given in *Use of Sarum II*, for the most part reproduces the rubrics of the Missal.
[3] For the reliability of this edition, see Lincoln II.868.

Whether an expert, a deluded obsessive or a charlatan, Clement Maydeston is our greatest pre-Reformation authority beyond the Sarum books themselves.

When the Sarum sources fail us, recourse has been had to authorities from other rites and uses. The uses of Lincoln,[4] Wells[5] and Hereford[6] have been consulted as representative of other mediæval English uses. For all its grandeur, that of Exeter, and its companion of Ottery St. Mary, have been avoided as much as possible, since they owe much to the industry of John Grandisson, who was much under the influence of the Roman rite as represented by the celebrations at the papal court of Avignon and was too active a mover in the prescription of rites to be regarded safely as a faithful recorder of inherited traditions. The *Cérémonial Romain-Lyonnais* of 1897, representing as it does a restored survival of an older form of the Roman rite, has been used, as have the *Ordines Romani* and the writings of John of Avranches. Some Roman and other Latin sources, mostly pre-Pian, have also been consulted, especially John Burckard's 1502 *Ordo Missae*.[7] These have been supplemented by the writings of more modern ceremonialists, especially A. H. T. K. Fortescue's *The Ceremonies of the Roman Rite Described*.

The Western religious orders have preserved not a few ceremonial details that were once common in the mediæval period, and their liturgies have also been consulted to supplement deficiencies in the Sarum authorities. Of these religious uses, the principal authorities followed are Dominican, on account of the wealth of material available, of the Preachers' care in regulating their liturgy from their early days and of the reputed similarity between the Dominican and Sarum rites, which developed in the same period. Two principal Dominican sources are used. The first is J. W. Legg's description of a Dominican High Mass from 1260 to 1275.[8] A modern authoritative work, *Caeremoniale juxta ritum S. Ordinis Praedicatorum* (1869), provides a view of the rite as it developed after the Reformation. Being heir to the mediæval ceremonialists, it has been a useful aid to the inevitable guesswork that a reconstruction of an ill-documented use such as that of Sarum entails.

Three other religious rites have been consulted, if in a lesser degree. That of the Præmonstratensians is represented principally by two works. The first is Pl. F. Lefèvre's *L'Ordinaire de Prémontré d'après des manuscrits du XIIe et du XIIIe siècle*, an edition of the late-twelfth-century Præmonstratensian Ordinary. This reflects the ritual of the Norbertines at an early period but can be used cautiously as a clue to understanding the origin and development of parts of the Sarum ritual. The *Ordinarius* of 1739, although reflecting the radical revision of the rite introduced at the general chapter of 1738, preserves some earlier ceremonies and so may be used with caution. The Cistercians'

---

[4] Chr. Wordsworth, *Lincoln Cathedral Statutes*, particularly the consuetudinary of ca. 1260 (I.364–96).
[5] H. E. Reynolds, *Wells Cathedral*. This customary is closely based on thirteenth-century practice at Sarum and sometimes gives further detail which may represent common practice and not merely ritual specific to Wells.
[6] W. G. Henderson, *Missale Ecclesiae Herfordensis*, a somewhat idiosyncratic edition.
[7] *Tracts*.119–78.
[8] *Tracts*.73–96, an edition of the British Museum's manuscript of Humbert's description. Inspection of an unpaginated Dominican missal of 1586, which reflects the decrees of the general chapter of 1551 but necessarily predates the 'Tridentine' reform of 1603 and therefore may be taken as representing the late mediæval rite, shews that it agrees closely with Humbert's text.

Liber Usuum of 1643 has also come in handy for understanding ceremonies that have dropped out of the modern Roman rite. B. Zimmerman's edition of a fourteenth-century Carmelite Ordinary which preserves the mediæval form of the rite and so is on occasion a better guide than the post-mediæval *Caeremoniale* of the Dominicans, supplemented by a rather unclear missal of 1621 and a film of a Carmelite High Mass celebrated in 1960, has also been helpful.

Altogether different is the tenor of Thomas Becon's *The Displaying of the Popish Masse*, a vituperative exhortation to abandon Catholic forms. It includes several ceremonial details, but these are presented often obliquely and described from memory after a decade in which the author had not offered the sacrifice that he condemns. Moreover, some of the ceremonies appear not to be of pure Sarum character. For these reasons, the work is to be read critically. Some of the ceremonies described have been adopted here, while others have not.

Also to be treated with reservation are the writings of the Anglican ecclesiologists of the nineteenth and early twentieth centuries, who, although Protestant in most of their cultural assumptions, have done much to further the understanding of the Sarum rite. Many of them sought to accommodate the accidentals of the rite to the requirements of the Anglican Book of Common Prayer, whether actual or imagined. Nevertheless, as pointers to other, more genuine authorities, their writings are often invaluable. The general bibliography owes much to these men.

For the many other sources, old and modern, consulted, see the general bibliography.

List of abbreviations

Apart from the abbreviations and symbols below, in the notes most works are cited under the author's name only (with page number) if this provides sufficient reference to the general bibliography. A short title also is sometimes included.

Acta OP	*Acta Capitulorum Generalium Ordinis Praedicatorum* (ed. B. M. Reichert). The numbers refer to volume and page.
B	*Breviarium Sarum* (edd. Procter and Wordsworth). The numbers refer to volume and column.
C	Frere, W. H. *Use of Sarum I* (*Customary*). The numbers refer to the chapters and sections used by Frere, substituting Arabic for Frere's Roman numerals.
CCC	The Corpus Christi customary, quoted as a footnote to C 47.
Col	*Missale Sarum* (ed. Dickinson). The numbers refer to columns.
Cons	Frere, W. H. *Use of Sarum I* (*Consuetudinary*). The numbers refer to the chapters and sections used by Frere, substituting Arabic for Frere's Roman numerals.
Crede Michi	Maydeston, C. *Crede Michi* (ed. Chr. Wordsworth in *The Tracts of Clement Maydeston*). The numbers refer to Wordsworth's sections.
Defensorium Directorii	Maydeston, C. *Defensorium Directorii* (ed. Chr. Wordsworth in *The Tracts of Clement Maydeston*). The numbers refer to Wordsworth's sections.
Durham	J. Raine's *Rites of Durham*. The numbers refer to pages.
Ebor	*Manuale ... Ecclesiae Eboracensis* (ed. W. G. Henderson). The numbers refer to pages.
F	Fortescue, A. H. T. K. *The Ceremonies of the Roman Rite Described*. Other works by Fr. Fortescue are indicated clearly.
G	*Graduale Sarisburiense* (ed. W. H. Frere). The numbers refer to the plates in Frere's edition.
HA	Hope, Sir W. St. J. and Atchley, E. G. C. F. *English Liturgical Colours*.
Hereford	*Missale ... Ecclesiae Herfordensis* (ed. W. G. Henderson). The numbers refer to pages.

Lincoln	*Lincoln Cathedral Statutes* (ed. Chr. Wordsworth). The numbers refer to volume and page.
Lyons	*Cérémonial Romain-Lyonnais.* The numbers refer to book and section.
M	*Manuale Sarum* (ed. A. J. Collins). The numbers refer to pages.
Missal	*The Sarum Missal* (ed. J. W. Legg). The letter refers to the manuscript as named by Legg (C=Crawford, B=Bologna, A=Arsenal, M=Morris); the numbers, to the pages of Legg's edition.
OCarm.	B. Zimmerman's *Ordinaire de l'Ordre de Notre-Dame du Mont-Carmel.* The numbers refer to pages.
OCist.	*Liber Usuum Sacri Cisterciensis Ordinis.* The numbers refer to pages.
Olalla	F. B. Olalla Aragón's *Ceremonias de las missas solemnes cantadas.* The numbers refer to sections.
OP	*Caeremoniale juxta Ritum S. Ordinis Praedicatorum.* The numbers refer to sections.
OPraem	*L'Ordinaire de Prémontré* (ed. Pl. F. Lefèvre). The numbers refer to chapter and line.
P	*Processionale Sarum* (ed. W. G. Henderson). The numbers refer to pages.
PG	*Patrologia Graeca.* The numbers refer to volume and column.
PL	*Patrologia Latina.* The numbers refer to volume and column.
Processions	Wordsworth, Chr. *Salisbury Processions and Ceremonies.* The numbers refer to pages.
Rock	Rock, D. *Church of Our Fathers.* The numbers refer to volume and pages.
S	Simmons, *The Lay Folks Mass Book.*
Tracts	*Tracts on the* Mass (ed. J. W. Legg). The number refers to the page.
Wells	Reynolds, H. E. *The Ordinale of Wells Cathedral.* The numbers refer to the pages of Reynolds' edition.

Key to the symbols used in the figures

 The celebrant in a chasuble

 The celebrant in a cope

 The deacon whether in a dalmatic or not

 The subdeacon whether in a tunicle or not

 Thurifer whether with or without thurible

 Cross-bearer

 Taperer

 Book-boy

 Water-boy

 Other clerks

 Verger

 The Gospel lectern

BOOK I

THE TREASURER'S PURVIEW

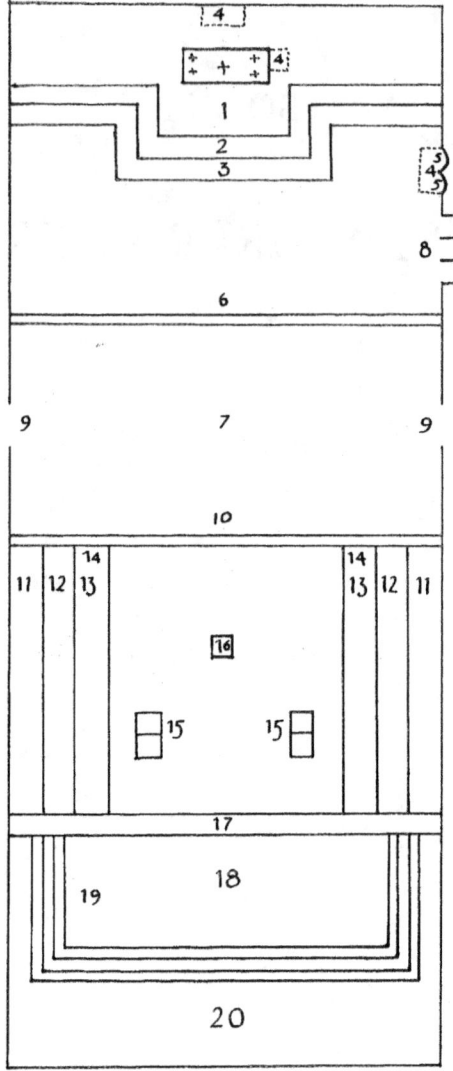

Figure I. Plan of a church. (1) Footpace (*supremus gradus*). (2) Deacon's step (*ante gradum supremum*). (3) Subdeacon's step (*tertius ab altari gradus*). (4) Possible locations of the credence (*locus administrationis*). (5) Piscina and aumbry. (6) *Gradus presbyterii*. (7) Presbyterium. (8) Sedilia. (9) *Ostia presbyterii* in Sarum church. (10) *Gradus chori*. (11) Choir stalls of the upper step (*de superiore gradu*). (12) Second form of the choir (*secunda forma*). (13) Lowest form of the choir (*prima forma*). (14) Place for the taperers at High Mass. (15) Seats for the rulers of the choir. (16) Great lectern in the choir (*pulpitum minus*). (17) Rood screen and chancel step. (18) Pulpitum. (19) Great Gospel lectern (*aquila*). (20) Nave.

I

THE CHURCH

Laying aside merely ecclesiological controversies, in this chapter the focus is not on how to reconstruct an English church of the time of our eighth Henry or our Catholic Mary but rather on what the rite itself requires of a church and its sacristan for the celebration of the Mass.[1] Much that is familiar to priests of the Roman rite is but mentioned in passing, and the antiquarian in search of further details will need to consult other works on the subject.[2]

The Sarum liturgy presupposes the existence of a church.[3] It will have a nave for the congregation, separated by a chancel arch[4] or equivalent structure from the choir.[5] This is the site of the Rood, at which processions make a station.[6] West of the choir is where the pulpitum should be located, a raised area in the north half of which the Gospel lectern is erected.[7] Marking the east end of the choir is the choir step (*gradus chori*).[8] At Salisbury Cathedral itself there was a further step, the presbytery step (*gradus presbyterii*), that marked the west end of the sanctuary, and between the two steps there was a space of considerable extent (*presbyterium*). It is in this area, on the south side, where the sedilia should be and where seats are placed for the spouses at weddings.[9] Processions also can be marshalled here. In many churches, however, it is likely that

---

[1] C 7.1: *Thesaurarii officium est ornamenta et thesauros ecclesie conservare, luminaria administrare.*
[2] Most importantly, Dr. Rock's *Church of Our Fathers*.
[3] See *Processions*, diagram after page 72, for a hypothetical reconstruction of the ground plan of Salisbury cathedral.
[4] The very word 'chancel' from the Latin *cancelli*, meaning 'lattice-work', refers in origin to the latticed screen that formed this division between the nave and the choir. The modern use of the word 'chancel' refers to the space beyond the *cancelli*. In many modern churches, the old chancel screen will not be present.
[5] For the disposition of the choir and sanctuary, see Figure I and Rock IV.242-5.
[6] P.ix.
[7] Rock IV.244 explains the development of the *pulpitum* from the two *ambones*. At Sarum, the Gospel-lectern was called the eagle, after its shape, and the Gospel was read from it on Sundays and most feasts only. For a complete list of the days, see C 66.11. For the possibility of the lessons being read from the rood-loft, see *Processions*.279. At Durham, where the great choir lectern bore the shape of an eagle (Durham.12), there was a rood-loft lectern for the Matins lessons, but this was no longer in use by the time of the suppression (Durham.14). Bonniwell, page 120, would have Dominican churches endowed with two minor *pulpita*, at the chancel screen, and one *pulpitum majus* in the midst of the choir, the Mass lessons being read from the former.
[8] Chambers, page 9.
[9] Col 836*. See Rock IV.201.

there was a single step, and the distinction drawn between the two steps in the books may not be too important in practice. On the presbytery step, two or four standard candlesticks may be placed,[10] and it is on the line of the *gradus presbyterii* (or over the first step east of the choir) that the Lenten veil should be hung.[11] The area east of the presbytery step is that which surrounds the altar, where the celebrant, ministers and servers conduct their business. In some place of the church, there should be a vestry.[12] The church is supposed to be orientated, that is to say, that the choir will be west of the sanctuary and east of the nave. In this book, as in the Sarum books themselves, this orientation is presumed.

The principal element of the sanctuary is the altar, raised on two or three steps.[13] The altar must be consecrated[14] and ideally should be freestanding, so that it can be walked round when incensing. The altar should be dressed in four white linen[15] altar cloths, of which at least two should be blessed. The topmost should be apparelled with a narrow frontlet as wide as the front of the altar.[16] There should be a frontal of the

---

[10] Cons 5; OP.468.

[11] HA.43; Bond, pages 102–3; C 60.2. If the winch mechanism on the north-eastern pier of the eastern transept in Sarum church was indeed that used for raising and lowering the Lenten veil, then the veil must have hung immediately to the east of the *gradus presbyterii*, impeding neither the ceremonies at the choir step nor those at the altar. C 60.4 has the veil fall on Spy Wednesday *in area presbyterii*. It is not clear by what route the acolyte brought the chalice at Mass while the veil was in use. Perhaps he entered the presbytery opposite Bishop Audley's chantry, where the Radnor pew is now.

Alfriston may be taken as an example of a parish church. There the hooks for the Lenten veil survive on the easternmost tiebeam in the chancel, immediately east of the sedilia and west of the piscina. Were the altar against the east wall, there would be enough space for the ministers to stand on their steps at the altar behind the veil. The hooks are at the extremes of the beam, but it is not clear whether the veil extended from wall to wall or only covered the width of the altar itself. Rock IV.257 would have the Lenten veil in parish churches hang between the chancel and the nave but provides no authority for this.

[12] Col 582 supposes that the celebrant and ministers vest in a place other than a sanctuary. The cathedral at Sarum possesses a *vestibulum* (*Processions*, diagram facing page 72), and this is mentioned explicitly in the Sarum books (e.g. *Processions*.71). The fifteenth-century bede roll of St. Mary's, Sandwich, makes explicit mention of a vestry (Rock II.306), and many structures survive throughout the country. Rock III.97–101 has more on these structures. S.163–6 argues against the existence of vestries in lesser churches (see also, e.g., S.134 and 136). Durham.28 and 82 reports that there was a revestry, but minor altars had their vessels and vestments kept in their chapels, not in the principal vestry.

[13] Presumably the *gradus altaris* of C 66.4, 66.16 and elsewhere.

[14] It is not an excessive exaggeration to say that, in churches remodelled in the second half of the twentieth century, a celebrant may need a certain amount of luck to find a suitable altar, and that, in churches offered for use through the generosity of the clergy of the Establishment, consecrated stone altars are practically non-existent. Nevertheless, the Council of Exeter (1287), cap. IV, leaves no room for doubt: *nec Missae nisi in altaribus et superaltaribus consecratis aliqualiter celebrentur* (Wilkins II.132).

For the *superaltare*, a form of mounted portable altar-stone, its appearance in a sixteenth-century painting and will, and its arrangement under the altar cloths, see Rock I.183–209. Sarum church possessed a superaltar-chest in 1222 (*Processions*.177) and P.63 supposes the superaltar itself to be in the vestry.

[15] *Processions*. 206 (quoting Thomas Becon's *Catechism*). See also Becon, page 102: 'white linnen clothes to be laid upon the altars'.

[16] Council of Exeter (1287) apud Rock I.188: *Sint ... quatuor tuellae ad majus altare quarum saltem duae sint benedictae, et una illarum cum parura; item ad quodlibet altare cum contigerit missam inibi celebrari.* This does not seem to include any cere-cloth (*chrismale*), but one of them may be intended as a frontal, thrown over the altar so as to cover at least the east and west sides as well as the surface. Elsewhere, three 'towels' are required, though one of these may be meant as a hand towel for the lavatory (S.173 and 333).

colour of the Mass.[17] On the altar is laudably kept the *Liber vitae*, a register of those faithful departed for whom the sacrifice is offered in that church.[18] The floor before the altar, where the priest stands at Mass, may be covered with carpet.[19] When not in use, the altar may be protected by a vesperal cloth.[20] During Mass, on the altar there should be a cross[21] placed between at least two candles.[22] The altar should be under a canopy of some sort.[23] The Sarum books do not presume Eucharistic reservation in a tabernacle placed on the altar.[24]

---

[17] As is often the case, the colour did not always match (see Rock's editors at Rock IV.309), but in modern celebrations such a match is probable and seemly. See also Rock I.183–90.

[18] Rock II.278 et seq.; S.329; Durham.14–15.

[19] *Processions*.299.

[20] OP.504.

[21] The cross is prescribed by Innocent III (ob. 1216) (King, *Roman Church*, page 100). This cross may often have been part of a fixed reredos, but movable crucifixes are also found (see e.g. Rock IV.290). The fifteenth-century bede roll of St. Mary's, Sandwich, records the existence of a foot designed to hold a movable cross (Rock II.305). The Sarum inventory of 1214–22 (*Processions*.176) mentions *cortine.ii. ad crucem supra principale altare*, which suggests a large cross hanging over the altar rather than a small portable cross, but these curtains may have been made for the church at Old Sarum. The altar cross should bear an image of Christ crucified. This, at least, can be deduced from the fact that the processional cross had such an image (C 66.18). Hope, *English Altars*, Plate V, fig. 1, shews an altar crucifix in a manuscript of ca. 1245, but the figure on the cross did not become general until the fourteenth century.

[22] Much ink and animus have been spent on the number of altar candles. It seems certain that six candles were coming in by the sixteenth century. Six candles were used on the High Altar of the chapel of St. Salvator at St. Andrews (King, *Roman Church*, page 105). Dix.420 contends that there was a hugely variable number of altar candles in England, generally in excess of two, and appears to demolish the myth of two candles only. Rock IV.243 and the Anglican ritualists follow Cons 5, which may prescribe two candles on the altar, at least for some days of the year, and also the famous two standard candles lit on the step before the altar. At Wells, it seems that there were two altar candles only, both at the High Altar (Wells.49: *super majus altare debent ardere duo cerei … quotiens legitur vel canitur in choro … Isti … cerei sufficiunt ad omnes horas per totum annum*) and at side altars (Wells.50: *ad omnes missas privatas ad altare utrumque Sancti Stephani Sancti Johannis et ad missam in capitulo quando canitur alias quam ad majus altare debent accendi duo cerei de quatuor lib: et ardere usque ad finem missae*), though at pontifical Low Masses there may have been four altar candles (Wells.51: *ad missam domini Episcopi duo cerei de Marca si ipse forte celebraverit privatim*). There was also a supplementary taper used in case of necessity when the light from the altar candles was insufficient (Wells.50: *Praeterea ministri altaris debent habere minutam candelam ad accendendum ad libitum cum opus fuerit quando cerei non possunt commode altari* [sic] *ad librum*). Since there seems to be no definitive evidence for late practice at Sarum (though, *prima facie*, six candles do not seem unlikely), we have conservatively assumed two candles here. Churches will need to make their own decisions. In the inventory of 1219–25 (*Processions*.182) the altar of St. Thomas possessed two brazen candlesticks. The modern Dominicans (OP.514–18) vary the number of candles according to the day's rank, not only the solemnity of the function. See also Chambers.285–96, and Morse §457 for this most vexed of questions.

Rock II.391 speculates that candles before the Reformation were generally less bleached than they are now. The implication, however, is that an attempt at bleaching candles was made, so bleached candles would be suitable for use on the modern altar. Specially bleached twisted candles, called white branches, were used in some funeral processions. The Council of Exeter (1287), cap. IV, prescribes *duo saltem luminaria* (Wilkins II.132).

[23] Council of Exeter (1287), cap. XII, requires a *caelatura super majus altare* (Wilkins II.139). See the picture of the altar of Westminster Abbey under its canopy in Rock II.393, the font at Great Witchingham, and Bond, pages 23–4. The *tabernaculum ligneum* given by Bishop Richard Beauchamp in 1471 (*Processions*.279) may refer to such a superstructure. The riddels that used to be so popular with Anglicans are the last remnants of the ciborium.

[24] Although tabernacles of some sort are mentioned as early as the thirteenth century (Pearson. xxxi), they were only mandated by Cardinal Pole in 1556, too late to make definitive changes in the celebration of the liturgy. Formerly, the most common method of reservation was from a

Either at the south side or behind the altar should be the credence table.[25] Altars sometimes have aumbries (*armariola*) which can be used instead of the credence table. These should be placed at the south side of the sanctuary, but when two side altars share a single aumbry it may be necessary for the clerk at Low Mass to operate from the north side instead and go round *in plano* to the south side. Piscinæ used to be built next to aumbries. They are highly desirable as the water from the various washings of the hands can be poured down them in the course of the Mass.

The celebrant and the sacred ministers have their seats on the south side of the presbyterium.[26] From east to west, they are occupied by the celebrant, deacon and subdeacon, respectively.[27] Other, provisional, seating may be provided for the acolyte and thurifer at High Mass. Otherwise, these servers may stand throughout or sit at the feet of the celebrant, as the Carmelites do, or in the lowest form of the choir.[28] This last is presumed here.

The Sarum books assume that the choir consists of three rows of stalls on each side.

The lowest row (*prima forma*) is occupied by clerks in minor orders (servers and choristers). The middle row (*secunda forma*) is that of the junior clerks in major orders (subdeacons, deacons, junior canons and priests below the rank of canon). The upper row (*superior gradus*) belongs to select[29] deacons and vicars and the senior canons of the cathedral chapter, pre-eminent among whom are the four dignitaries (*principales personae*) of the cathedral: the dean, the precentor, the treasurer (sacristan) and the chancellor. All these have stalls assigned to them.[30] The south side of the choir is called

---

hanging pyx. At Sarum, the Sacrament was reserved in a Eucharistic dove over the High Altar (*Processions*.285). The inventory of 1214–22 includes such a dove, made of silver (*Processions*.171). In 1220, the cathedral was given a *pulchram cuppam argenteam deauratam intus et extra ad reponendam eucharistiam* (Jones, page 13). Unlike the tabernacle, which attracts acts of obeisance that tend to modify the liturgy, the pyx probably had little effect on the conduct of the clergy during the Mass (but see King, *Roman Church*, page 233). The Dominicans introduced a genuflection before the Sacrament only in 1569 (King, *Religious Orders*, page 349).

[25] C 66.11 says that the subdeacon leaves his chasuble *retro magnum altare*, but later (e.g. C 66.17) there is no indication of the location of the *locus administracionis*, which, as *locus ministracionis*, is also mentioned in Cons 39.14. See also Rock II.393 for what might be a temporary credence table south of the altar in Westminster Abbey.

Ordo Romanus XIV mentions a *locus aptus*, which may be a credence table. At Lyons, an altar-credence table stood immediately behind the High Altar, as also at Lincoln I.378, but O'Connell, *Church Building*, page 217, claims that the credence table did not become common in England. A variant was the practice of using the south corner of the altar, as the Dominicans still do, and then moving the elements onto the altar stone at the offertory (Legg, *Ecclesiological Essays*, pages 126–30). There is nothing to shew whether the credence table was covered with a cloth or not. The credence table as such seems not to be mentioned explicitly in the Sarum books, but in the churchwardens' receipts of St. Edmund's, Salisbury, for 1550–51 is mentioned a table 'that was for the deacon and subdeacon', which may refer to the credence table at which the ministers prepared the chalice (*Processions*.307). See also Bond, pages 100 and 167–70.

[26] Bond, pages 176–203, and many other surviving examples.

[27] Surviving examples shew the three seats on different, descending, levels from east to west. See also Rock I.335.

[28] As John of Avranches (*PL* CXLVII.33) says of the subdeacon, some of whose functions the Sarum acolyte performs.

[29] C 1.1. Since the upper form alone was entitled to the almuce (Cons 19.3), it is understandable that some elderly clergy were promoted to the upper form.

[30] C 1.

the dean's side (*Decani*); the north, the precentor's (*Cantoris*). On certain days, the choir may be ruled by a varying number of rulers (*rectores chori*). These have their places in the midst of the choir, half of them on the north side and half on the south side.[31]

At the same time, the Customary allows for a simpler disposition of the choir in parish and conventual churches.[32] A choir of two forms on either side is assumed, of which the upper is occupied by the senior clerk of each side (the most senior clerk on the south side and the next most senior on the north), who sit in the westernmost stalls, then the clerks next to them in seniority (called clerks of the upper form) and, closest to the altar, the junior clergy (called clerks of the second form). The lower level is occupied by the boys, called clerks of the first form.

The other parts of the church, the narthex and the baptistery, play no part in the ordinary celebration of the Mass.

---

[31] See Rock II.165 for examples of the rulers' seating and Chapter XXII, note 96, for its orientation.
[32] C 11.

II

BOOKS, VESSELS AND INSTRUMENTS

§1. BOOKS

The books that will be needed are, first, the missal.[1] In addition to this, at High Mass, a book containing the Gospel lessons to be read throughout the year will be necessary.[2] Separate from this is the Text (Textus), a book containing the entirety of the Gospels.[3] On double feasts, two Texts may be used,[4] though in lesser churches there will often be no Text at all, and only the book of the Gospel lessons will be found. A book is needed by the subdeacon to read the epistle, and this book will also contain those additional lessons read on certain days by the acolyte and other lectors. The Gradual[5] and the Sequentiary contain the choral chants needed for High Mass. The Processional[6] has the directions and texts for processions on Sundays and other days throughout the year. The Manual is needed for the celebration of the sacraments, for blessings, funerals and other occasional offices.[7] The Ordinal contains directions for the selection of each day's liturgical texts and some ceremonial directions.[8] There are no altar cards.[9]

---

[1] Ordinarily known as the Mass book (S.155). The closest to a standard modern edition is Dickinson's *Missale ad Usum Insignis et Praeclarae Ecclesiae Sarum*.
[2] In its place, a second missal may be used. The same can be said of the epistle-book below. For the book of the Gospel lessons (as distinguished from the Textus), see C 66.19–22.
[3] In fact, the Textus did not always contain the entirety of the four Gospels, as the entries in the inventory of 1536 shew (*Processions*.168). The most famous examples of Textus, though much earlier in date than Sarum Use, are the Lindisfarne Gospels and the Book of Kells. Their artistry reflects their ceremonial status.
[4] C 66.3 and 66.24.
[5] Frere's *Graduale Sarisberiense* provides a facsimile reproduction of a thirteenth-century manuscript. There does not seem to be a readily available modern edition of the later Gradual.
[6] The standard modern edition is Henderson's *Processionale ad Usum Insignis et Praeclarae Ecclesiae Sarum*. This can be compared with and supplemented by Wordsworth's *Salisbury Processions and Ceremonies*.
[7] The *Manuale ad Usum Percelebris Ecclesiae Sarisburiensis* edited by Collins.
[8] There is no single edition of the ordinal that contains all the necessary information. B's broken-up Pie, C, Cons, the works of Clement Maydeston, Frere's *Use of Sarum II* and the rubrics of the other liturgical books themselves must be combined and interpreted. A modern, unified, edition of the *Pica Sarum* would be of inestimable benefit for regulating the choice of texts. An attempt at detecting, inferring and explaining the ceremonies is the object of this book.
[9] Altar cards came in gradually during the course of the sixteenth century. In 1570, the Roman rite knew only the central of its modern altar cards, and the others appeared only later. There is no evidence of the use of altar cards in Sarum. See *The Catholic Encyclopedia* s.v. 'Altar cards'.

§2. VESSELS

Most sacristies will possess the vessels required for a Sarum Mass: a basin[10] and towel[11] for the lavatory and the ablutions, to which may be added a ewer, if desired; a set of cruets,[12] preferably on a stand;[13] a pyx or ciborium for bringing the unconsecrated hosts[14] at High Mass and another for the reservation of the Sacrament; a paten and chalice for the elements of the sacrifice; and a second, non-sacramental, chalice or other suitable vessel for the purification after Communion.

The principal and most sacred vessels are the paten and the chalice. The chalice is dressed[15] with the purificator,[16] paten, pall (if used),[17] chalice veil or offertorium[18] and

---

[10] C 66.10, where a ewer is not mentioned. However, the inventory of 1389, apart from pewter cruets (*phiolae*), mentions also two pewter jugs (*olle*) to hold a pint of water each (*Processions*.299). A ewer was used at York (S.252). If there is a piscina and a ewer is to be used, the water could be poured away after each lavatory.

[11] C 66.10. This should be of absorbent material and fair size so that it may hang decently from the server's arm at Low Mass and be held decorously before the celebrant by the taperers at High Mass.

[12] C 66.10.

[13] The stand is nowhere mentioned but, since the same taperer brings in the cruets and the pyx, it is almost necessary.

[14] C 66.10.

[15] C 66.12 and 66.34; OP.1204.

[16] The purificator as such is not named in any rubric and appears to be found first in a Roman inventory of 1295 (King, *Roman Church*, page 99). The earlier custom seems to have been to keep a cloth at the piscina or on the altar for use at the ablutions, as enjoined in St. Edmund of Abingdon's constitution of 1236: *habeat quoque Sacerdos juxta Altare Pannum mundissimum circumdatum undique, et honeste ac decenter coopertum: in quo, post susceptionem Sacramenti Altaris digitos cum labiis ablutos emundet* (Wilkins I.639). The Carmelites and the modern Dominicans employ the purificator, and the early Dominicans (*Tracts*.82) bid the celebrant dry his fingers *cum panno ad hoc ipsum preparato qui semper intra calicem reservetur*. The conservative Carthusians preserve the use of a special cloth, the 'Agnus Dei', which they use for drying the celebrant's lips and fingers at the ablutions but not for drying the chalice (King, *Religious Orders*, page 56). It is reasonable to suppose that the use of the purificator had become more general by the mid-sixteenth century and Dominican practice has been followed here for the most part.

It is dangerous to argue from the silence of the rubrics that the purificator was not in use. The rubrics make no mention of the *pannus mundissimus* prescribed in 1236 either, yet this can be presumed to have been in use by the sixteenth century. It is improbable that the chalice was permitted to be made wet and sticky on its external surface after the second ablution as the omission of a purificator of some sort would necessitate, though the comment of Becon, page 292 ('What wiping of the mouth, and licking of the fingers is there then'), on the second ablution is intriguing. The existence of the purificator need not be incompatible with the practice of involving the chalice on the paten. In the sixteenth century, Goude, Plate XXXII, depicting a form of the Roman rite, pictures the involved chalice.

To the appearance of the purificator has been attributed the adoption of white wine in exchange for the red wine that was traditional in both East and West until that point (King, *Roman Church*, page 173).

[17] Both OP.1204 and Lyons II.55 place the optional pall under the veil. The Spanish tradition, however, is to use a lesser, round pall, probably of later origin, to separate the host from the chalice veil and to enclose the square pall in the corporal, so that when this is unfolded, that should appear in its middle right-hand square (Olalla.36–7 and also *Ceremonia y rúbrica*). *Tracts*.169 (Burckard) prescribes likewise for the Roman rite. That the corporals are always mentioned in the plural and appear to be treated as inseparable might be an indication that at Sarum also this practice may be more authentic historically but is not mentioned explicitly in the Sarum books. Accordingly, we presume the modern Dominican way of dressing the chalice, but either form may be followed without scruple. When the great corporal is used, of course, the pall will be omitted.

[18] This is the ancestor of the chalice veil and is not easy to distinguish from the humeral veil. Originally, the offertorium was long enough to cover the paten and have its end thrown over the

burse[19] containing the corporals. The offertorium and burse should match the colour of the vestments.

There are two sizes of corporal.[20] The little corporal is folded and used like that of the Roman rite, in combination with a pall or a second, folded, corporal to take the place of the pall. The great corporal is rectangular, the front part being used to place the host and chalice as usual and the rear part used to raise over the chalice to cover it. To fold the great corporal, it is first folded across its width, bringing the nearer corners over the further. It is then folded again, bringing the further corners over the nearer. The result is folded in three, bringing the left third over the middle and lastly the right third over the left.[21] Either form of corporal may be used at will, the only difference in

---

acolyte's shoulder (see *Tracts*, plate I) but, as the humeral veil (*mantellum*) grew in prominence, the offertorium shrank, being only held and no longer thrown over the shoulder. The early offertorium was often made of simple or decorated linen but sometimes of silk, especially later, and in this case would often match the colour of the vestments. It is used to envelop the paten before handing it to the acolyte to hold wrapped in his humeral veil, as the Dominican subdeacon still does (OP.1035). See Rock I.330-4 and IV.218.

[19] A Westminster missal of the fourteenth century shews a burse on the altar during what looks like a Low Mass (Legg, *Ecclesiological Essays*, plate 1 and page 31). The inventory of 1214-22 refers to burses: *viij paria corporalium, cum forell'. v.* (*Processions*.173); C 66.34 says of the deacon: *corporalia complicet et in loculo reponat*.

[20] C 66.34 uses the plural, *corporalia*, perhaps supposing the use of two little corporals. Practice varied, however. It appears from illuminations that a single large corporal was used which was folded up over the chalice from behind and so served to cover it, and the instructions to the priest to cover the corporal himself (e.g. Col 620), rather than allowing the deacon to do so, perhaps implies the use of the great corporal. See Chapter XIX, note 15.

Later, the use of two smaller corporals was introduced. Of these, one was spread on the altar as it still is in the Roman rite; the other remained folded and was used as a cover for the chalice, being the ancestor of the modern pall. Gavanti (1569-1638) was still discussing the liceity of using two smaller corporals instead of the greater corporal, so it is improbable that the use of the latter had ceased in England by 1558. Nevertheless, since both practices were probably to be found, there seems no objection to permitting either custom to be followed, as at Lyons.

There (Lyons I.94) the corporal is starched, but some (not all) mediæval depictions of the great corporal (e.g. Rock IV.175) shew clearly unstarched corporals. Chambers, page 270, quotes Lyndewode as an authority forbidding the starching of the corporal. An illustration of a single starched corporal being used at what appears to be a Low Mass of St. Gregory can be found in the Bodleian Library's MS. Auct. D. Inf. 2. 11. 217v.

In this work, the lesser corporal is presumed for Low Mass and the great corporal for High Mass, not because this practice is recommended, but because it enables the way of handling the pall (which is more complex) to be described among the ceremonies of Low Mass. At Lyons I.94, the great corporal is used for solemn Masses, but either form is permitted at Low Mass.

[21] This manner of folding the great corporal, which allows the furthest fold to fall better over the chalice, is deduced from OP.505, which assumes a corporal folded in four from front to back and in three from side to side. This great corporal remained in use among the Dominicans until the seventeenth century (King, *Religious Orders*, page 382). More recently, the Dominicans have adopted the use of the pall and the lesser corporal, which is folded as in the Roman rite (OP.1204).

The directions given by Lyons I.94 are more specific. There the corporal is about 43" by 29" and is folded differently: first across its width, bringing the further corners over the nearer, and then folding the remaining area as if one were folding a little corporal, namely, folding up the nearer third, then bringing the further third over the nearer and then folding the left third over the middle and lastly the right third. Lyons III.217 (note 1) explains how to cover and discover the chalice with the great corporal:

> il prend par les deux extrémités la partie supérieure du corporal, qui était repliée en trois contre la croix ou le tabernacle, et la porte sur le calice, de manière qu'il soit entièrement

ceremonial being that the great corporal requires both hands to handle when covering or discovering the chalice.

For general Communions, a second purificator and chalice[22] will be needed. This should not be a sacramental chalice, which laymen may never touch, but should be a noble vessel, as all that are employed in the sanctuary, and chalice-shaped. Under communicants' chins should be extended a houseling cloth.[23]

§3. INSTRUMENTS

For Mass, the church should possess at least one thurible with its boat and spoon;[24] two candlesticks for the taperers' candles; torches for use at the elevation;[25]

<blockquote>
caché, comme quand il est couvert du voile. Chaque fois que le prêtre découvre le calice, il prend de même le corporal par les deux extrémités, le lève avec précaution plus haut que la coupe, pour éviter les accidents, et le replie en trois derrière le calice.
</blockquote>

Chambers, pages 270 and 272, recommends square corporals. Chamber's suggestion in the same place that the corporal should hang over the front of the altar is contradicted by illuminations and by Gavanti, the very authority to which he refers in the same paragraph.

[22] *Tracts*.86 calls this vessel a chalice (*in calice alio quam sit calix cum quo celebratur*). It should not look like a sacramental chalice (S.381).

[23] *Processions*.88; Jerdan, page 22; Great Glemham and Gayton Thorpe fonts. For suitable lengths, see Bond, page 141.

[24] C 66.24 contemplates two thuribles at Pontifical Masses and P.11 does so for double feasts. Two thuribles are also used at the Sepulchre on Good Friday.

[25] The Council of Exeter (1287) requires two torches to burn during the Canon (see Du Cange s.v. *tortisius*), and torches held by *choristae* at High Mass were to be found in Sarum church in the fifteenth century (*Processions*.278). Apart from the torch lit by the clerk, it was not uncommon for laymen, whether of their own volition or in representation of some guild, to kneel in the vicinity of the altar holding additional lighted torches. In 1468, funds existed for the provision of torches at the Morrow-Masses in the Cathedral (*Processions*.294). Assuming that the Morrow-Mass was low, this detail confirms the use of torches at Low Masses in the cathedral itself. For details of this devotional custom and of the making of the torch, which took the form of thin tapers wound round each other, see Duffy, *Stripping*, page 96, where no authority is provided for the assertion that the torch remained until *Agnus Dei* or the Communion.

The torch's modern successors are, at High Mass, the torches held by torchbearers from the *Sanctus* until the elevation or Communion and, at Low Mass, the sanctus candle that is preserved among the Dominicans and by observers of the Roman rite in many places on the continent but which has mostly fallen into desuetude in England. Nowadays this also remains lit until Communion (*Missale Romanum: Ritus servandus*, VIII.6). However, *Tracts*.155 and157 (Burckard) has the minister light the torch at *Hanc igitur* and extinguish it after the elevation of the chalice. This avoids the difficulty of holding the torch and attending to the pax and is the usage suggested here.

A further problem arises. At Low Mass, it is impossible for a single server to raise the celebrant's chasuble at the elevation, ring the bell and hold the torch at once. Now, the possession of a handbell for use at the elevation is mandated by councils, e.g., that of Exeter in 1287 (see Rock IV.179), but it does not necessarily follow that this bell should be rung by the server at Low Mass: it could be rung by a sacristan, for example. Becon assumes the presence of both boy and parish clerk ('besides the boy and Parish clerke that wait upon you', page 106; 'the boy or Parish Clerke rings the little Sacry bell', page 144), though not always ('many times there is no bodie in the Church, but the Boy that helpeth you to say Masse', page 135). Nevertheless, there is a ritual clash. How, then, to resolve this clash, the product presumably of ritual accretion? It is most probable that local practice varied considerably. Certainly, there is varied pictorial evidence. An Anglo-Flemish Sarum book of hours from the 1440s at the Bodleian Library (MS Gough Liturg 3, fol. 72v, *apud* Rock II.394) depicts a rocheted clerk kneeling at the south side of the chancel at the foot of the altar facing north, holding a handbell;[26] a cushion for the Texts and another (or a book-stand) for the

a torch in his right hand and ringing a handbell with his left. Nobody holds the celebrant's chasuble. The picture, however, does not depict a typical Low Mass: six mourners hold torches round the bier, and a clerk in cope stands at either side of this, holding a book and apparently ruling an absent choir. On the other hand, a Norman Sarum Book of Hours of the 1470s in the same library (MS. Auct. D. inf. 2. 11, fol. 217v) shews a Mass of St. Gregory with the server kneeling behind and to the left of the celebrant, holding a torch in his left hand and the chasuble in his right. It is possible that at private Masses said at side altars, the handbell contemplated in the Council of Exeter of 1287 (*campanella deferenda*) was sometimes rung by the server, while at more public Masses, whether High or Low, the external bell commanded by John Peckham, metropolitan of Canterbury, in 1281 (Rock I.182) would be rung by the usual bell-ringer. These circumstances affect the ritual. In the former case, the clerk will need to light a standing torch at the south side of the altar (the ancestor of the modern sanctus candle, though it is remarkable that the Roman Burckard requires, not a miserly third candle, but a rather more spectacular *intorticium*: Tracts.155) and then operate the bell at the elevations. This is the compromise reached by the modern Roman and Dominican rites, although it destroys one of the most dramatic rituals surrounding the elevation. There is nothing to prevent laymen or others from holding other torches *devotionis causa*. In the latter case, the clerk can hold the torch himself during the elevations and leave the care of the bell to another. For what it is worth, in a Roman *Sacerdotale* of 1559 (foll. 79r–80r), the chasuble is held and the torch is lit for the elevations only at the expense of the bell, and that is the solution adopted here.

High Mass presents its own complications. Numerous illustrations from Northern Europe depict torches being held at the elevation. Some of these are more allusive than accurate (e.g. in Goude, Plate XIX, where the footless torch is standing unaided), but often they are held by the deacon and the subdeacon. *Tracts*.80 has the two acolytes of the Mass (*uno* and *altero*) hold tapers during the Sacrings themselves. This stipulation, however, is not compatible with the Sarum books, which state explicitly that the taperers remain in the choir until the *Supplices te rogamus* (C 66.28), thereby precluding their presence before the altar at the Sacring. That the sacred ministers or the taperers held torches at Sarum seems unlikely, therefore. Supernumerary torchbearers, however, do appear to have been employed in the fifteenth century in the cathedral, though it is unclear whether as a proper part of the liturgy or *devotionis causa* (see *Processions*.278), and so we have assumed their presence. Since there is no indication of when the torchbearers retired, the same approach has been followed as for Low Mass. However, practice may have varied in the parishes, and it could hardly be gravely wrong to follow the Roman practice of having the torchbearers remain until after Communion at Requiem Masses and when a general Communion is held.

[26] The modern altar bell is paraliturgical in origin, inasmuch as its use benefited people that did not form part of the congregation, and represents a conflation of two distinct bells, the development of whose use is not altogether clear. For one account of the history, see Thurston, 'The *Sanctus* Bell'.

On the one hand, there was the bell used as a signal to the faithful elsewhere in the church or outside it that the elevation was approaching. This was in origin a small bell rung by the clerk or by somebody else at some point before the Consecration. It was either handheld (when it may sometimes have been associated with low side windows; but see King, *Roman Church*, page 303) or suspended from a beam in the chancel, as are the arrangements to be found at Hawstead and Somersham, in Suffolk. A later technical improvement on this small bell was the use of an external bell in the tower or, in some churches, a small sanctus bell in its own bellcote above the chancel. A suspended bell in a side chapel, used to tell people elsewhere in the church that Mass was about to begin, as well as to give warning of the approaching Consecration, is mentioned in Rock III.88. See also Rock III.219. In this book, a handbell is presumed. This bell receives a variety of names, among which one may mention 'sance bell', 'sanctus bell' and 'sacring bell'. Confusingly, this sacring bell was not that rung at the Sacring itself but merely gave notice that the Sacring was approaching. It is not clear at what point before the Sacring this bell was rung. Fr. Thurston mentions that in the fifteenth century the scholars at Eton were summoned from their classroom by this bell to say certain prayers in the chapel and returned to their books after the elevations. Therefore, the bell must have been rung with sufficient time for this progress of schoolboys to take place. The name 'sance-' or 'sanctus-bell' also suggests that it was rung some time before the consecration, at the *Sanctus*, and not at *Hanc igitur*, for instance. The *Sanctus* also marks the moment when the preface (spoken aloud) is concluded and the inaudible Canon begins. If the torch was lit at the *Sanctus* also, this would argue for the bell being rung at this point: the server would be killing two birds with one stone. This, the

missal;²⁷ and a pax-brede with its cloth.²⁸ There may be a portable lectern for use on

sanctus bell properly so called, appears to be devotional in nature and not to be prescribed by any canon. From the point of view of the ceremonialist, this bell presents no difficulties and is adopted here with no reservation.

Distinct from this bell (but often also called 'sacring bell') is that which was rung at the elevation itself. We first hear of this bell in Cologne about 1200, when it is certainly a handbell (Thurston). S.38 and thereabouts and 281–2 speak of 'a litel belle'. Later conciliar decrees ordered a bell in the bellcote to be rung as well, to advise people outside the church, and often at a considerable distance from it, that the Sacring was taking place, so as to enable them to cease from work for a moment and join spiritually with the priest at the holiest point of the Mass (see Council of Exeter (1287), cap. IV apud Wilkins II.132 for the great bell to be rung thrice at the elevation). This bell was rung in the tower by an ordinary bellringer who could observe the altar from a window high in the west wall of the nave or elsewhere (Bond, pages 252–3). The Council of Exeter required a bell *ad elevationem Corporis Christi*, but there seems to be no mention of a second bell at the elevation of the chalice, which is of later introduction and still optional in the Sarum Missal we are following. For the measures adopted in the diocese of Worcester and the province of Canterbury in 1240 and 1281, respectively, see Rock IV.182. For further details concerning the origin of these bells, see Fortescue, *The Mass*, pages 342–4; King, *Roman Church*, pages 303 and 327–8; and Thurston.

From this, it appears that the ringing of the handbell at the elevation was a canonical requirement. However, it is quite probable that the requirement only applied to the solemn form of Mass: it is unlikely that the bell in the tower was rung at every Low Mass. The bell at the elevation appears in few pictorial sources. The font panel at Badingham may shew the parish clerk with a handbell at the elevation, but he is wearing neither surplice nor rochet, and the picture may well be a composite representation of the Mass, reminding the viewer of the characteristic bell usually used at High Mass, rather than an accurate depiction of a Low Mass. The same may be said of the Bodleian Library's MS Gough Liturg 3, fol. 72v, *apud* Rock II.394, described above in the note on the elevation torch. It is also possible that at Low Masses a little elevation bell was rung by a person other than the server of the Mass.

Whatever the status of the handbell at the elevation, it presents insurmountable difficulties for a single server at Low Mass. For the resolution of this difficulty and the reasons for the practice recommended in this book, see the note above on the elevation torch. At High Mass, we presume that the external bell will be rung and so there is no need for the little handbell. It could hardly be illicit, however, to use this.

For other treatments of the difference between the sance bell and the sacring bell, see Rock IV.179 and S.280–283.

²⁷ C 66.3 requires cushions for the two Texts on doubles. Illustrations shew the missal sometimes on a cushion and other times on a missal-stand. Missal-stands are included in the inventory of 1214–22 (*item lectricum.j. ad altare, Processions*.180). C 66.2 prescribes a cushion (*cervicale*) for the carrying of the Text, and presumably such a cushion could be used in place of a missal-stand on the altar.

²⁸ The pax-brede is found in numerous inventories and wills and needs little description here. Its use was ordered by the Council of Exeter (1287), cap. XII, where it is called *asser ad pacem* (Wilkins II.139), and became well-nigh universal. Bishop Bonner's articles of visitation in 1554 required it (S.296). Neither the liturgical books nor the ordinals nor the cathedral inventory of 1536 mentions a pax-brede explicitly, though its use is implied by Cons 114, which has the deacon of the Chrism take the vessel containing the Chrism to the choir *in loco pacis*. The inventory of St. Thomas's altar in 1389 (*Processions*.299) mentions two *deosculatoria vitrea*, and in 1470 a pax of copper parcel-gilt was assigned to the Morrow-Mass altar (*Processions*.293). In some places, an ornate Textus was used instead of a pax-brede (Rock IV.186–90; Duffy, *Stripping*, pages 497 and 588). In Spain, a cross was sometimes offered in place of the pax-brede (Olalla.283).

The pax-brede, with its cloth, was kept on the altar (cf. Duffy, *The Voices of Morebath*, page 65 note 1). As usual, illustrations can be inaccurate, and those that shew the pax-brede at the north end of the altar neglect the likely fact that the deacon, probably standing to the right of the celebrant, would find it more convenient to take the pax-brede from the south end of the altar. Goude, for example, shews the pax-brede on the north end of the altar in Plate V and at the south end in Plate

days when the lessons are not read from the pulpitum.[29] A great lectern in the midst of the choir may be used on other days, or the pulpitum, if sufficiently capacious, may be employed.[30] The lectern should be covered[31] with a rich cloth of the colour of the day[32] for the reading of the Gospel. If the choir is to be ruled, the rulers may carry staves.[33] There is no need for a flabellum.[34]

VI. As is often the case, such illustrations may be suggestive rather than accurate representations of the liturgy.

In the Roman rite, the pax-brede should be held through a cloth of the colour of the Mass, though this is generally omitted (F.18). In Spain, the acolyte charged with offering the pax sometimes wears a humeral veil of the colour of the Mass (Olalla.276-85). There is nothing to prove or disprove the existence of such a veil in England.

[29] *Crede Michi* [79]. B.I.1 prescribes this lectern for the lessons at Matins. The Bodleian Library's MS. Auct. D. Inf. 2. 11 (188v) shews choir rulers singing from a small lectern. See also OP.1024 and OP.1059.

[30] At Sarum, the great lectern in the pulpitum used for reading the Gospel on more solemn days was called the *aquila*. See C 66.14 and 66.41. The word *pulpitum* (originally meaning 'a stage') can bear more than one meaning. In some cases, such as when the choral chants are intoned at the pulpitum, it makes more sense to understand the choir lectern. On other occasions, such as when the lessons at Mass are read from the pulpitum, the western platform or elevated *jubé* might be meant. In practice, the layout of the individual church will often dictate the choice.

[31] Presumably it is to the laying of this veil that C 66.14 refers.

[32] HA.41.

[33] Rock II.164-7. *Processions*.177 records *baculi.viij. ad chorum regendum* in the inventory of 1214-22. At *Processions*.160-1, in the inventory of 1536, are recorded the following:

> Two staves, covered with silver and guilt, having an image of our Lady, and a priest kneeling, with this scripture, 'Ora pro nobis'; having also one knop with six buttresses and six windows in the midst; one of them wanting a Pinnacle and two little knops of the Pinnacles, with one top of a window ... Item, ... staves of wood, with branches of Vines in plates of silver upon them.

These, although listed as *baculi pastorales*, read more like rulers' staves than croziers. See also the woodcut at P.96 and elsewhere.

[34] The flabellum is one of the myths of Sarum Use. Generalist writings on the subject tend to mention it (e.g. King, *Liturgies of the Past*, and *The Catholic Encyclopedia*), and its use by the deacon is as dogmatically maintained as is the all-important question of two candles on the altar.

It is true that the flabellum was in use in many churches in the West, Old Sarum not excluded. The inventory of 1214-22 mentions *duo flabella de fusto et pargameno* and *flauellum unum argent'. quod dñus episcopus contulit ecclesie. fractum* and, for the altars of St. Peter and All Saints, *flabellum j* (*Processions*.177, 170 and 180).

Tracts.79 gives an indication of how the flabellum might have been used: *tempore quoque muscarum post inceptionem secretarum debet diaconus tenere flabellum. quo cohibeat eas honeste a molestando sacerdotem et abigat a sacrificio*. See also OP.1065. How the deacon juggled the flabellum and the thurible during the Consecration is not explained, nor when the flabellum should be laid aside. King, *Religious Orders*, page 290, reports that the Carmelite deacon laid aside the flabellum at the end of the Canon. Rock IV.225 would have the deacon take the flabellum at the preface but does not provide any authorities for his doing so. Rock IV.229-33 gives other particulars of the flabellum and its use but does not claim that its use survived into the sixteenth century. The flabellum is not mentioned in the Missal or the Consuetudinary or the Customary. King, *Religious Orders*, page 322, assumes that the flabellum disappeared from the Latin rites (with the exceptions of the Dominican and Carmelite rites, which retained its use in theory until the twentieth century) after the Council of Constance (1415), though it still appears in *Ordo Romanus* XIV. See also OP.502.

In conclusion, since neither any of the extant Sarum liturgical or rubrical books nor the cathedral inventory of 1536 mention a flabellum of any sort, it can be presumed that its use had ceased long before the end of the period when Sarum use was celebrated regularly. Therefore, its restoration, regretfully, is not envisaged here.

There should be at least two processional crosses:[35] one, with an image of the Crucified,[36] for use throughout most of the year; and a second, plain with no image and painted red, for use during Lent.[37] A third, made with beryl, may be used during Eastertide.[38]

For the Sunday procession, there should also be a holy-water stoup and sprinkler. On some occasions, processional banners are required.[39] Details of these are given in their appropriate chapters. For the blessing of bread on Sundays, there should be a plate.

Special functions throughout the year have their own requirements. On Ash Wednesday, a salver will be needed for ashes. On Palm Sunday, a lantern is borne before the chest of relics. On Holy Saturday, a triple candlestick[40] and a further candlestick for the Paschal Candle are required. On Corpus Christi and in certain other processions, a pallium, supported by at least four poles, is carried. There should also be a pall for funerals and another for weddings.

---

[35] At least in greater churches, two crosses were used on minor doubles and three on other doubles (P.11). Two crosses will be needed on Palm Sunday.

[36] Even Chambers, page 282, accepts that the processional cross bore on it the image of the Crucified. See also Rock II.158 for such a processional cross from Fountains Abbey.

[37] Throughout most of Lent, the processional cross had no image and was painted red. See C 58 and *Crede Michi* [76]. For Palm Sunday, *Crede Michi* [79] presumes a silver cross also: in parish churches this may be the ordinary cross.

[38] *Crede Michi* [87] supposes a processional cross made with beryl for use in Eastertide until the Ascension. See also Rock IV.290–1. At Durham, there was a crystal cross for use during Easter week.

[39] See e.g. P.12.

[40] P.74; Hereford.97. This triple candle may take the form of a serpent: P.76 and P.80 (woodcuts); Feasey, page 211–12; Rock IV.87.

III

THE VESTMENTS

Over their usual cassocks, the clergy at Mass wear vestments.[1] For the priest, these will be the apparelled[2] amice, the apparelled alb, the cincture, the maniple, the crossed stole[3] and the chasuble. At processions and solemn blessings, he will wear the cope in place of the chasuble and may remove the maniple.[4] The deacon wears the same vestments as the celebrant, except that he wears the usual diaconal stole and the dalmatic in place of the chasuble. The subdeacon vests like the deacon, but he wears no stole and dons a tunicle instead of the dalmatic. On certain days, however, the sacred ministers wear chasubles[5] instead of dalmatic and tunicle. When they do so, they keep their hands

---

[1] For an authoritative list of the necessary vestments, see S.167. Properly speaking, the surplice or a rochet should be worn under the amice. For the garlands worn in some places on certain occasions, see Rock II.340. Whether the garlands mentioned in the inventory of 1536 (*Processions*.167) are of the same sort or votive offerings is not clear.

[2] The apparels, while originally of merely ornamental nature, became something like vestments in their own right, a little like the *collarines*, their descendants found in some Spanish cathedrals, such as Seville's. They are here considered to be such, rather than of antiquarian interest alone, on the grounds that they are mentioned explicitly in a rubric of the Missal (Col 328) and at P.69. The existence of a rule for their omission supposes their existence as proper liturgical (rather than decorative) ornaments. See Rock I.367.

The amice should have one apparel along its edge closest to the throat, but the alb should have at least four: a large one just above the hem at the front, another just above the hem at the back (*parurae*) and one at the end of each sleeve, above the back of the hand (*maniculae*). The font at Westhall shews the lower apparel quite clearly, and HA.167 gives details of 'ij smalle parures for aube slevys' from London in 1466. Rock I.360–5 would have two further apparels, on the breast and the back of the alb (*spaulae* or *spatulariae*), and shews that these survived on the continent and among the Dominicans until a late period, though at I.368, in support of their use in England until the reign of Mary, he quotes Watson, bishop of Lincoln, drawing an analogy between the apparels of the alb and amice and the five wounds of Our Saviour. Chambers, page 30, would have apparels restricted to subdeacons and above, and claims Honorius of Autun as his authority.

As Rock I.382 points out, the apparelled amice should be worn quite loose, leaving the throat free. For consideration of when apparels should not be worn, see Rock I.367.

[3] Gayton Thorpe and Great Glemham fonts, among other sources of evidence.

[4] Of all the vestments, the maniple is that whereof the wearing is subject to the greatest variation. In the Roman rite, it is only ever worn for Mass and never outside it. It is removed for blessings and prayers that take place at the altar immediately after Mass. Even within the Mass, it is generally removed for preaching. Among the Dominicans it is worn sometimes outside Mass (OP.541) but never with the cope (OP.546). The Bodleian Library's MS. Auct. Inf. 2. 11 fol. 188v shews the celebrant in cope, with ministers in dalmatic and tunicle, wearing the maniple at a burial, in accordance with OP.541. The custom of Sarum church cannot now be ascertained and may have differed from practice elsewhere, so variation now may be permissible. See the notes on individual cases as they occur.

[5] HA.81 speculates that this rule may often not have been observed.

inside their chasubles, unlike the celebrant, who keeps his hands joined outside the chasuble's folds.[6] On vigils and Ember Days, and at some Requiem Masses,[7] the deacon and subdeacon wear neither chasubles nor dalmatic and tunicle.[8]

The acolyte wears the amice, the alb and the cincture only, though for parts of the Mass he wears a humeral veil (*mantellum*).[9] At Masses when the *Gloria in excelsis* is said, the acolyte also wears a tunicle.[10]

The thurifer, the taperers and the torchbearers[11] wear the amice, the alb and the cincture.[12] The alb is never worn without amice and cincture.

The clergy in choir wear their choir dress according to their rank and the season.[13] On many occasions, the clergy of the upper and second forms also wear silk copes[14] over their surplices,[15] as do the rulers of the choir.[16] The boy choristers wear surplices.[17]

[6] C 66.2.
[7] C 66.42.
[8] For the days when the ministers wear dalmatics, chasubles or neither, see C 66.2 and 66.3; also Cons 46.1.
[9] C 66.12. The nature, origin and development of this mantellum are somewhat obscure. See also Rock I.330–4. where the difference between the *mantellum* (the modern humeral veil) and the *offertorium* (the ancestor of the modern chalice veil as used by the Dominicans) is explained, together with the difficulties arising from confused terminology. Rock's interpretation, which is consistent with Dominican practice, is followed here. For a contrasting explanation, which would have the acolyte wear the *mantellum* only when the sacred ministers wear chasubles, see HA.202.
[10] Cons 55.
[11] C 66.2 (*ceteris vero ministris, ut ceroferariis turribulario et accolito in albis cum amictibus existentibus*). Ut suggests that the list of ministers is not exhaustive and so would include the torchbearers. The general principle seems to be that the alb, not the surplice, should be worn by those ministering at the altar.
[12] Col 582. Taperers still wear tunicles in some Spanish cathedrals, and they survived in some French cathedrals at least until the Revolution. In the Roman rite, a second subdeacon acting as crucifer wears a tunicle on some occasions. Rock I.327–8 adduces examples of tunicles worn by taperers and thurifers at York and London, and at IV.212 refers to an inventory of goods given by its founder, Archbishop Chichele, to the Oxonian College of All Souls (which was bound by its statutes to follow Sarum Use), in which can be found *item 2 tunic. pro ceroferariis cum parura*. Despite these indications, there seems to be no positive evidence of such a practice at Sarum. The statement that they wear albs and amices when the sacred ministers wear chasubles (C 66.2) might imply that they wore tunicles at other times. Likewise, B.I.mclxviii, dealing with the procession after first Vespers of the first Sunday after Trinity, has the taperers *albis tantum indutis*, as if they were otherwise attired at other times, though the contrast in these instances may be not with other days but with other ministers. Rock II.5 quotes the Processional of 1555, which, on the solemnity of Christmas, has the three cruciferes in tunicles, but the taperers and thurifers *albis cum amictibus induti tantum*. Col 350, when describing the procession to the font on Holy Saturday, has the acolyte crucifer wear a tunicle but the taperers and the thurifer in albs with amices. Although the question, therefore, must remain moot, and practice doubtless varied from church to church according to its inclination and the splendour of its appointments, the more authoritative representatives of the practice at Sarum itself seem to frown on tunicles for the taperers and thurifers. See King, *Roman Church*, page 137, for the use of the tunicle at Salisbury.
[13] Choir dress is not strictly liturgical and so its mediæval form is not explored here. For the details, see Rock II.63 seq. A liturgical use of choir dress, however, appears at the Vigils of Easter and Whitsun, when the canons remove their black *cappae chorales* at the *Gloria in excelsis* (C 46.2). This rubric may perhaps be considered to belong to the choral establishment and so treated as ceremonial rather than general (*Defensorium Directorii* [1]). See Chapter XXII.
[14] These are expected to be in major orders, that is to say, to have reached at least the subdiaconate (C 1). The rule seems to be, therefore, that the cope is restricted to these, *pace* Bailey, page 14, who has the boys don copes but provides no justification for this claim.
[15] Wells.63 imposes a fine on those rogue clergy who wear their copes over their black *cappae chorales*.
[16] The Council of Exeter (1287), cap. XII (Wilkins II.139), required each parish church to possess at least one *capa chori*.
[17] For the length of the surplice's sleeves, see Rock II.9.

Except by the servers, the head is covered when sitting,[18] when walking in procession outside the church and by the celebrant in vestments when going to or returning from the sanctuary. Either the amice or the biretta (or other canonical cap) may be employed.[19]

---

[18] In the Lincoln choir, the head was discovered when going to read or sing or when walking for any other reason (Lincoln I.390); but see *Tracts*.xii, which supposes different rules from those in force at Lincoln, and the Bodleian Library's MS. Auct. D. Inf. 2. 11 fol. 188v, which shews an external funeral procession with uncovered clergy.

[19] The Sarum books scarcely mention headgear beyond the bishop's mitre and the use of the amice on Christmas and All Hallows by the boys who take the part of angels at Matins (C 24.8). The black cap (*pilliolus*) formed part of the choir dress of *installati* (Frere, *Use of Sarum* I.263), so the head was undoubtedly covered at times as it was at Lincoln (with a cap, not the amice: Lincoln I.377) and is still done in other rites. See Rock I.389–94 and Bonniwell, page 181, for the use of the amice among secular priests before the sixteenth century. See King, *Roman Church*, pages 157–8, Rock I.389 seqq. and *Tracts*.237 for wearing the amice on the head. The woodcut at P.129 seems to shew the rulers of the choir with amices on their heads. Becon, page 70, thinks of the amice as a headpiece, so he is probably not alluding to the momentary placing of the amice on the head while vesting when he writes 'ye first put upon your head, an headpeece, called an *Amice,* to keepe your braines in temper, as I thinke'. Our suggestions are based on illuminations, and Lincoln, Dominican and Roman practice, which sometimes contradict each other. The ministers are nowhere mentioned but, by analogy with the celebrant, we assume that they also are sometimes covered.

IV

THE COLOUR OF THE VESTMENTS

Although the rite does not have a prescriptive colour sequence,[1] sacristans may wish to adopt the following guidance for the colour of the usual silk

---

[1] The Sarum colour sequence is preserved but imperfectly and is much more confusing (and less prescriptive) than that used now by the Roman rite. *Defensorium Directorii* [41] classifies the colour sequence as a ceremonial rubric, that is, of obligation only for the clerks of Sarum church and those who have bound themselves to follow the use of the cathedral. Moreover, it is likely that practice changed over time (see HA.40 and HA.155 for the change from red to white for the Epiphany in some places and the gradual increase in the use of white for Lent, respectively), and the sources that we have are too incomplete to judge the course of this evolution adequately.

The fundamental principle is that the finer vestments are used for Sundays and feasts, and older, poorer, vestments are relegated to ferias. The 1287 Council of Exeter (HA.11) prescribed two sets of vestments for parish churches: one festal and the other ferial. Naturally, the cathedral possessed many more vestments than ordinary churches, but the allocation of particular sets of vestments to particular days by the sacristans was more influenced by the quality and condition of the vestments than by their colours: even in the cathedral itself, four of the five side altars mentioned in the inventory of 1214–22 appear to have been endowed with no more than two sets of vestments (*Processions*.179–82).

With time, a colour sequence developed, and the Sarum books give a reasonable indication of what this was like, but there are significant gaps in the information provided in the Missal and the Customary, and these will prove frustrating to those accustomed to the rigid colour sequence of modern books. The detective work of Hope and Atchley has proved invaluable for moving beyond the explicit rubrics of the Missal (Col 583), the Consuetudinary (Cons 19.4 and 19.5) and the Customary (especially C 47, with its lengthy footnote taken from the customary now at the Oxonian college of Corpus Christi, and C 66.42) to infer from wills and the cathedral inventories (those of 1214–22, of 1389 and of 1536) plausible colours for days not mentioned there. The sequence suggested here owes much to their work and is limited to the liturgy of the Missal.

Even putting all these sources together, there are considerable gaps in the sequence, most notably the colours of Advent, Lent and ferias throughout the year. It is likely that, on the few unimpeded ferias *per annum*, poorer vestments were used, irrespective of colour. However, in an attempt to fill these gaps to the partial satisfaction of modern sacristans, the sequences of Wells (Wells.95-6 and 101-3) and Lichfield (HA.211-12) have been plundered to a considerable extent.

Rather than group Masses under colour headings, which would only repeat the confusion of the sources, it has been thought more convenient for the putative sacristan, especially if he is preparing for occasional Masses, to follow the example of the Wells statutes and work calendrically, giving first the colours for the temporal, then those for the sanctoral (by class, as in the commons of the saints), third those for some of the more confusing feasts in the proper of the saints (by month) and last those for votive Masses.

The colours mentioned in the Sarum books are: red (*rubeus*), white (*albus*, *candidus*), saffron (*croceus*) and black (*niger*). To this we add here green (*viridis*, *glaucus*) as an alternative to saffron and blue (*indius*), which are found in the inventories. A legitimate distinction can be made between festive (possibly reflected by *candidus*, 'shining white', of C 47.1), and penitential white. As for

vestments[2] and apparels, together with the humeral veil,[3] chalice veil and burse, along with the frontal and the altar curtains. On the most solemn feasts, the best vestments, irrespective of colour, may be used.[4]

When the Mass is of ...	the colour should be ...
[Masses of the Season]	
Sundays of Advent and throughout all the year outside Eastertide when the Mass is of the Sunday	red[5]
ferias in Advent	(no specified colour, perhaps dark blue, purple or Lenten white)[6]

patterns, starry (*instellatus*) and barry (*ex transverso stragulatus*; Chambers, page 274, explains the term) are mentioned in the customaries, and powdered (*poudratus*, generally referring to appliqué work) and paly (*stragulatus*, a term used of the primitive habit of the Carmelites in Du Cange s.v. *stragulati*) are found in the inventory of 1389. These descriptions are probably no more than references to particular suits of vestments and do not seek to create binding rules, any more than the undoubtedly thematic embroideries of the period.

Cons 19.4 and Cons 19.5 give two colours: white and red. The inventory of 1214–22 gives six: violet (*violetta*), red, white, blue (*indicus*), purple (*purpureus*) and *diversi coloris*. The inventory of 1389 gives three colours: white, red and green (both *viridis* and *glaucus*); it also mentions the patterns powdered (*poudratus*) and paly (*stragulatus*). C 47 and C 66.42 give four: white, red, saffron and black. To these CCC adds *colorum mixtorum* (which may mean that different clerks wore vestments of different colours: see HA.138) and the pattern barry (*ex transverso stragulatus*). Col 583 gives the same colours as the Customary: white, red, saffron and black. The inventory of 1536 mentions three colours only: white, red and green.

The acceptable alternatives may strike the modern reader as odd. So, black, dark blue and violet may have been but legitimate variants of a single colour, it being difficult to achieve a pure black colour in the absence of modern dyes. Illuminations often depict blue in use at funerals, e.g., the Bodleian Library's MS. Auct. D. Inf. 2. 11 (fol 188v), admittedly of Norman work, where the ministers wear their proper black dalmatic and tunicle but the celebrant, who appears to have worn black for the Mass (note the stole), has put on a blue cope for the burial. Rock II.217 and Hope and Atchely support this view. Blue is often called *indi(c)us* or *blodius*, both suggestive of dark blue. The modern sky-blue associated with the Immaculate Conception in Spain and some of its former territories does not seem to have been common in mediæval England, though it is recommended by John Grandisson to Exeter Cathedral in 1327 for certain, non-Marian, feasts (HA.138). Likewise, green and yellow appear to belong to the same family and may have been as interchangeable as scarlet and red, and black and violet (cf. *Tracts.178*, quoting from the *Missale Romanum* of 1501: *ad hos quatuor principales colores referuntur ceteri: quia coccineus refertur ad rebeum: croceus ad viridem*). This would explain why the Missal and the Customary require saffron vestments while the inventories mention green. At Wells, the two colours were used in combination or alone (Wells.5).

In the table, only those suggestions that are not taken from C 47 (including CCC) are given their own reference.

[2] Rock I.313 has the colour of the dalmatic match the celebrant's chasuble. Except when various colours are prescribed, it would seem preferable to have the vestments match in colour. Such a preference is implied at *Processions.117* (*preparetur processio in vno colore*) and is made explicit in Lincoln I.375.

[3] HA.205 finds a developed use of a colour sequence for the humeral veil only in the inventory of King's College, Cambridge, but it will be more seemly to have the humeral veil match the colour of the vestments when this can be managed.

[4] CCC; OP.564.

[5] Any doubt left by C 47.2 is removed by C 66.3, by CCC and by Col 583.

[6] At Lichfield, the Advent colour was black (HA.212); at Wells, it was probably blue (HA.213). Chambers, Appendix, page v, suggests that indigo or purple was used for Advent and Lenten ferias,

Ember Days in Advent	(no specified colour; perhaps as on Advent ferias; on Ember Wednesday perhaps white)[7]
Christmas Eve	(no specified colour)[8]
Christmas Night and Day	white,[9] but the best vestments of mixed colours[10] should be worn irrespective of their principal colour[11]
St. Stephen (and his octave day)	red[12]
St. John the Apostle in December (and his octave day)	white[13]
the Holy Innocents (and their octave day)	as for St. Stephen
any day from Christmas until the eve of the Epiphany (save for occurring saints' feasts)	white[14]
the Epiphany and its octave	red, but on the feast day itself the best vestments of mixed colours should be worn, as on Christmas Day[15]
Sundays after the octave of the Epiphany	red

and for Ember Days and vigils outside Whit Week, basing this deduction on the presence of indigo vestments in the 1222 inventory.

[7] At Wells, the sacred ministers wore white on Ember Wednesday, on account of the prominence given to the Annunciation. At Sarum, the Gospel at Mass is of the Annunciation. At Exeter, the deacon wore white for the Annunciation Gospel at Matins (HA.139). HA.108 recommends Lenten white for these Ember Days.

[8] The Advent ferial colour would seem appropriate, but at Evesham, c. 1377, white was used (HA.142), and Morse §464 justifies white by analogy with French uses which, like Sarum, had special choir offices for this day without ferial prayers.

[9] So most probably, but there can be no certainty concerning the underlying theoretical colour, since in practice the best vestments would always be used.

[10] *Colorum mixtorum* (CCC). This customary gives colours for the rulers' copes but implies that, unless otherwise mentioned, the dalmatics and tunicles were of the same colour (*similiter ministri altaris dalmaticis et tunicis*). In principle, it is not improbable that the celebrant might follow the same rule.

[11] CCC. For one idea of what vestments of mixed colours might have looked like, see the rather early (thirteenth century) Gösser vestments now kept at Vienna's Museum für Angewandte Kunst.

[12] On the feast itself, CCC would have the second-best copes worn, irrespective of colour, provided that the dalmatics and tunicles be red.

[13] C 66.3. On the feast itself, CCC would have the second-best copes worn, irrespective of colour, provided that the dalmatics, tunicles and copes be white.

[14] C 47.3. The only doubtful day would be Epiphany Eve, but that is suppressed in favour of the octave of St. Thomas. In practice, this rule applies only to 30 (within the octave of Christmas) and 31 December (St. Silvester). When 30 December falls on a Sunday, the colour is white, not red, since the service is of Christmas, not of the Sunday: cf. the Pie for year G (B.I, cxxxi).

[15] CCC requires that the dalmatic and tunicle should be sprinkled with stars.

ferias after the octave of the Epiphany	(no specified colour)[16]
Septuagesima, Sexagesima and Quinquagesima Sundays	red
ferias in the weeks following Septuagesima, Sexagesima and Quinquagesima	(no specified colour)
Ash Wednesday	red[17]
the six Sundays in Lent	red[18]
Lenten ferias up to Spy Wednesday	probably white,[19] but from Septuagesima to Maundy Thursday, on Sundays and simple feasts of nine lessons, the tract is sung by four clerks in red copes (Candlemas, the Annunciation, the First Sunday in Lent and Palm Sunday being excepted)[20]
Maundy Thursday	red[21]
Good Friday	red[22]

---

[16] In 1389, the altar of St. Thomas in Sarum Church had a *vestimentum, pro ferialibus diebus, poudrat' coloris steynat.'* (*Processions*.299). Morse §464 assumes white as the colour of the season until Candlemas or Septuagesima, whichever should fall first.

[17] C 66.3.

[18] See Sundays of Advent in the table. This certainly seems to be the rule (C 47.2), but HA.83 surmises that white was gradually taking over from red as a Lenten colour, even on Sundays.

[19] The Sarum books do not specify a colour and, very unhelpfully, the inventory of 1389 gives merely *vestimentum, pro ferialibus in xlma*, with no mention of colour (*Processions*.299). HA.42 argues for the widespread use of white vestments. While these seem to have been often of materials inferior to silk, such as linen or fustian, undyed and sometimes painted with red, black, purple or brown crosses, the royal wardrobe in 1547 possessed Lenten vestments of white damask with red crosses (HA.83). Lady Hungerford's chapel in Salisbury cathedral possessed Lenten altar cloths decorated with purple crosses (HA.66) but the colour of the 'lynnen' is not specified. The argument at HA.153 that red was used on the ferias of Passion and Holy Week seems neither convincing (change from purple does not necessitate change to red) nor applicable (the pontifical in question assumes purple for the other Lenten ferias and does not appear to conform to the Sarum sequence), whereas the very fact that Col 583 and C 66.3 make a point of mentioning the colour of Ash Wednesday and Maundy Thursday as red implies that this colour was not that of the other ferias. Likewise, Rock's argument (II.216) that the mention of red for Ash Wednesday, Maundy Thursday and Good Friday implies the constant use of red throughout Lent and Passiontide is inconclusive.

[20] C 66.18 and 47.2 as interpreted by HA.128–9. Cons 19.5 has the rulers of the choir wear red copes on simple feasts in Lent.

[21] Col 583; C 66.3. Red is used also for the Chrism Mass, according to HA.148.

[22] Col 316.

Easter Eve	red up to the blessing of the font,[23] but the deacon and subdeacon use dalmatic and tunicle that are transversely striped; on the way back from the font, the litanies are sung by three clerks of the first form, one in a white cope and the others in red;[24] white for the Mass[25]
Easter Day	white, but the best vestments of mixed colours should be worn, as on Christmas Day
Easter Monday and Tuesday	white, but the second-best vestments should be worn, irrespective of colour, provided that on Easter Monday the dalmatics and tunicles should be white
the Easter octave thereafter	white
any day from Low Sunday until Ascension Day	white,[26] except on the Invention of the Holy Cross
Rogation Masses	(no specified colour)[27]
Ascension Day	as on Christmas Day
the octave of the Ascension	white[28]
Whitsun Eve	probably as for Easter Eve. The deacon and subdeacon could use transversely striped dalmatic and tunicle
Whit Sunday	as on Christmas Day
Whit Monday and Tuesday	as on Easter Monday and Tuesday, provided that on Whit Monday the dalmatics and tunicles should be white
Whit Week thereafter, not excepting the Ember Days	white[29]

---

[23] Col 348; P.74.
[24] HA.148, HA.211 and P.90.
[25] HA.148, where it is also assumed that the best vestments would be used, the Mass being festal and the first of Easter. This is borne out by Cons 69, which, however, is plagued with apparent inconsistencies, in part because it attempts to distinguish between the vigil celebrated with and without baptisms. The solution offered here is as good a compromise as any.
[26] C 47.1. The words *de quocunque fit servicium* imply that the rubric applies only to the Mass of the day and not to votive Masses.
[27] P.104 directs red banners to lead the procession but is silent on the colour of the vestments. The colour of the Advent and Lent Ember Days would not be unsuitable.
[28] CCC; HA.89.
[29] *A quarta feria ebdomade pasche et pentecostes per ebdomadam … ministri altaris utuntur candidis indumentis* (CCC). The apparently contradictory instruction further down *feria quarta ebdomade pentecostes uiribus* [sic] *utuntur dalmaticis et tunicis*, being corrupt, may be disregarded.

Trinity Sunday	as on Christmas Day[30]
ferias following Trinity Sunday	white
Corpus Christi and its octave	white,[31] but on the feast itself as on Christmas Day[32]
Sundays after Trinity	red
ferias from Corpus Christi until Advent	(no specified colour)[33]
Ember Days in September	(no specified colour)[34]

[Masses from the Commons and Proper of the Saints]

vigils other than Christmas, Epiphany, Easter, Ascension and Whitsun	(no specified colour; perhaps Lenten white)[35]
octaves	(no colour specified; perhaps the same colour as on the feast, unless otherwise specified)
apostles and evangelists outside Eastertide	red
martyrs outside Eastertide	red
confessors outside Eastertide	saffron[36] or green[37]
virgins, whether martyrs or not, throughout the whole year	white[38]

---

[30] Since Eastertide was reckoned to last until the Saturday after Trinity (Col 631), the theoretical colour, replaced by the best vestments, should be white, *pace* HA.89, which alleges red with no explanation. Red was not uncommon in other churches.

[31] The colour of Corpus Christi varied within England and is not specified in the Sarum books. Nevertheless, as the feast falls within Eastertide, the colour of the feast itself should be white according to the rule when C was written, and it would be remarkable if the colour changed halfway through the octave. White, therefore, has been suggested for both the feast and the octave, even though red is not uncommon and was very widespread in France, presumably on account of the passional nature of the feast, and may have spread in England in later years. Since at Sarum Maundy Thursday was celebrated in red, it would not be too surprising if red were used for the new feast of Corpus Christi also, as it was at Wells. The now-covered wall-painting at Alfriston of the Sacrament procession shewed a scarlet cope (Pagden, pages 31–2).

[32] The CCC does not mention Corpus Christi. However, Trinity is assigned the best vestments and Corpus Christi is of the same rank (*duplex majus*).

[33] The inventory of 1389 gives a rather annoying *vestimentum, pro ferialibus diebus, poudrat' coloris steynat.'* (*Processions*.299).

[34] HA.108 recommends Lenten white for these days, as for the Ember Days in Advent.

[35] Lenten white is found in Lincolnshire (HA.35 and HA.90) and would not be unsuitable.

[36] Also Col 583.

[37] Green and saffron appear to have been considered equivalent (HA.4). See note 1 above. The inventories of 1389 (*item. ix. vestimentum coloris glauci, pro confessoribus* (*Processions*.299) and 1536 mention green but no saffron vestments. Chambers, Appendix, page vii, identifies *glaucus* with yellow but this seems improbable.

[38] C 47.1: *cuiuslibet virginis*. Morse §463, after the Emmanuel College MS missal: *et in festo quaelibet* (sic) *Virginis per totum annum*.

women not virgins outside Eastertide	(no colour specified; perhaps saffron or green)[39]
saints of all classes in Eastertide	white
angels	white[40]
Our Lady	white[41]
the church's title (*festum loci*) and its octave	(no special colour indicated but presumably that corresponding to the class of saint; probably the best vestments should be worn on the feast itself)[42]
the dedication of the church	on the feast itself as on Christmas Day; throughout the octave, white
the Conversion of St. Paul (25 January)	(no colour specified)[43]
Candlemas (2 February)	white
the Chair of St. Peter (22 February)	(no colour specified)[44]
the Annunciation (25 March)	white
St. Mark and the Greater Litanies (25 April)	white for St. Mark;[45] for the procession and litanies no colour is specified
the Invention of the Holy Cross (3 May)	red
St. John before the Latin Gate (6 May)	white[46]

---

[39] HA.151 suggests that non-virgins were allocated the same colour as confessors, with the exception of St. Mary Magdalen, but no authority is given for this assertion. This seems to be the rule at Wells.

[40] C 47.1 for both feasts of St. Michael. At St. Thomas's altar in Sarum Cathedral in 1389, there was a *vestimentum, pro angelis, coloris albi poudratum* (*Processions*.299). But HA.104-6 suggests that red for St. Raphael was intended by the founder of the feast to be used throughout the country.

[41] According to Morse §463 after the Emmanuel College MS missal, this colour is to be used at all Masses of Our Lady, whether of a feast or at her weekly commemorations or during her octaves or at votive Masses.

[42] Since the best vestments are to be worn on Trinity Sunday (CCC), which is only a major double, it would be reasonable for them to be worn also for the *festum loci*, which is a principal double (C 19.1).

[43] At Wells, red, this being the most notable feast of St. Paul. However, not being the feast of his martyrdom, some uses adopt another colour: at Exeter, if after Septuagesima, blue; at Rome, white. This feast is somewhat analogous to that of the Nativity of St. John the Baptist (for which Sarum adopts white while Wells uses blue and Lichfield the colour of confessors, but which is of higher rank and so possibly not representative) and to that of the Chair of St. Peter (for which Wells and Lichfield adopt the colour of major confessors). Red, or more probably saffron or green, or even white are all possibilities.

[44] See on the Conversion of St. Paul (25 January), which presents similar difficulties.

[45] Because his feast will always fall after Easter (C 47.2).

[46] Because it will always fall after Easter (C 47.2), *pace* Morse §463, who assumes red.

the Nativity of St. John the Baptist and its octave (24 June)	white[47]
the Commemoration of St. Paul (30 June)	red[48]
the Feast of Relics (Sunday after 7 July)	(no proper colour specified);[49] in practice, the best vestments of mixed colours should be worn[50]
St. Mary Magdalen (22 July)	white
St. Anne (26 July)	as for holy women not virgins[51]
St. Peter ad Vincula (1 August)	(no colour specified; perhaps saffron or green)[52]
the Transfiguration (6 August)	(no colour specified)
the Name of Jesus (7 August)	(no colour specified)[53]
the Assumption and its octave (15 August)	on the feast itself as on Christmas Day; for the octave, white
the Beheading of St. John the Baptist (29 August)	(no colour specified; possibly red)[54]
the Exaltation of the Holy Cross (14 September)	red
All Saints (1 November)	as on Christmas Day[55]
All Souls (2 November)	black[56]

---

[47] Also Morse §463, after the Emmanuel College MS missal, and HA.102, who give white for the feast. The colour may have been kept throughout the octave.
[48] This feast commemorates St. Paul's martyrdom, overshadowed by that of St. Peter, so red is the obvious colour.
[49] In the Roman rite, red (after martyrs). Otherwise, the colour proper to the class of the principal saint whose relics are kept in the church might be reasonable.
[50] So CCC, even though at Col 23** the feast is ranked as only of nine lessons.
[51] If the suggestion at HA.151 is followed, St. Anne's colour will be saffron or green. See note on non-virgins.
[52] At Wells, as for greater confessors (saffron and green); at Rome, white.
[53] HA.96–7 offer examples in support of the popularity of red for Jesus Masses and deduce from this that the Mass of the Holy Name is also to be offered in red.
[54] Red was used at Lichfield (HA.129) and Westminster, which possibly represents the use of London (HA.132). Elsewhere, violet is marked as the practice of the Roman court (HA.153) and so peculiar. Red for St. John the Baptist's martyrdom would not be unreasonable.
[55] The proper colour, displaced by the use of the best vestments, is more likely to have been red than white (HA.152).
[56] C 66.42 but the inventory of 1536 mentions a blue velvet frontal with images of souls coming out of Purgatory for use at the High Altar on All Souls' Day (*Processions*.167).

[Votive Masses]

Requiem	black[57]
the Holy Trinity	(no specified colour)[58]
the Holy Ghost	(no colour specified; possibly white)[59]
Corpus Christi	(no colour specified; possibly red)[60]
the Passion (Holy Cross, Five Wounds, *de Corona Domini*)	(no colour specified; possibly red or Lenten white)[61]
Our Lady	white
other saints and angels	(no specified colour; probably the saint's usual colour)
Salus Populi	(no specified colour)[62]
for Peace	(no colour specified; perhaps Lenten white)[63]
Ad invocandam gratiam Spiritus Sancti and *Ad poscendum donum Spiritus Sancti*	(no colour specified; possibly white)[64]
the Nuptial Mass	(no colour specified; perhaps green)[65]
all other votive Masses printed in the Missal[66]	(no colour specified)

---

[57] C 66.42. In the case of the funeral, trental and anniversaries of a canon of the cathedral church, however, Cons 118 prescribes white silken vestments, a practice perhaps found also at St. Paul's Cathedral, where the white suit had black apparels (HA.108).

[58] See Trinity Sunday in the table, and also HA.158 for a discussion of the colour at weddings, which were followed by a votive Mass of the Holy Trinity. The font at Great Witchingham shews the priest vested in green for a wedding.

[59] At Wells, red was used for votive Masses of the Holy Ghost, as also at Whitsun, whereas at Sarum Whitsun was celebrated in white, an English peculiarity (HA.149).

[60] See note 31.

[61] By analogy with the feasts of the Cross, the colour of passional Masses should be red (C 47.2), but the Mass *de Corona Domini* opens up a doubt. This Mass, with some variations, is included in the Roman Missal as granted *aliquibus locis*, sometimes during Lent and sometimes after Easter. In the Roman Missal, the preface of the Holy Cross (which Sarum lacks) is said. The rule of the Roman Missal before the twentieth century was that Masses *de Passione Domini* had purple vestments (*Rubricae Generales Missalis*, XVIII.5), even though the feasts of the Invention and Exaltation of the Holy Cross are said in red. On the one hand, therefore, the colour red would be in accordance with Sarum practice as concerns feasts of the Cross; on the other, however, a more penitential and Lenten colour, possibly white, would not be unreasonable. HA.96–7 gives no clear guidance but seems to incline towards red for the Jesus Mass.

[62] Red was used at Eton College and blue (*blodius*) at Exeter (HA.97).

[63] White at Wells.

[64] By analogy with Whitsun, though as a Mass of supplication rather than of celebration, Lenten white would also be reasonable.

[65] See note 58.

[66] *Pro rege, Pro seipso, Pro peccatoribus, Pro poenitentibus, Pro inspiratione divinae Sapientiae, Pro tribulatione cordis, Pro infirmo, Pro salute amici, Pro serenitate aeris, Pro pluvia petenda, Tempore belli, Pro eo qui in vinculis tenetur, Contra mortalitatem hominum, Pro peste animalium, Pro quacunque tribulatione, Pro iter agentibus.*

BOOK II

LITURGICAL GESTURE

V

CERTAIN COMMON RITUAL ACTIONS

Most ritual actions conform to those of the Roman rite and so are not described at length here. Others deserve a brief note.

§1. DEPORTMENT AND POSITIONS OF THE HANDS

When approaching or receding from the altar, the celebrant and the sacred ministers always do so *per longiorem*, that is to say, they stand in the middle at the foot of the altar and bow.[1]

Other than when a man is sitting, the hands' position of rest is folded on the breast, as in the Roman rite, except that the thumbs are not crossed.[2] However, when the deacon and the subdeacon wear chasubles, they keep their hands inside these.[3]

The elbows should be joined to the sides and, when the arms are extended in prayer, the extremities of the fingers should barely project above the shoulders.[4] The exception to this rule is at the *Unde et memores*, when the celebrant extends his arms fully in the manner of a cross.[5]

---

[1] OP.830.
[2] Rock IV.178 gives a picture, taken from a fourteenth-century manuscript (British Museum, Royal MS. 10, E. 4, f. 257) illustrating this. Chambers, plate facing page 392, gives another, from fourteenth-century France. A further example may be found in the thirteenth-century East Anglian Carrow Psalter, fol 178r, now in the possession of the Walters Art Museum (W.34). As late as 1557, Leonhard Badehorn, mayor of Leipzig, and his family were painted holding their hands thus (Pastoureau, page 103). OP.812 omits any mention of crossing the thumbs, though it gives the inferior servers the option of holding their arms crossed over the breast according to the custom of the province. This posture is found also in Goude, Plates XXIX and XXXII, and is sometimes used by junior ministers in the rite of Lyons. The fourteenth-century Morris Missal (*Tracts*, Plates I and II) appears to accept both forms. Whichever posture is to be adopted, it is desirable that there should be uniformity among the servers. The Roman Burckard would have the thumbs crossed (*Tracts*.130).
[3] C 66.2.
[4] Col 647 (*Cautelae Missae*). OP.1225 has the priest hold his palms away from himself as is still customary in Spain, but practice may have varied. The British Library's Sarum *Hours of the Umfray Family* (illustrated in France c. 1420) shews the celebrant's palms facing each other.
[5] Col 617.

§2. CROSSINGS

Signing oneself or another person or a thing is done as in the Roman rite,[6] with the exception that the thumb and first two fingers only of the right hand are extended, the last two fingers remaining bent into the palm.[7] When making the sign of the cross over something, the index finger should be over the middle finger.[8] When signing oneself, the other hand may rest meanwhile on the breast below the lowest point of the cross that is to be formed. When signing other people or things, the left hand may be placed on the altar if standing at it or on the breast if elsewhere.

§3. THE DIFFERENT KINDS OF OBEISANCE

The Sarum books employ several words to refer to different kinds of obeisance: *inclinatio*,[9] *inclinatio capitis et corporis*,[10] *humiliatio, genuflexio, prostratio*. Of these, the first two are clearly bows, and, although no categorical distinction is made between them, it is highly probable that some bows are deeper than others. Apart from the individual instances when the rubrics prescribe bows, a bow to the altar is always made when crossing from one side of the church to the other,[11] and it is likely that bows should also be made when approaching or departing from the altar[12] or the choir, when crossing from one side of the altar to the other,[13] when a junior server or minister approaches a senior server or minister or the celebrant or recedes from him,[14] and at the holy names of Jesus and Mary;[15] also at the words *Humiliate capita vestra*

---

[6] Blunt, page 80, gives: 'And in thys blyssynge ye begynne wyth youre honde at the hedde downewarde. & then to the lyfte syde. and after to the ryghte syde ... And after this, ye bryng your hande to your breste.'

[7] Col 648 (*Cautelae Missae*). *Tracts*, Plate II, shews the thumb hidden behind the first two fingers, making the gesture agree with Humbert's rule for the Dominicans (Bonniwell, page 385) rather than the modern Dominicans (OP.1242). Chambers, plate facing page 76, shews a bishop in the act of blessing; the plate facing page 4 shews a variant gesture. See also Rock III.176, IV.155–6 and Blunt, page 80.

[8] *Tracts*.80.

[9] E.g. Col 587.

[10] E.g. Col 594. When bowing at the altar, Col 648 (*Cautelae Missae*) gives *toto curvatus corpore*.

[11] At least when crossing from one side of the choir to the other (C 3). O.Praem.I.11–12 prescribes a deep bow when crossing the middle of the altar.

[12] Col 629 prescribes a bow before leaving the altar at the end of Mass, but the Dominican and other rites expect everybody to bow profoundly whenever they approach or depart from the altar (OP.830).

[13] OP.822.

[14] OP.810–11.

[15] Chambers, page 92, refers to this bow at the name of Jesus and to indulgences granted by Urban IV and John XXII. *The Catholic Encyclopedia* s.v. 'Holy Name of Jesus' makes a similar claim. An additional indulgence was granted by John Grandisson, bishop of Exeter, in 1328, in his decree, *Ineffabilis misericordiae*, in which he includes bowing at the name of Mary in the indulgences granted by these two popes (Dalton, page 141).
  At the *Communicantes* in the Canon, Col 614 instructs the priest to bow, but it is unclear whether he is to bow at the name of Mary only or also at the name of Jesus. Given the difference in dignity between the two, the former is unlikely. It is more probable that the priest should bow constantly from *Mariae* to *Christi*. M.89 has a similarly ambiguous rubric in the embolism, but again it is unlikely that the bow should be made at the names of Ss. Peter, Paul and Andrew rather than at

Deo;[16] when cantors or lectors at the step, having bowed to the altar, separate to go to their stalls, they bow slightly to each other;[17] when receiving holy water or incense;[18] when the choir greets the celebrant on his arrival and departure.[19] The term *humiliatio*[20] is discussed at the places where it occurs.

Genuflection in the Roman sense of the term does not seem to be contemplated as a habitual gesture.[21] Kneeling, however, occurs frequently. The Sarum books distinguish between kneeling erect and prostration. This latter consists of a profound bow made while kneeling and is defined by the Dominicans as *'quando flexis genibus cum cubitis et corpore procumbimus et prosternimur super formas, vel super genua, quando non habemus formas'*.[22] When rising from such a prostration, the books sometimes require that the floor or the form be kissed.[23] On some occasions, a full prostration, lying flat on the floor as in the Roman rite, might take place.[24]

---

that of St. Mary. These rubrics encourage us to assume that the bows indulgenced by Urban IV and John XXII, and promoted in England since at least 1328, had entered the liturgy at Sarum. The Dominican (OP.817) and other rites also have adopted this bow. Becon, pages 54 and 120, has the congregation make a 'courtesie' when the Holy Name occurs in the Gospel.
C 13.2 makes no mention of bowing at *Gloria Patri* (cf. OP.748).

[16] OP.749.
[17] OP.751(1).
[18] OP.752.
[19] The cases at OP.754 are not dissimilar.
[20] E.g. Col 626. This term may imply a profound bow or a genuflection or kneeling. It is prescribed for the deacon when asking for the priest's blessing before the Gospel and for the celebrant at *Ave in aeternum* before Communion, and is discussed more fully at those places.
[21] It may occur at *Flectamus genua* (e.g. Col 135, where *genu flectant* may be the same as *genuflectant*), by the subdeacon at *Dominus vobiscum* before the collects and postcommons at Mass (see Chapter XIV, note 53), and at the *Gloria in excelsis* on Holy Saturday (Col 353) and Whitsun Eve (Col 423). Becon, page 80, has: 'Christ sate, yee sometime stand upright, sometime leane upon your elbowes, sometime crouch downeward, sometime kneele', where 'crouch downeward' may allude to genuflection, and 'I passe over your monstrous and apish toyes, your inclinations and prostrations, your complications and explications, your elevations and extensions, your incurvations and genuflexions, your inspirations and exosculations, your benedictions & humiliations, your pulsations and pausations, with your consignations, and all other abominations' (pages 297–8) where, however, 'genuflexions' may mean no more than 'kneeling'. *Genuflectio* is specifically forbidden at the verse *Adjuva nos* in the Tract *Domine non secundum* (Col 137). OP.775 prescribes a genuflection *utroque genu* at *Flectamus genua*, thereby making certainty concerning Sarum ritual doubly impossible. It is generally thought that, by the sixteenth century, genuflection was probably taking the place of some of the bows during Mass. However, if this was the case, the rubrics had not caught up with the practice by the death of Queen Mary and so we have not presumed their introduction. For the genuflection before the *Gloria in excelsis* at Low Mass, see Chapter VII, note 17.
[22] OP.781. The lack of clarity concerning prostration is almost total. Some attempt at elucidation is made in the notes, but often through no more than a quotation of the ambiguous Latin. A passage that may be attempting to distinguish between genuflection and prostration may be found at M.129.
[23] E.g. *Processions*.62, 66, 71.
[24] Rock IV.199 and Col 839*. Also, from *Miscellanea quoad Sarum* (*Processions*.148). In the absolution from excommunication, the stripped excommunicate places himself before the doors of the church *prostratus, vel flexis genibus* (*Processions*.257). From Missal C.453 (of blessing a pilgrim): *deinde dicat has oraciones super illos in terram prostratos*. Hereford.xxxv tells the ministers to be diligent *nec jacere prostrati, sed stare et considerare processum Sacerdotis*. Jerdan, page 22, has the king and queen at their coronation lie prostrate as they say the *Confiteor* before their Communion and then 'somewhat arise kneeling' to receive the Sacrament. For the spouses during the nuptial Mass, see Chapter XXIV.

§4. INCENSING

When incensing, the modern distinction between double and simple swings is not observed.[25] The usual bows before and after incensing should be retained, however.[26] Additionally, the person being incensed bows the head slightly while receiving the incense.[27] When two persons minister to the celebrant at the imposition of incense, the act may be carried out as in the Roman rite, with the exception that the deacon holds out the incense on the spoon to be blessed by the celebrant and then imposes the single spoonful in the thurible himself.[28] When the thurifer ministers on his own, he will do so most conveniently as in the Dominican rite. The manner of wielding the thurible in this way is explained admirably by Fr. A. Thompson, O.P., and those of his words that are not incompatible with the Sarum rubrics are worth quoting *paene in extenso*:

> The thurifer holds the chains near the disk (or the disk ring) with the little finger of the left hand; with his left forefinger and thumb he holds the boat (which must have a little pedestal base). With his right hand he holds the chains just above the cover, holding the thurible at about waist height on his right side. This is how he always holds the thurible when it is not in use: it is never carried or held with the chain at full length, except during the singing of the Gospel … [To minister,] he lowers the thurible and, with his right hand, pulls up the center chain ring and hooks it on the ring finger of his left hand. This will raise the thurible cover about four or five inches: more than enough to get access to the coals. Then, with his right hand, he grasps the four chains just above the cover and raises them up so that he can grasp them with the last three fingers of his left hand.
>
> The open thurible is now at waist height, and the thurifer's right hand is free. With it, he opens the boat, and takes out a spoonful of incense. He offers this to the priest, saying, 'Benedicite'. The priest blesses the incense, the thurifer responding 'Amen'. The thurifer then puts the incense in the censer, places the spoon back in the boat, closes the boat, and takes the chains off the three fingers of the left hand, letting the chains extend completely. He then takes the center chain ring off the left ring finger and lowers the cover of the thurible. He then takes the chains just above the cover with his right hand, so as to assume the position for holding or walking with the thurible. One should note that the sliding ring around the chains,

---

[25] O' Connell, *Celebration of Mass*, III.33–4, includes an informative note on the development of this distinction.
[26] OP.751 (implicitly) and OP.752 (explicitly).
[27] So the Dominicans of whatever rank, whether celebrant (OP.1114), sacred minister (OP.1066 and OP.1033), junior server (OP.1000) or clerk in choir (OP.752).
[28] This is the usual Dominican practice. By blessing the incense in the spoon, rather than in the boat, more incense can be blessed later, at the Gospel and the offertory, without blessing the same incense repeatedly. See Chapter XVII, note 2. A corollary of this practice is that, unlike at Rome, only one spoonful of blessed incense can be imposed each time. So also Lyons III.209. Morse §63, influenced perhaps by the Roman rite, has the celebrant bless the incense in the thurible. However, he has neglected the word *prius* in the rubric (Col 581). It seems unlikely that the deacon should ask the priest to bless the incense and then whip the spoon away and impose the incense before the priest actually blesses it.

if present, is never pushed down onto the cover of the thurible. It remains at midpoint of the chains at all times. If it is pushed down, these movements would be hindered or impossible. ...

When the thurible is carried, whether there is incense lighted in it or not, it is never held with the full chain extended. It is held or carried as explained above. This means that the chains are in the proper position if the thurible is to be given to a major minister to hand to the priest. If the thurifer is to hand the thurible to the priest himself, he must reverse his hands first – so that the priest will receive the thurible correctly oriented for use. ...

When the thurifer (or priest or deacon) incenses, this is done without any swinging of the censer during the *ductus*. Thus there is no chain-clanking. The motion is straight up and down, entirely silent.[29]

---

[29] Thompson, 'Incense and Thuribles in the Dominican Rite'. See also OP.957.

BOOK III

LOW MASS

VI

PREPARATION

Low Mass[1] would have been said between daybreak and noon.[2] There is no provision for evening Masses in the Sarum books. The celebrant must be in a state of grace and fasting.[3] He should have said at least Matins, Lauds, Prime and Terce.[4] The assistance of one clerk is presumed.

Before Mass, the following preparations must be made. The altar has a cross between two lit candles, which should stand at either end. The missal-stand is at the south nook[5] of the altar, straight, so that its front line is parallel with the front of the altar. Also on the south part of the altar, if the Pax is to be given, stands the pax-brede on its foot, with its cloth and, at least if the bedes are to be bidden at the altar, the *Liber vitae*. There are no altar cards.[6]

The elevation torch stands elsewhere, on the south side.[7] In the aumbry or on the credence table the cruets stand, filled with wine and water, with the dish and towel. If the people will make its offering, there should be a plate or cloth to receive this. If there is to be a general Communion, the vessel with watered[8] wine for the purification of the communicants' mouths, covered by its napkin, will be needed. If there will be a great number of communicants and two clerks available, a second vessel and napkin may be set out. When there is to be a general Communion, it is better to use hosts consecrated at the Mass or to celebrate at the altar of reservation. If a handheld bell is to be employed, it may be in the aumbry or at the south side, near where the clerk will kneel. In the sacristy, the vessels and their dressing are prepared and the vestments are

---

[1] Ceremonial directions are given in C 66, Cons 39 and Coll 1–17, 577–638 and 647–51. Most suggestions taken from other sources are indicated as such in the notes.
[2] Col 629 assumes that Mass is ordinarily sung before None. Chambers, page 309, explains the canonical position.
[3] In the sixteenth century, probably at least from midnight. For modern celebrations, it is probable (by analogy) that the rule given in *Universae Ecclesiae*, §27 (*Acta Apostolicae Sedis*, Vol. CIII, N.6, pages 413–20), that the discipline of the 1983 *Codex Iuris Canonici* applies, should be followed.
[4] Council of Oxford (1322) *apud* Rock IV.170. Lyndwode (Chambers, page 309) allows private Masses to be said early in the day before Terce is sung in choir. Perhaps a priest who will assist in choir later may be excused the praying of his hours privately before an early Low Mass.
[5] This is where it will first be used, for the Officium (Col 581). See also S.10 (B.87–8).
[6] Altar cards do not appear before the sixteenth century and seem not to be mentioned in an English context even then. For a brief account of their history, see *The Catholic Encyclopedia* s.v. 'Altar Cards'.
[7] This seems to be also the primitive practice of the Dominicans (OP.494).
[8] S.381.

laid out on the vesting table. The missal will be placed near the vestments, so that the priest may first find and mark the places in it.

At Low Mass, three tones of voice are employed.[9] Everything that is sung at High Mass is read aloud, so that it may be heard by all who assist. Whatever is spoken between the celebrant and the clerk, such as *Benedicite* and the prayers at the foot of the altar, *Orate fratres et sorores* and *Nobis quoque peccatoribus*, is said in a middle voice, such that the interlocutors, but not other bystanders, may hear each other clearly. Everything else is said secretly, so that the celebrant alone may hear himself. Nothing is to be said so quietly as to be inaudible to the speaker.

When the priest is ready, he washes his hands, combs his hair[10] and prepares the chalice. On the chalice, he places the purificator, the paten, having on it the host,[11] the pall,[12] the veil and the burse, with a corporal inside.

Then he puts on the vestments.[13] First, he takes the amice and places it on his head, where he keeps it while he puts on the other vestments in order:[14] alb, cincture, maniple on the left arm,[15] stole crossed before his breast,[16] and chasuble. If he will wear a cap, he pulls the amice back, leaving the apparel as a collar outside the other vestments. While vesting,[17] he says *Veni creator*, &c. When vested, he says ℣. *Emitte Spiritum tuum* and its collect with joined hands.

Once he has vested, he says *Introibo ad altare Dei* and the Psalm *Judica me*. He repeats *Introibo ad altare Dei* and proceeds *Kyrie eleyson. Christe eleyson. Kyrie eleyson. Pater noster*. He continues the prayer silently up to *Sed libera nos a malo. Amen*. He then says the first part of the *Ave Maria*[18] silently.

He now[19] takes the chalice, covered, in the left hand, and lays the right on the burse. The veil should cover the chalice in front, so that it cannot be seen. Holding the chalice so, with head covered with a cap or the amice, he bows to the cross in the sacristy,

---

[9] OP.1196-9, where, however, some of the prayers at the foot of the altar and *Nobis quoque peccatoribus* are said aloud, and the Last Gospel is said in the intermediate voice.

[10] Rock II.101-4.

[11] Alternatively, after the model of High Mass, the host may be presented in a pyx by the server when the chalice is made.

[12] For the reasons why the use of the pall is presumed and its placing on the chalice, see Chapter II, notes 17 and 20.

[13] For vesting at the altar when there is no vestry, see *Tracts*.238 and S.6 and 163. The Sarum books often mention a vestry (*vestiarium*), e.g. C 36.2 and C 66.15.

[14] This is the order of the vesting prayers in Missal BM.216. See also S.167.

[15] S.168; Becon, page 71: 'upon your left arme ye put on a Fannell.'

[16] S.168. The Gayton Thorpe font seems to shew this done left over right; that at Great Glemham, right over left. Modern Dominican practice is to cross the stole right over left.

[17] Missal C.216: *sacerdos albis indutus dicat ymnum*.

[18] The text used was probably that given at M.30: *Ave Maria gratia plena Dominus tecum: benedicta tu in mulieribus: et benedictus fructus ventris tui Jesus. Amen*. See also *The Catholic Encyclopedia* s.v. 'Ave Maria' and Rock III.258 and III.261 for further reasons for this supposition. Procter and Wordsworth, in their edition of the Great Breviary of 1531 (B.III.xxx), state that that is the only Sarum breviary to include the second half of the *Ave Maria* and call its inclusion a blunder. None of the editions printed under Queen Mary include the second half. Littlehales, page 20 *et alibi*, illustrates in English the form of saying these prayers. Blunt, page 79, defends the 'short' *Ave Maria* as official, though it tolerates additional words for private use. See also S.184.

[19] Col 579: *his finitis*.

then follows the clerk into the church. At the door of the sacristy, the priest may cross himself with holy water.

At the foot of the altar, he bows profoundly.[20] Then he goes up to the altar, puts the chalice on his left, places the burse on the north side and spreads the corporal in the middle of the altar. He must take care to do this so that room is left in front of the chalice for him to kiss the altar.

In order to make the chalice,[21] the celebrant now removes the veil and places it, folded, on the altar to the right of the corporal. He places the pall on the right of the corporal, the paten with the host in the middle of the corporal and the purificator alongside the right of the corporal.

Holding the chalice in his left hand by the node, he goes to the south end, takes the wine cruet from the clerk with his right hand and pours some wine into the chalice. When the clerk says *Benedicite*, the priest makes the sign of the cross over the water, saying, *Dominus. Ab eo*, &c. and then pours a few drops of water[22] into the chalice. Returning to the middle of the altar, he places the chalice on the corporal and, having wiped it with the purificator, dresses it, leaving the burse and the purificator on the altar as before.[23]

With joined hands he then goes to the missal, opens it at the Officium[24] and returns to the middle. He turns by the right[25] and goes to the top step (the first step below the foot pace, that is, the first step below the level where he stands while saying Mass).[26] Where the foot pace has no steps leading to it, the celebrant stands on the floor. If the bedes will not be bidden and there will be no sermon but there are any notices to give out, he does so now.[27] When he is ready to begin the Mass, the celebrant bows profoundly to the altar.

---

[20] The Sarum books do not mention this bow explicitly, though its companion, at the end of the Mass, is prescribed at C 66.35. OP.1215 commands it for the Dominicans when the Sacrament is not reserved or exposed; in the other cases, it commands a genuflection, but this was introduced only in 1569 (King, *Religious Orders*, page 349) and is not mentioned in the Sarum books. Becon, page 296, might mention some form of genuflection at the end of Mass ('solemnly making curtesie to your God, that hangeth over the altar, ye trudg out of the Church'), but he also uses 'courtesie' of bowing at the Holy Name (page 54) so the question cannot be considered closed.

[21] There is no certainty as to when the chalice was prepared at Low Mass. This moment varied considerably from use to use (cf. Legg, *Ecclesiological Essays*, chapter V). By the sixteenth century, the chalice was generally prepared at the altar. Becon, pages 117–18 (see Chapter VII, note 34), suggests that at Low Mass the chalice has been made well before the Gospel, presumably before the beginning of Mass. The Dominicans prepare the chalice at the altar before coming down for the prayers at the foot of the altar, and we have followed them here. The question should not be given excessive importance: as late as the 1590s, Suarez, in *De Sacramentis*, maintained that in choosing a moment for making the chalice *nulla est praecepti necessitas* (*Tracts*.239).

[22] Col 649: *parvissima quantitate*.

[23] OP.1217.

[24] S.190.

[25] With the exceptions to be noted, the celebrant at Mass always turns from the altar and back to it by the south side, that is, on turning from the altar by his right hand, on turning back to it by his left. See OP.1225-6.

[26] C 66.4.

[27] Cons 123.7 has the notices given after the procession and before Mass but does not seem to contemplate notices being given at private Masses. They are not to be given out after the Gospel. Since even now in the Roman rite the priest sometimes announces his intention after preparing the missal and before beginning the prayers at the foot of the altar and the Sarum books presume the Mass to begin with the Officium, the moment chosen here for the notices has seemed the most suitable.

VII

TO THE GOSPEL

With joined hands, the celebrant begins in the middle voice[1] ℣. *Et ne nos inducas* and ℣. *Confitemini*. As he says this last, he makes the sign of the cross.[2]

While he says the *Confiteor*, he bows profoundly.[3] He does not strike his breast at *mea culpa*.[4] He remains profoundly bowed while the clerk says the prayer *Misereatur* and his own confession.[5] As he says *Absolutionem*,[6] he does not make the sign of the cross.[7] Standing erect, he continues[8] with ℣. *Adjutorium* and ℣. *Sit nomen Domini*.

---

[1] In a low voice because these prayers form part of the celebrant's and server's preparation for Mass. If we accept as a rule that everything that is sung at High Mass is said aloud in a clear voice at Low Mass, the implication is that everything else is said quietly, presumably including everything before the Officium. On the other hand, the prayer *Aufer a nobis* is directed to be said *tacita voce* (Col 581), as though that which precedes it had been said aloud. According to Fortescue, *The Mass*, page 227, the Roman Missal of 1550 allowed either voice for the psalm *Judica* before the celebrant went to the altar. It is possible that different priests used different tones of voice for these prayers, as still happens in practice in the Roman rite. As these prayers became less the private preparation of the priest and more the beginning of the public service, there was a general move towards saying them aloud (cf. OP.1196 and OP.1198). In any case, they must be said sufficiently loudly for the server to be able to answer, so a quiet but audible voice may be the most judicious.

[2] No sign of the cross is mentioned in the Sarum, Hereford or York books. The Dominicans do make the sign of the cross, but their example is less valuable in this instance because they have introduced *In nomine Patris*, &c. before *Confitemini* (OP.1219). Although the books keep silent on the matter, perhaps because at the time when they were written these prayers were still the semi-private preparation of the priest and so their ceremonial was less codified than that of the rest of the Mass, yet Becon, page 105, supposes this crossing, which indeed is to be expected at the beginning of any Christian act: 'Now standing before the Altar, after yee have crossed your selves upon your forheads and breasts for feare of wicked spirits, ye say the *Confiteor*.'

[3] The Missal does not mention bowing, but it seems a reasonable assumption by analogy with other uses. Cf. OP.831.

[4] Striking the breast is not mentioned in the Missal or B.I.xiii and is prohibited by OP.1220.

[5] OP.1221.

[6] Col 580 gives the reading *vestrorum*, but C 66.4 gives *nostrorum*. In the Roman rite, *vestrorum* is classed as an abuse that proved very difficult to eradicate and so may represent an earlier tradition. Since there is no way of ascertaining the 'right' reading, perhaps one may take refuge in that catch-all instruction of the Congregation of Sacred Rites: *servetur rubrica*. The Dominicans say *vestrorum*. See also Chapter XIV, note 5.

[7] The sign of the cross is mentioned neither by the Missal nor by the Customary nor in *Tracts*.74 and is proscribed by OP.1220. But see Chapter XIV, note 5.

[8] C 66.5 gives verses and ceremonies that were interpolated here in churches other than the cathedral itself. The Dickinson Missal makes no mention of these.

During all this time, the priest holds the hands joined before the breast. As he says *Oremus*, he separates the hands and joins them again, but does not raise them.[9]

He now bows deeply[10] and goes up to the middle of the altar.[11] There, bowing profoundly and with folded hands, he silently says *Oremus* again and the prayer *Aufer a nobis*. He stands erect, kisses the altar in the middle, resting his hands extended on the altar on either side of the corporal.[12] Standing erect, he signs himself saying *In nomine*.[13]

Making no further reverence to the cross, he goes with joined hands to the missal at the south corner.[14] Here he reads the Officium of the Mass in a clear voice without making the sign of the cross and repeating the Officium as many times as the day's rank requires.[15] He continues immediately with the *Kyrie* in the same voice alternately with the clerk, still standing at the missal. At the end of the Kyries, he uncovers. If the *Gloria in excelsis* is to be said,[16] he goes to the middle to begin it.[17] At the words *Gloria*

---

[9] So the Roman rite.
[10] Cons 39.6. See Chapter XIV, note 5.
[11] Col 581.
[12] From F.45:

> This position of the hands is to be observed every time he kisses the altar. During Mass, except from the Consecration to the Communion, whenever the celebrant lays his hands on the altar, he places them, not on the corporal, but one on either side of it. Between the Consecration and the Communion, when the forefingers and thumbs are joined all the time, he lays his hands on the corporal.

Missal C.220 makes a point of stating that, at *Hanc igitur*, the celebrant lays his hands on the altar outside the corporal: *submittat manus suas super altare ex utraque parte corporalium*.

[13] Col 581. In this instance, Becon, page 109, reports a use that is clearly at variance with true Sarum ritual, for he has: 'yee approach to the Altar, and making a crosse upon it, yee kisse it.' As is often the case, ceremonies evolve differently in different uses. Perhaps as relics from the old beginning of the Mass at the introit, it is almost universal for the celebrant to kiss the altar and make the sign of the cross upon arriving at the altar after his preparation. While kissing the altar is a fairly fixed ceremony, the manner of crossing varies considerably. In some, as at Sarum, the celebrant crosses himself; in other missals, he kisses the foot of a crucifix (Évreux, in Martène, Lib.I. Cap.IV. Art. XII. Ordo XXVIII) or a picture of a cross in the missal (e.g. that of Antoine de Longeuil, bishop of St. Pol-de-Léon, in Martène, Lib.I. Cap.IV. Art.XII. Ordo XXXIV); in yet others, he might trace a cross with his thumb and then kiss it (OP.1221). It is a ceremony of this kind that Becon seems to be describing here. Duplication can easily creep in (cf. OP.1222). The restrained Roman rite makes the celebrant kiss the altar during *Oramus te, Domine* and sign himself at the missal as he begins the introit. Neither the Sarum books nor OP.1222 has a crossing at the Officium, probably for this reason.

[14] Col 581.
[15] Coll 581–2.
[16] The ordering of the prayers lies outside the remit of a book on ceremonial. The rules may be found in the Missal and the Customary. In addition to these, a mnemonic verse is given at M.181 for the days when *Gloria* and *Credo* are said.
[17] Col 583. Becon, page 111, describes an additional ceremony: 'After these things', viz. Kyrie, 'ye goe unto the midst of the Altar, and look up to the pixe, where you thinke your God to be, and making solemne curtesie, like womanly *Ioane*, ye say the *Gloria in excelsis*.' The comparison with 'womanly Ioane' makes it almost certain that a genuflection in the modern sense is meant. Coll 353 and 423 prescribe genuflections for the choir at this point in the unparalleled Vigils of Easter and Whitsun, and it is not inconceivable that the genuflection at the *Gloria* was usual and mentioned there merely on account of the accompanying ceremony of the canons doffing their black *cappae chorales*. On the other hand, this genuflection is not mentioned in the Sarum books, does not appear in other rites and is not observed by the Dominicans, and so is not recommended here. Becon must be referring to a genuine ceremony, however, and it may be that it was to be found as a semi-private devotion of priests, who were prompted to adore the Sacrament in the pyx as it hung overhead *in excelsis*.

in, he lays his hands extended on the altar;[18] at *excelsis*, he elevates them; at *Deo*, he joins them, bowing his head moderately to the cross.[19] Then he returns to the missal from which he reads the rest of the hymn in a clear voice, taking care to bow[20] his head moderately to the book at the words *Adoramus te, suscipe deprecationem nostram* and *Jesu Christe*. At the end, he signs himself[21] at the words *In gloria Dei Patris*.[22]

Having crossed himself, even when the *Gloria in excelsis* is omitted,[23] still standing at the book, he turns[24] by his right[25] to face west and says *Dominus vobiscum*, extending and elevating his arms somewhat and joining his hands.[26] In turning, he pivots about in the same spot, so that his back will be directly in front of the missal. He turns back to the missal, turning by his left, not completing the circle. Facing the altar and extending his hands,[27] he says *Oremus* and reads the collects, joining his hands at the end of the last. Only the first and second are preceded by *Oremus*; only the first and the last have their own conclusion[28] and *Amen*.

---

[18] As at the creed (see Chapter VIII, note 8), only the Dominicans have the hands laid on the altar at this point (OP.1224).

[19] These gestures are found in *Tracts*.75 and OP.1224.

[20] G.11+ *& seq*: *inclinando*.

[21] See Pearson, page xlv.

[22] Col 587.

[23] The celebrant crosses himself before turning for *Dominus vobiscum* but does not kiss the altar. He does this before the collects, before the Offertory and before the postcommon. This last instance suggests that the crossing is associated with turning to greet the people rather than with the *Gloria* and the creed, the rubric at Col 587 (*ad* Gloria in excelsis, *quando dicitur* In gloria Dei Patris, Amen) notwithstanding. Missal B.217 seems to reflect a more primitive practice: *Hiis completis signet se sacerdos in facie dicens* In nomine Patris. et filii. et. spiritus. sancti. *et reversus ad populum dicens* Dominus uobiscum. The former existence of special words to accompany the sign of the cross suggests that the crossing was originally independent of the end of the *Gloria* but was anticipated to *In gloria Dei Patris* when the *Gloria* was said. So, even though he crosses himself towards the end of the *Gloria* and the creed and does not repeat the signing before *Dominus vobiscum*, the celebrant should still cross himself when the *Gloria* and the creed are not said.

[24] At this point, the Dominican rite (but only since 1622: Acta OP.VI.325) makes a distinction between Mass celebrated at an altar at which the Blessed Sacrament is reserved and one at which it is not (OP.1225 and OP.845). Although there appears to have been a tabernacle at Holyrood before the Reformation (King, *Roman Church*, p. 94), it was not until Cardinal Pole's Legatine Synod of 1555 that tabernacles came into use in England. Since the Dominican stipulations become otiose in the absence of a tabernacle, we have followed the Domincan Low Mass when the Sacrament is not reserved at the same altar.

[25] OP.1225.

[26] Col 588 does not make it quite clear whether the celebrant raises his joined hands or raises them extended and then joins them as is done at Rome and among the Dominicans (OP.1225-6). However, Hereford.116, which contains this same stipulation in a very similar wording, goes on to add that the hands are separated for the *Dominus vobiscum* and then joined again. The priest then turns back to the altar and separates them again for *Oremus* and the collect. Describing the *Orate fratres*, OP.1238 gives a similar wording to that of Col 588 here (*elevatis et extensis*) to describe a movement that is identical to that at *Dominus vobiscum* before the collects, so the traditional practice, as it has survived among the Dominicans, is recommended here.

It is perilous to take such rubrics too literally: imprecise language is as possible in a missal as in any other writing. The Roman rite itself used to contain a similar difficulty. Its *Rubricae Generales* VI.3 directed the celebrant to begin the creed *elevans et extendens manus*, whereas the *Ordo Missae* contradicted this, saying *extendens, elevans et jungens manus*, the latter being the traditional and general practice.

[27] Hereford.116, differing from OP.1226.

[28] C 68 gives the rules for the different conclusions.

After the last collect, he lays his hands on either side of the book[29] and reads the epistle. He then goes on at once[30] to read, in the same tone of voice, the gradual, tract, Alleluya or sequence[31] as these occur in the missal. He must remember to repeat the gradual's antiphon after the verse on the days appointed.[32]

He then comes to the middle of the altar[33] with hands joined, leaving the book open at the south side. In the middle, he raises the front of the chalice veil with both hands and folds it back over the pall or paten. Steadying the foot of the chalice with his left hand, he raises the pall (or the veil) a little, enough to check that the host is present on the paten. He then folds the veil forwards as it was before.[34] Then, bowing to the cross[35] with joined hands, he says *Jube, Domine, benedicere. Dominus sit.* Standing erect, he signs himself as he continues *In nomine Patris*, &c.[36] When there is no minister to move the missal, the celebrant himself does so before returning to the middle to peep at the paten and say *Jube, Domine, benedicere.*[37]

---

[29] O.P.1228. *Tracts*.140 (Burckard) allows the hands to be joined before the breast or laid either on the book or the altar.

[30] O.P.1228 has the chants read with joined hands.

[31] The sequence never ends in *Amen* (Col 11). *Tracts*.95 directs the priest to omit the sequence *in missis privatis*. Similarly, in the Roman rite, the sequence may be omitted in daily Masses for the Dead. The omission of the (frequently lengthy) sequence at Sarum may have been usual in Low Masses. On the other hand, Rock IV.173 presumes, on no cited authority, that the sequence was read at Low Mass, and he seems to be supported by Becon, page 49.

[32] See Col 8 for these days.

[33] Col 589 states that, except for beginning the *Gloria in excelsis*, everything from the Officium to the epistle and from the Communion to the end of Mass is said at the south end of the altar, and that (except for the Gospel when there is no deacon) everything else is said at the middle. There is no mention of where the blessing before the Gospel is said, but, in the light of this rubric and the Roman and Dominican practice, it seems reasonable to assume that it is said at the middle.

[34] The *Alphabetum Sacerdotum*, after the missal has been moved to the north corner, instructs the priest: *Deinde visitet hic sacrificium surgendo* (alias *levando*) *patenam supra quam debet esse hostia, respiciendo infra calicem si sit vinum et aqua et dicat:* Jube domine benedicere ... (*Tracts*.39). See also *Tracts*.294. Although the Sarum books make no mention of this ceremony, Becon, pages 117–18, appears to confirm that this was also contemporary English practice: 'Yee take up your Massebook, and away ye goe to the other end of the Altar to reade the Gospel. But first of all yee uncover the chalice, and look whether your drinke bee there or no.' King, *Roman Church*, page 279, appears to base his sweeping assertion that the ceremony was observed 'in England immediately before the Reformation' on Becon, since besides this he mentions only French sources. Legg, *Ecclesiological Essays*, pages 133 and 147–8, makes a similar claim and refers to a half-uncovering of the chalice at this point in the Stowe Missal (Warner, page 7). The ceremony, therefore, has a long British history and, since it belongs especially to Low Mass, its omission from the rubrics of the Missal and customaries may be to be expected. Although the Dominicans have not preserved this peeping at Low Mass (unlike at High Mass: O.P.1058), it is presumed here.

[35] Unless a genuflection was made at this point, it could be that Becon, page 118, purposely misinterprets this bow when, after peeping at the host, he has the celebrant 'make solemn curtesie to your little Idoll, that hangeth over the Altar, and so goe in hand with the Gospel'.

[36] Col 12. At High Mass, he blesses the deacon, saying *In nomine*, &c. At Low Mass, both the Roman and the Dominican rites omit this blessing. At Col 12, however, the celebrant is instructed to say *In nomine Patris*, &c. so we presume that he signs himself also.

[37] So the *Alphabetum Sacerdotum* and Becon, for which see the note above, both of which seem to assume that the celebrant will move the missal himself. Indeed, the former provides a prayer to accompany the action. Since the Sarum books are silent on the question, Dominican practice (O.P.1229) has been followed here.

VIII

FROM THE GOSPEL TO THE PREFACE

§1. THE GOSPEL TO THE CREED

After the priest has said *Dominus sit in corde meo*, &c. he comes with joined hands to the book at the north side,[1] facing northeast. There he says *Dominus vobiscum*.[2] As he says *Sequentia* (or *Initium*) *sancti Evangelii secundum N.*, he lays the left hand on the book and makes the sign of the cross with the thumb upon the beginning of the Gospel.[3] Then, laying the left hand on his breast, he makes the sign of the cross with the thumb on his forehead and breast, saying *secundum N.*[4] As the clerk replies *Gloria tibi, Domine*, the celebrant turns to face the altar cross and signs himself from his forehead to his breast and shoulders.[5] Turning back to the missal, he then reads the Gospel.[6]

When the Gospel is finished, the celebrant kisses the book.[7] Then he brings the missal to the middle of the altar, but on the north side of the corporal, turning it diagonally towards the middle. It should not stand on the corporal but as near to it as possible. If the creed is to be said, he begins it at once in the middle of the altar. As he says *Credo in unum Deum*, he extends his hands, lifts them to the height of the shoulders, joins them as he says the word *Deum* and bows the head.[8] He says the creed with joined hands at the middle of the altar.[9] As he says the words *Et incarnatus est de Spiritu sancto*, he bows and stands erect again. He does likewise at the words *Et homo factus est* and again at *Crucifixus etiam pro nobis*.[10] As he says the last words, *et vitam*

---

[1] Col 589.
[2] Dominicans place their hands on the book to say *Dominus vobiscum* (OP.1230), while at Rome the priest keeps his hands joined.
[3] Hereford.117. See also S.16 and S.206.
[4] Hereford.117.
[5] At Col 587, the *lector Evangelii* turns to the altar and all the clergy cross themselves. OP.1230 does not instruct the celebrant to turn here. Should the celebrant bow to the altar? See Chapter XVII, notes 34 and 35.
[6] There is no indication as to the position of the hands during the Gospel. At Rome, the hands are held joined before the breast. At Low Mass, the Dominicans place their joined hands upon the book.
[7] Col 14. OP.1231 has this done at the beginning of the text without raising the book. The Sarum books do not have the celebrant cross himself here.
[8] OP.1232, Hereford.117 and the Roman books. Only the Dominicans mention placing the hands flat on the altar at the word *Credo*.
[9] This is implied by Col 589 and confirmed by Hereford.117. OP.1232-3 has the celebrant begin the creed in the middle, then continue it at the north side, returning to the middle only for *Incarnatus*.
[10] Col 14, quoting the Gradual.

venturi saeculi, he bows again[11] and immediately makes the sign of the cross,[12] laying the left hand on the breast.

§2. THE OFFERING OF THE SACRIFICE

After the creed, he turns to the people by the south side, his arms raised somewhat and his hands joined, as before the collects, and says *Dominus vobiscum*. If there is no creed in the Mass, he crosses himself and turns to say *Dominus vobiscum* as soon as he is at the middle, after the Gospel. Facing the altar again, without completing the circle, he says *Oremus*, extending and joining his hands.[13] In the same voice he then reads the Offertory with joined hands.

The offertory act now follows. The celebrant uncovers the chalice. He takes the veil from the chalice with both hands, folds it and lays it on the altar at his right, just outside the corporal beyond the purificator. He lays his left hand on the altar, outside the corporal. With the right[14] he takes the pall from the chalice and lays it on the folded veil. He now takes the chalice by its knop, holding its foot with the left. With his head slightly bowed,[15] he lifts the chalice, still having the paten upon it, to the level of the breast, and so holding it says the offertory prayer *Suscipe, Sancta Trinitas*. This said, he puts the chalice down in the middle of the corporal.[16] Removing the paten from the chalice with his left and then taking it in both hands, he puts it on the corporal before the foot of the chalice.[17] With both hands, he tips the paten slightly away from him so as to let the bread slip from the paten onto the corporal. His left hand once again on the altar, he brings the upper edge of the paten to his lips with his right and kisses it; then he lays it on the altar on the right, so that one half lies under the corporal and the other half on the purificator. With his right hand, he covers the chalice with the pall. Touching the foot of the chalice with his left hand to steady it, he makes the sign of the cross over the chalice and the bread, saying secretly, *In nomine Patris*, &c.

With joined hands, he now goes to the south end of the altar for the lavatory.

---

[11] Col 587. Although the rubric in the Missal refers to the choir and bids it bow from this moment to the offertory, which the celebrant cannot do, there is no reason why he cannot bow for the last words of the creed only as he has done for the other phrases in the creed where the rubric is also destined for the choir's use.

[12] Col 587 et seq. At Lincoln, the choir signed itself at the end of the creed (Constitutions of Lincoln (1212) *apud* Wilkins I.535).

[13] OP.1234.

[14] OP.1235.

[15] Col 593.

[16] The rubric after the offertory prayer (Col 593) is confused: it is inconceivable that the celebrant should lay down the chalice with paten on top, then cover the chalice, then remove the paten from under the pall, then slip the bread from the paten onto the corporal. Moreover, the words *In nomine Patris*, &c. suggest a sign of the cross somewhere. The reconstruction proposed here, which is close to OP.1236, is based on the rubric in Missal B.218 (*deinde ponat calicem in loco suo et cooperiatur cum corporali et insignet dicendo* In nomine Patris) and the silence of the customaries. The Carmelites, having covered the chalice, bless the offering while saying the prayer.

[17] Col 593 in a development from the earlier practice described by Rock I.208.

§3. THE PEOPLE'S OFFERTORY

However, if oblations of the people are to be received,[18] as soon as he has said *In nomine Patris*, &c. the celebrant removes his maniple and, holding it in his right hand,[19] turns again in the middle of the altar and comes down the steps.[20] There, facing west,[21] he receives with his left hand the offerings made by the clergy, who approach in order of rank, and deposits the offerings in the plate or cloth held before him by the clerk. On certain occasions, a worshipful layman may assist in receiving the offerings.[22] As he receives the offering, he extends his right hand or the end of the maniple to the person making the offering to kiss.[23] When the clergy have made their offerings, the celebrant

---

[18] The Sarum books themselves give no directions for the offertory of the people, the sermon or the bidding of the bedes beyond the vaguest of hints. Col 408 locates the sermon between the offertory anthem and the secret prayer. P.8 has the bidding of the bedes in parish churches take place *post evangelium et offertorium* and the offering seems not to be mentioned at all.

A Roman *Sacerdotale* of 1559 (fol. 76v–77v), describing a Low Mass, has the celebrant read the offertory antiphon, then receive the people's gifts, then preach a sermon followed by prayers and finally embark upon the offertory act. This retains the primitive place of the people's offertory. Jerdan, page 21, also supposes that the King presents the obley for his houseling before the offertory act, together with the wine for his purification. However, several authors (Fortescue, *The Mass*, page 285; King, *Roman Church*, page 262; S.232) appeal to Chaucer's *Pardoner's Tale* (lines 711–16) as an English authority for having the sermon after the offertory anthem has been sung (not read secretly). In corroboration, Martène, Lib.I. Cap.IV. Art.XII. Ordo XXIV and Ordo XXVIII, gives the custom at Bayeux and Évreux of receiving the gifts of the people after the offertory act and the incensation of the altar and before the lavatory. Rock III.23 relates how at the funeral of the ill-fated Prince Arthur, elder brother of Henry VIII, the sermon began immediately after the nobility had presented its gifts. In the Church of England, the reformed bidding of the bedes survived as the opening of the sermon (*Constitutions and Canons Ecclesiastical* LV apud *The Book of Common Prayer*), and this was the order that was retained in France until the demise of its local rites (S.318). That this order remained customary and was eradicated only with difficulty transpires from Olalla.205. Some case, therefore, can be made for Simmons's preferred order, and this has been adopted here.

The Sarum books, possibly because they were written to reflect practice at the Cathedral, where the bidding prayers and sermon did not interfere with the offertory, do not presume any interruption of the liturgy between the incensing of the altar and the lavatory (Col 595), and it falls to us to attempt to reconstruct how these ceremonies were performed. See S.142, 231–8 and 315–22 but also, for the reconstructed ceremonial, Solans, Part 2, pages 408 seq.

Since this offering would normally only take place at the principal Mass, it is generally omitted in Low Masses.

[19] *Sacerdotale* (1559), fol. 76.

[20] Olalla.205. The Roman *Sacerdotale* (1559) would have the offerings received at the south side of the altar, but in most English churches, with long choirs and proper chancel screens, it would be more practical to receive the offerings as suggested here. Olalla.206 also contemplates this possibility.

[21] S.238.

[22] S.236.

[23] Either the celebrant's hand or some object of devotion, such as the maniple, a cross or other image, was probably offered to the recipient to kiss. The use of the paten for this purpose has been reproved. See the Roman *Sacerdotale of* 1559 (fol. 76) and Olalla.205–6, which prescribe the maniple or image for women, lest they kiss the celebrant's hand.

The *Sacerdotale Romanum* of 1585 would have the celebrant say to each as he offers the maniple to kiss, either *Acceptabile sit sacrificium tuum omnipotenti Deo* or *Centuplum accipias et vitam aeternam possideas*. The priest should say this aloud in a low voice, so that the offerer should hear him. Solans reports the local custom of his diocese (Urgel), which was to say *Oblatio tua accepta sit Deo*, and that the Congregation of Sacred Rites wished the offering to be received in silence, a practice which smacks almost of discourtesy. If the offering be received in the modern manner, from a representative of the people who has gathered a collection, it would not be unreasonable for the celebrant to utter the formula in the plural. Olalla.206 would have the person offering kiss that

comes down to the chancel arch to receive the offerings of the laity,[24] first the men's and then the women's, in order of rank, as he received the clergy's. Returning to the altar, with the usual bow at its foot, he puts on the maniple again and continues with the Mass.

§4. THE BIDDING OF THE BEDES AND THE SERMON

At the principal Mass on Sundays and on certain other days,[25] if no procession has preceded the Mass, the bidding of the bedes[26] will take place at this point, immediately before the sermon,[27] if there be one. Standing either at the south end of the altar or in the pulpit,[28] and facing the people,[29] he[30] delivers the exhortation *Oremus pro ecclesia Romana*[31] in the vernacular. If the bedes are bidden by the rector of the church, he should omit the phrase *Vel rectore istius ecclesiae*. Turning east, he recites the psalm *Deus misereatur* and the following prayers in Latin. After the collect *Deus qui caritatis dona*, he turns again to the people for *Oremus pro animabus* and the bede roll in the vernacular. Finally, turning back to the east, he proceeds with *De profundis* and so to the end. If the celebrant will preach or announce any notices,[32] he may do so from the middle of the altar step, or he may go to the pulpit.

If the sermon follows the bidding of the bedes, he will preach from the same place as the prayers have been said. If another is to preach, the celebrant will retire to the sedilia. At the end of the sermon, the celebrant returns to the altar and continues with the Mass.

§5. THE LAVATORY TO THE *SANCTUS*

On days when he does not bid the bedes, if he so wishes, or if he has been placed under an obligation to do so, the celebrant, standing at the south corner, turns by his right

---

which he offers before he gives it and the celebrant's hand or the maniple afterwards. These kisses are omitted at Masses of the Dead.

[24] See S.235, for an interesting treatment of whether the laity should come up with their offering or this should be collected from the pews.

[25] P.8.

[26] For the bidding of the bedes, see Rock II.286–98. For their placing at this point of the Mass, see P.8. For the *Liber vitae* that sometimes lay on the altar, see Rock II.278–9 and S.329. For the longer roll read on All Hallows and on other special occasions, see Rock II.303.

[27] Rock II.287; S.316. Preaching the sermon immediately after the Gospel entered the Roman books only in the revision of 1604 (S.317).

[28] P.8.

[29] The directions for facing the people and turning to the altar are taken from P.6–7.

[30] Generally this will be the celebrant, but Rock II.294 thinks that this duty often fell to the curate.

[31] This exhortation, and that preceding the bedes for the faithful departed, are incomplete in P, as can be deduced from the words *(et cetera) more solito* (P.6–7). Rock II.295 provides an abbreviated form of the exhortation, taken from the hostile Becon. *Processions*.22–32 gives a form of the bidding of the bedes as used in the cathedral. For this, see Appendix II.

[32] See Chapter VI, note 27.

to face the congregation and announces his Mass intention. If he has undertaken to say certain prayers for the departed, most usually a *Pater noster* or *De profundis* with following verses and collect, he announces their intention, generally in the vernacular, facing west, and then says the prayers in Latin, with joined hands, once he has turned to face the altar again.[33]

For the lavatory, the priest stands at the south end of the altar, facing the clerk, and holds his hands over the dish[34] to receive water over his thumbs and forefingers; or he may dip his fingers in the bowl. Then he takes the towel and dries them. In doing this, he should hold the hands, not over the altar, but outside and in front of it. As soon as he begins to wash his hands, he begins silently the prayer *Munda me Domine* and continues it while drying them. From now on, he should not turn the pages of the missal or touch anything other than the host with his thumbs and forefingers.[35] Then he comes to the middle with joined hands. He bows low, lays his hands, joined, on the altar in front of him and so says the prayer *In spiritu humilitatis* silently. He stands erect, places his palms on either side of the corporal and kisses this[36] to the right of the sacrifice.[37] Immediately, he stands erect, steadies the foot of the chalice with his left hand,[38] makes the sign of the cross over the sacrifice and, placing his left hand on his breast, crosses himself, saying *In nomine Patris*, &c.

Joining his hands, he turns by his right to the people. Facing them, he extends his hands and joins them again,[39] as at *Dominus vobiscum*. Meanwhile, he says *Orate fratres* quietly, that is, in the intermediate voice.[40] He turns back to the altar[41] completing the circle,[42] while he continues *et sorores pro me*, &c. in the same voice. The clerk answers *Spiritus Sancti gratia*, &c. quietly.[43]

---

[33] See Rock III.106 and the details on the preceding page of plaques placed at the south end of the altar where the priest may be reminded for whom to pray. Rock III.107 gives a form of words for announcing such prayers. At Paris, the *De profundis* for the Bishop was said here, just before the lavatory (Martène, Lib.I. Cap.IV. Art.V.II). These prayers survived in the Spanish diocese of Oviedo under the name of 'amentaciones', and perhaps elsewhere, until the second half of the twentieth century (García-Rendueles, page 15).

[34] At an earlier stage in the development of the rite, the priest may have washed his hands in the piscina now as he certainly did after Communion. See Rock IV.194.

[35] *Tracts*.79; OP.1237.

[36] So the Dominicans later during the Canon (OP.1252). S.24 (A.264) and 264 also presupposes this kiss.

[37] Here again, Becon, pages 134–5, is at variance with the Sarum rubrics: 'After ye have washed your hands, ye returne again to the Altar, holding your hands before you, like maidenly Priests, and manerly bowing your selves to your lettle great god that shal be, ye make a crosse upon the Altar, and kisse it.'

[38] *Tracts*, Plate II, shews an illustration from the Morris Missal that seems to shew the celebrant about to steady the foot of the chalice with his left as he makes the sign of the cross over it with his right. We presume that this was done whenever the sign of the cross was made over the chalice. The modern Dominicans do this only during the Consecration (OP.1249). Modern Roman usage is to steady the chalice with the left when handling the pall with the right.

[39] OP.1238.

[40] OP. 1198 and *Tracts*.79: *ita alte ut possit audiri a ministris*.

[41] The 'solemn curtesie' mentioned by Becon, page 135, at this point is nowhere mentioned in the Sarum books.

[42] OP.1238 and the Roman books.

[43] The meaning of *privatim* is less than clear. On the one hand, the response, which was originally spoken aloud, is directed at the priest and so should be heard by him. In other words, *privatim* may

At the end of this answer, the priest extends the hands as before the collects. So he says *Oremus* and the secrets, reading them silently from the missal. He may stand a little to the left of the centre of the altar to read the secrets more easily from the book, but he must return to stand in the middle and face east when he lays his hands on the altar for their conclusion.[44] Only the first and last secrets have the conclusion *Per Dominum nostrum*, &c. At the end of the first secret he says *Amen* secretly. At the end of the last secret (therefore of the first, if there is only one), he says the words of the conclusion as far as *in unitate Spiritus sancti Deus*, like all the rest, silently; then he pauses, lays the right hand on the altar and with the left finds the place of the preface in the missal. When it is found, he lays the left hand also on the altar and says aloud *Per omnia saecula saeculorum*. The clerk answers *Amen* and replies to each verse of the following dialogue. The celebrant, keeping the hands on the altar,[45] says *Dominus vobiscum*. Then he raises the hands to the height of the shoulders or breast, holding them as during the collects and secrets, to say *Sursum corda*. He joins the hands as he says *Gratias agamus*. As he begins the preface, he holds the hands extended again on either side and remains in that position till it is ended.

At the end of the preface, he says the *Sanctus*,[46] remaining erect throughout.[47] As he begins it, he raises his extended arms for a moment and joins his hands[48] until the words *In nomine Domini*, at which he crosses himself.[49] Then, laying the right hand on the altar, he finds with the left the beginning of the Canon in the missal as he finishes the *Sanctus*. He kisses the representation of our crucified Lord's feet on the title page of the Canon.[50] This being done, he begins the Canon,

---

refer to the intermediate voice. On the other hand, the use of *secrete* in other missals may incline one to suppose that the server should no more than whisper the response. See S.255–7.

[44] This movement is often seen even in the Pian Roman Mass and is mentioned in S.26 (B.279–80 and B.300–2), and S.269–70 (where it is also ascribed to the Cistercians) and OPraem.IV.108–9. OP.1238 and OP.1240 certainly do not exclude it.

[45] Chambers, page 336, would have the celebrant turn to the people for *Dominus vobiscum*, and gives John of Avranches as his authority. However, Chambers has confused this *Dominus vobiscum* with the *Orate fratres* (PL.CXLVII.36).

[46] At Rome, the *Sanctus* used to be said in the middle voice, sufficiently loud to be heard by the server but quietly enough not to be heard by the congregation. That the bell is rung at this point and that the *Sanctus* is said quietly at High Mass both suggest that the same practice was followed at Sarum, but Becon, page 139, explicitly says of the *Sanctus* that 'lifting up your hands, ye speake with a loud voice', as some Roman celebrants do also. The Dominicans say the *Sanctus* aloud (OP.1196 and 1241).

[47] OP.1241. However, it is worth bearing in mind that the Monastic Constitutions of Lanfranc (quoted by King, *Roman Church*, page 302) does enjoin the choir to bow. As usual, Dominican practice is followed here, supported, perhaps, by the silence of the Sarum books at a point when other details (e.g. the joining of the hands) are not omitted.

[48] This seems to be the great gesture of invocation that the Roman rite now has at *Te igitur*, displaced hither perhaps by the raising of the hands there. *Tracts*.153 (Burckard) omits this.

[49] C 13.5, however, has the choir cross itself at *Benedictus*. The difference is so slight as to be immaterial.

[50] Missal C.220, and Rock IV.175–6. *Tracts*.23–4, quoting Langforde's *Meditations* (late fifteenth to early sixteenth century): 'From the begynnyng of the Canon. which is when the prest after the *Sanctus*. and after that he haith kyssyd the Crucifix on the masse book. dothe Inclyne A fore the Avter vnto the sacring be done.' Kissing the cross, or the crucifix in the missal, at this point was common in the Middle Ages, and Rock's account, corroborated by Becon, page 140, suggests that the practice endured into the 1550s. The variant included in the schismatic *Book of Ceremonies* (S.274), of making a cross on the altar and then kissing this, may be adopted if the missal does not

which he will pronounce secretly and slightly more slowly than the rest of the Mass.[51]

---

present a suitable cross or initial T at the beginning of the Canon. We are inclined, against *Tracts*.238 and S.207, but with *Tracts*.258, to consider this kiss additional to that at *ac petimus*. Whether the celebrant laid both hands on the missal to kiss it or laid both hands on the altar or joined his hands cannot now be ascertained. The first method could lead to the chalice being upset, and the second could look undignified, so perhaps the third, which is closest to the kissing of the altar at *Supplices te rogamus* in the Canon, is the least unlikely. This last may also be the German practice hinted at in Rock IV.177: *compositis manibus*.

The prayer in the fifteenth-century manual cited by Rock IV.176 (*Adoramus te, Christe, et benedicimus tibi quia per crucem tuam redemisti mundum, miserere nostri qui passus es pro nobis*) does not appear in the Missal and may be no more than a private devotion.

[51] Col 649 (*Cautelae Missae*): *morosius*.

IX

THE CANON TO THE COMMUNION

§1. THE FIRST PART OF THE CANON

The celebrant joins his hands and, so joined, raises them to the level of his face as he lifts his eyes[1] and says *Te igitur*. Lowering his hands to his breast, he immediately looks down, bows low and continues. When he has said *supplices rogamus ac petimus*, he stands upright and then lays the hands on the altar, one on either side, outside the corporal, kisses the altar on the corporal to the right of the sacrifice as he says *uti accepta*, then stands erect, joins the hands, lays the left hand on the foot of the chalice and with the right makes the sign of the cross thrice over the chalice and bread as he says *haec* ✠ *dona, haec* ✠ *munera, haec* ✠ *sancta sacrificia illibata*. After the third cross he does not join the hands but holds them extended and uplifted before the breast.[2] This is the normal position of the hands throughout the Canon. At the words *una cum famulo tuo Papa nostro N.*, he adds the name of the reigning Pope. At the words *et antistite nostro N.*, he adds the name of the ordinary bishop only, not the archbishop. At the words *et rege nostro N.*, he should add the name of the King.[3]

As he says *Memento Domine famulorum famularumque tuarum*, he joins the hands.[4] He then stands a moment in this position, bowing slightly while he remembers any persons for whom he wishes here to pray. Then, standing again erect with the hands

---

[1] This, an interpretation of *manus eleuet iunctas* of Missal B.221, introduces a vivid gesture of supplication for the acceptance of the sacrifice that is not found in the Roman rite. The joined hands betray the mediæval character of the ritual.

[2] Col 613, against OP.1242.

[3] This mention of the King has been removed from the Roman books since 1604 and retained only in the Catholic monarchies (Fortescue, *The Mass*, page 329; *The Catholic Encyclopedia* s.v. 'Canon of the Mass'). This is coherent with the nature of the prayer, which is indicative of communion. Benedict XV's permission to name the King of the Belgians in the Canon (King, *Roman Church*, page 314) suggests that personal, and not institutional, communion is enough to warrant the retention of these words. The substitution in the Roman rite for the prayer for the Roman Emperor of that *pro res publicas moderantibus*, which is said even in heathen countries, when Pius XII reconstituted the Holy Week liturgy could be used to justify retaining the prayer for the King on Good Friday in the Sarum rite, but this prayer is of an altogether different nature from the commemoration in the Canon. Although neither question can be settled definitively other than by a dormant authority, we are inclined to think that both the clause *et rege nostro N.* and the Good Friday prayer should probably be omitted in modern celebrations of the Sarum Mass while the Protestant Monarchy endures, even if the words remain in the Missal 'for a day'.

[4] OP.1243. Col 650 (*Cautelae Missae*) merely enjoins the priest to pray mentally. Cf. Col 650.

extended, he continues *et omnium circumstantium*. In the *Communicantes*,[5] he bows briefly at the name *Mariae* and continues bowing until he has said the word *Christi*.[6] At *Per Christum*, &c. he joins his hands.

He lays his hands on the altar outside the corporal[7] and, bowing slightly,[8] looks at the host with great devotion and so begins *Hanc igitur* until he has said *quaesumus Domine*. At *ut placatus*, he extends his hands again, raising his eyes slightly and immediately lowering them to their normal angle, and so concludes the prayer.[9]

At *Quam oblationem*, he looks at the host again and, steadying the chalice with his left hand, makes the sign of the cross thrice, as before, over the sacrifice, at the words *bene ✠ dictam, ascri ✠ ptam, ra ✠ tam, rationabilem, acceptabilemque facere digneris*. Then he makes the sign of the cross over the bread only as he says *Cor ✠ pus* and over the chalice only as he says *San ✠ guis*. He joins the hands and continues, bowing the head as he says *Jesu Christi*.

§2. THE SACRING

As he says *Qui pridie quam pateretur*, he extends, lifts and joins his hands, and then wipes his thumb and forefinger, either rubbing them together or on the fore corners of the corporal[10] or on the altar cloth,[11] and takes the host between the thumb and forefinger of each hand, raising it somewhat but not so much that the people can see it.[12] He lowers it immediately until it is a little above the corporal and places the other fingers of each hand, joined and extended, behind it.[13] Still standing erect he continues *accepit panem*, &c. As he says *elevatis oculis in coelum*, he looks up to the cross and at once looks down. As he says *gratias agens* he bows and then stands almost erect. At the word *bene ✠ dixit*, he holds the bread in the left hand only and makes the sign of the cross over it with the right. In doing this, he does not keep the thumb and forefinger joined but holds the fingers straight out, in the usual way when blessing. At *fregit*, he touches the bread[14] with his right forefinger and then again holds the bread in both hands as before, and, bowing,[15] continues, *deditque discipulis suis dicens: Accipite et*

[5] Rock IV.179 reports a papal permission, given during the Fourth Lateran Council (1215), to mention the name of saints whose relics are held by the church in which Mass is said, but the Missal shews no sign of this practice and so there seems no reason to warrant its observance.
[6] See Chapter V, note 15, and S.106 and 356. Cf. the Carthusians (*Tracts*.101).
[7] Missal C.220: *ex utraque parte corporalium*. Rock IV.180 has the celebrant place his hands on the corporal itself, but elsewhere, e.g., C 66.24, it is clear that *ex utraque parte* need not mean 'from the interior of', and so there seems no reason to depart from the common modern practice that has the celebrant place his hands outside the corporal before the Consecration and on it afterwards. See also Chapter VII, note 12.
[8] Missal M.221, and *Tracts*.258. Becon, page 143, gives: 'yee fall to crouching and beholding the little cake and chalice.' Durandus (IV, cap. 39, 1) gives *Sacerdos in quibusdam ecclesiis profunde se inclinat*. Hereford.127 has *hic incliniet se parum versus Hostiam*.
[9] Missal C.220 and Rock IV.180, quoting an undated manual.
[10] F.53.
[11] *Tracts*.80.
[12] Col 616.
[13] This, Roman, practice is also supported by pictorial evidence, e.g., Duffy, *Stripping*, plate 43.
[14] For the evolution of this rubric see *Tracts*.259–61.
[15] M.86.

manducate ex hoc omnes. Holding the bread before him, bowed,[16] he says, in a single breath and without a break, the words of consecration, *Hoc est enim corpus meum.* He should say these words in a low voice, but so that he can hear himself. When the words have been said, without delay, he stands erect, then inclines[17] profoundly to the Host over the altar, still holding the Host with both hands over the altar, as before. He rises at once[18] and holds up the Blessed Sacrament above his forehead, so that it may be seen by the people. He lifts it straight up before him to such a height that it may be seen from behind, over his head.[19] He lowers it again, lays his left hand on the corporal[20] and with his right makes the sign of the cross with it over the corporal, and places it reverently on the corporal in front of the chalice, at the same place as before. He makes no second reverence to the Host.

From this moment till the ablutions at the end, the celebrant keeps the thumb and forefinger of each hand joined except when he touches the consecrated Host or extends his fingers in blessing. In turning over pages, holding the chalice, or doing any other such action, he must be careful to use the other fingers so as not to separate these. Likewise, every time he lays his hands on the altar he does so on the corporal.[21]

He uncovers the chalice, taking care not to separate his thumb and forefinger, and lays the pall on the right side. Then he rubs the thumb and forefinger of the hands over the chalice, to let any crumb there may be fall into it.[22] Standing erect, he takes the chalice in both hands, holding it by the middle with his right and laying his left on its foot. Without raising it, he says *Simili modo postquam coenatum est.* He continues the words, still holding the chalice with both hands. As he says *gratias agens*, he bows.[23] As he says *bene* ✠ *dixit*, he makes the sign of the cross over the chalice with the right (separating the thumb and forefinger to do so),[24] his left remaining on the foot as before. Then he holds the knop with his right hand and the foot with his left as he says *deditque discipulis suis dicens: Accipite et bibite ex eo omnes.* He bows slightly over the altar and lifts the chalice a little, putting the second, third and fourth fingers of his

---

[16] Hereford.128; OP.1247. Although the rubrics are silent on the matter, it is possible that some celebrants laid their elbows on the altar. Becon, page 80, has: 'Christ sate, yee sometime stand upright, sometime leane upon your elbowes, sometime crouch downeward, sometime kneele.'

[17] On this vexed question, see also Morse §225 and §444, who advocates the half-genuflection employed at Lyons. However, it may not be insignificant that the Missal uses the same verb here (Col 617: *inclinet se*) as it does at *Supplices* (Col 618: *corpore inclinato*), when Morse accepts that the celebrant kept his knees stiff. *Tracts*.244 quotes a Carmelite ordinal of 1532: *sine genuflexione*. At their equivalent of *Te adoro, Te glorifico* (Col 625: *inclinet se*), other rites bow with stiff knees. A more convincing case for a genuflection of some kind could perhaps be made for *cum humiliatione* at Col 626, before the celebrant's Communion. See Chapter V, note 21, and note 77 of this chapter.

On the other hand, Becon, pages 178–9, assumes a bending of the knees of some sort: 'After ye have once spoken these five words, Hoc est enim corpus meum, over the bread ... yee kneele down to it, and worship it ... and afterward ye hold it up above your ... heads.'

[18] M.86.

[19] For the very convenient custom of drawing a dark curtain behind the Host at the elevation to enable those distant from the altar to see better and for the survival of this custom in Spain, see *Tracts*.234–6.

[20] OP.1247.

[21] See Chapter VII, note 12, and note 7 of this chapter.

[22] OP.1249. He does this every time after he has touched the Host. See note 28.

[23] Unlike at Hereford, where he raised his eyes (Hereford.128).

[24] Col 617.

left hand joined under the foot and the thumb and forefinger over it.[25] He holds the chalice quite straight, not sloping towards him. So, in the same low but audible voice as before, he says the words of consecration over the chalice:[26] *Hic est enim calix sanguinis mei novi et aeterni testamenti mysterium fidei qui pro vobis et pro multis effundetur in remissionem peccatorum.* Holding the knop with his right and the foot with his left partly under it as before, he raises the chalice up to the height of his breast or above his head,[27] as he says: *Haec quotiescumque feceritis in mei memoriam facietis.* He sets the chalice down on the corporal, rubs[28] his thumbs and forefingers together over its bowl and covers it with his right hand, his left lying on the corporal.[29]

§3. THE SECOND PART OF THE CANON

Standing erect and holding the arms extended on either side in the manner of a cross,[30] but now always keeping the thumbs and forefingers joined, he continues the Canon at the words *Unde et memores*. As he says *hostiam* ✠ *puram, hostiam* ✠ *sanctam, hostiam* ✠ *immaculatam*, he lays his left hand on the foot of the chalice and with the right, separating his thumb and forefinger,[31] makes the sign of the cross thrice over both the

---

[25] OP.1249.

[26] The particulars of these directions are taken from OP.1249 and Roman practice. The Sarum books give very sparse directions.

[27] If the Sarum books mention no bow or genuflection at this point, Becon, pages 230–1, has:

> After the aforesaid words … yee kneele downe, lift up your hands, and honour it … After that yee stand up againe … and taking the chalice in your hands, yee hold it up … above your … heads, that the people also may worship it… This done, yee set the chalice downe againe upon the Altar, and yee cover it with your Corporasse cloath … Then once again kneele ye downe, and up againe … and kisse the Altar, and spread your armes abroad.

> *Tracts*.24, quoting Langforde's *Meditations*: 'In the secund Elevacyon at your pleasure yow may say thus … ffrome the last Elevatyon of the sacryng.'

[28] This rubbing seems indicated explicitly only here (though it is implied by the corrupt text at *Tracts*.262–3), but it is universal in other uses whenever the Host has been touched and this was probably the practice at Sarum. We have assumed this throughout. The practice is an obvious consequence of the doctrine of the Real Presence and corresponds to the spirit of the words of St. Cyril of Jerusalem in his oft-quoted *Mystagogical Catechesis* V.21: Μετ' ἀσφαλείας οὖν ἁγιάσας τοὺς ὀφθαλμοὺς τῇ ἐπαφῇ τοῦ ἁγίου σώματος μεταλάμβανε, προσέχων μὴ παραπολέσῃς τι ἐκ τούτου· ὅπερ γὰρ ἐὰν ἀπολέσῃς, τοῦτο ὡς ἀπὸ οἰκείου δηλονότι ἐζημιώθης μέλους. Εἰπὲ γάρ μοι, εἴ τίς σοι ἔδωκε ψήγματα χρυσίου, οὐκ ἂν μετὰ πάσης ἀσφαλείας ἐκράτεις, φυλαττόμενος μή τι αὐτῶν παραπολέσῃς καὶ ζημίαν ὑποστῇς; Οὐ πολλῷ οὖν μᾶλλον ἀσφαλέστερον τοῦ χρυσίου καὶ λίθων τιμίων τιμιωτέρου διασκοπήσεις ὑπὲρ τοῦ μὴ ψῖχαν ἐκπεσεῖν; (PG.XXXIII.1126).

[29] Unlike in other, later, uses, the celebrant bows once to the Host before its elevation but not after it, and no bows accompany the (lesser) elevation of the chalice. As late as 1587, the Dominicans had no elevation of the chalice.

[30] Col 617 (*elevet bracchia sua in modum crucis*) is much closer to that in the Præmonstratensian missal of 1530 (*extendat bracchia in modum crucis*) than to that in the Dominican missal (*extendat bracchia plus solito, mediocriter tamen*). The post-1738 Præmonstratensians make no mention of this special posture. Since, however, the Rt. Rev. J. M. Gallagher, O. Praem., the last White Canon in Europe to use the traditional Norbertine rite before the recent movement for its restoration, and the calced Carmelites still extend their arms fully, it is reasonable to assume that the same was done at Salisbury.

[31] Col 617.

Host and the chalice. As he says *Panem* ✠ *sanctum*, he makes the sign of the cross over the Host only; at *calicem* ✠ *salutis*, over the chalice only.

He extends his hands in the usual manner[32] and says the prayer *Supra quae*, looking at the sacrifice.[33] At *Supplices*, he crosses his hands before his breast, right over left,[34] and bows profoundly up to the word *quotquot*. Here he stands upright and kisses the right side of the corporal, his hands still crossed,[35] as he continues *ex hac altaris participatione*, &c. Laying his left hand on the corporal, at the word *Cor* ✠ *pus*, he makes the sign of the cross over the Host; at *San* ✠ *guinem*, over the chalice as before. As he says *omni benedictione caelesti*, he signs himself with the cross,[36] holding the left under the breast but so that the right hand should not touch the forehead or the chasuble, keeping his thumb and forefinger joined, using the remaining three fingers.[37] Then he joins his hands.

Keeping his hands joined,[38] he begins *Memento etiam Domine*. At *N. et N.*, he prays silently for those faithful departed[39] whom he wishes to commemorate. At the words *qui nos praecesserunt*,[40] he extends his hands and continues the prayer. At the conclusion, *Per Christum Dominum nostrum*, he joins the hands.[41]

---

[32] This can be inferred from C 66.28.

[33] Maskell, page 98, quoting a Sarum missal of 1492.

[34] OP.1252. Other Dominican documents disagree among themselves: *Tracts*.81 agrees with the modern Dominicans, but the missal of 1586, in ambiguous wording depending for its sense on word order, gives *brachio sinistro superposito dextro*. *Tracts*.101 has the Carthusians fold their arms right over left.

[35] OP.1252. At Rome, the celebrant kisses the corporal in the middle with his hands laid on the corporal. The Carmelites lay their hands on the corporal and then kiss it at its right. Col 618 says nothing of the position of the hands at this point.

[36] Does he separate the thumb and forefinger of his right hand for this crossing? We do not think so. The rubric at Col 617 has *non disjungendo pollicem ab indice nisi dum facit benedictiones tantum*. This certainly includes the crosses made over the sacrifice. However, throughout the ordinary of the Mass, *benedicere* and *benedictionem dare* are used of making the sign of the cross over other things or people, and *se signare* and *signaculum crucis in facie facere* are used of making the cross on oneself. The purpose of keeping the thumbs and forefingers joined is to avoid the risk of dropping crumbs. The risk is much greater now than when it is merely to move through the air over the sacrifice and corporal. Both from reason and from textual analysis, therefore, we conclude (with OP.1252) that at this point the priest keeps his thumbs and forefingers joined.

[37] OP.1252.

[38] The Dominicans (OP.1253) and Carmelites keep their hands joined, whereas Hereford.130, the Roman rite and the Præmonstratensians (at least since 1738) have the hands extended. The Præmonstratensian missal of 1530 says nothing either way. Unlike at the former *Memento*, the Sarum books are silent and the true gesture cannot now be known. Either possibility is reasonable. On the one hand, it seems reasonable to follow the Dominicans and Carmelites, since they agree. On the other hand, at the *Memento pro vivis*, the Sarum celebrant prayed with hands extended, and, unlike at Col 613, no deviation from the usual position of the hands is indicated here.

[39] C 66.28 states explicitly that he makes his mental prayer here, as the Dominicans do, and not after *pacis*. Given typical sensibilities, and Roman and Dominican usage, it is likely that the priest looked at the Host during this mental prayer. For other, less edifying, habits at this point see *Tracts*.254. The post-1738 Præmonstratensian Ordinarius directs the priest to hold his hands joined *ante pectus vel usque ad faciem elevatas*. This is a very natural gesture and, although not prescribed, may well have been common.

[40] OP.1253.

[41] So both OP.1253 and the Roman Missal. At Rome, the celebrant also bows the head, but there seems no authority for the Dominicans to do this and the Sarum Missal is silent on the matter. For a hypothesis to explain this curious (and very late) rubric, see King, *Roman Church*, pages 337–8.

He says *Nobis quoque peccatoribus* in the middle voice.[42] At the same time, he lays the left hand on the corporal and strikes his breast once with the right. He does so with the second, third and fourth fingers extended, not touching the chasuble with the thumb or forefinger.[43] He continues *famulis tuis*, &c., erect, with hands extended.[44] At the conclusion, he does not join his hands[45] but continues to hold them extended until the words *sancti* ✠ *ficas, vivi* ✠ *ficas, bene* ✠ *dicis*, at which he makes the sign of the cross three times with the right over the Host[46] and chalice together.

Laying his left hand on the corporal, with the right he uncovers the chalice and lays the pall on the right. He takes the Host with his right hand between the thumb and forefinger; with the left he holds the chalice by its foot[47] and makes the sign of the cross five times with the Host. The first, extending beyond the diameter of the cup, as he says *Per ipsum*; the second, of the same size as the cup of the chalice and from lip to lip, as he says *et cum ipso*; the third, inside the cup of the chalice and slightly deeper, as he says *et in ipso*; the fourth, same as the first, as he says *est tibi Deo Patri omnipotenti*; and the fifth, over the corporal and low down before the foot of the chalice, as he says *in unitate Spiritus Sancti*. Then, holding the Host in his right hand over the bowl, he raises the chalice[48] with his left hand, holding it by the knop. Lowering the chalice again, he places the Host where it was before, in front of the chalice, laying the left hand meanwhile on the corporal. He rubs his fingers[49] over the bowl and lays his left hand on the corporal while the right covers the chalice with the pall as he says *Omnis honor et gloria*.[50] Then he lays the right hand also on the corporal, keeping them there up to the words *Pater noster*. He stands erect, the hands still on the corporal, and says aloud, *Per omnia saecula saeculorum*.

---

[42] The Missal does not mention this change in tone of voice. However, Maskell, page 102, argues from Bede (*ob*. 35), Amalarius of Metz (*ob. post* 850) and the *Micrologus de ecclesiasticis observationibus* for its antiquity, and it occurs in the Roman, Dominican (OP.1254), Carmelite and Præmonstratensian (1530) rites. It is also mentioned by Missal B.224: *Hic percuciens sacerdos pectus suum aliquantulum alcius dicat*. At High Mass, it serves as an early signal to the sacred ministers of the end of the Canon (King, *Roman Church*, page 339).

[43] OP.1254.

[44] OP.1254.

[45] OP.1255 and the Carmelites.

[46] Col 6149 and M.88 state that the crosses are made over the chalice. However, such crosses are generally made over both the Host and the chalice, unless there is a good reason to the contrary. So the host only is signed before the first Consecration and the chalice only before the second. At other times, such as at the *Unde et memores*, the Host and chalice are signed together and then individually, but nowhere is the chalice signed alone without specific reference to it. Both the Dominican (OP.1255) and Roman books make the signs of the cross over both elements at this point, so it is reasonable to suppose that Sarum practice was also to do this and that the word *calicem* here is but a synecdoche.

[47] *Tracts*.81; OP.1255.

[48] For the little elevation, which is not mentioned by any of the Sarum books, see Chapter XIX, note 15.

[49] The Dominicans strike the thumb and forefinger of the right hand only over the chalice; at Rome, the celebrant rubs the thumbs and forefingers of both hands over the chalice. The Carmelites also cleanse the thumbs and forefingers of both hands. The Sarum books mention nothing, but see note 28. Col 617 suggests that rubbing, rather than tapping, was the Sarum method.

[50] Missal B.224.

§4. THE FRACTION AND THE PRIEST'S COMMUNION

When the clerk has answered *Amen*, with hands still on the corporal,[51] he says *Oremus. Praeceptis salutaribus moniti*, &c. As he begins *Pater noster*,[52] he raises and extends the hands. In this position he says the prayer. When the clerk has answered *Sed libera nos a malo*, the celebrant answers *Amen* silently. Keeping the hands extended,[53] he says the embolism privately. He bows slightly at the name of Mary.[54] At *Da propitius*, as he continues the prayer, he places the left hand on the corporal and takes the paten in the right from under the corporal. He holds the paten in the right hand between his forefinger and the second finger.[55] He kisses the paten at its upper edge, puts[56] it to his left eye and then to his right, and then makes the sign of the cross with it[57] in the air from above his head (so that it may be seen from behind) to his breast[58] and from his left shoulder to his right. As soon as he has made this sign, he slips the paten under the Host,[59] pressing the left edge of the Host lightly with his left forefinger to ease the

---

[51] This is the clear implication of the rubric and concords with OP.1256, although differing from Roman practice.

[52] So Col 620 and M.89, against C 66.30 and B.II.494, which indicate a raising of the hands between the words *noster* and *qui*. If the celebrant raises his hands as he says *Pater noster*, the difference becomes imperceptible.

[53] So the implication of Col 621, which mentions no change until *Da propitius*, and of OP.1257.

[54] M.89, and Col 621, note c, in a rubric that could be taken to refer to Ss. Peter, Paul and Andrew. Missal B.225 more clearly restricts the bow to *Maria*. In combination with the rubric ordering a bow at the name of Our Lady in the *Communicantes*, the interpretation here seems more likely. See Chapter V, note 15.

[55] At this point, he may have touched the Host with the edge of the paten where he will kiss it presently, but Col 621 makes no mention of this. However, see Missal B.225 (*Hic assumat patenam et tangat Eukaristiam cum patena deinde deosculet patenam*) and Tracts.26 (Langforde's *Meditations*): 'When the prest takith the Patteny. and towcheid the Ooste, and kyssyd the Patteyn Saing *Da Pacem & cetera*'; Tracts.47 (the French *Alphabetum Sacerdotum*): *hic tangat de patena corpus christi postea calicem in tribus locis dicendo*: Petro et Paulo, &c. and Tracts102 (of the Carthusians): *signat se cum patena, Cum qua tangit hostiam*.

[56] *Ponat* (Col 621) suggests that the paten is to touch the eyes (presumably the shut eyelids), though the rubric in the Lund Missal (1514) suggests otherwise: *ventilet ex ea* [sc. *patena*] *oculos* (King, *Roman Church*, page 351). Tracts.211 (Ciconiolanus) has *non opus est tangere oculum*. The Carmelites touch the eyelids.

[57] The fifteenth-century York Missal preserves here the older form of making the sign of the cross: 'ad dextram (*sic*) usque ad sinistram' (King, *Liturgies of the Past*, page 345), but there is no indication that the cross was other than from left to right at Sarum.

[58] As far as the cincture, according to the Roman Ciconiolanus (*Tracts*.211).

[59] This is done at Rome but differs from Dominican (OP.1257) and Carmelite practice. Col 622 says only *reponat eam in locum suum*, which is ambiguous, since it could mean that the paten should be placed under the corporal or, as at Rome, under the Host itself, or, as the Dominicans and Carmelites do, on the altar to the right of the corporal. However, C 66.31, speaking of the blessing at this point at a pontifical Mass, states that the celebrant bishop places the Host back on the paten (*eukaristia super patenam reposita*), and Missal M.225, despite following earlier practice in some details, gives a rubric at the end of this prayer, *Tunc duas partes eukaristie super patenam ponat*, thereby suggesting that the paten has not been placed under the corporal. Likewise, *Tracts*.264, quoting the (admittedly variant) Blew MS, has: *Hic accipiat sacerdos patenam et deosculetur et supponat corpori domini*. These two indications, combined, imply that the paten had already been returned to its place in front of the chalice, and the Roman analogy suggests that this was the moment when this was done.

process if necessary. At *Per eundem Dominum*,[60] he uncovers the chalice and takes the Host in the right hand with an inclination. He holds its lower edge between his thumb and forefinger, pushing it up somewhat by laying meanwhile the forefinger of the left hand on the farther edge of the Host. Then, steadying the foot of the chalice with his left, he holds the Host over the bowl of the chalice while he continues the prayer. With both hands, he now breaks the Host reverently in a straight line down the middle, using both hands to do this, holding each half between the forefinger and thumb of either hand as he continues the doxology.

At *Qui tecum*, he turns that half of the Host which he holds in his right hand and lays it across and over the other half[61] with the fracture upwards,[62] and from the former half (which he had held in his right) he breaks off a particle, about a quarter of the original whole in size,[63] between the thumb and forefinger of his right hand. If possible, he should avoid touching the line of the fracture.[64]

Holding the first and second parts of the Host in his left hand, and the third in his right touching the second as if they were still whole,[65] over the bowl of the chalice, he says aloud *Per omnia*, &c. He makes three crosses within the chalice with the third particle in his right hand, saying *Pax Domini sit semper vobiscum*. When the clerk has made his reply, the celebrant at once begins the *Agnus Dei* still holding the Host over the chalice as before.[66]

If the *Preces in prostratione* or equivalent prayers are to be said,[67] they are said immediately before *Pax Domini sit semper vobiscum*. The priest lays the three parts of the Host on the paten, arranged so as to form a whole, and covers the chalice. He reads the *Preces* as at High Mass, in a clear spoken voice with his hands joined, while all in the church kneel. When they are concluded, the celebrant uncovers the chalice, takes up the Host as before and continues immediately with *Pax Domini*.

Then, keeping his left hand in place and beginning secretly *Haec sacrosancta commixtio*, &c., he makes the sign of the cross with the particle inside the bowl and lets it fall into the chalice. While he concludes the prayer, he arranges the first two parts of

---

[60] The description of the details of the fraction given here is heavily influenced by OP.1258-9, which is easily compatible with the later Sarum rubrics. These, however, while giving an outline of the actions to be performed, do not give sufficient detail to reconstruct, e.g., the position of the two halves of the Host before the second fraction.

[61] *Tracts*.82 and the Carmelites, against OP.1259.

[62] So the Carmelites and Bonniwell, page 388.

[63] *Tracts*.82: *dividat eam in duas alias [partes]*.

[64] *Tracts*.82.

[65] OP.1259.

[66] This seems a reasonable deduction, supported by Becon, page 252 ('Thrice doe yee call that Bread which yee hold in your hands, the Lamb of God'). The particle is held over the chalice at *Pax Domini* and dropped into the chalice at *Haec sacrosancta*. No mention is made of moving the Host for the *Agnus Dei*. The course here suggested concurs with OP.1260. Becon, page 151, also has: 'When ye have broken your new formed God in three parts, two pieces you keepe still in your hands for flying away, and the third yee let fall downe into the chalice.'

[67] The agreement between the convent of Durham and Henry VII (Rock IV.185) says *statim post fraccionem postea et decantacionem vel leccionem* Per omnia secula seculorum, thus implying that such *preces* could be said at Low Masses.

the Host on the paten[68] neatly so as to form a better circle.[69] Then he rubs the fingers of both hands over the chalice.

He covers the chalice in the usual way,[70] joins his hands[71] and so says the prayer *Domine, sancte Pater*.

If the Pax is to be given,[72] this is done as at High Mass. The celebrant turns to the right with joined hands and kisses the pax-brede held up to him by the clerk, saying *Pax tibi et Ecclesiae Dei*.

---

[68] Here the rubrics, the Dominicans and the Carmelites all fail us. Col 624 states that, after the prayer *Domine Sancte Pater*, the priest kisses the right end of the corporal, the lip of the chalice and the deacon. The difficulty lies in the fact that it is impossible to kiss the corporal in a seemly fashion while simultaneously holding the Host in the left above the chalice and holding the knop of the chalice in the right. This is the most likely position for the right hand. See OP.1261. At no other point is the right hand alone laid on the corporal.

Even if the left hand is wrapped round the bowl of the chalice while holding the Host, it is unlikely that no other support should be employed. It is true that the Carmelite rite allows for this as an option for the Pax itself but not during the delicate moment when the corporal and chalice are kissed and only if there is no pax-brede. Laying the Host on the paten would prove a neat solution to the difficulty. The Host is laid on the paten at Rome, where the altar is kissed. The rubric before the prayer *Deus Pater fons et origo* (Col 625), by drawing attention to the holding of the Host (*tenendo hostiam duabus manibus*) is consistent with the notion that the Host has lain on the paten for the Pax.

Neither the Dominicans nor the Carmelites face the same problem because they do not kiss the corporal or the altar. The Dominicans hold the Host over the chalice with the left and the knop of the chalice with the right, and then kiss the lip of the chalice at the right. At High Mass, the celebrant then kisses the pall presented to him, but this is omitted at Low Mass. At a Carmelite High Mass, the celebrant holds the Host over the chalice with the left and places the right hand round the bowl of the chalice as a mirror of the position of the left hand but without touching the Host. Then he kisses the pall presented to him and the lip of the chalice at the closest point to him. Keeping the Host in his left hand, he embraces the deacon with his right. At Low Mass, the Carmelites omit the Pax altogether.

[69] Roman practice is to lay the two halves of the Host on the paten next to each other. The Carmelites hold the Host in the left hand and arrange it into a circle.

[70] This is pure speculation but consistent with the general rule that the chalice should be kept covered when not in direct use. The Dominicans and Carmelites keep the chalice uncovered for this prayer because they hold the Host over it; at Rome, where the Host is on the paten, the chalice is covered.

[71] So at Rome, where celebrant does not hold the Host in his hand at this point. As a rule, the priest holds his hands together for what were originally private prayers and extended for public prayers. With the exception of the secrets and the Canon, the latter survived as sung prayers, while the former were said secretly. At Rome, the celebrant bows as he says the prayer for peace, whereas the Dominicans and Carmelites do not, presumably because they are holding the Host over the chalice. There is nothing in the Sarum books to indicate bowing at this point, and *Deus Pater fons et origo*, which is also addressed to the Father, is later said erect. Nevertheless, since the argument from silence is inapplicable in the case of rubrics, the question must remain moot.

[72] The survival of the old kiss of peace varies considerably by rite and time, and it is not easy to tell what Sarum practice was, if indeed it was uniform. In the Sarum, Roman, Dominican and Carmelite rites, it survived at High Mass (with a few specified exceptions, e.g., at Requiems) and retained popular vigour (see Duffy, *Stripping*, pages 126–9 and 558). The practice at Low Mass is more complex. Some chantries and nave altars that would not have had solemn Masses celebrated possessed their own pax-bredes (Duffy, *Stripping*, page 114), and some laymen will have been attracted by the chance to receive the Pax at 'their' Mass more prominently than in their usual place at the Sunday Mass. It is quite possible that the Pax survived at some Low Masses, borne by the clerk, or even at private Masses, exchanged with the clerk alone. Becon, who for the most part describes a Low Mass, supposes the Pax: 'Shortly after the Agnus, yee kisse the Pax' (page 261). *Tracts*.83 prescribes that the Pax should be given to the server and to nobody else unless local custom dictate otherwise. Even five hundred years later, and after the Tridentine reform sought to curtail the ceremony as a way of eliminating the abuses associated with it, the Pax is given at some Low Masses in the Roman rite,

If the Pax is to be omitted, after the prayer *Domine sancte Pater*, the celebrant lays his left hand on the corporal and uncovers the chalice.

Taking the Host in both hands, he holds the two parts together over the chalice[73] so as to form an imperfect circle in his hands cupped round the bowl.[74] Standing almost erect,[75] he says silently the prayer *Deus Pater, fons et origo*. At the words *Te adoro*, he bows;[76] at *Te glorifico*, he bows a second time, and a third time at *Te tota mentis ac cordis intentione laudo*. It will appear more seemly if he allows more time for saying *Te adoro* and *Te glorifico* so that all three bows take the same amount of time. Still bowing and holding the Host over the chalice, he continues with the prayers *Domine ... Fili Dei vivi* and *Corporis et sanguinis tui*.

He addresses the Host with a low bow,[77] saying the prayer *Ave in aeternum*. At *In nomine*, leaving his left hand cupped round the chalice,[78] he makes the sign of the cross

---

[73] when celebrated in the presence of prelates and princes. The Roman Missal's *Ritus Servandus* X.3 as it stood immediately before the alterations inspired by the Liturgical Movement presumed that the Pax would be given even at Low Masses, but only if a pax-brede and clerk were available.

If the Pax was not given, did any relics of the rite survive at Low Mass? In the Roman and Carmelite rites, only the prayer for peace is said and all other ceremonies are suppressed, but at Requiems even this prayer is omitted. Thus, there is a difference between the simplification of the rite at Low Mass and its suppression when it would be omitted at High Mass also. The Dominicans, who lack the prayer for peace, kiss the lip of the chalice and omit all other ceremonies, with no distinction between Requiem and other Masses (OP.1261). In Hereford.133, the celebrant kisses the chalice, then the altar and then the clerk, but in Masses for the dead, when the rite is omitted, the priest merely kisses the chalice and then continues with the prayers before Communion. In the two rites (Rome and Hereford) where the altar is kissed, therefore, this kiss is omitted when the full rite is not followed. *Crede Michi* [33] has the priest omit the kissing of the altar and the chalice at Requiem Masses, but says nothing of the prayer *Domine, sancte Pater*. It being impossible to tell for sure whether there was a difference between ordinary Low Masses without the Pax and Requiem Masses, the more cautious solution appears to be, *pace* the Dominicans, to assume that the prayer *Domine, Sancte Pater* was never omitted but that both kisses, touching the chalice with the Host, *Pax tibi* and the kiss itself were all omitted whenever the Pax was not given, irrespective of the character of the Low Mass.

[73] Again, recourse must be had to the earlier missals. Missal C.226, has the priest hold the Host with both hands above the chalice. Missal B.226 has the priest raise the paten with the Host and hold it over the chalice for the duration of the following two prayers. Holding the Host above the chalice agrees with OP.1260 and Carmelite practice and gives better sense to the words in the prayer (*in manibus meis teneo*).

[74] So the Carmelites.

[75] The celebrant is told to bow at the end of this prayer, when he begins to address the Son, so it can be presumed that he stands erect until then.

[76] The Missal does not specify how many times the celebrant should bow. B.II.497, however, specifies the three bows and the tricolon with anaphora lends itself to a threefold bow. Col 625 implies that the rest of the prayer also is said bowing.

[77] The word used here is *humiliatione*, literally, 'a going down to the ground'. Although conventionally it is thought that officially Sarum had introduced no genuflections in the modern sense, some English missals (e.g. the York Missal of ca. 1470 reproduced in Hope, *English Altars*, Plate XII, fig 1) depict the priest kneeling before the Sacrament. If the priest did kneel at this point, then Cranmer's instruction in the Prayer Book of 1549 (Gibson and Ratcliff, page 225) that 'the Priest turnyng him to gods boord, knele down, and say' the prayer of humble access would be a less striking innovation.

At the equivalent prayer in the Carmelite missal, the rubric is: *Genuflectens, sed non usque ad terram*. The effect is a bow while the Host is held over the chalice and the elbows come close to leaning on the surface of the altar.

M.93 and *Tracts*.266 give *inclinatione* as a variant reading.

[78] So the Carmelites, who unlike the Dominicans make this sign of the cross and communicate from the right hand. See King, *Religious Orders*, pages 390-1, for the difference between the Sarum

in front of himself with the Host and receives his Communion.[79] As he swallows the Host, he holds his hands joined;[80] then he again bows low[81] and says *Ave in aeternum caelestis potus*. At *Amen*, he takes the chalice in the right, holding it by the knop between the forefinger and the other fingers, while supporting it under the foot with his left.[82] He makes the sign of the cross before him with the chalice, saying *In nomine Patris*, &c. Raising the chalice, he drinks all the precious Blood with the particle in it, cautiously, in two or three sips,[83] and replaces the chalice on the corporal. As soon as he has drained the chalice, he covers it, bows with joined hands and says the prayer *Gratias tibi ago*.[84]

If he is to renew the reserved species, he does so now, consuming the old hosts before he proceeds to the ablutions.[85] If there is to be a general Communion within Mass, the time to renew the species will be after the Communion of the congregation.

and Dominican rites, and also Bonniwell, page 187, whose insistence that at Sarum the celebrant received the Host with both hands seems insufficiently justified by the rubrics of the Missal.

[79] For this sign of the cross, see Col 626, note i; C 66.34; and M.93. The sign of the cross in itself supports Communion from the right hand, since crossing with the left is unheard of and crossing with both hands is less easy than with the right alone. Rock's 'making the sign of the cross upon his mouth with that precious body' (IV.191) may be an exaggeration of the sense meant by *ante os*.

[80] Both the Dominicans and the Carmelites join their hands for the prayer after the first Communion. Although their prayer is a meditation on the Communion received rather than an address to the chalice, the analogy still stands, since at least part of the point of these prayers is to allow time for the Host to be swallowed properly.

[81] This bow is not mentioned in the rubrics and neither the Dominicans nor the Carmelites bow here. However, a bow here is reasonable, since this prayer reflects that just before the first Communion, and the nature of the Dominican and Carmelite prayers is different.

[82] OP.1263; so also the Carmelites.

[83] Col 650 (*Cautelae Missae*); OP.1263.

[84] Col 626. The manuals and C 66.34 place this prayer after the ablutions and omit *Adoremus crucis signaculum*. The early missals used by Legg and *Tracts*, however, which also omit *Adoremus crucis signaculum*, have *Gratias tibi ago* here. *Tracts*.266 quotes B.M. Harl. 4919 as giving this prayer immediately after *Adoremus*. These prayers surrounding the ablutions must have remained in a state of flux up to the Marian period. The solution adopted here seeks to combine the practice of the missals with that of the manuals and the Customary.

Gratias tibi ago is preserved here because it looks a lot like a personal thanksgiving immediately after Comumnion and makes much less sense halfway through the ablutions, even though similar prayers are said in other rites at that point (see King, *Roman Church*, page 380). Being printed here in the missals (and with a healthy manuscript tradition behind it), it also seems the most probable practice of real priests at the altar.

[85] Col 650 (*Cautelae Missae*), which contemplates the renovation of the Sacrament in the pyx but not a general Communion within Mass. In the latter case, it is more expedient for the celebrant to purify his mouth before administering Communion and to consume the additional hosts immediately before washing his fingers. The reasons for delaying the general Communion until after *Quod ore sumpsimus* are given in Chapter XI, note 1.

X

FROM THE ABLUTIONS TO THE END OF MASS[1]

As soon as he has finished the prayer *Gratias tibi ago*, the priest takes the paten[2] in his right hand and scrapes up any crumbs on the corporal, lifting its edge with the left if necessary. Having uncovered the chalice and holding the paten over this, he uses his left thumb and forefinger to wipe the crumbs into the bowl. He then replaces the paten on the corporal in front of the chalice and removes the purificator towards the south corner of the altar, where he will be able to reach it at the time of the second ablution.

Taking the bowl of the chalice in both hands[3] and holding his thumbs and forefingers still joined but not over the chalice, he goes to the right corner.[4] There, facing south, he holds out the chalice to the clerk, who pours wine and water.[5] The celebrant rubs his thumbs and forefingers over the chalice to dislodge any crumbs.[6] Having done so,

---

[1] The missals, manuals and Customary, as well as the Hereford, Dominican and Roman books, all vary considerably at this stage. What follows here is a composite conjecture, which happily agrees with S.305–6. There appear to have been four *lotiones*. The first, with wine and water; the second, with wine alone; and the third, with water alone, were all poured into the chalice. The fourth, originally performed at the piscina but later at the altar, served to wash the celebrant's hands. As often, the directions for High Mass are clearer than those for Low Mass, which are not easily deducible from the former. See also Morse §450.

[2] The Sarum books do not specify what is done about the paten and the crumbs. It is consistent with Eucharistic theology that the crumbs should be gathered up (see Chapter IX, note 28), and both the Dominican and Roman rubrics make provision for this. At Rome, this takes place after Communion of the Host and before receiving the chalice. The Dominicans, on the other hand, purify the paten after communicating from the chalice (OP.1263). As generally, Dominican practice is followed here, *mutatis mutandis*.

Dominican ceremonialists differ as to whether the paten should be purified before or after the laity's Communion. Here we assume that the paten is purified after the laity's Communion because there could be occasions when the hosts for a general Communion might lie on the corporal and paten rather than in a ciborium.

[3] *inter manus* (C 66.34).

[4] C 66.34.

[5] Morse §139 contends that the phrase *vinum et aquam* is a summary of the whole process and assumes two ablutions, the first with wine only and the second with wine and water over the celebrant's fingers. He quotes a manuscript missal in the possession of Emmanuel College, Cambridge, in support of this theory, but provides insufficient context for the claim to be assessed. Missal B.228 mentions three washings explicitly (*ad terciam locionem*).

[6] Col 627 and C 66.34 require of the celebrant that he should *resinceret manus suas*. This verb, which is rare (v. Du Cange s.v. *resincerare*) and entered the English language as 'rinse' in this context, implies cleaning by washing in water and rubbing. Indeed, the *Oxford English Dictionary* gives as its first,

he faces the altar,[7] still standing at the corner[8] and, still holding the chalice in the same way by the bowl (or, if he can do so safely without putting the chalice down on the altar,[9] taking the knop with his right hand and the foot by his left), tilts and revolves the chalice so as to collect any remaining drops of the precious Blood; next, holding it with both hands, he drains it[10] and then says the prayer *Quod ore sumpsimus*.

If there is to be a general Communion within Mass, he returns to the middle, lays the chalice on the corporal, covers it and proceeds to administer the Sacrament. Otherwise, he remains at the south nook. Turning to face south again, and holding his thumbs and forefingers slightly separated inside the bowl, he holds out the chalice to the clerk, who now pours wine only[11] over the celebrant's fingers.[12] Turning east, the celebrant lays the chalice on the altar before him, strikes his thumbs and forefingers on the rim of the chalice and wipes them on the purificator, which he has picked up with his left hand. From this moment, the celebrant no longer holds his thumbs and forefingers together. Then, holding the purificator under the lip of the chalice with his left hand,[13] he takes the chalice with his right and so drinks the ablution, saying nothing. As he lays the chalice down again, he says the prayer *Haec nos Domine communio*.

For the third ablution,[14] turning to face the clerk again, with the purificator in his left, he holds out the chalice in both hands by its knop and foot for the clerk to pour water only. Facing east, the celebrant drains the chalice as before. He should do so thoroughly so that no drips should run from it later. Directly, he goes to the middle, taking with him the chalice and the purificator. He replaces the chalice on the corporal,

---

albeit obsolete, definition of 'rinse': 'Of a priest: to clean the chalice and fingers with wine and water after the Eucharist.' See also S.301.

Other uses, e.g., the early Dominicans and the earlier Præmonstratensians, like the Roman rite, use this first ablution to purify the chalice and the mouth, not the fingers. Moreover, the second ablution requires the celebrant to wash his fingers in the bowl of the chalice. It is likely, therefore, that the rubric *Qua dicta … calice* (Col 627) describes the ablutions in general and that at the first ablution the celebrant merely rubbed his dry fingers. It is a natural instinct to rub one's fingers over the chalice at almost any opportunity. Alternatively, perhaps *resinceret* could be forced to bear the meaning of 'cleaning by rubbing' to take the place of the modern Dominicans' striking of the fingers on the edge of the bowl.

[7] *Habens faciem ad altare* (OPraem.IV.184–5). This seems more seemly than drinking in sight of the choir and congregation.
[8] Since the second ablution is drunk at the corner (C 66.34: *qua hausta, eat sacerdos in medio altaris*) and there is no indication that the celebrant goes to the middle now, the first ablution also was probably taken at the corner. Tracts.188 (pseudo-Roman *Indutus Planeta* of 1507) and Tracts.245 (quoting a Carmelite ordinal of 1532) have the ablutions drunk at the south corner though the less unfamiliar Roman *Ordo Missae* of John Burckard (Tracts.164) implies the middle.
[9] Neither his hands nor the chalice, being unpurified, should be laid on the altar outside the corporal.
[10] It is not quite clear from the Sarum books themselves, among their variant readings, that this first ablution is drained. M.94 gives *post primam ablutionem* and mentions *infusionem* as a variant in the Harleian Ordinal; C 66.34 gives *effusionem*; some missals (Col 627) have *ablutionem vel effusionem*. The fifteenth-century manual quoted by Rock IV.193 is the closest to a proof, since it mentions drinking in the context of the first infusion. Nevertheless, since the books include this instruction among the directions for bination, and since in all other uses the celebrant drains this first ablution, our suggested course of action seems not improbable.
[11] Not wine and water. So the missals, the manuals and the Customary, against Morse §139 (see note 5).
[12] The rubric (Col 627) is *lavet*, not *resinceret*.
[13] A convenient detail borrowed from Roman ritual.
[14] C 66.34.

and, with his right hand, lays the purificator in its place to the corporal's right. Using both hands, he then lays the chalice down on its side to drain[15] by tipping it towards himself so that the rim of the bowl lies on the paten, close to the celebrant, and the foot lies on the middle of the altar east of the paten, probably (unless it is very ample) beyond the corporal.

While the chalice drains, the celebrant, raising his eyes to the cross and immediately bowing before the altar,[16] with joined hands says the prayer *Adoremus crucis signaculum*, after which,[17] with folded hands he goes to the south side and there washes them as at the offertory, saying nothing[18] and drying them on the towel or the purificator.[19] The water should be poured down a special piscina.[20]

Returning to the middle, he takes the chalice and sets it to his lips to receive the last drop. Then he places the chalice on the corporal in the middle and wipes his lips and then the inside of the bowl with the purificator,[21] which he lays over the chalice, as it was at the beginning of Mass, and the paten (and pall) on this. Finally, he lays the veil on the chalice so as to cover it completely in front.[22]

---

[15] *ponat* (Col 628); *involvat* (M.95). Goude, Plate XXXII, shews the chalice lying as described here. Since at High Mass the deacon has to put the chalice to the celebrant's lips *redeunte sacerdote ad dextrum cornu altaris* (C 66.34), the chalice must be within the deacon's reach, which it would not be if it lay with its foot to the right of the cup. The position suggested here, therefore, seems to make sense and be corroborated by pictorial evidence, albeit from a non-Sarum source.

[16] This is an attempt to reconcile M.95 (*respiciendo crucem*) and Col 628 (*inclinando se*).

[17] At High Mass, the celebrant washes his hands at the south end while the deacon folds the corporal. If the hands were washed at Low Mass with one clerk, one of these actions must take place before the other. In the Roman rite, this washing of the hands at Low Mass only takes place when a bishop celebrates. Then, in the absence of the customary two chaplains, the celebrant washes his hands before the chalice is dressed (Ahearne and Lane, page 137). By this analogy, the same order is adopted here. Becon, page 293, seems to agree: 'yee goe to the Altars end, and there once againe, yee wash your hands ... After this yee returne to the Altar, and take another licke or two of the dropping of the Chalice.'

[18] The fifteenth-century Harleian ordinal (*Tracts*.266) has the celebrant wash his hands at the sacrarium, but M.95 has the celebrant wash his hands at the right corner of the altar while the deacon folds the corporals. C 66.34, I think, mispunctuates (*Diaconus interim corporalia complicet ad dextrum cornu altaris. Subdiaconus librum portet*) and so suggests that the deacon folds the corporals at the right corner, thereby leaving no room for the celebrant. The manuals, however, give *diaconus vero interim corporalia complicet: et ad dextrum cornu altaris subdiaconus librum portet*, which makes more sense. *Tracts*.83 gives the option of washing the hands at the piscina or (preferably) in the chalice and then drinking the water. The third ablution, with water only, may be a duplication of this lavatory. It appears, however, that this duplication, if such it is, is official. *Tracts*.102 ascribes three ablutions to the Carthusians.

[19] *Tracts*.83.

[20] *Tracts*.83.

[21] OP.1264.

[22] At High Mass, the deacon dresses the chalice and folds the corporals while the celebrant washes his hands and then, during the first postcommon, hands the chalice to the acolyte to take back to the vestry (C 66.34). The Dominican subdeacon (OP.1041) dresses the chalice, folds the corporals and returns to the vestry during the postcommons. At Low Mass, however, the Dominican celebrant veils the chalice before saying the Communion but does not fold the corporals until the very end of the Mass (OP.1272). Since both rites are similar at High Mass, it is reasonable to assume that they may have been also similar at Low Mass. Hence, the folding of the corporal is here presumed to be postponed until after the *Placeat*. The use of York's blessing with the chalice may be an indication that there also the corporals were folded after the *Placeat*. For Becon's description, see note 37.

In case of bination,[23] the ablutions are conducted in the usual way but not drunk. Instead, the chalice is put in the sacrarium or the wine and water are poured into a clean vessel until the next Mass, when they are consumed with the ablutions.[24]

Going to the book at the south nook,[25] he reads the Communion antiphon aloud[26] with folded hands.[27] Then he crosses himself in the usual way, turns where he stands and says *Dominus vobiscum* and the postcommons as he said the collects earlier.

On days when the prayer over the people is to be said,[28] as soon as the clerk has responded *Amen* to the last postcommon, the celebrant says *Oremus* in the usual manner. Without turning to the people, with joined hands he subjoins *Humiliate capita vestra Deo*, inclining his head as he says these words, and says the prayer as he did the postcommons.

After the last postcommon, or after the prayer over the people, he crosses himself again, turns[29] and says *Dominus vobiscum* and *Ite missa est* facing the people. However, he faces the altar to say *Benedicamus Domino*[30] and *Requiescant in pace*.

After *Deo gratias*, turning back to the altar, he closes the book[31] and goes to the middle of the altar, where, bowing with joined hands, he says the prayer *Placeat* secretly. At its end, he stands erect, lays his hands on either side of the corporal, kisses the altar[32] in the middle[33] and crosses himself, saying *In nomine Patris*, &c.[34]

[23] The Missal contemplates the possibility of legitimate bination (Col 627). Rock II.383 quotes the Council of Oxford (1222), cap. VII (Wilkins I.586), on the subject: *Ne sacerdos quispiam Missarum solennia celebret bis in die; excepto die Nativitatis et Resurrectionis Dominicae, vel in obsequiis defunctorum, viz., cum corpus alicujus in ecclesia eodem die tumulandum, et tunc prior missa de die, posterior vero pro defuncto celebretur*. The English Cistercians, who followed their own rite, had peculiar permission to binate also on the feast of St. Thomas of Canterbury (Rock III.180). Trination seems contemplated by the Missal at Christmas, when the three usual Masses are provided. See also Rock IV.249. With less legitimacy a lack of available priests could also lead to bination and even trination (*Processions*.158).

[24] Col 627. At Rome, they are consumed after the first ablutions of the second Mass.

[25] Coll 589 and 628, corroborated by Becon, page 294 ('ye come againe to the Altars end, where yee began your ... Masse') and by S.54 (B.578–9) and 308.

[26] S.308.

[27] OP.1265. *Tracts*.164 (Burckard) allows the priest to hold his hands joined or on the book or on the altar, as for the epistle and the following chants. If he has to move the book himself, he will take it after he has arranged the chalice.

[28] See this point at High Mass for an explanation of the ceremonial indicated here.

[29] C 66.35 and Becon, page 294 ('After a few Collects mumbled over, yee turne you to the people, and say, *Dominus vobiscum*, bidding them adieu, and with *Ite Missa est*, yee bidde them goe'), imply that *Ite missa est* is said at the south corner, against *Tracts*.83. See note on this place at High Mass.

[30] *Ite missa est* is said only when the *Gloria in excelsis* has been said. At all other Masses, apart from Requiems, *Benedicamus Domino* is said (Col 2).

[31] The Roman and Dominican rites, in which *Ite missa est* is said in the middle, have the celebrant close the book after the postcommon. Becon, page 296 (see below on the Last Gospel) has the book shut immediately before the priest departs, which would require crossing over to the south and so seems unlikely. *Ite missa est* seems the most natural place for the book to be closed.

[32] Very peculiarly, since this is the priest's farewell to the altar, there is no mention of a kiss, against the Dominicans (*Tracts*.84) and the Carthusians (*Tracts*.103). Recourse must be had to the earlier Missal C.229: *et sic erigens se osculetur altare et signet se dicens*.

[33] So at *Aufer a nobis*, the equivalent point at the beginning of the Mass.

[34] The tone of voice is not mentioned. At Roman and Dominican High Masses, the blessing, which evolved from this crossing, is spoken in the moderate voice. At Roman Masses for the dead, there is neither crossing nor blessing. At Sarum, the blessing took place at pontifical Masses before the Communion, and it may be supposed that the words here are said in the same low voice as the *Placeat*. That presbyters' blessings were common, though, is seen from Blunt, page 332, which states

He moves the chalice away from the corporal, on the left side,[35] takes the corporal, folds it and puts it back into the burse, which he lays down to his right. He sets the chalice in the middle of the altar, then lays the burse on the top of all.

Taking the chalice in his left hand by the knop and laying the right on it, he comes down to the foot of the altar.[36] Having made a bow, he returns to the vestry, preceded by the clerk and saying secretly the Gospel *In principio*.[37] If he wears the cap, he should

---

that 'euery preste may blysse the peple in the ende of his masse. yf there be no bysshop presente. that wyl blysse' and that this blessing should be given after *Ite missa est*. Cf. also Goude, Plate XXXIII. Rock IV.196 gives a form of blessing with the chalice and folded corporal taken from the use of York. Occasional blessing with the chalice seems to be hinted at by Becon, page 156: 'to blesse the people with an empty cup, as ye doe at your high and solemne feasts.' The phænomenon was not novel: in the early twelfth century, the author of the *Micrologus* said that this blessing could not be omitted *absque gravi scandalo* and appeals to Leo the Great and Pope Gelasius to forbid presbyters from blessing at the end of Mass only when a bishop is present (*PL*.CLI.990-2). See also *Tracts*.28 (Lanforde's *Meditations*): 'After *Ite missa est*. the prest stondeith in the mydes of the Awter. and so blessyd the people.' *Tracts*.84 allows the blessing where it is customary. *Tracts*.267 gives a supposedly Sarum form for a blessing with the chalice.

[35] OP.1272.

[36] The rubric states that he bows but does not mention that he comes down the steps before doing so. However, this is a reasonable supposition in the case of altars with steps.

[37] The rubric at Col 629 is explicit, *in redeundo*, but presumes the cathedral's public High Mass at the High Altar, since the choir is expected to begin None as soon as it has replied *Deo gratias* to *Ite missa est*. The rubric also supposes that the celebrant departs immediately (*Et sic, inclinatione facta, redeant*). However, it is conceivable that the Gospel was begun at the north corner and the celebrant packed up the chalice and retired while saying *In principio* quietly. See Bonniwell, page 301, for this custom among the Dominicans.

In churches where the priest unvested at the altar (*Tracts*.238), this Gospel in its entirety may well have been said there before unvesting. See also Rock II.410 on what was done at the funeral of Prince Arthur in 1502, admittedly in the Benedictine cathedral priory of Worcester, when the absolutions were performed after the Last Gospel. Most significantly, Col 849*, dealing with the blessing of bread on Sundays, specifies that the blessing begins with the reading of the Gospel *In principio*. While other sacramentals sometimes began with this lesson (Duffy, *Stripping*, page 216), there is no reason to posit a duplication in this instance. S.309 shews that 'the people were exhorted to "abide the end"', which supposes that *In principio* was recited publicly. See also the interesting note at S.383-4. The existence of indulgences attached to hearing this Gospel (Duffy, *Stripping*, page 215) also suggests that, except when the choir service was resumed immediately after Mass, as contemplated in Col 629, the Last Gospel may well generally have been said at the altar. In this case, it is reasonable to assume that it would have been said at the north corner, as at Rome, in the same way and with the same crossings, and so forth, as the first Gospel was said earlier, and that the celebrant went on to perform the requisite blessing immediately afterwards, keeping his maniple (a detail deduced by analogy with the procession, at which the maniple was probably sometimes worn: see Morse §105). When the Last Gospel is said at the altar, it would be reasonable for the corporal to be folded after it, just before the celebrant is to recede (OP.1272).

It is worth reading Becon's words here, since for the most part he is describing an ordinary Low Mass in an ordinary church, one with no vestry. After *Ite Missa est*, he continues (pages 295-6):

> Then fall yee once againe to kneeling downe at the altar, and because yee are our Ladies knights, yee salute her most humbly with some devout Orison. That done, ye rise up againe, like tall fellowes, and saying the beginning of S. *Iohns* Gospell, ye blesse you Secrosse you as though a thousand Devills were about ye. After all these things, yee trusse up your trinkets, yee shut your booke, ye fold up your corporasse cloath, yee winde up your chalice ye put off your fooles coate, your vestment, your stole, your Fannell, your girdle, your Albe, and your Amice, yee put out the candle, & solemnly making curtesie to your God, that hangeth over the altar, ye trudg out of the Church.

Tracts.245 connects this prayer to Our Lady with the Carmelite *Salve*, said before the Last Gospel.

receive this from the clerk immediately before departing; but if he wears the amice, he should cover at the altar before taking up the chalice.[38] Once he has unvested, he begins the antiphon *Trium puerorum* and says the appointed psalms and prayers.

---

[38] OP.1272.

XI

ADMINISTRATION OF HOLY COMMUNION[1]

The ceremonial of a general Communion will vary greatly depending on whether the Sacrament will be administered outside or within Mass.

---

[1] There is no detailed description of a general Communion in the Sarum books, probably because general Communions were rare and perhaps more so in the cathedral, where the ratio of priests to inferior ministers and laymen was considerably higher than in parishes. Remarkably, Margery Kempe sought and obtained leave of Thomas Arundel, Archbishop of Canterbury, to choose 'hyr confessowr and to be howselyd every Sonday, yyf God wold dysposen hir therto, undyr hys lettyr and hys seel thorw al hys provynce' (Kempe, I.16.22–24). Lady Margaret Beaufort is famous for communicating monthly (Duffy, *Stripping*, page 93). The XV Articles of the Catholic rebels in 1549 included Article 3: 'Item we will haue the masse in Latten, as was before, & celebrated by the Pryest wythoute any man or woman communycatyng wyth hym' and Article 5: 'Item we wyll haue the Sacrament of þe aulter but at Easter delyuered to the lay people, and then but in one kynde' (Rose-Troup, page 220).

Primitively, the congregation received Communion during Mass, after the celebrant's own Communion. That this practice survived in England up to the sixteenth century, at least on occasion, is certain. The device for the coronation of Henry VII has the King communicated 'after the Cardinall hath commoned his self' (Jerdan, page 22). The same had been observed by Richard II in 1377 (Walsingham, page 337). At Sarum itself, ca. 1445 at the High Mass on Easter Day, the Communion of those below the presbyterate took place *postquam* [*domnus episcopus*] *se ipsum communicaverit in altare* (*Processions*.88). Maskell, page 124, assumes the practice.

On the other hand, throughout the Latin West, it became common over time for the congregation to be communicated outside Mass, a practice that endured well into the twentieth century. Rock IV.197 quotes *Piers Ploughman*: '(I) dude me to churche, / To huyre holliche þe masse. and be housled after.' The story of Nicholas Tyting, parishioner of Little Plumstead in Norfolk, who, refused Communion, went out weeping into the churchyard after Mass (Duffy, *Stripping*, page 94) implies this practice, as the poor man would hardly wait until the end of Mass before retiring in tears if Communion were being administered before the ablutions. The Roman *Sacerdotale* of 1559 assumes that Communion will be administered after Mass (fol. 97) though it permits it within Mass (fol. 83). M.63 prescribes Communion after Mass at the blessing of a pilgrim, thus making Communion after Mass a normative practice for Sarum Use. However, a Mass after the blessing of a pilgrim was very probably not a public High Mass, and even the Easter Mass at which the laity received 'their rights' may be considered different from a High Mass in its most solemn form.

Since, however, the Oecumenical Council of Trent desired Communion to be administered within Mass (Sess. XXII, cap. vi: *Optaret quidem sacrosancta synodus, ut in singulis Missis fideles adstantes, non solum spirituali affectu, sed sacramentali etiam Eucharistiae perceptione communicarent*), it seems impossible to decry the practice in a work of pastoral more than merely archæological character, though a reasonable cause, such as a great number of communicants, is sufficient to justify the administration of the sacrament outside Mass. Indeed, for the congregation to receive both the Pax and Communion would create a certain amount of disturbance and lengthening of the function.

The precise moment of the general Communion within Mass cannot be determined easily. The indications given in the sources above are that the Sacrament was administered after the celebrant's own Communion, but whether before or after his *purificatio oris* is not mentioned. *Tracts*.85 is equally vague. Post-mediæval Roman practice is for the laity's Communion to take place before *Quod ore sumpsimus*, but Burckard's *Ordo Missae* (*Tracts*.164) and the *Sacerdotale* of 1559 (fol.

If Communion is to be administered immediately before Mass, the priest will be in his Mass vestments; if after Mass, having removed the maniple and chasuble, in amice, alb, cincture and crossed stole only.[2] At other times he will wear a surplice and stole.[3]

On the altar should be an unfolded corporal and at least two lights. The veiled chalice is removed to the north of the altar, but if the celebrant will remove his chasuble in the vestry after Mass before giving Communion, he will take the chalice as usual and come out again. The burse should lie to the north of the corporal. A bowl of water, later to be poured into the sacrarium, and a purificator, should also be present on the altar. The houseling cloth[4] should lie extended on the Communion rail or be held by suitable servers or laymen or by the communicants themselves.[5] Communion will be administered most conveniently at the altar of reservation. If Communion will neither follow nor precede Mass, the priest will bring the corporal in the burse with him and extend it as soon as he has arrived at the altar.

Once the Sacrament lies on the altar, all kneel, with the exception of the celebrant, who bows profoundly.[6] All adore the sacrament for a short while.[7] The clerk, kneeling at the south side,[8] says the *Confiteor*.[9] As soon as he has finished, the priest turns by

---

83) have it, much more sensibly, when the celebrant has purified his mouth but not his fingers. Nor was this the moment chosen by Roman books alone: the same instruction is found in a fifteenth-century missal from Benediktbeuern (Daniel, page 147). Col 650 (*Cautelae Missae*) would have the Sacrament in the pyx renewed before the ablutions (*demum desuper ablutiones, et non prius*), but it is not clear whether the *purificatio oris* (which is different from the subsequent washings of fingers and hands) is counted as being part of the ablutions. The existence of contemporary (if continental) authoritative evidence, the ambiguity of the Sarum books and the argument from congruence all lead us to suggest the moment after the priest's purification but before his ablutions as that for the laity's Communion. The modern Roman (and Dominican) practice could hardly be condemned, however.

In the absence of detail in the Sarum books, the ceremonial put forth here follows the Dominican practice reported in *Tracts*.84-7 and the iconographical evidence provided by the fonts of Great Glemham, in Suffolk, and Gayton Thorpe, in Norfolk. These, incidentally, depict a priest administering Communion vested in amice, alb, cincture, stole and no maniple, rather than surplice and stole, which suggests that the priest is either about to say Mass or has just said it. De Herdt (t. I. p. 2. nn. 28 and 54), providing as he does details of the older ceremonial of the Roman rite, has also been consulted.

Tracts.84-7 supposes that, even during Mass, only members of the house will communicate at the High Altar, *extranei* communicating at a side altar. Communicating at a side altar outside Mass remained common until the reforms of Pius X.

[2] Great Glemham and Gayton Thorpe fonts, against the Roman books as understood by OP.1331.
[3] This seems not implausible. For the colour of the stole (either that of the day, or white or red, most plausibly), see above on the colour to be used for Corpus Christi. De Herdt (t. I. p. 2. n. 28. cap. V) prescribes the colour of the day.
[4] Jerdan, page 22.
[5] Jerdan, page 22: 'ij [of] the grettest astate then present holding befor the King and the Quene a long towell of silke.'
[6] *Tracts*.85.
[7] *Tracts*.85.
[8] This reflects modern Dominican and Roman practice and is the natural position for the clerk, since it is where he kneels for Communion during the Mass.
[9] The *Confiteor* before a general Communion is common in many uses both before and after Trent. There is no mention of its use at Sarum itself, but Walsingham, page 337, when dealing with Richard II's coronation, in 1377, tells us: *Percelebrata Missa usque ad Communionem, reductus est Rex ad altare, et genu flexo coram Archiepiscopo, dixit – 'Confiteor.' Quo absoluto, communicatus est, et iterum reductus est ad sedem suam.* From Jerdan, page 22 (see also Rock IV.199), we learn that Henry VII

his right to the clerk and congregation, withdrawing slightly to the north so as not to turn his back to the Sacrament, and says *Misereatur* and *Absolutionem*.[10] Turning back to the altar, the priest takes the pyx in his left and, holding a host in his right hand over the ciborium,[11] comes down to the place where the people are kneeling to receive Communion.[12] The clergy, in descending order of rank, should receive Communion at the altar itself, kneeling on the footpace or at the foot of the altar; the laity, outside the chancel, or at a greater distance from the altar, if a side altar be used.[13]

After the absolution, the clerk goes to the aumbry to fetch the vessel of watered wine and the napkin.[14] The people kneel in a row, the houseling cloth stretched out before them.[15] The priest communicates the people, walking along the row from south to north,[16] holding in his right hand a Host before each communicant[17] and, making a small sign of the cross with the Host over the ciborium,[18] says *Corpus Domini nostri Jesu Christi custodiat corpus tuum et animam tuam in vitam aeternam. Amen*,[19] before laying the Host on the communicant's tongue.[20] He is followed by the clerk or a sacristan, who administers the wine to the communicants to purify their mouths immediately after Communion,[21] holding out the vessel and putting it to the communicants' lips.[22] Between communicants, the clerk wipes the lip of the vessel with

and his queen also said the *Confiteor* themselves when they communicated (within Mass) at their coronation. They lay prostrate on the floor for the *Confiteor* and the general absolution (cf. OP.796), rising somewhat to kneel for their Communion and standing for the purification. Nothing suggests the use of *Ecce Agnus Dei*, and even the modern Dominicans seem to say this somewhat under protest (OP.1328).

[10] Using the *vestrorum* form. So modern Roman and Dominican practice. See also Chapter VII, note 6.
[11] *Tracts*.85.
[12] See the Gayton Thorpe font.
[13] This reflects (if faintly) the distinction between *fratres* and *extranei* in *Tracts*.85.
[14] Jerdan, pages 21–2; Gayton Thorpe font.
[15] See the Gayton Thorpe font and cf. Becon, page 94: 'and this is the goodly God whom the people may not receive sitting nor standing, but kneeling upon their marrowbones.' This contrasts with the practice of the Dominicans at High Mass (*Tracts*.85–6). Jerdan, page 22, has the King and Queen lie prostrate for the *Confiteor* and then 'somewhat arise kneling' after *Absolutionem*. It seems that no uniformity of posture for the laity may be prescribed but all must be left to the individual's piety.
[16] So it appears from the Gayton Thorpe font. *Tracts*.85 has the friars approach *bini et bini*.
[17] The Royal Injunctions of 1549 proscribed 'shewing the Sacrament openly before the distribution of the Communion' (Burnet, page 243), but it is not clear whether this had formerly taken place before the whole congregation before the priest came down from the altar or before each communicant.
[18] There is no explicit authority for the making of a cross with the Host as this formula is said, but it is a practice common in other uses (e.g. OP.1329), would reflect the cross made before the priest's own Communion and may be supported by the peculiar use of the word *recipientis* in *cruce prius facta ex ipso corpore.scilicet. christi/ante os recipientis* at M.93, which, while dealing ostensibly with the celebrant's own Communion, appears to describe him, most unnecessarily, as *recipientis*. It is therefore included here as being probable.
[19] This is the formula found twice in the Manual (M.37, at baptism; M.111, at Communion of the sick). Missal C.131, dealing with the first Communion of neophytes on Holy Saturday, gives what is presumably an older form: *Corpus Domini nostri Jesu Christi custodiat te in vitam eternam. Amen*. The celebrant receives with the short formula *In nomine Patris*, &c. (Col 626).
[20] Aside from the relevant canons, Becon, page 156, has 'wee will put it in your mouths'. The Prayer Book of 1549 retained Communion on the tongue (Gibson and Ratcliff, page 230).
[21] See the Gayton Thorpe font and S.381.
[22] This seems to be the import of Becon's unclear words (pages 224–5): 'Neither can ye abide, that the people should touch your Pope-holy chalice when they drinke the wine, but ye your selves holding the chalice in your hands give them drinke, as though they were babes of three dayes old, and could not put the Cuppe to their mouth.'

the napkin.[23] The communicants kneel upright to receive the Sacrament and stand up to receive the wine.[24] Otherwise, the clerk may stand at the south end and administer the wine and napkin there, the communicants coming to him.[25]

When the last communicant has received, the priest returns to the altar, lays the Sacrament on the corporal, shuts the pyx and reserves the Sacrament. He then washes his fingers in the bowl and dries them on the purificator. Bowing, he retires as he came.

If Communion must be administered within a Low Mass, the priest is fully vested. He exposes the Sacrament as soon as he has said the prayer *Quod ore sumpsimus*, while the clerk is saying the *Confiteor*. He turns by his right, withdrawing slightly to the north, to say *Misereatur* and *Absolutionem*. Turning back to the middle, he takes the pyx in his left hand and descends to communicate the congregation as above. After he has communicated the last communicant, he returns to the altar and consumes or reserves the remaining hosts. He scrapes any remaining crumbs on the corporal and proceeds with the Mass as normal.

---

[23] Among the Dominicans, the communicants use this purificator to wipe their lips (*Tracts*.86). De Herdt (t. I. p. 2. n. 28. cap. I) prescribes the same for the Roman rite. However, this wiping of the lips seems to be of little ritual importance, and, pastorally, it seems more prudent to apply the purificator to the lip of the chalice.

[24] *Tracts*.86 (which has friars bow immediately before rising) and also Jerdan, page 22.

[25] So the Roman *Caeremoniale Episcoporum*, Lib. II, cap. xxix.3 and *Tracts*.86.

XII

THE DUTIES OF THE CLERK AT LOW MASS

Ordinarily, no priest should say Mass without an assistant.[1] This assistant should be a clerk, that is to say in traditional parlance, he should have received at least the tonsure. However, a layman[2] may take the place of the clerk if necessary. He should be arrayed in cassock and surplice[3] and have clean hands.[4]

The clerk should see to it that the vestments are laid out for the celebrant and that the missal is ready. If he has been ordained to the subdiaconate, he should also make sure that the chalice has been prepared. He also sees that the candles have been lit,[5] that the missal-stand is in its place on the altar at the south nook and that the cruets, the bowl and towel for the lavatory, the sanctus bell and the elevation torch[6] (with the

---

[1] The liturgical books give some details of the ministers' duties at High Mass, but the server's duties at Low Mass are touched upon but once and then in a contested reading: at Coll 595-6, the response to *Orate fratres* is made by a *clericus*. It is on the strength of this word that we call the server a clerk, instead of the Dominicans' *servitor*. His duties probably varied considerably from church to church and even from server to server. Such is still the case within the Roman rite. Not only are there considerable differences between Spanish, French and English styles of serving, but within England alone great variation can be seen. The indications given here have been deduced from the presumed requirements of the celebrant and influenced by the practice of the Dominicans. See the notes in preceding chapters for the reasons why we have assumed the ceremonies suggested here.

[2] Becon, page 106, contemplates the presence of both a boy and the parish clerk ('For many times besides the boy and Parish clerke that wait upon you, there bee in the Church as many white bulls and fat oxen, as there bee men and women'), and the untonsured St. Thomas More sang in a surpliced choir (Rowse, page 66).

[3] The *vestis talaris* was enjoined upon all clergymen. Mediæval illustrations of clerks serving at Low Mass sometimes feature surplices and sometimes rochets, often sleeveless, and the Sarum inventory of 1214-22 mentions rochets (*Processions*.180). Chambers, page 30, refers to a gloss of Lyndewode's in his *Provinciale*, in which the rochet is prescribed for clerks ministering to the priest. Morse §294 reports a constitution of Archbishop Raynold in 1322 to the same effect. The rochet was gradually replaced by the surplice as the vestment common to all clerks, and nowadays the use of the rochet is limited to prelates and those who have received this privilege by papal indult. Rock II.7-8 advocates the surplice, but see also his treatment of the rochet at II.14-15. For the abusive omission of the surplice (or rochet), see *Processions*.155.

[4] OP.932.

[5] Or he may light the candles after placing the missal on its stand and before going to the credence table for the cruets, as the modern Dominicans are supposed to do (OP.936) and as was the former practice in the Roman rite. Becon, pages 295-6, supposes that after Mass the candles are extinguished before the priest leaves the altar ('After all these things ... yee put out the candle, and ... ye trudg out of the Church').

[6] For the difficulties involved in combining the use of the torch and that of the bell at Low Mass, see Chapter II, notes 25 and 26.

means to kindle it) are ready. The torch will most conveniently be on the south of the sanctuary. If the bedes are to be bidden at the altar, the *Liber vitae* should be thereon, behind the stand for the missal. Otherwise, it will be available in a convenient place. The pax-brede, if it is to be used, is placed on the south part of the altar. If there is to be a general Communion, the vessel with watered wine for washing the communicants' mouths covered with a napkin is placed in the aumbry. The houseling cloth is laid out in its accustomed place.

The clerk assists the celebrant to vest and makes the responses to the preparatory prayers. He takes the missal, supporting its front cover on his breast, holding it in his left hand, with the spine resting on his lower left arm. With the right hand, he holds its lower fly.[7] He bows to the principal image in the vestry with the priest and precedes the celebrant to the altar. At the door of the vestry, he hands holy water to the celebrant and rings the bell if customary.[8] At the foot of the altar, he bows profoundly with the celebrant,[9] standing to his right. He places the missal on the stand, going round the footpace by the south side to do so. He descends and goes to the aumbry. There he takes the wine cruet in his right hand and the water in his left. Returning to the south side of the altar, he bows at the bottom[10] and goes up to the celebrant. He hands the wine cruet to the celebrant[11] and moves the water cruet to his right. Receiving the wine cruet in his left hand, he holds up the water cruet in his right, says *Benedicite* and waits while the celebrant blesses the water. He hands the cruet to the celebrant. Upon receiving it again (with his left hand), he bows and descends to the aumbry. Leaving the cruets, he goes round the bottom of the steps to the north side,[12] bowing moderately in the middle as he passes.[13] He kneels on the bottom step or, if there is only one step, on the floor. Throughout the Mass, he kneels with joined hands on the bottom step opposite to where the missal is, except during the Gospel and when otherwise ministering.[14]

---

[7] C 66.19; OP.1018.
[8] S.149.
[9] OP.936, where the server is to make the same obeisance as the celebrant.
[10] These bows are practised among the Dominicans (though not mentioned in their ceremonial until the lavatory (OP.940)) and are presumed to take place whenever the clerk attends at the corner of the altar.
[11] At this point, the vexed question of the *solita oscula*, as they are called by Roman authors, must be pondered. At High Mass, the deacon hands the thurible (Col 581) and the chalice to the celebrant, kissing his hand each time (C 66.23). Whether from this one can legitimately extrapolate the observance of *solita oscula* whenever something is handed to or received from the celebrant at either High or Low Mass is uncertain. For the Dominicans' practice, see OP.809.
    Among the Dominicans, a server ordained to the subdiaconate may infuse the wine and water into the chalice (OP.936).
[12] OP.937.
[13] He should bow whenever he passes the middle of the altar (OP.938).
[14] OP.938. Hereford.xxxiv–xxxv instructs the ministers to stand and not lie prostrate (*nec jacere prostrati, sed stare*), but it is clear from reference to the deacon that this instruction is to be understood of the sacred ministers at High Mass. It seems safer to assume that at Low Mass the minister knelt: cf. *Tracts*.95.
    Should the server minister at the celebrant's chasuble when he turns to say *Dominus vobiscum*, as the subdeacon does at Mass? *Tracts*.95 has *trahere casulam cum expedierit non omittat*. This necessity will not exist with modern chasubles and the modern Dominicans do not do so. (Indeed, OP.938 seems to exclude this possibility.)

Kneeling in his place, he makes the responses. He bows throughout the celebrant's confession as well as his own. At *mea culpa* in the *Confiteor*, he does not strike his breast. He alternates with the celebrant during the *Kyrie*. If the celebrant wears a cap, the clerk receives it from him at the end of the *Kyrie* and lays it down in a suitable place. In this case, it will be more convenient for him to go round to the south steps during the Officium and alternate the *Kyrie* there. At the end of the epistle, he makes no response.[15] Towards the end of the sequence or during the alleluya or tract, unless the celebrant will flit the book himself,[16] the clerk rises and goes round the steps to the missal, bowing moderately in the middle as he passes. He takes the missal with its stand to the north nook, again walking round the front of the steps,[17] and sets it on the altar at an angle. Standing on the top step below the footpace and facing the celebrant, he responds to *Et cum spiritu tuo*. At *Sequentia*, &c. he crosses himself with his thumb on his forehead and breast. As he replies *Gloria tibi Domine*, he crosses himself in the usual fashion from his forehead to his breast and shoulders, and bows to the cross.[18] He then goes down the steps on the north side and goes round the steps to the south side, bowing in the middle as he passes. He stands at the corner facing the celebrant. At the end of the Gospel, he signs himself but makes no response.[19] He kneels down until the celebrant has read the Offertory.

If the people are to make their oblations, the clerk rises after the celebrant has read the Offertory and brings from the aumbry the plate on which they are to be received. Standing to the south of the priest, he holds the plate before him so that the celebrant may conveniently deposit the offerings on it. When the oblation is over, he returns directly to the aumbry.

If the bedes are to be bidden or the celebrant will preach, the clerk, having accompanied him to the pulpit if customary, may go to a seat. At the end of the sermon, he accompanies the priest back to the altar, goes to the aumbry and returns with the water for the lavatory.

More usually, when the celebrant has finished reading the Offertory, the clerk, going straight to the aumbry, puts the towel over his left arm and then takes the basin in his left hand and the water cruet (if employed for this purpose) in his right. He goes up to the south side of the altar, bowing at the bottom of the steps.[20] If the priest says

---

[15] OP.939.
[16] See Chapter VII, note 37.
[17] Ceremonialists of the Roman rite, such as De Herdt, Solans and Fortescue, have the server go round *per planum* when going to fetch the missal and when returning to his place after moving the book, but do not always specify the route that he should follow while carrying the book across. In practice, three possibilities exist: (1) to go round *per planum*; (2) to go round as close behind the celebrant as decent, i.e., neither going *per planum* nor coming down the steps in the middle; and (3) coming down the steps in the middle. O'Connell and universal modern English practice follow the third method. Writing of moving the missal after Communion, De Herdt (t. I. p. 2. n. 34. cap. IV) seems to favour the second option: *transfert missale, et collocat ut ad introitum, incedens per planum*. Since at High Mass the subdeacon must needs transfer the missal after Communion going *per planum* (because the celebrant is standing at the south corner), and it seems more comely to adopt the same method for both transfers of the missal, we recommend the second option here.
[18] But see Chapter VIII, note 5, and Chapter XVII, notes 35 and 36.
[19] OP.939.
[20] OP.940.

prayers for the dead, the clerk will make the responses. Going up for the lavatory, he may extend the towel on the altar,[21] or he may keep it on his arm for the celebrant to take. He then pours water over the celebrant's fingers or holds out the basin for the celebrant to dip his fingers in the water. When the celebrant has replaced the towel, the clerk bows and returns the cruet, bowl and towel to the aumbry. He returns to his place at the south corner of the steps and kneels. When the celebrant has turned back to the altar after *Orate fratres*, the clerk replies *Spiritus Sancti gratia* privately.[22] He kneels there and makes the responses until the celebrant approaches the end of the preface.

If the bell is handheld and has been placed at the foot of the altar, the clerk rings it as the celebrant begins the *Sanctus*.[23] At some point during the first part of the Canon, he rises to go and light the torch. If a fixed bell is to be rung elsewhere in the chancel,[24] the clerk rises towards the end of the preface so that he may ring the bell at the beginning of the *Sanctus*. After ringing the bell, he goes to light the torch.

If another is to ring the external bell at the elevation,[25] the clerk, when the celebrant has begun *Hanc igitur*,[26] with the lighted torch in his right hand, goes straight up the south side to the highest step and kneels behind the celebrant to his right,[27] holding the torch aloft so as to illumine fully the elevated Host. At the elevation, he raises the celebrant's chasuble[28] a little with his left hand. As *Unde et memores* is begun, the clerk returns the torch to its place, extinguishes it and goes back to his place at the foot of the altar on the south side.

He remains here until the Pax, or, if this is to be omitted, until the celebrant has communicated himself from the chalice, and makes the necessary responses.

---

[21] O.P.940.
[22] Col 595. See Chapter VIII, note 43.
[23] O.P.615 seems to consider the *Sanctus* to be the moment shortly before the elevation. Three rings are now usual, but see O.P.941. The bell is not rung at all at Low Mass said at a side altar when Mass or any part of the Office is being said at the High Altar of the church. See O.P.616.
[24] S.272 supposes an external bell at Masses said at the High Altar.
[25] S.285 considers three rings at each elevation, but there is no authoritative source for this. If there is no elevation of the chalice, the bell is not rung then.
[26] Two principles must be reconciled: (1) that the clerk should arrive in plenty of time for the Sacring; and (2) that he should not go up too soon. He will probably have just over a minute and a half to ring the bell, light the torch and return to his place, but he must not dawdle unnecessarily. *Hanc igitur* is chosen because the celebrant, in laying his hands on the altar, signals the approach of the Sacring. (This is also the moment appointed by John Burkard for the pre-Tridentine Roman rite: see *Tracts*.155.) If the clerk is to ring a fixed bell elsewhere, he will not have time to return to his place before lighting the torch but, if he uses the handbell, he need not leave his place until slightly later, perhaps during the *Memento pro vivis*.
[27] So many, but by no means all, illustrations. It is not unusual to see the clerk depicted on the left of the celebrant (e.g. the Bodleian Library's MS. Auct. D. Inf. 2. 11 fol. 217v). The right, however, seems simpler, as it does not involve the clerk crossing to the other side, and it may be no accident that the Dominicans' candle is lit on the south side (O.P.494).

Some illustrations (as above) shew the clerk facing east with the celebrant; others (e.g. *The Mass of St. Giles* by the Master of St. Giles) shews him facing north. The latter position allows the torch to be held closer to the Host, but no doubt there was local variation in this also.
[28] Morse §305 claims that there is no English authority for raising the chasuble, and it is true that this ritual does not appear to be mentioned in service books or other liturgical ordinances. It is found in illuminations, however (e.g. the Bodleian Library's MS. Auct. D. Inf. 2. 11 fol. 217v), and is prescribed by the Dominicans (O.P.941). For the difficulty of reconciling the raising of the chasuble with the bell and the torch, see Chapter II, note 25.

If the Pax is to be given, he comes up to the right of the priest after the commingling, takes the pax-brede from the altar, kneels on the footpace and holds up the pax-brede for the celebrant to kiss, answering *Et cum spiritu tuo*.[29] He then kisses the pax-brede and takes it to the nave as at High Mass. Alternatively, since the Pax might take some time and be prolonged until after the celebrant's Communion, another clerk in a surplice could come up to receive the Pax and take it to the nave.[30]

Upon his return,[31] as soon as the celebrant has communicated from the chalice, the clerk goes to take the cruets from the aumbry, the wine in his right hand, the water in his left. He brings them to the south nook of the altar, bowing at the bottom. When the celebrant approaches, the clerk pours wine and then water into the chalice. He stays in his place until the celebrant turns towards him for the second ablution, when the clerk pours wine only into the chalice over the celebrant's fingers. When the priest turns for the third ablution, the clerk pours water only into the chalice, bows to the priest and returns to the aumbry with the cruets. There he takes the water cruet, the bowl and the towel and attends the celebrant while he washes his hands as was done earlier at the lavatory.

Returning from the aumbry after laying down the towel, &c., the clerk moves the book back to the south corner, making the same moves as before the Gospel but in reverse, and then goes to kneel on the north side, where he makes the responses. As the celebrant says the *Placeat*, the clerk goes to the south nook, collects the missal and returns to the foot of the altar, bringing the celebrant's cap if it is to be worn. There he bows with the celebrant, standing at his right, and leads him to the vestry.

In the vestry, he assists the celebrant to unvest and makes the responses at the prayers after Mass. Lastly, he tidies up after Mass and removes his surplice.

If there is to be a general Communion after Mass, the clerk accompanies the celebrant to the altar and says the *Confiteor* kneeling on the south. After *Absolutionem*, he rises and brings the houseling cloth from the aumbry to the communicants. Returning to the aumbry, he brings the vessel with wine and the napkin, and administers the purification to the communicants, following the celebrant or standing at the south end of the chancel arch. If there are two clerks, each with a vessel, the second should stand at the north end. At the end, he returns the chalice and purificator to the aumbry and returns to the foot of the altar to bow and accompany the celebrant back to the vestry.

If there is to be a general Communion within Mass, the clerk returns the cruets to the aumbry as the celebrant drinks his purification. He comes back immediately, kneels on the south side and bows to say the *Confiteor*. After *Absolutionem*, he goes to the aumbry to bring the vessel and napkin for the purification. He assists with the Communion as above, returns the vessel and napkin to the aumbry and proceeds to administer the cruets for the ablutions as usual.

At Requiem Masses, the clerk does not say *Benedicite* or hold up the cruet to the celebrant, as the water is not blessed. At the offertory, he must not delay after washing

---

[29] *Tracts*.162 (Burckard) and Col 623.
[30] For the clerk as bearer of the Pax to parishioners, see Chapter XIX, notes 50 and 51. On restricting the Pax to the server at Low Mass, see Chapter IX, note 72 and *Tracts*.83.
[31] If the server is to administer the Pax, he must return before the ablutions. So Becon, page 291: 'When the boy or Parish Clerke commeth againe with the Pax, yee hold forth your chalice.'

the celebrant's hands, but leave the cruet, bowl and towel in the aumbry and directly return to his place so as to be ready to reply aloud[32] *Tu suscipe*, &c. if the celebrant says *Hostias et preces*. In answer to *Orate fratres*, the clerk says *Requiem aeternam*, &c. aloud.[33] The Pax is not given. At the end, he replies *Amen* to *Requiescant in pace*.

[32] Col 595.
[33] Col 596.

BOOK IV

HIGH MASS

XIII

PREPARATION

The Sarum books assume that the proper time for the High Mass is after Sext has been sung in choir.[1] On penitential days, Mass is sung after None.[2]

The altar is prepared with lit candles[3] on either side of the cross and the missal-stand at the south corner[4] parallel with the front of the altar. On doubles only (if two Texts will be employed), the missal, open at the Officium, is laid upon this; on other days, the deacon may bring the missal with him. To the left of the missal-stand or behind it is laid the epistle-book.[5] Except on doubles, when the subdeacon will bring it with him, somewhat to the left of the middle of the altar at the back[6] may be laid a cushion[7] for the Text. If a Text is to be used later at the Gospel, the Gospel-book itself

---

[1] Col 629. This was the later custom. The earlier practice was to bless the water before Terce (Rock IV.208) and to sing Mass immediately after that hour (Cons 39.2). Although giving no primary authority, *Processions*.198 suggests eleven o' clock for the High Mass in Sarum church. These 'proper' times are comparable to those in the Roman books, which assume Mass after Terce (or None on penitential days). There neither is (nor was) any impediment to the celebration of solemn Masses at other times.

[2] Cons 46.4.

[3] See Chapter I, note 21.

[4] *Tracts*.73 would have the missal cushion covered with a veil.

[5] *Tracts*.73; OP.493.

[6] OP.980.

[7] Among the modern Dominicans, who do not use the Text and adopt a cushion for the book of the Gospels, these book-cushions are of the colour of the day (OP.493). The woodcut at P.129 includes a representation of such a cushion.

The disposition of the books and cushions according to the rank of the day is quite intricate and is affected further by the question of whether the church possesses a Textus or not. The arrangements may be summarized as follows.

In churches where a Text is used, on doubles, the missal is placed on the altar, on its stand or cushion, before Mass begins. The subdeacon brings in the first Text on a cushion (C 66.3) and lays it on the north part of the altar at *Aufer a nobis*. The deacon carries the second Text on another cushion (C 66.3) and lays it on the south part of the altar at the back of the mensa to the left of the missal. On days other than doubles, the missal-stand or cushion, with no missal, is placed at the south end of the altar before Mass. At the north end of the altar, an empty cushion (OP.493) is laid for the Textus. The subdeacon will bring in the Textus (C 66.3) and lay it on its cushion at *Aufer a nobis*. The deacon will do likewise with the missal (OP.1050). Otherwise, the deacon may come in with no book (a possible interpretation of C 66.3 and the implied custom at Wells.35) and the missal may be placed on the altar, open at the Officium.

The Sarum books always presume the use of the Text. However, it may be imagined that when no Text will be used, both on doubles and on other days, the empty missal-stand is placed on the altar before Mass, but there is no cushion at the north end. The subdeacon may bring the book of the

is laid on the altar at its north end balancing the epistle-book. On the south side of the altar, in line with the candlesticks, is placed the pax-brede with its cloth of the colour of the day.[8]

Places should be prepared for the celebrant and the ministers at the sedilia, and the easternmost places in the lowest rank on either side of the choir for the taperers.[9] The acolyte and the thurifer may have places there also, next to the taperers, or they may sit near the sedilia.[10] If the lessons are to be read from a portable lectern, this should be prepared in a suitable place and brought out when required. If the choir is to be ruled, seats for the rulers are set out in the middle of the choir, in front of the first form. The book for the prophecy may be prepared in the choir or, if preferred, at the lectern, aumbry or credence table, together with the handbell, if it is to be used. The plate or cloth for the people's offertory, if it will be needed, is prepared in a convenient place.

In the vestry, the dressed chalice without a host, the humeral veil, the host in a pyx, the cruets on their tray, the basin, ewer and towel, the taperers' candles in their candlesticks, the lit thurible and full incense boat with its spoon,[11] the processional cross,[12] the torches and the vestments are prepared. Copes should be laid out for the cantors, the rulers of the choir and the choir, if they will be needed. If the church possesses a Text, this also is laid out. On doubles, two Texts, if available, both on cushions,[13] are prepared. On other days, the missal is made ready for the deacon to bear it to the altar. There should also be a covering for the Gospel lectern and the book from which the Gospel will be read.

The clergy go to the altar[14] in the following order: first,[15] the acolyte[16] (carrying the processional cross, at least on doubles); then two taperers side by side, the first to the

---

Gospel lessons (OP.1018) and place it on the altar at *Aufer a nobis*. The deacon does likewise with the missal (OP.1050). The celebrant is offered the book of the Gospel lessons to kiss after the Gospel (C 66.22), but all other kisses of the Textus are omitted.

[8] Olalla.285; OP.981.
[9] C 66.28. In practice, they will be busy elsewhere most of the time other than during the Canon.
[10] See page 6. Rock IV.223 suggests the latter, though he quotes no authority.
[11] Frere, *Use of Sarum* II.2, includes a hint that incense may not have been used when the choir was not ruled (*ad missam incensum habeatur et sic in omnibus festis cum regimine chori*), but this is contradicted by C 66.41.
[12] C 66.19 has the cross carried before the Gospel only on doubles. P.1 has the acolyte carry the cross in the ordinary Sunday procession. Cons 25 and 33 also give directions for the cross at the procession, but it is not made clear whether the cross is ever carried on the way to and from the altar at Mass as we presume here. C is silent. Morse §36 thinks that it was not.
[13] Unveiled, unlike the missal's (*Tracts*.73). The woodcut at P.129 shews an unveiled cushion at the Saturday Evensong procession.
[14] It is likely that the Missal's rubrics and C are both defective, since they mention neither crucifer nor acolyte, and yet both these functions are required later on. P.1 requires an acolyte carrying the cross to go in front with the taperers, thereby giving both functions to the same person. In the same way, the directions for the vestments worn are also defective. The acolyte is here described as wearing only an alb, but he wears a tunicle when the *Gloria is excelsis* was said (Cons 55). That the model Mass is that of the first Sunday of Advent gives excessive prominence to details that do not obtain for most of the year.
[15] At Sarum itself, processions were at least sometimes preceded by vergers. See P.5 and *passim*. At Durham, the verger preceded the procession only between the choir and the revestry, presumably because there was no need for anybody to clear the way in the priestly precinct itself (Durham.8).
[16] The acolyte is not mentioned with the other ministers at the entrance (Col 582), but his presence is assumed lower down when the vestments of the servers are discussed. P.1 has him carry the cross in the procession on ordinary, i.e., non-double, Sundays, and the woodcut there shews him advancing

right of the second; then the thurifer;[17] then the subdeacon carrying the Text[18] book (on a cushion on doubles) or, in its absence, the Gospel-book, lying on its cushion only on doubles;[19] then the deacon, carrying the missal on his breast[20] or, on doubles, a second Text on a cushion;[21] and finally[22] the celebrant. The last three walk covered.[23] The choir, including the choristers who will act as torchbearers,[24] are presumed to be already in the stalls, singing the preceding hour. Apart from the choir and the several cantors, there should also be two surpliced boys to help with the water, salt and book before the procession on Sundays and, if desired, with the preparation of the lectern.[25]

The clergy bow to the cross in the vestry and set out for the sanctuary. They approach the altar[26] at different times depending on the rank of the day.[27] On ferias and feasts and within octaves, when the choir is not ruled, they enter the chancel as the Officium is intoned, but at other times as the choir begins the *Gloria Patri* of the Officium (or the verse when the *Gloria Patri* is omitted).[28] At the presbytery step, all bow[29] profoundly to the altar and then to the choir,[30] with the exception of the crucifer, who never bows or kneels while bearing the cross.[31]

---

between the two taperers. However, perhaps with greater authority, P.5 has the taperers follow the crucifer. At the Christmas procession, P.11 prescribes three acolytes in albs, not in tunicles, which implies that there is no relation between the acolyte of the procession and that of the Mass, who may wear different vestments (the tunicle is worn on Christmas Day, since the *Gloria in excelsis* is said). Similarly, the presence of three acolytes at the procession does not imply that three acolyte-crucifers served at the Mass.

[17] The Missal gives *thuribularii*, in the plural, but C 66.2 gives the singular, *turribularius*. Two thurifers are employed at Pontifical Masses (Col 594) and in processions (P.5).

The existence of a boat-bearer is nowhere mentioned, as is also the case with the liturgical books of the Roman rite. He is unnecessary and merely clutters up the sanctuary. The dictum *entia non sunt multiplicanda sine necessitate* comes to mind.

[18] The Dominicans (OP.1018) carry the Gospel-book, so this is presumed from *textum* (C 66.3.). By the same analogy, if a Text is not to be used, the subdeacon may carry the Gospel-book.

[19] C 66.2.

[20] OP.1050. At the Pontifical Mass on Maundy Thursday, the missal and the lesson-books are borne in the procession by three acolytes, while the principal subdeacon and the principal deacon carry Texts (*Processions*.72).

[21] C 66.3. This, the deacon's, Text seems to be the second copy for kissing by the choir later.

[22] At Durham.7, the subdeacon comes out of the revestry in front of the deacon, so we presume that the ministers did not walk at the celebrant's sides.

[23] Lincoln I.377.

[24] *Processions*.278.

[25] C 66.10 and C 66.41. P.1–2.

[26] C 66.2 (*presbyterium intret*); Col 582 (*accedant ministri ad Altare*). At Durham.7, the clergy, preceded by a verger, set out from the vestry as the Officium is intoned and pause (the celebrant and ministers in a row) at the south choir door until *Gloria Patri* has been begun, when they enter the choir and go up to the altar.

[27] C 66.36.

[28] OP.1050 *et alibi*, fleshing out the details of Col 582, C 66.2 and C 66.36. The reason for this difference seems to be that, when the Officium is sung thrice, there is plenty of time for the procession to arrive at the altar and the initial prayers to take place but, when the Officium is shorter, the procession should set out earlier.

[29] So at Durham.7, where the bow is directed at the hanging Sacrament.

[30] OPraem.IV.18–19, at the presbytery step, having entered the choir through its west door. In other words, the clergy had to turn west to greet the choir. At Durham.7, the clergy enter through the south presbytery door and no bow to the choir is mentioned.

[31] OP.946.

XIV

FROM THE ENTRANCE TO THE COLLECTS

The acolyte goes to leave the cross in its place and retires. The taperers stand aside with their candles.[1] The thurifer stands at the south side, some way behind the first taperer.[2] The celebrant and ministers go up and stand on the highest step of the altar, just below the footpace, the celebrant in the middle, the deacon on his right and the subdeacon on the left.[3] The celebrant begins *Et ne nos inducas*, &c. The ministers and taperers[4] make the responses. At the *Confiteor*, &c.[5] the ministers bow throughout the celebrant's confession as well as their own,[6] and the taperers turn to face each other,[7] still holding their tapers. After the following versicles and *Oremus*, the celebrant turns to the deacon and kisses him; then he turns to the subdeacon and kisses him also.[8] While he does so, he says *Habete osculum pacis*, &c. once only, breaking off for the kisses themselves. When the priest has kissed the subdeacon, the taperers go round

---

[1] The taperers should take care never to stand between ministers of higher rank or between them and the altar, but should always stand and cross behind them (*Tracts*.75).

[2] This seems to be the practice of the Carmelites.

[3] C 66.4. The Dominican ministers lay down their books at this point on the footpace before them and pick them up again later to go up to the altar (OP.1019 and 1050). At Lincoln, in agreement with Durandus, the ministers seem to have held the Texts in their hands and did not lay them down (Morse §109; Lincoln I.376). This is also the implication of OPraem.IV.24–5. At Wells.35, the subdeacon is described as bearing the Text during the *Confiteor*, the deacon apparently not holding the missal but merely assisting. Durham.7 is unclear. The Sarum books are silent but, on balance, the practice of Wells and Lincoln seems preferable. If the ministers held the books, it is practically certain that the breast was not beaten at *mea culpa*.

[4] OP.986.

[5] At Lincoln, the deacon and subdeacon, holding their Texts, came before the celebrant for *Absolutionem*, &c. (Lincoln I.376). If this ceremony was observed at Sarum, it is likely that the ministers bowed and that the celebrant made the sign of the cross over them. The ceremony has not been preserved by the Dominicans.

[6] OP.1019; OP.1051.

[7] *Tracts*.74; OP.986. At Vespers, the taperers face each other across the priest for the collect (C 38.1).

[8] Wells.35 has the celebrant kiss the Text before the ministers, and this kiss is the original kissing of the Text mentioned by Durandus (IV, cap. 6, 8) and preserved in Pontifical Masses of the Roman Rite. The kissing of the Text after the incensation of the altar, done at Sarum and also (by duplication) at Wells, seems to be a later development. By analogy with Wells, it would not be unreasonable for the celebrant to kiss the Text twice, but is the *statim* of C 66.5 an indication that the Text was no longer kissed at this point? The Consuetudinary mentions the kissing of the Text after the incensation of the altar only (Cons 39.5 and 39.6). Kissing the subdeacon holding the Text cannot have been easy. The best method will be for the celebrant to place his hands on the ministers' shoulders and kiss them as he will later at the Pax.

the sides of the steps and put down their tapers, still lit,[9] by the bottom step of the altar *in plano* in line with the altar candlesticks or on the presbytery step[10] and go to their usual place. When their candles are placed in line with the altar candlesticks, this place will be standing[11] *in plano* before the altar at its foot, facing east, the first taperer at the south and the second at the north. When the tapers are set down on the presbytery step, the taperers will stand behind their tapers, facing east, and will then come to the foot of the altar when they need to do so.[12]

Having made a profound bow[13] with the ministers, the celebrant goes up to the altar, repeats *Oremus*, says *Aufer a nobis*, kisses the altar and signs himself as usual. The ministers go up with the priest, the deacon to the south corner where he places and opens the missal at the Officium[14] if he has brought it with him, and the subdeacon to the north side, where he places the closed Text on the cushion.[15]

When the celebrant has blessed himself, he turns to the right as the thurifer comes up the south steps.[16] The deacon takes the incense boat from the thurifer. Offering incense in the spoon to the celebrant, he says *Benedicite*, and the celebrant blesses the incense with a single sign of the cross, saying *Dominus*, &c. The deacon then imposes the incense,[17] returns the boat to the thurifer, takes the thurible from the thurifer and hands it to the celebrant, kissing his hand.[18] This kiss is observed whenever the thurible is delivered up to or received from the celebrant.[19] The celebrant, accompanied by the ministers, incenses the altar.

---

[9] Cons 39.6.
[10] C 66.6, C 66.12 and Cons 39.6 would have the taperers set down their candles *ad gradum altaris*. OP.986 specifies *infra gradus altaris … id est, in utroque latere, et in eadem linea ac candelabra altaris*, assuming that the altar steps go round the altar. In practice, this means that they will be outside any curtains. If the steps do not go round the sides of the altar, the candles could be placed on the presbytery steps if these are distinct from the altar steps (OP.986). It would hardly be wrong to set the candles at the foot of the altar if sufficient space were allowed for the various ministers to go about their business (Morse §33 and §398). Doubtless, when this rite was celebrated frequently, questions such as this were answered differently in different parishes.
[11] Col 586.
[12] Tracts.75 would have them either at the presbytery steps or, on condition that they return to the altar when the celebrant does so, in the choir. Either place seems legitimate. OP.987 permits the taperers to retire to the choir, particularly when there is a dearth of singers, or to sit on either side of the sedilia.
[13] Cons 39.6 is ambiguous, since the bow could be prescribed either before ascending to the footpace or before incensing the altar. Here the former is understood for the following reasons: (1) *humiliatio* seems more likely to refer to an obeisance made when approaching the altar rather than to a bow made before a particular ritual act performed when already at the altar, even though OP.1221 prescribes no bow at all at this point and OP.1291 a modest bow when incensing before the chalice at the offertory; (2) OP.1107 prescribes profound bows both when ascending to the altar and before incensing the Cross in the divine office; and (3) the bow before incensing the altar is naturally considered an integral part of that act, whereas it is more reasonable to prescribe explicitly the bow at the ascent to the altar. Col 581 omits mention of either bow.
[14] Tracts.74; OP.1051. On doubles, he lays the closed second Textus with its cushion on the altar, between its middle and the missal-stand.
[15] Tracts.74: *appodiando illud*. OP.1019 has the Text leant against the reredos.
[16] Morse §69 has the thurifer go up the middle but provides no authority for this. The Carmelites (at the introit and the offertory) and OP.965 (at the offertory) have the thurifer come up the side, and this practice has been followed here.
[17] Col 581; C 66.6.
[18] Col 581.
[19] OP.955. See also Chapter XII, note 11.

To do this, the celebrant,[20] with the deacon[21] at his right holding the chasuble out of the way and the subdeacon at his left, bows profoundly with them in the middle to the cross,[22] incenses the cross with three swings[23] and bows again. Walking between the ministers along the altar towards the south horn, he incenses its surface with three swings of the thurible. At the corner, he swings the thurible twice along the side[24] and then returns to the middle, incensing the frontal of the altar with three swings.[25] In the middle, all three bow and do exactly the same on the northern side, finishing in the middle. There he incenses the principal image with a triple swing[26] and any relics on the altar. The thurifer may remove and replace the missal while the south corner is being incensed.[27]

Still standing at the middle of the altar, the celebrant hands the thurible to the deacon, who retreats somewhat down the southern altar steps,[28] turns and faces the celebrant. The celebrant turns to face the deacon and, observing the usual courtesies, is

---

[20] The rubrics for incensing the altar are very unclear. The altar was incensed at the Officium (Col 581; C 66.6; Cons 39.6), before the Gospel (Col 12; C 66.19; Cons 39.19) and after the offertory (Coll 593–6; C 66.24–5; Cons 39.24–5) at Mass, and in the Divine Office (C 23.2, 23.3, 37, 70; Cons 21.2, 27.4, 43.1, 51.2, 52.1, 52.6–7, 52.9, 52.11, 54.1-2, 74.1). There is no suggestion that, as at Wells (Wells.9), incense was also used after the intonation of the *Gloria in excelsis* or that fewer incensations were carried out on less solemn days.

At Matins and Evensong, and at the Offertory of the Mass, the altar was incensed on its surface and then on all four sides, but at the Officium there is no indication in either the Sarum or the Wells books that the altar was circuited, nor is mention made of the principal image or the relics. Col 581 and C 66.6 have the celebrant incense the middle *et utrumque cornu Altaris*. Some missals add, confusingly, *primo in dextera, secundo in sinistra parte, et interim in medio*. The phrase *interim in medio* is not found elsewhere and may be a corruption for *iterum in medio*, which is found elsewhere (e.g. C 37), or may indicate that, the south corner having been incensed, the celebrant swings the thurible at the altar as he crosses over to the north corner.

The insistence on incensing the horns of the altar may be designed to distinguish the celebrant's incensing of the altar at the Officium from his incensing the middle of the altar only at the offertory, while *ipse sacerdos* may be designed to distinguish between the celebrant walking along the length of the altar here and the deacon incensing the whole altar *in circuitu* at the offertory.

At Evensong (C 37), the altar was incensed three times in the middle (possibly the altar cross), three times on the right, three times on the left, again in the middle, then the principal image (of St. Mary, in Sarum church) three times and then the relics in a manner not unlike that described by OP.1108. No further details are given. The reconstruction suggested here seems as good as any and will not seem too strange to a congregation accustomed to the Roman Mass (cf. F.121). Wells.9–10 gives the, rather simpler, manner of incensing the altar there.

[21] Cons 39.6, *pace* Morse §148, who seems to have understood *solus sacerdos* (as at Wells.9) for *ipse sacerdos*. Wells.36 has *ipsum altare thurificet Diaconi ministerio*.

[22] The bow of Cons 39.6 probably refers to the bow before ascending to the footpace, but a second bow after blessing the incense is not implausible and would correspond to the Roman rite's.

[23] C 37 and OP.1291. The incensing of the cross is not mentioned explicitly anywhere but is supposed here by analogy with other rites and by inference from the words of the Customary. King, *Roman Church*, page 233, considers that the incensation in the middle of the altar may be directed to the hanging pyx.

[24] The *cornu* of Col 581, as opposed to the simple *ter in dextera parte* of C 37.

[25] An interpretation of *interim in medio*. See the note above.

[26] C 37.

[27] Neither the Sarum nor the Dominican books mention this and there is much less point to this ceremony here than in the Roman rite, where there are no Texts on the altar. When going up to the altar for whatever purpose, he and the other lesser servers will laudably avoid standing on the footpace (OP.464).

[28] OP.1064.

incensed with three gentle swings.²⁹ To do so, having folded up the chains, he holds the thurible in his right hand and raises the front hem of the celebrant's chasuble slightly with his left.³⁰ Once incensed, the celebrant turns by his left to face north³¹ and, with hands joined, kisses the closed Text, held out to him by the subdeacon, on the cross or image with which it is decorated.³² If there is no Text, this kiss is omitted. Finally, he turns by his right and goes immediately to the south corner to read the Officium. The deacon, having returned the thurible to the thurifer, points out the Officium to the celebrant and goes to stand on his step. Throughout the Mass, the deacon assists at the missal as necessary, pointing out the texts and turning the pages.³³ The subdeacon stands on his own step behind the deacon.

The celebrant then reads the Officium from the missal in a low voice, standing at the south corner, the deacon and subdeacon standing immediately behind him on their respective steps.³⁴ After the Officium, the celebrant and ministers alternate the *Kyrie*.³⁵ If the *Gloria in excelsis* is not to be said and they will not sit for the *Kyrie*, they remain standing there until the collects. If he wishes, the celebrant may say privately by sections the prayer *Summe sacerdos et vere pontifex* while the Officium, *Kyrie*, *Gloria in excelsis* and Creed are sung, though it is better if he should say this as part of his preparation before Mass.³⁶

Otherwise, having alternated the *Kyrie* quietly, they go to the middle and bow *in plano* before going to the sedilia *per longiorem*: first the subdeacon, followed by the deacon, and finally the celebrant.³⁷ They sit with the celebrant nearest to the altar, the deacon to the celebrant's left and the subdeacon to the deacon's left.³⁸ There they remain for the sung *Kyrie*.³⁹

---

[29] For the Dominican manner of wielding the thurible and making the swings while incensing the altar, see OP.1107.

[30] Despite the silence of the Sarum books, this detail is preserved because it is found in at least three religious rites. The Dominicans (OP.1064) and also the Carmelites (King, *Religious Orders*, page 306) both observe this ceremony. The older Præmonstratensians pulled the middle of the chasuble down (*trahat ei deorsum*), presumably because its old cut made the chasuble ride up after the celebrant's energetic fuming. This is unlikely to be the case with most modern chasubles.

[31] Dickinson (Col 581) punctuates so that it may seem that the Text is to be kissed at the south corner of the altar. C 66.7, on the other hand, by omitting to punctuate, permits a more likely sense, namely, that it is the Officium followed by the Kyrie that takes place at the south corner.

[32] C 66.24 and Cons 56 specify that the book is open for the Bishop, implying that it is closed for priests. So the Præmonstratensians (Lefèvre, *Coutumiers liturgiques*, page 15). Rock IV.216 adduces no authority for having the celebrant kiss the Text as it lies open in the middle of the altar

[33] OP.1054.

[34] C 66.8. The Dominican ministers, to whom the missal is equally inaccessible, are instructed to recite the Officium with the celebrant. In the Roman rite, the ministers remain silent.

[35] Presumably without farsing them.

[36] Col 567.

[37] OP.1279.

[38] An order suggested, not only by *Tracts*.75 and OP.1020, but also by not a few surviving English examples of sedilia. See Rock I.335. OP.552 preserves the use of the *mappula*, a lap cloth not unlike the silken pontifical *gremiale*, which is spread over the knees of the celebrant and the sacred ministers. Grandisson prescribed a linen lap cloth for Ottery St. Mary (Rock I.335), but there seems no positive evidence of its survival at Sarum.

[39] C 66.7 prescribes that the celebrant and ministers should sit for the sung *Kyrie*. With the triple chanting of the Officium and farsed *Kyrie*, this is not unreasonable. There is no indication that sitting depended on the day's rank, as it does with the Dominicans.

During the sung *Kyrie*,[40] or, if there is little time, while the celebrant is reading the Officium, the two taperers, leaving their tapers, by which they have been standing,[41] and the thurifer, who is to return the thurible to the vestry, come to the middle round the steps. They bow to the altar, the thurifer standing between the taperers, and go to the vestry. The taperers, preceded by the thurifer, who retires to his place, return forthwith: the first carrying the cruets on their stand and the pyx containing the hosts;[42] the second, the basin and towel and, if it is to be used, the ewer. On arriving, they bow to the altar in the middle and place what they have brought in the aumbry or on the credence table.[43]

Towards the end of the *Kyrie*, the celebrant and ministers return to the altar and ascend so that the celebrant stands on the footpace in the middle, the deacon behind him on his step and the subdeacon on his own behind the deacon. There the celebrant discovers his head. If he uses the cap, he should hand this to the deacon or to a clerk who has come up to receive it.[44] The ministers discover also, the deacon arranging the celebrant's amice, if necessary.[45] They will not cover again until the end of the function.[46] The celebrant now intones the *Gloria in excelsis*, if this is to be said. As he does so, all turn to the altar.[47] As soon as the *Gloria* has been intoned, or as soon as the celebrant has reached the footpace, if the hymn is omitted, they all go to the south corner and read the *Gloria* privately, the deacon on the celebrant's right and the subdeacon on the left.[48]

The celebrant and ministers stay at the south side until the choir has finished the *Gloria in excelsis*.[49] As the choir sings *Adoramus te* and *Suscipe deprecationem nostram*,

---

[40] Col 589 says *post Introitum*. Singularly, this appears to refer to the Officium, though it could simply mean 'at some point after the procession has entered'. The most sensible moment is after the celebrant has read the Officium privately, and this is the view adopted by Rock (IV.218). The question is immaterial, since it is only once the celebrant and ministers are out of the way, during the *Kyrie*, that the taperers, who have only recently laid down their tapers, are in a position to leave without cluttering up the sanctuary and distracting from the operations of the ministers.

Legg, *Ecclesiological Essays*, chapter V, writes that there was considerable indifference in the Middle Ages concerning the moment for preparing the elements, of which this rubric indicates the beginning. Legg identifies three principal moments at which the elements were prepared: the beginning of Mass (varying from before vesting to the time of the introit), between the lessons and after the Gospel (varying from immediately after the Gospel to after the offertory antiphon). It is possible that at Sarum the process was begun at the beginning of Mass (*post Introitum*) and continued, after a gap, before the Gospel, when the chalice was made.

[41] This seems much more convenient than having them retire to their places in the choir. There is no indication that the Dominican practice, whereby the taperers stand to the right of the celebrant and ministers while the Officium is read privately, was followed at Sarum. The difference may be explained by the fact that in Dominican convents the acolytes are bound by the Office, whereas at Sarum the *pueri* were not, and so had no need to pronounce every word of the choral texts.

[42] In principle, a single host only, but there is no reason why he should not bring a ciborium with many hosts, the topmost of which will later be placed on the paten.

[43] The aumbry will not really be suitable for High Mass and a credence table should be used.

[44] Lincoln I.377. Or this may be done more discreetly at the sedilia, as at Rome, before returning to the altar.

[45] *Tracts*.xii.

[46] The Dominican celebrant and ministers, who wear the amice, remain uncovered for the entire function. However, if the cap be worn, as at Rome, this may perhaps be worn at other times when sitting. For the celebrant sitting covered in fourteenth-century France, see Rock II.104.

[47] C 13.5.

[48] C 66.7.

[49] There is no indication that they sit during the *Gloria*.

all in the choir and the sanctuary stand facing the altar and bow.[50] As the choir sings *In gloria Dei Patris*, all bow and sign themselves with the celebrant.[51] At the conclusion of the *Gloria*, the ministers descend to stand on their steps behind the celebrant as before. The celebrant crosses himself and turns round for *Dominus vobiscum*. As he does so, the deacon does likewise.[52] The subdeacon, who has been standing behind the deacon, turns to his right and goes to genuflect briefly to the south of the celebrant, facing north. As the celebrant extends his hands to sing *Dominus vobiscum*, the subdeacon, with his left hand on his breast, raises the front of the celebrant's chasuble slightly with his right hand, and, rising immediately, returns to his place behind the deacon.[53] All three stand facing the altar as the celebrant sings the collects, the first under its own *Oremus* and conclusion, the rest under one *Oremus* and a single conclusion. The deacon points out each collect[54] and then returns immediately to his step.

When he has finished the last collect, the celebrant goes to the middle and then follows the deacon to the sedilia, where they sit for the lessons. The taperers may assist the celebrant with his chasuble as he sits down.[55] If there are several lessons, the

---

[50] G.11 et seqq.
[51] C 13.5.
[52] C 66.8.
[53] This rubric, found at Col 7 note+, at Col 589 and at C 66.8, is mysterious on two counts: the meaning of *ca(p)sula aptanda*; and whether the subdeacon kneels or genuflects.

(a) The Missal and Gradual confirm that the chasuble in question is the priest's, not the subdeacon's. On the face of it, since the subdeacon is instructed to occupy his own step, behind the deacon, it would be impractical for him to handle the celebrant's chasuble. However, *ita ut* is susceptible of bearing concessive force. Thus interpreted, the rubric would mean:

> And always, when the priest stands at the Office of the Mass, the deacon should stand immediately behind him on the next step down, and the subdeacon likewise on the second step down, but subject to the condition that, whenever the priest should turn to the people, the deacon should likewise turn, but the subdeacon meanwhile, *genuflectendo*, should assist the celebrant to compose his chasuble.

In other words, the subdeacon need not be on his own step immediately west of the deacon but should go round and kneel (or genuflect) south of the celebrant, facing north, and assist with the chasuble.

What *aptanda* itself means is also unclear: raising the front of the chasuble to lessen its weight as the celebrant raises his arms for *Dominus vobiscum* is one possibility; rolling up its sleeves for a similar purpose is another, though more far-fetched. A third, more likely possibility, is that the subdeacon is to pull down the front edge of the chasuble, which is presumed to be conical and so liable to ride up and in need of being pulled down from time to time. Cf. *Tracts*.75, *Tracts*.78 and OPraem.IV.41. Modern chasubles are less likely to ride up, and so it might be easier to observe the ceremony by raising the front of the chasuble slightly, as the modern Dominican deacon does while incensing the celebrant at the offertory.

(b) Genuflection can be of three classes: worship (of God or of people); prayer (as at *Flectamus genua*); practicality. The first was a late liturgical development and much has been speculated on the part it played in Sarum Use. The second is ancient and had its place at Sarum (cf. e.g. Col. 324). The third engages us here. Doubt concerning genuflection in worship does not preclude genuflection made for practical purposes. Everything indicates that *genuflectendo* here falls under our third category. Since the subdeacon is to genuflect only while the celebrant faces the people and carry out his mysterious duty, it is unlikely that he would be able to kneel and deal with the celebrant's chasuble in such a short time. We expect, therefore, that a simple genuflection is meant.

[54] OP.1054.
[55] OP.991.

taperers may go to sit[56] and return to their places in the sanctuary when the celebrant goes to sing the collects.[57]

[56] OP.987 and OP.993. Rock IV.219–20 adduces no authority for having both taperers wait by the sacrarium.
[57] OP.990.

XV

FROM THE COLLECTS TO THE SEQUENCE

On days when an additional lesson precedes the epistle, the celebrant goes to sit with the deacon and the subdeacon. The acolyte[1] collects the book during the collects and, bowing to the altar, goes unaccompanied to the place where the epistle will be read.[2] There, facing east, he sings the lesson and returns to his place. When more than one such lesson is to be sung, as on Ember Saturdays, the acolyte reads the first lesson as above, the others being read by clergy taken in order from the second form of the choir, the last being read by a priest from the upper grade.[3] These lectors come to the choir step[4] to sing their lessons.

On days when the deacon and subdeacon wear chasubles, during the last collect, the subdeacon and the first taperer[5] go behind the altar or to the credence table in order to remove the chasuble.[6] This done, the subdeacon returns to his place behind the deacon until the last collect is finished. Having bowed with the celebrant at the foot of the altar, the subdeacon goes up to collect the epistle-book. Returning to the foot of the altar in the middle, he bows and, unaccompanied,[7] proceeds down the

---

[1] C 66.38, where it is not explained whether this acolyte is to be the crucifer or another acolyte sitting in choir. Col 435, treating of Ember Wednesday in Whit Week, has the prophecy read from the pulpitum by a surpliced acolyte. The peculiar character of the Whit Ember Days and the use of the pulpitum might be taken to suggest that the Customary refers to the ordinary practice. Most churches will not have spare acolytes.

[2] C 66.38; Cons 46.2. This will generally be the presbytery step but may sometimes be the pulpitum (Col 45).

[3] C 66.39.

[4] This detail is not specified in the Customary but seems a reasonable inference. C 70.1, which also has clergy *de superiori gradu* sing, but specifies *ad gradum chori*, supports this conclusion.

[5] The first taperer is already situated on the south side of the sanctuary. The Dominican subdeacon, who does not use the chasuble, is assisted later by the junior acolyte (OP.990), the senior ministering to the deacon (OP.991).

[6] The assistance of the first taperer is nowhere stated explicitly, but it makes sense. Neither the Dominicans nor the Carmelites use folded chasubles. At Rome, the second acolyte helps the subdeacon, but there the acolytes stand by the credence table and are to hand. The Roman master of ceremonies, who appears to be related to the Sarum acolyte, has no part in this preparation, and this job appears to be too menial, if the word may be used of the service of the altar, for him.

[7] At Lincoln I.377, the second subdeacon, who seems to take the place of the Sarum acolyte, accompanied the subdeacon. Among the more restrained Dominicans, the subdeacon is accompanied by the junior acolyte (OP.990), but the former practice on days when the epistle was read at the presbytery step was for the acolyte not to accompany the subdeacon (*Tracts*.76). However, at Sarum, although the books are silent on the matter, it is likely that the subdeacon was unaccompanied, since the taperers and the acolyte will be engaged in bringing in the chalice. If,

middle[8] of the sanctuary to the place where the epistle is to be read that day. He chants the epistle in the middle,[9] facing the altar.[10] In the cathedral, the epistle will be read at the choir step,[11] except on Sundays, on all days when the choir is ruled, on Maundy Thursday, on Holy Saturday, on Whitsun Eve and on All Souls' Day. On these days, the epistle is sung from the pulpitum.[12] In other churches, local custom and the disposition of the building may impose other requirements. When the epistle is read at the choir step, a portable lectern may be erected there for the purpose.[13] The taperers will set it up after the collects and remove it after the epistle.

The gradual, Alleluya, tract and sequence follow. For the choral ceremonial to be observed, see Chapter XXII.

When he has finished singing the epistle,[14] the subdeacon shuts the book and goes to bow at the foot of the altar. If the acolyte has not yet receded after laying the corporals on the altar, the subdeacon must wait in his place until he has done so, so as not to get in the acolyte's way. At the foot of the altar, the subdeacon is met by the acolyte,[15] who stands at his right and to whom he hands the book. Both bow to the altar and go their separate ways: the subdeacon to the sedilia to sit at the deacon's left and the acolyte round the altar and up its southern steps to replace the epistle-book where it lay before.[16]

The acolyte now picks up the missal[17] so as to hold it open away from him, and goes to the sedilia.[18] There he stands[19] in front of the celebrant, holding the open missal

---

as at Hereford.116, a portable lectrinum is placed at the choir step from which to read the epistle, the thurifer may be given this task and could then accompany the subdeacon as the Dominican acolyte does.

[8] This is supposed from the fact that the subdeacon proceeds *per medium chori* when going to the pulpitum. The Dominican subdeacon proceeds down the north side of the choir to the pulpitum and returns by the south side (OP.1024).

[9] OP.1024; OPraem.IV.43–4. Rock IV.219 has the subdeacon stand on the south side, near the sedilia, but offers no authority. Singing the epistle at the choir step in the middle would suit the ample layout of Sarum church, since the southern *ostium presbyterii* used for the acolyte's entrance with the chalice (C 66.12) is east of the choir step. In lesser churches, it might indeed be more practical to sing the epistle somewhat to the south side, thus allowing the acolyte to enter under the chancel arch and up the middle of the choir.

[10] OP.1024. The Dominicans cross their hands over the bottom part of the book while they read the epistle.

[11] C 66.11.

[12] C 66.11. On doubles and Sundays, *Tracts*.76 has the epistle read *retro chorum*, which suggests the pulpitum step west of the choir screen, adding *vel alibi loco eminenti* of the Gospel (*Tracts*.77). For the layout of primitive Dominican churches, see Bonniwell, page 120.

[13] OP.1024, OP.1059.

[14] There is no mention of the subdeacon kissing the celebrant's hand either in the Sarum books or in those of Wells, Lincoln or the Dominicans, though the custom is mentioned by Durandus (King, *Roman Church*, page 249).

[15] At Lincoln I.378, the subdeacon is met by the thurifer, since the second subdeacon goes to the vestry to help with the chalice; at Durham.7, he places the book on the altar himself.

[16] OP.990. *Tracts*.76 has the book replaced on the altar until the acolyte has occasion to take it back to the vestry.

[17] So the Dominicans and, since it is still the practice on Good Friday, presumably also the former practice of the Roman rite (F.307).

[18] The Dominican acolyte, who is accompanying the deacon, goes round to the middle of the altar step to bow, but in this rite the trip seems otiose.

[19] OP.991.

before him so that he and the ministers may read the gradual,[20] Alleluya or tract, and sequence, in a low voice.[21]

The acolyte takes the missal[22] back to the altar, bowing in the middle, and going straight up to the south corner replaces the missal on its stand. He then goes to the credence table to assist at the washing of the subdeacon's hands and the making of the chalice.

---

[20] Presumably on the days when the gradual is repeated by the choir, the ministers at the sedilia should do so as well.

[21] C 66.17 has the celebrant and ministers read the chants privately, though whether at the altar or the sedilia is not clear. However, the blessing of the water, which is presumed to follow immediately, takes place at the sedilia (Col 587), so, since the Dominicans read the chants at the sedilia, it may be assumed that the same was done at Sarum. C 66.9 also implies very strongly that the lessons and chants were not read at the altar, though the rubric may refer to 'public' prayer rather than the celebrant's private reading at this point. The rubrics (Col 587) do not indicate that the celebrant reads the lessons themselves privately. At Lincoln I.377, he does read them and at the altar, but the Dominicans did not do so until 1656 (Acta OP.VII.390). For the obligation of learning liturgical texts in the context of another secular cathedral (Hereford), see Pfaff, page 470, note 75. For the texts to be learned and sung from memory by the vicars at Sarum, see *Processions*.274–5. It is here presumed that the celebrant does not read the lessons privately. For the way in which the Dominican celebrant and deacon alternate the chants, see OP.1057.

[22] The Dominican subdeacon takes the missal himself, but he has a reason to go to the altar, since he will prepare the chalice there. It seems unlikely that on a detail such as this, involving a sacred minister, the Sarum books should remain silent, so it seems more probable that another server takes the missal.

XVI

THE MAKING OF THE CHALICE

While the epistle is being sung,[1] the acolyte, bowing in the middle, goes to the vestry.[2] In the acolyte's absence, the taperers go to the middle, bow[3] and go to pick up their tapers. They return to the middle, bow and go to the entrance of the sanctuary[4] to meet the acolyte[5] who is bringing the dressed chalice enveloped in the humeral veil (*mantellum*), carrying it raised before his face.[6] They return to the sanctuary, the taperers on either side of the acolyte or, in smaller churches, preceding him. Bowing before the middle of the altar, they go to the credence table where the acolyte leaves the chalice and paten. He removes the burse and lays it to one side. He then takes off the humeral veil, the taperers assisting if necessary,[7] and covers the chalice and paten

---

[1] Ambiguously C 66.12 says *interim*. On the face of it, this should mean during the epistle, described in C 66.11. However, C 66.13 begins *dum epistola legitur* and having the boys who are coming to sing the gradual distract attention from the μεγάλη εἴσοδος might seem improbable. Rock I.332 interprets Cons 39.13 as indicating a moment 'just before the epistle'.
  Wells.36 may provide the answer: *Et dum Epistola legitur, duo pueri in superpelliciis facta inclinatione ad gradum in chori* [sic] *in pulpito ipso se ad cantand' Gratiam preparent. Interim etiam veniant duo Ceroferarii obviam Accolito ad ostium presbyterii cum veneratione ipsum calicem ad locum predicte administrationis deferenti.* This seems unambiguously to place the μεγάλη εἴσοδος during the epistle, unlike at Lincoln I.378, where the chalice was brought in by the subdeacon after he had chanted the epistle. OPraem.IV.30–9 has the chalice prepared before the epistle.
[2] Morse §92 would have the acolyte wait in the vestry from the beginning of the Mass, but even if the cross be not carried at the entrance, it would become a member of the community better to sit (e.g. in the choir) and go to the vestry now.
[3] None of this going to the middle and bowing is mentioned in the books, but it can reasonably be presumed. It is a neater alternative to having one taperer crossing the altar to get at his taper while having the other simply amble up to his.
[4] C 66.12.
[5] What is the canonical status of this acolyte? Although Cons 25 ranks him among the *pueri majores*, ordinarily he should be a cleric and have at least received the order of acolyte. Since 1972 (by Paul VI's motu proprio *Ministeria quaedam*) this order is no longer conferred to *clerici*, and so only deacons, presbyters and bishops may ordinarily carry out the functions of this acolyte. Extraordinarily, for the traditional form of the Roman rite, a layman who has received the novel ministry of acolyte may, with some restrictions, act as subdeacon. Consequently, it seems at least probable that such a lay 'instituted acolyte' could be permitted to act as a Sarum acolyte in an extraordinary capacity, since he would at no point touch the chalice or the paten other than through the humeral and chalice veils. See King, *Roman Church*, page 109, on the Roman acolyte carrying the chalice.
[6] C 66.12. Tracts.75: *eleuatum ante faciem suam*. OP.1022: *elevatum ante pectus suum*.
[7] At Lincoln I.378, the first subdeacon brought in the chalice holding it through a humeral veil and the second subdeacon brought in the corporals in a second humeral veil, but there is no indication

with it.[8] Taking the burse, he goes to the foot of the altar between the two taperers.[9] All three bow and the taperers go round to the bottom step where they were before, while the acolyte goes up the middle, places the burse and pall on the altar in front of the cross,[10] kisses the altar, holding his hands joined without placing them on the altar,[11] and comes down again.[12] As he kisses the altar, the taperers put down their tapers[13] and come round to the middle to meet the acolyte. All three bow and go to their usual places. These ceremonies must be completed before the subdeacon returns to the altar after singing the epistle. If necessary, the taperers should go out to bring the elements before the collects have been finished.

Meanwhile,[14] the subdeacon[15] rises, bows to the celebrant[16] and goes to the credence table, timing his arrival so as not to have to wait for the acolyte, who will assist him. The subdeacon's hands are now washed, either at the piscina or in the basin. He dries his hands on the towel offered by the acolyte. He removes the humeral veil from the chalice and puts it round his shoulders[17] with the acolyte's assistance,[18] then removes the chalice veil (and pall, if used), takes the host from the pyx held out to him by the acolyte and places it on the paten. He then takes the paten from the chalice and lays it to one side. He wipes the inside of the chalice (held through the humeral veil)[19] with the purificator.[20] Leaving the chalice veil and the purificator on the credence table,[21]

---

that this was done at Sarum, and neither the Dominican nor the Roman rites bring the corporals to the altar through a humeral veil.
[8] This is the position of the humeral veil in the Roman rite. The Dominicans, who use the altar as their *locus administrationis*, place the chalice on the humeral veil instead. The solution adopted here will not impede the making of the chalice later.
[9] C 66.12, *pace* C 66.18, which is contradicted in many of its details by both the Missal and the Consuetudinary.
[10] He does not unfold the corporal. Cf. C 66.18, where the ambiguous *deferat* should probably be taken to mean that he extracts the corporals from the burse and places them directly on the altar.
[11] As the deacon at Rome does when receiving the Pax (De Herdt, t. I. p. 2. n.53).
[12] C 66.12.
[13] This is the last mention made of the taperers until the vesting of the eagle after the epistle. What follows here is taken from OP.992-4.
[14] A literal reading of C 66.18 would have the making of the chalice not take place until after the gradual is finished. Nevertheless, it would be unseemly for the chanting to be finished before the preparations for the Gospel were concluded, so it is advisable for the subdeacon to go to wash his hands as soon as the celebrant and the ministers have finished reading the chants privately.
[15] The preparation of the chalice is ascribed unambiguously to the subdeacon in the Consuetudinary and in the Missal, but C 66.18 later has the deacon do most of this preparation at the altar. The Missal is here followed, which is consonant with the practice of other uses, not least the Dominican, and with the *traditio* of the chalice to the subdeacon at his ordination. Since the deacon is about to busy himself with preparations for the Gospel, it also makes practical sense to leave most of the preparation of the chalice to the subdeacon.
[16] This is the Roman practice, but it could be considered common liturgical courtesy, so it has been presumed here. See Chapter V, note 14.
[17] OP.1026.
[18] OP.992.
[19] OP.1026.
[20] Lincoln I.378 explicitly requires this cleansing: *et tunc secundarius mundabit calicem ab omni sorde.*
[21] The Dominicans leave the purificator on the altar and place the paten directly on the chalice (OP.1026).

he places the paten (with the host and, if used, the pall) on the chalice[22] and through the humeral veil takes the chalice in his left and covers it with his right. He goes to the celebrant at the sedilia, preceded by the acolyte[23] bearing the cruets. There he uncovers the chalice and gives the paten and host, covered with the pall, to the sitting[24] deacon, who shews the host on the paten to the celebrant, removing and replacing the pall to do so. The subdeacon takes the wine cruet from the acolyte, who stands at his right,[25] and pours in the wine, stopping at the celebrant's signal.[26] Then he takes the water from the acolyte and holds it up to the celebrant, who, still sitting,[27] blesses it, saying *Benedicite*. After the blessing, the subdeacon pours a few drops of water into the chalice, returns the cruet to the acolyte, receives the paten from the deacon[28] with his right and puts it back on the chalice, covers the chalice as before with the humeral veil and returns preceded by the acolyte to the credence table. There he lays down the chalice, redresses it, not forgetting the purificator, covers it with the humeral veil, which he removes with the acolyte's help, and returns to his seat.

On days when the subdeacon wears a chasuble, before returning to his seat, with the assistance of the first taperer, he resumes the chasuble, either behind the altar or at the credence table itself.[29]

---

[22] The Dominicans cover the host with the pall. Obviously, this cannot be done when a single corporal is used, but if the pall be employed, this would protect the host from the veil and would not make things more difficult at the sedilia.

[23] Cons 39.14 and C 66.17: *ministerio acoliti*.

Chambers, page 332, has the water only taken to the celebrant, but the Sarum rubrics and the Customary are less than clear on this question. C 66.18 has the obviously garbled *benediccionem* [sic] *prius a sacerdote petitam* [sic] *hoc modo ... Sacerdote sic respondente Dominus*. Col 587 has *Accipiat subdiaconus panem ... et praeparet; benedictione prius aquae a sacerdote petita hoc modo Benedicite; sic respondeat sacerdos Dominus*. The question is whether *prius* means that the water is blessed before the chalice is prepared or merely that the subdeacon says *Benedicite* just before the celebrant begins *Dominus*. As usual, it has seemed better to follow the Dominican practice, supported here by Lincoln I.378, which has the cruets borne to the celebrant by the secondary subdeacon. Taking the chalice also allows the celebrant to check that the host is there. See OP.1058 and Chapter VII, note 34.

[24] OP.1058.

[25] OP.992.

[26] OP.1027. At Lincoln I.378, the celebrant pours the wine and water into the chalice himself, but Col 587 implies that it is the subdeacon who prepares the elements.

[27] C 66.18.

[28] OP.1027.

[29] See Chapter XV, note 5. Alternatively, the acolyte could assist, since he is already present and has assisted with the humeral veil. The Roman rite and OPraem.IV.18–19 have the chasuble resumed immediately after the epistle, but the Sarum books do not mention explicitly when the chasuble is resumed, only that the subdeacon wears it for the Gospel (C 66.19), and the Dominicans, whose customs we follow in these cases, do not use the chasuble at all. The tenth-century *Regularis Concordia* (*apud* Rock I.314) has the subdeacon remove the chasuble for the epistle only and the deacon remove it *antequam ad Evangelium legendum accedat* and wear it in the manner of a broad stole until after Communion, when he resumes it before the postcommon is concluded.

Since the subdeacon will be very busy with the preparation of the chalice, it would be reasonable for him not to resume his chasuble until shortly before the Gospel, and this possibility is not excluded by C 66.19. HA.38 says that, at Exeter, the subdeacon resumed his chasuble after making the chalice, and, despite our habitual reticence at adopting Exonian features, since this detail is unlikely to have been influenced by Roman or Avignonese customs, we have followed this practice here.

The deacon takes off his chasuble after the subdeacon has made the chalice (C 66.18) and resumes it after Communion (C 66.35).

During the Alleluya,[30] the deacon, when the subdeacon has returned from dressing the chalice, rises and, bowing to the celebrant, goes to the credence table.[31] On days when he wears the chasuble, he removes this (assisted as the subdeacon was) and puts it over his stole, binding it under his right arm.[32] He washes his hands in the same way as the subdeacon did, assisted by the acolyte, and then goes up to the middle of the altar, bowing first at its foot. He removes the corporal from the burse and unfolds it completely on the middle of the altar. Then he folds the furthest part back over the third.[33] Finally, he places the burse to the left of the corporal at the back of the altar. Coming down,[34] he bows in the middle and returns to his seat.

---

[30] Cons 39.18.

[31] The books do not specify where the hands are washed. The Dominican ministers wash their hands at the south corner of the altar, which is their *locus administrationis*. C 66.17 implies that the subdeacon washes his hands at the credence table, but then he has much business there and none at the altar. The deacon, on the other hand, will be unfolding the corporals at the altar, so it is possible that he may have washed his hands there. Nevertheless, there is no indication of this, and the unclear C 66.18 implies that the deacon washes his hands before going up to the altar.

[32] C 66.18. Or, nowadays, he could probably use the broad stole. Wells.36 gives a different order: the deacon washed his hands before removing the chasuble.

[33] *Tracts.*76.

[34] Should he kiss the altar before coming down? Nothing is mentioned, either in the Sarum books or in *Tracts.*76, but it seems strange that the acolyte should do so and not the deacon.

XVII

FROM THE GOSPEL TO THE OFFERTORY

While the celebrant and the ministers read the chants after the epistle privately, the taperers come to the altar step, bow and withdraw to the vestry, whence they return with the silken veil and go to prepare the Gospel lectern.[1]

While the deacon is preparing the corporal at the altar, the thurifer goes to the vestry to get the thurible. Meanwhile, the taperers, having prepared the Gospel lectern, resume their habitual positions. When the deacon has returned to sit, the thurifer comes back and approaches the sedilia,[2] where he stands before the priest. Handing the boat to the deacon, he holds up the open thurible. The deacon,[3] who remains seated,[4] offers the celebrant incense on the spoon, as at the Officium, saying *Benedicite*. When the celebrant has blessed the incense, the deacon answers *Amen*[5] and, imposing it on the coals, returns the boat to the thurifer, who goes to stand behind the first taperer, as at the beginning of Mass.

---

[1] If the epistle has been chanted at the choir step, the Gospel will be chanted at a small lectern placed in front of the lowest altar step at the north corner of the altar, facing north (C 66.41). If the epistle has been sung from the pulpitum, the Gospel also will be sung from the pulpitum, always facing north.

  C 66.14 supposes that only one taperer will go to prepare the eagle, accompanied by *aliquo puero de choro*, though this second boy is not mentioned in C 66.41, perhaps because a small lectern was easier to prepare than the great eagle. However, there seems to be no reason why both taperers should not undertake this duty if two people are needed.

[2] This is nowhere to be found in the Sarum books. However, it is probable that the incense was blessed and the Dominicans do so at the sedilia. Although, unlike at Sarum, the Dominican deacon is also blessed at the sedilia, it has seemed better to place the blessing of the incense here also, because blessing it at the altar would involve awkward choreography.

  Against the blessing of the incense at this point, it may be argued that the Dominicans bless it here because it has not been blessed at the Officium. Moreover, their thurifer offers incense on the spoon for blessing. At Rome, the incense is blessed both at the Introit and before the Gospel, but there the incense is imposed first and blessed in the thurible, so the incense in the boat is not blessed twice. In general, the Church seems to avoid blessing sacramentals repeatedly. So one year's Paschal Candle may not be used and blessed again the following year. However, it is likely that incense would be left in the boat from one Mass to another, so this blessing would in fact be repeated, since the Sarum books do not place any condition on the blessing of incense at the Officium. On balance, therefore, it seems reasonable to suppose that the incense was blessed before the Gospel and probably only that offered in the spoon.

[3] Since the deacon is about to go to the altar for the Gospel-book, OP.963 has the thurifer offer and impose the incense, though this is not the universal practice. Here we keep the deacon at the sedilia, and, since he has imposed the incense at the Officium, it seems better that he should do so also here.

[4] As earlier during the making of the chalice.

[5] OP.963.

All three ministers now return to the foot of the altar, where they bow. The celebrant goes up the middle. Meanwhile, the subdeacon goes round to the south corner, whence he takes the missal and transfers it to the north, going round the front of the steps, as the clerk does at Low Mass.[6] When the subdeacon has removed the book, the celebrant goes to the south nook and stands facing the altar. Meanwhile, as soon as the subdeacon has gone up to the north nook, the deacon goes up the middle, followed by the thurifer, and receives the thurible. The thurifer waits at the foot of the altar, standing between the taperers, in front of the acolyte (who on doubles only has come thither and stands there with the cross).[7]

The deacon incenses the middle of the altar[8] and returns the thurible to the thurifer, who has come up the steps and now returns to stand between the taperers. The deacon takes up the closed Text that lies on the north side of the altar. The celebrant turns in his place to face north and the deacon bows deeply[9] in front of him, facing south, holding the book in both hands. If the Text is not used, the deacon will hold the Gospel-book in its place. Bowing so, he asks for the blessing in a low but intelligible voice, without note: *Jube, domine, benedicere.* He remains bowing as the celebrant imparts his blessing with joined hands, making the sign of the cross over the deacon and saying *Dominus,* &c. The celebrant turns back to the altar, standing at the south corner, and remains there, crossing himself on his forehead and breast at the sung *Sequentia,* &c. and blessing himself again at *Gloria tibi Domine.*[10]

---

[6] See Chapter XII, note 17. The flitting of the missal is implied (C 66.9) but not explained in the Sarum books. OP.1026 has the subdeacon transfer the missal before the chalice is made, but he is already at the altar. *Tracts.*76 has *unus ministrorum* flit the book towards the end of the chants. The Roman subdeacon transfers the missal immediately after singing the epistle and just before the celebrant reads the Gospel privately at the altar. Morse §154 has the deacon transfer the missal before unfolding the corporal but gives no authority for this. The solution proposed here seems as good as any: the duty should probably be assigned to the subdeacon, by analogy with other rites, and this moment is the first that the subdeacon has occasion to return to the altar.

[7] The books do not mention whether the acolyte takes part in this procession when he does not carry the cross.

[8] No details are given as to how this incensation should be done, unless the cryptic directions of *Crede Michi* [30] should be applied to this moment. In this case, the deacon will incense the middle of the altar with seven, twelve or nine casts (*jactus*) of the thurible. Otherwise, three swings, to the middle, to the right and to the left, should be sufficient. C 66.19 states clearly that the deacon incenses *medium altaris,* rather than *in medio.* In other words, it appears that he does not incense the Text but the altar where the corporal has just been spread.

[9] Col 12: *humilians se.* Du Cange presents *humiliare se* as *per adorationem inclinare se, genua flectere* and as the equivalent of the Greek προσπίπτειν. This last certainly implies falling to the ground before another, but, of the examples given, some seem to indicate bowing and others a form of genuflection. The ambiguity of the term remains throughout the Sarum books, and no definitive meaning can be ascertained. On the one hand, the Anglican ecclesiologists, who seem to have conceived a horror of the Romanist genuflection, wish to believe that nothing more popish than a bow was ever practised in England before the Reformation. On the other hand, the movement throughout different uses in the sixteenth century was clearly towards genuflection, though in the Roman Missal this gesture did not become official until 1570. Furthermore, the practice at Sarum was to observe gestures of obeisance that would seem excessive in modern Latin rites. Apart from the equally ambiguous *prostratio/prosternere,* C 23.2 and 37 have the celebrant at Vespers kneel and kiss the altar step before incensing the altar. OPraem.IV.49–51 has *stans ad sinistrum cornu altaris, sacerdote surgente et stante ad dexteram partem, humiliter inclinans petat benedictionem. Tracts.*76 and OP.1059, which we follow here, have the deacon bow at this point.

[10] OP.1286; OPraem.IV.52–3.

On doubles, the deacon's taking of the Text acts as a signal to the acolyte to come up from his place in the choir, take up the cross and stand at the foot of the altar between the taperers and behind the thurifer.[11]

While the deacon is being blessed, the subdeacon takes up the book from which the Gospel will be read.[12] The Gospel procession is now formed: first, the acolyte, with the cross on doubles;[13] then the taperers with their tapers;[14] then the thurifer swinging his thurible;[15] then the subdeacon carrying the book of the Gospel lesson;[16] finally, the deacon with the closed Text. The subdeacon and deacon carry their books in this way:[17] with the front cover of the book against the chest, the spine of the book rests along the lower left arm, the lower end of the spine resting in the cupped left hand, while the right hand holds the fly of the book near its bottom end. Thus, they proceed down the middle of the choir[18] to the place where the Gospel is to be read. If the epistle was read from the pulpitum, the Gospel is read there also,[19] but if the epistle was read at

---

[11] C and Cons disagree and are unclear. C 66.19 says *commonicione puerorum ministrancium a choro ad ministeria sua redeuncium*. The ablative *commonicione* suggests that the deacon sees or hears something behind him and chooses this moment to take up the Text. Who, however, are these *pueri*? If they are the taperers, then who has been assisting during the gradual et seq.? If they are the second taperer and the lector who have been preparing the eagle, why has the lector come all the way to the altar before going away again, and why is he described as returning to the altar *ad ministeria sua*? If they are the cantors, how can they be returning *a choro ad ministeria sua*? Chambers, page 333, has 'when advised that the Eagle in the Ambo or desk is duly vested'. Cons 39.19 and Wells.36 have *ad commonicionem* and this is the text that we have followed here. In practice, since there should be plenty of time to prepare the lectern and, especially in a large church, the acolyte will need some time to collect the cross and come up to the altar, neither of these signals will be necessary and so these admonitions may be ignored.

[12] *Librum evangelice leccionis* (C 66.19). It is nowhere explained whence this book comes. Without multiplying the number of servers, and remembering that the Roman master of ceremonies had no function at Sarum, there are two practical possibilities: (1) that the book of the Gospels should be laid on the altar at the north side before Mass corresponding to the book of epistles; and (2) that the plenary missal was removed from its stand and used to read the Gospel. The final sentence of C 66.19 appears to confirm that two books were used: one, the book from which the Gospel was read; second, the Text, a precious object containing the full text of the Gospels. The second Text carried to the altar on doubles and used for kissing later on presumably remains untouched on the altar. Cons 39.19 also presupposes two books, so the custom must have been long-standing. The presence of the two books in the procession, therefore, should not be omitted by having the book placed on the lectern at the moment when this is veiled.

After the Gospel, the celebrant is offered either the Text or the Gospel-book to kiss (C 66.22; Coll 14 and 593). This suggests that at some Masses no Text was used but only the Gospel-book. Certainly, the precious Text book would have been unaffordable for lesser churches. Here we contemplate both possibilities.

[13] C 66.19: *Et si duplex festum fuerit, crux precedat*.

[14] C 66.20. The single taperer of C 66.19 and Col 12 must refer to occasions when the full complement of servers may not be had. Cons 39.19 corroborates the presence of both taperers.

[15] The use of incense at the Gospel began with the thurifer carrying incense before the Gospel-book, so having the thurifer swing his thurible, which is not found in the books, is at least consonant with the reason for having incense in the first place. See King, *Roman Church*, page 166.

[16] *Tracts*.77 has the early Dominicans, who did not juggle the books as at Sarum, take a cushion for the book.

[17] C 66.19.

[18] C 66.19. Presumably they also return up the middle of the choir after the Gospel has been read.

[19] C 66.19. See Figure III.

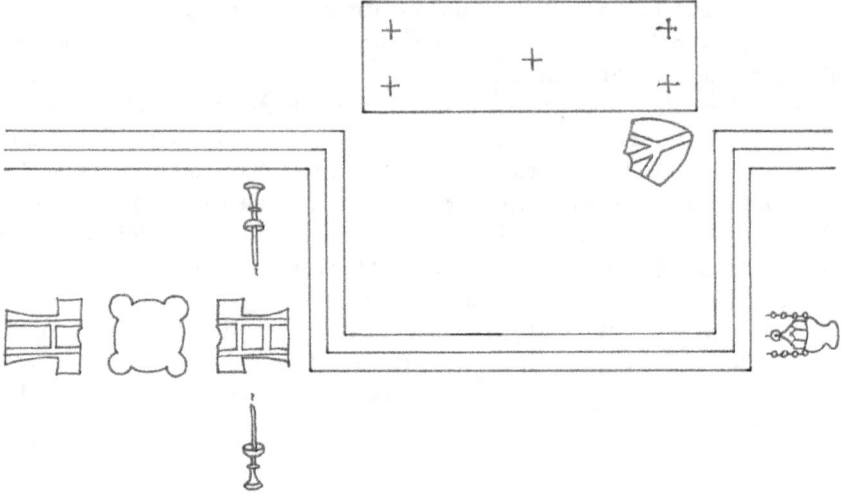

Figure II. High Mass: The Gospel sung from the altar step

the choir step, the Gospel is read next to the bottom step of the altar at its north end.[20] In either case, the Gospel is always read facing north.[21]

On days when the Gospel is to be read next to the altar (Figure II), the acolyte takes no part in the procession but remains standing at his place. The thurifer stands by the bottom step of the altar on the south side, behind the deacon and facing him.[22] If the Text is to be used, a lectern is erected next to the lowest altar step on the north side of the sanctuary, at which the deacon will sing the Gospel, facing north.[23] The subdeacon, standing behind the lectern and facing south, holds the Text before the deacon's face. The taperers with their candles stand on either side of the deacon,[24] facing him. If the Text is not to be used,[25] the lectern may be omitted and the subdeacon will hold the open book of the Gospels for the deacon to read therefrom.

On other days, when they have arrived at the appointed place (Figure III), the acolyte with the cross takes his position to the right and slightly in front of where the deacon will sing the Gospel, facing west, with the image of the cross towards the reader. The taperers stand to the immediate right and left of where the deacon will sing, facing each other, so that the taperer who faces west will stand to the left of the acolyte. He should allow enough space for the subdeacon to pass between him and the deacon when offering the

---

[20] The Gospel is read next to the altar when the choir is not ruled (C 66.41, describing the ceremonial on the days mentioned at C 66.36).
[21] C 66.20.
[22] C 66.41. See Figure II.
[23] C 66.41; Cons 45.3. Rock II.393 shews this lectern on the deacon's step at Westminster Abbey.
[24] C 66.41.
[25] Even in churches endowed with a precious Text, it might be reasonable not to use it on ferias and other days of lesser solemnity. We presume that the Text will not be used when the Gospel is read at the step, though C 66.41 makes allowance for the Text to be used on these occasions.

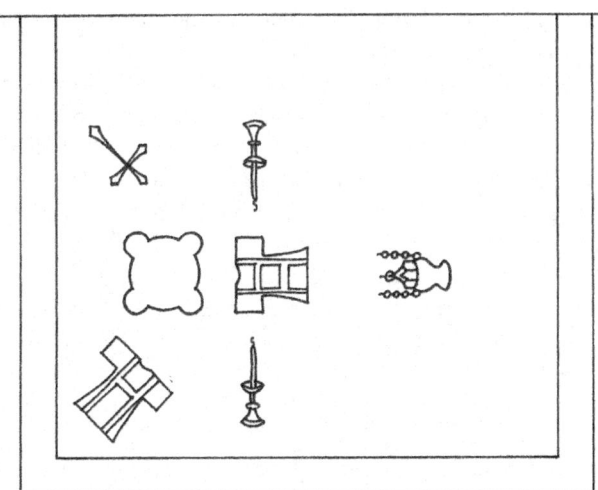

Figure III. High Mass: The Gospel sung from the pulpitum

Text after the Gospel has been read. The thurifer, after letting the ministers pass, will stand immediately behind the deacon, facing him, letting the thurible hang freely or swinging it gently[26] throughout the reading of the Gospel. The subdeacon, having left the book of the lesson on the lectern and having opened it at the correct page, turns to receive the Text from the deacon and then stands to the west of the lectern, facing the deacon at an angle, holding the closed[27] Text leaning upright on his breast[28] before him in both hands while the deacon sings the Gospel.

The deacon, having handed the Text to the subdeacon, approaches the lectern and, with joined hands,[29] sings *Dominus vobiscum*.[30] As he sings *Sequentia Sancti Evangelii*, he lays the left hand on the book[31] and makes the sign of the cross on this with his right thumb.[32] At *Secundum N.*, he signs his forehead and breast with his right thumb.[33] As *Gloria tibi Domine* is sung, he turns to the altar, signs himself[34] and bows.[35] The choir and all not otherwise engaged do likewise.[36] Turning back to the lectern, the deacon with joined hands sings the Gospel. After signing himself at *Gloria tibi Domine*, the

---

[26] Cons 69.3 of the thurifer during the *Exultet* on Holy Saturday has *cum thuribulo fumigante*, which seems to imply active smoking.
[27] Cf. Morse §159.
[28] Rock's very sensible supposition (IV.221).
[29] So the Dominicans (OP.1060), whose practice here differs from that observed by them at Low Mass.
[30] For the actions here, see C 66.20.
[31] So the Carmelites; OP.1060 is less clear.
[32] Presumably at the start of the day's Gospel (OP.1060).
[33] The Carmelites place the left hand extended on the breast. OP.1060 does not say.
[34] OP.1060 and the implication of Col 587. However, C 66.20 makes no mention of this sign of the cross.
[35] Col 587, but it is unclear whether only the choir should bow.
[36] Col 587; C 13.5.

celebrant turns by his left to face the deacon and listens to the Gospel standing thus, with his hands joined.

At the end of the Gospel, the deacon kisses the book.[37] With joined hands[38] he then kisses the Text held shut[39] to him by the subdeacon,[40] who has passed round to his right, between him and the taperer. All turn to the altar and stand still as the celebrant intones the creed.[41] Leaving the Gospel-book on the lectern and taking the Text, holding it upright before his chest, the deacon returns to the altar,[42] preceded by the subdeacon. If, however, a Text is not used, the deacon should take the Gospel-book for the celebrant to kiss. The acolyte, taperers and thurifer lead the way in the same order as they came.[43] On arrival at the foot of the altar, the acolyte lays aside the cross, if he has been carrying it, and comes to stand behind the deacon;[44] the taperers return to their usual places, where they stand holding their candles;[45] the thurifer stands at the foot of the altar, a little to the south side, to the right of where the deacon will stand and a little behind.[46]

As soon as the deacon has kissed the Gospel, the celebrant goes to the middle of the altar and intones the creed.[47] As he does so, all turn to stand erect facing the altar.[48] The celebrant turns round when the ministers arrive at the foot of the altar, the taperers

---

[37] Col 14; C 66.21. Neither the place where the book is kissed nor the manner of holding the hands is made clear. However, kissing the book at the beginning of the text seems most likely. He may place his hands on the book as he kisses it or hold them joined as he has held them while singing.

[38] Since he is not holding the book.

[39] There seems little point in opening a book whose purpose is mostly symbolic. At Lyons III.309, the Text is kissed (by the celebrant) shut, though the book of the Gospel (instead of the Text) is kissed open. Martène, Lib.I. Cap.IV. Art.V.VI, reports the common French custom of offering the Text open to a bishop to be kissed but shut to all others. He also mentions not kissing the book when there is no creed.

[40] There is some ambiguity (Col 14, C 66.21) as to whether the subdeacon should pass to the right of the deacon (thereby standing in place for the procession back to the altar) or whether the deacon should kiss the Text at its right edge. Pearson, page liii, interprets the rubric as meaning that the book to be kissed is presented on the right side of the deacon, and this is our preferred solution. The subdeacon, therefore, should pass to the right (east) of the deacon before offering him the Text to kiss.

[41] As may be inferred from Col 14 and by analogy with the *Gloria in excelsis*.

[42] Col 14, contradicting Rock IV.221.

[43] OP.948, 964, 1029, 1061.

[44] This seems the only reasonable way of allowing him to receive the Text to present to the subdeacon (Col 593).

[45] This is pure speculation, but it seems comely that they should hold their candles until the kissing of the book is over and the crowd round the altar begins to disperse.

[46] Unlike the Carmelites, but having the thurifer on the south side enables the subdeacon to stand to the deacon's left and replace the Text on the altar later. The Dominicans do not use incense at this point.

[47] Col 14. This whole section is the fruit of a combination of deductions from the Missal, the Consuetudinary and the Customary, all of which give apparently contradictory but complementary instructions.

[48] On balance, it seems more probable that C 13.5. and Col 587 mean that the choir turns for the intonation of the creed and then bows for *Et incarnatus est*.

bowing profoundly,[49] the deacon and subdeacon making no bow.[50] The deacon stands in the middle, the subdeacon at his left.

The deacon hands the Text to the subdeacon, takes the thurible from the thurifer, bows to the celebrant and incenses him with three swings, bowing before and after.[51] Returning the thurible to the thurifer, he receives the Text from the subdeacon. Both ministers go up to the celebrant. The deacon offers the book to the celebrant, who kisses it[52] and turns to the altar. The deacon hands the Text back to the subdeacon and goes to stand at the celebrant's right to continue the creed quietly with him.[53] They do not bow when they say *Et incarnatus est* privately but do so when the choir sings the words.[54] Meanwhile, the subdeacon comes down to the middle with the Text.

---

[49] OP.995.

[50] OP.1061.

[51] The number of swings recommended here is taken from Roman and Carmelite practice. C 66.24 has the Bishop first incensed and then offered the Text after the Gospel. Why should the deacon go to the foot of the altar to incense the celebrant? At Rome, this is done from the place where the Gospel is read. But the Carmelite deacon follows the subdeacon and incenses the celebrant from the foot of the altar, the thurifer standing at his left. The necessity for the deacon to incense the celebrant and offer him the Text suggests that both should be done together, therefore near the altar.

[52] On its right edge (Col 593); on its left edge (Col 15 quoting the Gradual); *in sinistris ejus* (C 66.22). See Pearson, page liii, for his proposed solution of the contradiction between left and right. His solution does not fit with Col 15, which contemplates either the Text or the Gospel-book. The Sarum books make no mention of a cross traced on the book (OP.1061).

The rubric at Col 593 (*deinde acolyto ministrante subdiacono, subdiaconus ipsi diacono*) is not found in some other editions or in the Customary. On the face of it, the deacon is here instructed to kiss the Text a second time, but only after the subdeacon and the acolyte, thereby breaking the usual hierarchical order. There are two possible explanations: (1) that this rubric is an elaboration by the printer of at least the 1526 edition, on which Dickinson's text is founded, and that it is somewhat confused; (2) that it is the result of a partial transposition from a rubric describing the passing of the chalice at the beginning of the offertory. That the wording here is identical to that at the beginning of Cons 39.23 inclines us to favour the latter explanation. Here we have been guided by Lincoln I.379-80 (see note 55), and, since the deacon has already kissed the Text after the Gospel, we have omitted the repeated kiss here.

Tracts.77 has the Dominican deacon omit the kiss at the end of the sung Gospel but kiss the book after the celebrant, who kisses it held up before him by the subdeacon in the place indicated by the deacon. This possibility is not entirely inconsistent with Cons 39.22 or Col 14.

[53] Col 589. The ministers say the Officium (C 66.7), *Gloria in excelsis* (C 66.7) and gradual, &c. (C 66.17), and Offertory (Cons 39.23) with the celebrant, so it is reasonable that the deacon should say the creed with him also.

Chambers, page 306, would have the celebrant and ministers sit for the sung creed, but gives no authority for this. Sitting might perhaps be permissible during a lengthy polyphonic creed, but such a style of singing seems at variance with the rubric at Col 14 for the choir to sing the creed straight through. In this case, since there would not really be much time to sit and the Sarum rubrics are silent on the matter, it would be better for the celebrant and his ministers to remain standing at the altar. OP.1289 does not contemplate sitting for the creed.

[54] OP.1288.

The choir is now incensed.[55] All three bowing to the altar,[56] the thurifer, bearing his thurible[57] and walking to the left of the acolyte, precedes the subdeacon[58] carrying the closed Text down to the choir.[59] In its midst, the thurifer imposes new, unblessed, incense.[60] They now go first to the precentor and the rulers in the middle of the choir, incensing first the precentor, then the principal and secondary rulers; then they go to the upper stalls (*superior gradus*) on the dean's side as that of greater dignity, where they visit each man in descending order of rank, the subdeacon going up into the stalls with the Text while the acolyte and the thurifer cense the canons from the floor.[61] When they have concluded with the upper rank on the dean's side, they do the same with the upper stalls on the precentor's side; then they go to the lower stalls (*secunda forma*) on the dean's side, then to the lower stalls on the precentor's side, then to the lowest stalls (*prima forma*) on the dean's side and finally to the lowest stalls on

---

[55] That the choir was incensed and kissed the Text during the creed was a widespread practice earlier in the Middle Ages and the rite of Lyons preserves this ritual. Fortescue, *The Mass*, pages 282-3, gives the history of the ceremony and its discouragement. Cons 39.22 seems to prescribe the practice and that this is so is confirmed by the late-thirteenth-century *Ordinale* of Wells, which tends to follow the Consuetudinary fairly closely (Wells.37). Unlike at Lyons III.310, Col 594 indicates that even the boys of the first form kiss the Text (*ab omnibus deosculando*). The Missal and Customary, however, give details of the incensation of the celebrant and choir and of the concomitant kissing of the Text after the offertory act, although the rubric is not the clearest (the same can be said of the rubric at C 66.41, which, however, merely reproduces Cons 45.3 and so might not represent later practice), and it is possible that the rite was moved at some point during the fourteenth century. In the context of the nuptial Mass, at which the creed is not said, both Col 838* and M.52 appear to assume that the choir and congregation are incensed after the offertory. The later rubrics concerning the celebrant's kissing of the Gospel (Col 14; C 66.22) make no mention of incense at this point (other than at pontifical functions), nor do the Dominicans use incense here. However, Becon, page 121, reports that the altar was incensed after the creed and before *Dominus vobiscum*, thereby making the use of incense during the creed in the sixteenth century at least credible. How to square the circle? Lincoln I.379-80 may provide the answer. There, when the creed was said, the celebrant kissed the Text and was incensed; then (though at Sarum this is not mentioned and so is omitted here) the deacon was incensed by the thurifer; then the choir was offered the Text and incense (*tunc incensetur chorus antequam tumbe incensantur*); then, after the creed, the celebrant incensed the sacrifice and was himself incensed by the deacon; then the altar and the relics were incensed. When the creed was not said, however, the relics were incensed before the choir (*tunc incensentur tumbe antequam chorus incensetur*). In other words, when the creed was said, the celebrant was incensed twice (once after the Gospel and once after the chalice), but when the creed was not said, all incense before the offertory was omitted and the choir was incensed only after the offertory, the celebrant being incensed first but not afterwards. It is this procedure that we follow here. For the relevant passage from Lincoln I.379-80, see Chapter XVIII, note 10.

That the choir is visited in the same order irrespective of whether the creed is said or not is inferred from the Gradual's *Eodem quoque modo sequatur textus post* Credo (Col 16).

[56] Lyons III.310.

[57] This can be assumed from the usual practice that the thurifer looks after the thurible when not in use and hands it to a more senior minister only when it is to be swung.

[58] C 66.24, Cons 39.22 and Col 594, against the Gradual (Col 16), which gives the deacon.

[59] The rule for incensing the choir of Sarum is given here. In other churches, the same principle is followed, *mutatis mutandis*. The reference to two Texts at C 66.24 is applicable to pontifical functions only.

[60] Col 838*-839*; OP.956.

[61] C 38.1 (*thurificando extra formulas vel infra formulas*). When the seats are raised and the choir is standing, there is space for the subdeacon to advance from canon to canon. At Lyons III.372, the thurifer *entre ensuite dans les hautes stalles, si elles sont assez larges, et encense chacun d'un seul coup*, rather in the manner recommended here for the subdeacon to offer the Text.

the precentor's side.[62] As they reach the first person of each rank, the acolyte takes the thurible from the thurifer, who will stand to the acolyte's left and a little behind him, and incenses each person individually with as many swings as the custom of the church requires,[63] bowing before and afterwards. Without returning the thurible to the thurifer, they move on to the next person and repeat these actions, while the subdeacon, following, offers the Text to each person to kiss, not bowing beforehand but bowing afterwards.[64] When they get to the end of each form, the acolyte gives the thurible to the thurifer. To cross to the other side, they come to the middle, advance to the end closer to the ranking person on the side to which they are going and bow to the altar there, the acolyte and thurifer standing behind the subdeacon. They repeat the operation as many times as necessary.

When the choir sings *Et incarnatus est*, all, including the thurifer, acolyte and subdeacon, pause, face the altar and bow three times with the choir.[65] At *Et incarnatus est de Spiritu Sancto ex Maria virgine*, they bow once, and again at *Et homo factus est*, and a third time at *Crucifixus etiam pro nobis sub Pontio Pilato*. At *Vitam venturi saeculi*, all turn and stand facing the altar, remaining so until the Offertory antiphon is begun.[66]

Once the whole choir has been incensed and has kissed the Text, the acolyte, with the thurifer to his right, precedes the subdeacon to the foot of the altar, where they stand aside to let the subdeacon pass. The subdeacon comes up to the altar, replaces the Text in its place between the middle and the north corner, brings the missal near the corporal,[67] placing it at an angle and leaving enough space for the celebrant to incense the altar to the left of the sacrifice, and, if the sung creed has not been concluded, stands at the celebrant's left. The acolyte and thurifer retire.[68]

As soon as the subdeacon has left the altar on his way to the choir, the taperers put down their candles and resume their habitual stations. If the Gospel has been sung

---

[62] In contrast, Lyons III.310 has only the clergy in the upper stalls, if vested as presbyters, kiss the Text.

[63] This varies considerably and in the past has been the subject of many acrimonious disputes. The Roman *Caeremoniale Episcoporum* (Lib. I. cap. XXIII.32) gives the standard rules for most churches nowadays.

[64] Lyons III.310.

[65] That the subdeacon, acolyte and thurifer pause is assumed only from the silence of the Sarum books. At Lyons III.310, the subdeacon continues offering the Text throughout these words, even though the choir genuflects.

[66] C 13.5. The unclear rubric probably means to prescribe a turning towards the altar, but not a bow.

[67] At Rome, the subdeacon used to bring the missal immediately after the celebrant had finished reading the Gospel privately, but here we presume that the celebrant does not so read the Gospel. See Chapter XV, note 21.

[68] Should the ministers be incensed here, immediately after the choir, or later, after the offertory, even when the creed is said? In the other rites consulted, even when the Text is kissed during the creed (Lyons III.374), the choir is incensed after the offertory and so little can be learned from them. Nevertheless, a clue, however tentative, may be found in the fact that Lyons III.374 and OPraem. IV.107 do not offer the Text to the ministers at the creed but have the deacon incensed after the offertory. Therefore, the incensation of the ministers (and, by extension, the congregation) could be said to be linked more to that of the celebrant at the offertory than to that of the choir, whose incensation is more closely connected with the veneration of the Text. For the reasoning behind having the ministers incensed at all, see Chapter XVIII, note 10.

from a portable lectern at the foot of the altar, the taperers now remove this and return to their places.

When the creed is finished, the ministers take up their places on their steps behind the celebrant, who crosses himself, turns and sings *Dominus vobiscum*, the deacon turning with him and the subdeacon assisting with the chasuble as before.[69] Having turned back to the altar, the celebrant sings *Oremus*. The ministers go up to the altar and stand at either side of the celebrant, the deacon on his right and the subdeacon on his left.[70] So they recite the Offertory quietly.

After reading the Offertory, the subdeacon crosses over to stand at the deacon's right, bowing moderately as he passes the middle.

However, if there is no creed, the celebrant sings *Dominus vobiscum* and *Oremus* while the ministers are still at the lectern, and kisses the Text[71] after *Oremus*.[72] He is not incensed,[73] nor is the choir.[74] Turning back to the altar, he waits for the ministers to join him before reading the Offertory.[75]

---

[69] C 66.8. Cf. OP.1063.
[70] Cons 39.23.
[71] The celebrant is to kiss the Text even when the creed is not sung (C 66.41).
[72] Cf. Lyons III.307.
[73] At least on the days mentioned at C 66.41.
[74] Col 594.
[75] OP.1290. That the celebrant is to wait for the ministers to join him before proceeding with the Offertory suggests that he sings *Dominus vobiscum* and *Oremus* as soon as the Gospel has been concluded. In this case, his chasuble is not arranged.

XVIII

FROM THE OFFERTORY TO THE PREFACE

§1. THE OFFERING OF THE SACRIFICE

As the celebrant reads the Offertory, the taperers, leaving their candles in their places, bow in the middle and go to the credence. There they assist the acolyte to put on the humeral veil, who now takes up the sacred vessels still covered by the chalice veil,[1] envelops them in the humeral veil[2] and so takes them to the altar.

When the Offertory has been read and the subdeacon has taken his station to the right of the deacon,[3] the acolyte brings the chalice to him[4] up the steps of the south side. The subdeacon removes the end of the humeral veil to uncover the chalice, which he places, veiled, on the altar in front of him. The acolyte returns to the credence table and removes the humeral veil. The taperers, having assisted the acolyte to remove the humeral veil, resume their usual places at their tapers. The subdeacon places the veiled chalice before the deacon, who removes the veil. Covering his hands with it, he hands the paten with the host to the priest.[5] The celebrant lays the paten with the host on the corporal in front of him, leaving enough space for the chalice to stand behind the paten, and holds out his right hand for the deacon to kiss.[6] The deacon kisses the

---

[1] The Dominican subdeacon brings the chalice to the altar during the *Gloria* covered by both its veil and the humeral veil. The chalice, covered in its own veil, then sits on the humeral veil on the south side of the altar (their *locus administrationis*). In the much-simplified Roman rite, the chalice, covered in its veil and the humeral veil, stands on the credence table from before the beginning of the Mass. The subdeacon takes it to the altar at the offertory enwrapped in the humeral veil, but the chalice veil is left on the credence table until after Communion. The Sarum books do not mention when the chalice was taken from the *locus administrationis* to the altar. Here, reading between the lines of Col 593, C 66.23 and Cons 39.23, we assume that the chalice is taken up after the Offertory has been read and, following the Dominicans for the most part, that the chalice veil remains on it as the acolyte takes it to the altar, even though the humeral veil is also employed, because it will be needed later in order to pass the paten after the secrets.
[2] The use of the humeral veil is not mentioned at this point, but the use of a veil to protect the handler from direct contact with the sacred vessels is widespread (e.g. in the Roman rite), and the humeral veil is used for this purpose by the acolyte when bringing the chalice earlier.
[3] The most sensible position if he is to pass the chalice from the acolyte to the deacon (Cons 39.23).
[4] This appears to be the meaning of Cons 39.23 and is understood thus by Rock IV.223.
[5] An interpretation of Cons 39.23.
[6] *Deinde* (Cons 39.23), clarifying Col 593 and C 66.23. There is no mention of the deacon kissing the paten as well, and, unlike when handing the celebrant the thurible at the Officium, the deacon is here told to kiss the celebrant's hand after passing him the paten. These kisses, then, differ from the *solita oscula*.

celebrant's hand and, holding the chalice's foot with his veiled[7] left hand, wipes any loose drops inside the bowl of the chalice with the purificator, lays this to the right of the corporal and passes the chalice, his hands still covered by its veil, to the celebrant. The priest places the chalice in the middle of the corporal, behind the paten, and holds out his hand again for the deacon to kiss. The deacon, having kissed the celebrant's hand as before, lays out the chalice veil on the altar, where it remains until used at the preface. The offertory act now follows, as at Low Mass.[8] The celebrant places the paten to his right, half-covered by the corporal. He covers the chalice himself[9] and blesses the offerings.

§2. THE FIRST PART OF THE INCENSATIONS

While the offertory is taking place, the thurifer comes up the southern steps.[10] The subdeacon crosses to the left of the celebrant. When the celebrant has blessed the offerings, he turns to the right. Incense is blessed and imposed and the thurible is

---

[7] Both Chambers, page 341, and OCist.101 would have the deacon pass the paten and chalice veiled to the celebrant. This would be consistent with the subdeacon not being allowed to touch the paten when passing it to the acolyte.

[8] There is no mention of the deacon holding the chalice with the celebrant, but the Carmelite deacon supports the right arm of the celebrant as he offers. OP.1064 has the deacon busy himself with the thurible during the offering.

[9] At Rome, the deacon uncovers and discovers the chalice with the pall. C 66.23, however, is explicit in saying that it is the celebrant that covers the chalice himself. This may be a survival from the use of the great corporal, which it would be more convenient and safer for the celebrant to use himself. The Dominican celebrant also covers and uncovers the chalice himself.

[10] Tracts.78.

The whole matter of the incensation of the offerings, altar, celebrant, choir and ministers is very confusing.

From C 66.24 and Coll. 593–5, the indisputable facts are that: (1) the offerings are incensed with three crosses and three circles; (2) the celebrant performs an uncertain number of incensations of some kind on either side of the offerings and in the space between himself and the altar; (3) at least when the creed is said, the celebrant is incensed by the deacon and then kisses the Text; (4) the celebrant washes his hands while the deacon performs further incensation involving the left corner of the altar, the relics and incensation *in circuitu*.

Beyond these facts, there is much that is unclear. With how many swings were these incensations performed? Was the thurible held in both hands or in one hand? Did the celebrant incense the whole altar or merely the offerings and possibly their immediate surroundings? Was the celebrant always incensed? How did the deacon perform his own incensation of the altar? Clockwise, or anticlockwise? Were the ministers and assistants also incensed?

In seeking plain answers to these questions, we are doomed to disappointment. The Roman rite as celebrated in the various churches of Western Christendom throughout the Middle Ages varied considerably in the matter of incensation at the offertory, presumably in part because this incensation was a fairly late addition to the rite. Consequently, there is no conclusive way of knowing how incense was used at the offertory in Salisbury cathedral in the sixteenth century. In our search for answers, it is worth considering how different uses (whether purely mediæval or later survivals) prescribe that these incensations should be made. Doing this should make any ultimate guess (for it cannot be other than a guess) at least more plausible.

The Sarum Consuetudinary and the Sarum Customary give details of the incensation of the altar at Matins and Vespers. These details give us some insight into how incensation was done at Sarum, but the presence of the offerings on the altar at Mass and the part possibly played by a deacon may have modified the ritual considerably.

Cons 27.4. gives us the following:

Interim autem ceroferarii introeant, et, acceptis candelabris, veniant obviam sacerdoti ad gradum presbiterii. Deinde sacerdos ponat thus in thuribulo benedicendo, et procedat ad altare, et, facta genufleccione ante altare, illud incenset, primo in medio, deinde in dextera parte, postea in sinistra; exinde ymaginem beate marie, et postea archam in quo continentur reliquie: deinde thurificando altare circumeat: hoc peracto sacerdos accedat ad extremum gradum ante altare, et ad altare se inclinet: et, precedentibus ceroferariis et thuribulo, in stallo huic officio deputato se recipiat.

C 37 has the following:

Et sic inponat thus in thuribulum et procedat ad altare, et, facta genuflexione ante altare terram deosculando, incenset ipsum altare primo ter in medio deinde ter in dextera parte postea ter in sinistra parte: deinde iterum in medio; exinde ter ad imaginem beate marie hoc est in medio altaris, postea arcam in qua continentur reliquie, deinde thurificando altare circueat altare.

Crede Michi [30] gives the following, though it is not clear from the context whether the Mass or Divine Service is being dealt with, or whether the Gospel or the offertory is meant: *De thurificatione chori a dyacono. Dyaconus thurificans altare debet thurificare medium altaris non cornua secundum vsum Sarum. sed quot jactus dubitatur. aliqui dicunt.vij. quidam .xij* [or ix: see apparatus].

Wells.37: *Sacerdos sacrificium ministerio diaconi ter in signum crucis thurificet, deinde ter in circuitu, postea ex utraque parte sacrificii; quo peracto sacerdos manus abluat ministerio subdiaconi et aliorum ministrorum; diacono interim ipsum altare in sinistro cornu incensante, et reliquias more solito, et ipsum altare in circuitum.*

Lincoln I.379–80 seems to establish a link between incensing the altar *in circuitu* and incensing the tombs of the saints, and so points the reader to deduce that, when the creed is not said (i.e. when persons are incensed at the offertory), the choir is incensed after the altar.

Et Credo dicto veniant thuriferarij ad altare et diaconus principalis acceptum turibulum dabit sacerdoti ad incensandum calicem et corporale et hoc facto debent diaconus principalis et secundarius sacerdotem incensare. deinde circa altare. Deinde tumbas sanctorum. et dummodo ipsi predicti diaconi incensent tumbas; subdiaconus principalis stabit cum diacono ante altare vsque ad aduentum diaconorum absencium, vnde sciendum quando dicitur. credo. tunc incensetur chorus antequam tumbe incensantur. et quando non dicitur. Credo tunc incensentur tumbe antequam chorus incensetur.

The unreformed rubrics of the Cistercian, Præmonstratensian and Carmelite rites shew variation in the incensing of the altar.

The Cistercian celebrant probably incensed the surface of the altar while standing still in the middle, and the deacon incensed the cross and round the altar.

Cistercian *Consuetudines* (as quoted by King, *Religious Orders*, page 141):

Sacerdos accipiens (thuribulum), thurificet calicem isto modo, semel volvat illud circa calicem, semel thurificet dexteram partem altaris desuper, semel et sinistram, semel quoque anteriorem ... Diaconus autem thurificet prius dexteram partem ipsius altaris [bis deforis add. Liber Usuum 1643]. Deinde elevans manus [manum (Liber Usuum 1643)] thurificet bis crucem, et inde transiens per retro altare ad sinistram partem thurificet eam similiter et crucem.

Before 1738, the Præmonstratensians incensed the choir at the creed, their celebrant did not move from the centre when incensing at the offertory and the deacon also incensed the altar. The celebrant and sacred ministers only were incensed at the offertory.

The Old *Ordinarius* of the twelfth century (OPraem.IV.91–108):

Unus ministrorum preparatum thuribulum cum incenso diacono tradat. Qui ad benedictionem sacerdotis imponens incensum, tradat sacerdoti, osculans ei manum. Quod sacerdos accipiens, calicem thurificet hoc modo: facta cruce desuper, circumvolvat ter calicem, deinde dexteram partem altaris semel, semel et sinistram desuper tantum, semel quoque anteriorem thurificet. Diaconus vero, posita manu sub ascella, teneat ei casulam, ut expeditius possit agere. Quo facto, reddat thuribulum diacono, et conversus ad chorum dicat Orate mediocriter ut possit audiri. *Quem conversum diaconus thurificet, et trahat ei deorsum medium casule. Cum autem ad altare vultum reduxerit, non ex ea parte qua se ad chorum convertit, et ad librum in sinistra parte accedens secretas dicere ceperit, diaconus thurificet prius dexteram partem altaris, deinde*

> altare quod retro positum est, deinde sinistram partem altaris, non desuper sed deforis tantum thurificans. Postea, thurificato subdiacono, reddat ministro thuribulum, et minister ipsum thurificans, reponat illud in locum suum.

The Præmonstratensian *Ordinarius* of 1739, page 174, retained the old mode of incensing for minor doubles and days of lower rank (King, *Religious Orders*, page 212):

> Incensatis Oblatis Celebrans, facta Cruci inclinatione, stans in medio triplici ductu incensat Crucem, (aut loco Crucis Ven. Sacramentum genuflexus, supple si sit expositum,) dicens Dirigatur Domine Oratio mea. Et iterum facta inclinatione stans ibidem, in Duplici minori et infra, ter ducit thuribulum ad cornu Evangelii simul dicens: Sicut incensum in conspectu tuo; iterum facta inclinatione ter mittit thuribulum versus cornu Epistolae dicens: Elevatio manuum mearum Sacrificium vespertinum. *Cum incensatur Crux (vel Venerabile Sacramentum) Diaconus amovet Calicem ad partem Epistolae, quem incensata Cruce (vel Ven. Sacramento) reponit in loco suo, tum Celebrans reddit thuribulum Diacono, dicens* Accendat in nobis Dominus &c. et ab eo incensatur ad cornu Epistolae.

The Carmelites have the celebrant incense the altar more completely, moving to its corners not unlike at Rome, and the deacon does not incense the altar. The Carmelite Ordinal of the fourteenth century (as quoted by King, *Religious Orders*, page 305):

> Qui (sacerdos) accepto thuribulo, faciat cum eo super calicem signum crucis. Deinde thurificet ante se in directum et super calicem versus sacramentum, postmodum ad dexteram primo et ad sinistram secundo, procedendo in thurificando a medio altaris usque ad cornua, et dum ad sinistrum cornu venerit et illud thurificaverit, ipsum altare anterius thurificet de sinistro ad dextrum cornu progrediendo, et deinde super altare thurificando ut prius ad medium altaris revertatur.

The modern Dominican celebrant incenses the offerings in a much simpler manner and then the altar much as at Rome, so in this instance their ritual is not necessarily a useful guide to Sarum usage. However, *Tracts*.78 has the celebrant incense the chalice in the form of a cross, then the space in front of him (three times: OP.1291) and the host, and then the altar, walking to its corners. Then the deacon incenses the celebrant, and then the thurifer incenses the deacon, the subdeacon, the other servers, and finally, having imposed more, unblessed, incense, the cantors and the brethren in choir. For the manner of incensing the altar in the divine office, see OP.1106–11.

The *Ordo Romanus XIV* has the celebrant incense the offerings and altar as now but then the deacon takes over: [diaconus] *thurificet altare per circuitum, primo a parte dextra, deinde a sinistra; postea thurificet capellanum qui servit pontifici* (PL LXXVIII.1164). How many assistants may be incensed is left fluid (*prout videbitur faciendum*).

In the modern Rite of Lyons, the celebrant incenses the altar much as at Rome and then hands the thurible to the deacon, who incenses the altar going round it clockwise and holding the thurible in one hand *de toute la longeur des chaînes*. This method of censing is not seen in Rome, where things are not incensed at a distance, but is much more sensible when incensing distant objects while walking. The Carthusians also employ this method when incensing the choir *en passant*.

Lyons III.263:

> A la fin de l'encensement il reçoit l'encensoir des mains du célébrant, qu'il salue simplement par une inclination de tête, et se tournant sur la droite, il s'éloigne un peu et l'encense de deux coups, en lui faisant une génuflexion avant et après. Ensuite il encense autour de l'autel, hors des cancels, de toute la longeur des chaînes, et tenant la main gauche pendante sur la côté. En passant devant le milieu de l'autel, il ensence trois fois la croix, avec une génuflexion avant et après, ce qu'il fait aussi derrière l'autel. Ayant achevé le tour, et étant arrivé à l'ouverture des cancels, du côté de l'épître, il remet l'encensoir au premier acolyte, et il se rend à sa place ordinaire, où il fait une inclination à l'autel et une autre au chœur.

Incensing the altar clockwise allows the celebrant and the deacon to conduct their offices without impeding each other. Of the celebrant, Lyons III.219 (with note 2) reads: *Il se lave pour la seconde fois les mains, ou plutôt les doigts, en disant:* Lavabo, *etc., revient au milieu de l'autel* (2: *Mais il attend auparavant que le diacre ait encensé le milieu de l'autel.*), *et continue comme à la messe basse.*

Rock IV.224 has the deacon cense 'the north end of the altar, the shrine, and what relics lay around the presbytery'.

handed to the celebrant as at the Officium. The deacon lays his bare right hand's fingertips[11] on the foot of the chalice to prevent accidents, while the celebrant incenses the offerings, first with three horizontal crosses, drawing the thurible towards him for the first stroke and then from left to right for the second; and then with three horizontal circles surrounding both chalice and host, starting between the host and himself, the first and second drawing the thurible anticlockwise, and the third drawing it clockwise.[12]

Next, while the deacon holds the edge of the chasuble so as to prevent it hampering the celebrant's right hand as it wields the thurible,[13] and the subdeacon stands to his left,[14]

> Morse §208 prescribes that 'the celebrant then blesses incense as before. Receiving the censer from the deacon he censes the oblations with three crosses and three circles saying as he does so: "Let my – Prayer be – Set forth, – O Lord in thy – Sight as the – Incense"; and concludes with one swing on either side.' §164:
>
> The deacon at once receives back the censer from the celebrant and at once censes him as at the Introit, which done he goes *in plano* round the altar-steps, censing as he goes. In the centre he will stop and bow eastwards towards the altar; at the north end he will stop again, face south, and cense up towards the north end of the altar, giving three swings with long chains. He then goes on passing behind the altar and going quite round till he comes to the right hand of the subdeacon standing in the centre on his own step, facing east. If the altar is close to the east wall or reredos the deacon returns, after censing the north end, and passing behind (i.e. west of) the subdeacon thus gets to his right hand.
>
> Bond, page 98, also supposes that the deacon goes all the way round the altar.
>
> The Sarum books do not mention the incensing of the ministers and other servers, possibly because the rubrics governing the incensation of the choir during the creed and those describing the incensations after the offertory are not clearly distinguished. Among the Dominicans (*Tracts*.78), once the celebrant had been incensed, the deacon handed the thurible to the thurifer, who incensed the deacon, the subdeacon, the acolytes, the cantors and the choir. When adapting this ceremonial for Sarum, one has to bear in mind the special character of the Salisbury acolyte. As to whether the junior ministers were incensed at all, it is perhaps worth considering that the congregation was incensed after the offertory (Col 838*; M.52), but no mention is made of this either at Col 594 or in the Customary, even though the practice had been considered normal as far back as the days of St. Thomas (*Summa Theol.* III, Qu LXXXIII, Art 5. Ad ij.). It seems odd that the choir and the congregation should be incensed, but not the ministers, and so we have presumed that they were.
>
> It is in the light of these variants and suggestions that the ritual outlined here is, tentatively, proposed. The White Canons have been followed for the celebrant's part in the incensations; the Cistercians' *Liber Usuum* has been mined for the deacon's incensation of the altar; the Use of Lincoln has proved useful in clarifying the order in which sacrifice, altar and choir were incensed; and, for the incensing of the clergy, despite the ensuing complication of the ritual, the Roman rite's order of precedence has been taken into account: it seems unlikely that the exalted choir of Sarum was incensed after the humble taperers.

[11] We have had the deacon hand the chalice to the celebrant through its veil before the offertory (see note 7, after OCist.101) but, after OCist.105 (see Chapter XIX, note 15) we will have him touch the chalice at *Per ipsum*. See also note 54 and Chapter XIX, notes 20 and 24. What the actual custom of Sarum church was cannot now be known.

[12] The Sarum books mention the three circles but do not specify the change in direction. This detail is taken from the Roman, Carmelite and Præmonstratensian books. The Dominicans incense the offerings in an altogether different way.

[13] Is this what is meant by *ministerio diaconi* (Cons 39.24)? So OP.1064 and the Roman rite. The Carmelite subdeacon also raises the chasuble a little. OPraem.IV.97 has the deacon place his hand under the celebrant's armpit (*ascella*) and hold the chasuble.

[14] So the Carmelites. The Roman, Præmonstratensian and Dominican subdeacons play no part in the incensation of the altar, being engaged in other duties. At Sarum, however, where the subdeacon needs to attend to the Text, something closer to Carmelite practice appears more plausible.

the celebrant incenses the corporal.[15] To do so, while standing in his place,[16] he swings the thurible once[17] over the right of the corporal;[18] immediately, he repeats the action over the left of the corporal,[19] the subdeacon removing the missal somewhat and replacing it presently if necessary. Stepping back a little, with three[20] further swings he incenses the front of the altar in the middle, before himself.[21] As he incenses the offerings and the altar, he says the prayer *Dirigatur*.

He hands the thurible to the deacon[22] and is incensed and kisses the Text[23] as at the Officium. Then he turns to face the altar in the middle until the deacon has incensed the cross, when he goes to the south corner to be met by the subdeacon and the acolyte with the tapers for the lavatory.

Having incensed the celebrant, the deacon turns by his right and incenses the southern part of the front of the altar with two swings,[24] walking towards the corner as he does so. At the corner, he turns, raises the thurible and incenses the cross with a triple swing,[25] bowing before and afterwards. He continues incensing the side of the altar, going round, with two swings and then the back of the altar with three swings. At the middle, he turns to the cross and bows. If there are relics, he incenses them now[26] and repeats his bow to the cross. He then continues incensing the back part of the altar

---

[15] Presumably this is what is meant by *ex utraque parte calicis et sacrificii* and *locum inter se et altare*. Lincoln I.379 gives: *ad incensandum calicem et corporale*. The rubric runs straight from incensing the offerings to incensing either side of them. There is no mention of the cross being incensed between the one and the other.

[16] Col 593 (*ex utraque parte calicis et sacrificii*) seems to link the action closely to the position of the sacrifice and is very distant from the wording at the Officium (*ipse sacerdos thurificet medium Altaris et utrumque cornu Altaris*, Col 581).

[17] So OPraem.IV.95–6 and OCist.102, *pace* C 37, which refers to the choral office, at which the celebrant may well have walked to the horns of the altar, as he does at the Officium. C 66.24 does not mention a triple swing here, despite mentioning the three crosses and three circles immediately before this. Three swings, adopted by the later Præmonstratensians, may be a later development.

[18] OPraem.IV.95 and most other rites begin the incensation on the south side. The later Præmonstratensians are exceptional in incensing the north side first.

[19] Col 593.

[20] So Col 593 in what may be a doubtful reading. OPraem.IV.95–6 has one swing to the right of the chalice, one to the left and one in front; their modern successors have three swings on each occasion but omit the incensing of the front of the altar; the Dominicans omit the swings on either side of the sacrifice but have three simple swings in front of the corporal, in the middle, to the left and to the right (though this distribution is not mentioned by OP.1291).

[21] Col 593; C 66.24. *Deinde iterum in medio* (C 37), i.e., after incensing right and left. *Partem ... anteriorem* (Cistercians and Præmonstratensians). *Inter se et altare* (Col 593) suggests that this refers to the front of the altar, not merely to the part of the corporal between himself and the offerings.

[22] How is the celebrant incensed? OPraem.IV.100 has the deacon incense the celebrant as he says *Orate*, turned to the choir; the newer Præmonstratensians, at the south corner, where the lavatory is about to take place. However, at Col 594, the celebrant is instructed to go to the right corner only for the lavatory. Since, moreover, the celebrant is to kiss the Text, it seems sensible to have him incensed at the middle, as at the Officium.

[23] C 66.24.

[24] So the Cistercians, perhaps because the middle of the frontal has already been incensed by the celebrant. There is no mention in the Sarum books of the incensation of the cross, but this occurs in the Roman, Dominican, Cistercian and later Præmonstratensian rites and is included here speculatively.

[25] So the Dominican celebrant when he incenses the cross (OP.1291). See Chapter XIV, note 23. OCist.102 has the deacon, who incenses the cross at the corners, swing the thurible but twice.

[26] Cons 39.25.

with three more swings. Coming round, he incenses the northern end with two swings. At the corner, he incenses the cross as before,[27] again bowing before and afterwards. If there is a principal image distinct from the altar cross, it should be incensed now.[28] He finishes by incensing the northern half of the frontal with two swings. If he has done so at the Officium, as soon as the subdeacon has gone to assist at the lavatory, the thurifer comes up the northern steps and removes the missal, replacing it once the deacon has incensed the north part of the altar.

When the altar is not free-standing, the deacon incenses the southern part of the frontal and the cross as above, swings the thurible twice round the south horn and comes down to his step in the middle (or to the bottom if the steps are insufficiently broad). Thence, as the celebrant goes to the south corner, the deacon goes up to the north corner. There he swings the thurible twice round the corner and then incenses the cross and the northern part of the frontal as above. If there are relics, he incenses those on each side after he has incensed the cross from that side and then repeats his bow to the cross.

Having finished incensing the altar, he comes straight down to the middle of his step and returns the thurible to the thurifer, who has come round the steps to receive it. He then faces east immediately.

The subdeacon, when he has replaced the Text on the altar, while the deacon is beginning his incensation of the altar, comes down the north steps and so proceeds round the steps to the middle, where he bows, and then goes to the south side to assist at the lavatory while the deacon incenses the altar's north end.[29]

§3. THE PEOPLE'S OBLATION, THE BIDDING OF THE BEDES AND THE SERMON

If the people is to make its oblation,[30] the celebrant waits in the middle while the deacon incenses the altar. The subdeacon, having replaced the Text, comes down to his step and stands behind the celebrant. When the deacon has finished circuiting the altar and has returned to his step, all three come to the foot of the altar and face west,

---

[27] So the Cistercians, whose ritual we have followed for the most part.
[28] C 37.
[29] At first reading, the words *his itaque peractis* (Col 594) suggest that the lavatory and the deacon's incensing of the altar should take place after the choir has been incensed. This is absurd and would make a mockery of the rubric at Coll 838*–839* that blessed incense should be offered on the altar and unblessed incense to the choir and the congregation. It is plain that the rubrics concerning the incensation of the choir have been interpolated between the celebrant's kissing of the Text and the lavatory, presumably because the incensation of the choir was linked originally to the incensation of the celebrant and the kissing of the Text at the creed. Cf. Wells.37.
[30] For the placing of this rite, see Chapter VIII, note 18. The complete silence of the Sarum books on this question presents two especial difficulties for High Mass. The first is that the deacon's incensing of the altar is made more difficult by having the celebrant delay his departure to the south corner. The second is that the dissociation between the incensation of the altar and celebrant and that of the choir and ministers is stressed much more when the offering, bidding of the bedes and sermon are interpolated, thus making the displacement of the choir's incensation from the creed to the offertory more awkward. For the ceremonial recourse has been had to Solans and Olalla, as for Low Mass.

the celebrant between the deacon on his right[31] and the subdeacon on his left. They go to the choir step,[32] where, the taperers holding the cloth or plate between them before him, the celebrant receives the offerings of the clergy, handing them at once to the subdeacon[33] to place in the basin or cloth held by the taperers and then going down to the chancel arch accompanied by the ministers and preceded by the taperers, those of the laity, as at Low Mass. If a cross or image is to be offered to the people to kiss, it should be held by the deacon,[34] to whom the taperers should have brought it. The taperers return to the credence table, and the celebrant with his ministers returns to the altar to continue the Mass. If a single offering of money is to be received, only one taperer need assist. In this case, he stands next to the subdeacon and holds the basin.[35]

If the bedes be bidden, or if other prayers are to be said, the celebrant will bid them, either from the footpace or from the pulpit, as at Low Mass, aloud but without note. The Psalm *Deus misereatur* is alternated by the choir without note, begun by the principal side.[36]

If there is to be a sermon, the celebrant and ministers go to the sedilia. If one of the ministers will preach, he accompanies the celebrant to the sedilia before departing for the pulpit. If the celebrant himself will preach, he may go to the sedilia to remove his maniple and chasuble.

Returning to the altar in the usual way, the deacon remains in the middle on his step, while the celebrant and subdeacon go to the south for the lavatory. Mass continues in the usual way.

§4. THE LAVATORY

At the south horn, the celebrant is met by the acolyte, who stands to the subdeacon's left, and the taperers,[37] the first of whom, who stands behind the subdeacon, has brought the towel, and the second, who stands behind the acolyte, the basin and, if it is to be employed, the ewer.[38] If he is to say certain prayers for the dead, he does so exactly

---

[31] Olalla.206; Lyons III.216.
[32] This is where the choir is sprinkled at the *Asperges* (P.4) and seems to be the place where the celebrant and the choir meet, as the chancel arch is the boundary between the clergy and the laity.
[33] S.236.
[34] S.236.
[35] Olalla.206.
[36] P.6.
[37] C 66.25 and Cons 39.25 specify that the celebrant washes his hands with the help of the subdeacon *et aliorum ministrorum*, but no further indications are given. *Tracts*.78–9 contemplates both ewer and basin and has the subdeacon pour the water while the towel is held by the deacon and one of the taperers. OCarm.80 has the subdeacon administer the vessels as the taperers, holding the towel extended between them, stand, facing east and west, between the celebrant and the subdeacon. Chambers, page 346, dispensing with the ewer, has the subdeacon administer the water and the acolyte the towel. The solution here is a composite adaptation to allow for the presence of the Sarum acolyte. The wording of Col 595 (*diacono interim ipsum Altare in sinistro cornu thurificante*) supposes that the deacon is absent at this point, and so we assume that the subdeacon is assisted by junior *ministri* only.
[38] *Tracts*.79 allows for the omission of the ewer. The water is to be poured either directly into the ground or into a different piscina from that used for the ablutions later. See Bond, pages 154 and 156.

as at Low Mass, without note, the subdeacon and his assistants making the responses. As the celebrant turns for the lavatory, the subdeacon and acolyte go up the steps to meet him, followed by the taperers. Standing on one of the steps, the subdeacon turns by his left to receive the ewer and the acolyte turns by his right to receive the basin. The taperers come to stand, facing east and west, between the celebrant and the others. There they stretch the towel between them so as to protect the celebrant's chasuble. The subdeacon and the acolyte bow to the celebrant. The subdeacon pours water over the celebrant's hands[39] into the acolyte's basin. The celebrant dries his hands on the towel. If there is no ewer, the celebrant himself washes his hands in the basin. All bow again to the celebrant. As the priest returns to the middle, the first taperer takes back the towel. Resuming their places behind the subdeacon and the acolyte, the taperers take back all their equipment and return it to the credence table, whence they go to their places. On days when the creed has been said, the acolyte retires to his place; but on other days he goes straight to the middle to await the subdeacon and the thurifer.

The subdeacon goes round *in plano* to the middle, where he stands on his step, timing his progress to arrive at the same time as the celebrant. *In spiritu humilitatis* follows as usual.

§5. THE SECOND PART OF THE INCENSATIONS

As he does so, on days when the creed has not been said, the subdeacon goes up to the Text, which he brings down directly. Bowing and turning with the acolyte and the thurifer, who has taken the thurible back from the deacon, they go to the choir. There a goodly quantity of more, unblessed, incense is imposed and the choir is visited in the same manner as described above at the creed.[40]

Upon their return, the subdeacon replaces the Text and comes down to his step. Meanwhile, the acolyte takes up his station behind the subdeacon. Standing *in plano* to the right of the acolyte, the thurifer, bowing before and after, incenses successively the deacon,[41] the subdeacon and the acolyte, who from their steps turn to face him and bow in reply. The deacon and subdeacon are incensed with two swings each; the acolyte, with one. Next, standing in the middle, a little to the west of the taperers, he incenses these as they turn to face him, bowing before and afterwards, with one swing each, first the senior, then the junior. Bowing to the altar, the thurifer goes to the west of the chancel and, bowing as usual before and afterwards, incenses the congregation[42] with three swings, to the centre, to the south and to the north.[43] Bowing again to the altar, the thurifer retires and removes the thurible to the vestry.

---

[39] Unlike at Low Mass, since the celebrant has handled the thurible, and possibly also the offerings of the people, more than merely the tips of the fingers should be washed. So the Roman rite.

[40] Col 16. The rubric at Col 594, *Chorus non thurificetur*, seems unanswerable. However, from C 66.24, where the details of the choir's incensation come before *Dominus vobiscum*, it can be seen that this instruction merely prohibits the incensation of the choir before the offertory when the creed is not said. On these days the Mass, the choir's incensation omitted, continues at once with the Offertory.

[41] See Chapter XVII, note 68, and note 10 of this chapter.

[42] Col 838*; M.52.

[43] A detail taken from the Roman rite.

§6. THE CONCLUSION OF THE OFFERTORY AND THE PREFACE

The torchbearers[44] come from their places in the first form of the choir to the step, bow with the thurifer and accompany him to the vestry to put on albs[45] and fetch their torches. They return during the *Hanc igitur* and kneel at the presbytery step, holding their torches aloft,[46] until after the elevation.[47] They then return their torches to the vestry, going thither with the thurifer, and, having laid aside their albs, return with him presently, resuming their places in the choir.

When the celebrant says *Orate fratres*,[48] the deacon arranges the front fringe of the celebrant's chasuble and then comes up to move the missal closer to the corporal.[49] He replies *Spiritus sancti gratia* quietly, points out the secrets and finds the preface. Then he returns to his step behind the celebrant.[50]

As the deacon goes up to the celebrant's left, the acolyte and the taperers go to the credence table, where the latter help the former put on the humeral veil. At *Per omnia saecula saeculorum*,[51] the deacon goes to stand at the celebrant's right. The acolyte, wearing the humeral veil, comes between the taperers to stand behind the subdeacon, on the next step down. The deacon takes the paten in his bare hand[52] and, returning to his step,[53] hands it, covered with the chalice veil,[54] to the subdeacon, who in turn hands it to the acolyte, who holds it through both the chalice veil and the humeral veil[55] and remains holding it until the Lord's Prayer. To do so, he holds his left arm horizontally across his breast and holds the paten aloft in his right hand, supporting his right elbow on his left hand.[56]

---

[44] See *Processions*.278 for the existence of two torches held by choristers before the altar for the elevation at High Mass on all doubles, feasts of nine lessons and the weekly commemoration of Our Lady. There seems no reason why more torchbearers (preferably even in number) should not be present on very solemn occasions. Likewise, the possibility cannot be excluded of there being torches also on other days, as is the custom elsewhere.

[45] C 22.2 and 36.2 have the choristers who will act as taperers and thurifers at Vespers go to vest after the third psalm. Presumably they resume their surplices for Compline, which follows immediately. See also Chapter III, note 11.

[46] The torchbearers are described as *torchetos tendentibus* (*Processions*.278), which, if not a scribal error for *tenentibus*, suggests holding the torches aloft, an action that, indeed, would make the Host, elevated high above the altar, itself raised above the floor of the sanctuary, more easily seen.

[47] Or until Communion. See Chapter II, note 25.

[48] OPraem.IV.100-1, OP.1065 and *Tracts*.79, which has the deacon also arrange the celebrant's chasuble at *Orate fratres*, but without kneeling.

[49] OP.1065.

[50] For the flabellum, see Chapter II, note 34.

[51] C 66.27 gives *tunc*, which probably refers to *Per omnia* rather than to *Sursum corda*. Rock IV.225 and Wells.37 agree.

[52] OP.1070.

[53] So the Dominicans. In the Roman rite, the subdeacon receives the paten at the altar and comes round the south side, since he is already at the altar for the offertory. There is no reason to assume that at Sarum the subdeacon and acolyte came up to the altar at this point.

[54] It is clear from C 66.27 that the subdeacon receives the paten in the offertorium, but it is not said whether the deacon picks up the paten from the altar with his hands or through the offertorium also. The Dominican deacon uses his bare hands (*Tracts*.82; OP.1068). See note 1.

[55] The Dominican subdeacon holds the paten through either the chalice veil or the humeral veil (OP.1035; OP.1068), but handing the bare paten to the acolyte is another matter. It is also unclear how the veil would return to the altar if it were retained by the acolyte at the *Pater noster*. The arrangements suggested here, though imperfect, may be considered adequate.

[56] *Tracts*.79; *Tracts* (Plate I) and OP.1035.

Having accompanied the acolyte to the altar and having assisted him with the humeral veil, if necessary, the taperers stand at their tapers. As the *Sanctus* is begun,[57] they bow and go to their places in the choir, at the end of the first form of stalls, leaving their burning tapers in their usual places before the altar.[58] They remain there, standing and kneeling with the choir,[59] until they see the celebrant bow at *Supplices te rogamus*. However, if the taperers are to hold torches for the elevation, they go to the vestry to fetch them at this point, accompanying the thurifer, who waits at the south of the sanctuary until now.

At the end of the preface, the deacon goes up to the celebrant's right and the subdeacon to the celebrant's left.[60] There all three say the *Sanctus* quietly. At *Benedictus*, all three sign themselves.[61] When they have finished saying the *Sanctus*, the ministers return to their steps, where they remain, and Mass proceeds immediately as usual[62] while the choir continues the *Sanctus*.[63]

As the *Sanctus* is begun, the church's sanctus bell is rung three times.[64] There should be no need for a supplementary handbell to be rung at this point.[65] At *In nomine Domini*, all sign themselves and the choir faces the altar.[66]

---

[57] C 66.28. The taperers are to go down into the choir *dum secretum misse tractatur*. This ambiguous expression could refer to the secrets onwards or to the *Sanctus* onwards. The latter moment (supported by S.267) seems more likely, makes for neat choreography and allows the taperers to assist the acolyte with the humeral veil. See Missal.xi and Maskell, page 78.

[58] The reasonable supposition of Rock IV.225.

[59] Of the taperers, C 66.28 has *in choro moram faciant, exteriorem locum prime forme tenentes*. Of the ministers round the altar, C 14.2 has *non genuflectent sed quilibet in suo gradu stet*. Chambers, page 361, quoting no complete authority, has the taperers observe the postures of the choir and this prescription seems reasonable.

[60] Cons 39.23.

[61] OP.1067.

[62] From now on, the books give but sparse directions for the ministers. Consequently, the customs of other churches and uses become much more influential. So does speculation, principally concerning three matters: (1) whether the deacon and subdeacon held torches at the elevation; (2) whether incense was used at the elevation; and (3) whether the flabellum should be used. The vexed question of the bells is dealt with in Chapter II, note 26. For (1) and (3), see the explanations given in Chapter II, notes 25 and 34. *Ad* (2) incense at the Consecration was apparently in use at Chichester in the early fourteenth century (King, *Roman Church*, page 168) and was adopted by the Dominicans. It seems likely, therefore, that it was also used at Sarum, *pace* Morse §82, who misinterprets the rubric at Col 861*, which deals with the incensing of tombs at Requiems, not with the use of incense at Mass per se. Likewise, Morse's appeal to the consuetudinary of Wells (*loc. cit.*) is ineffective: incensation at Wells was carried out on a different scheme from that followed at Sarum, as the passage adduced shews. The Dominican practice of having the deacon swing the thurible at the Consecration (not the only approach found, cf. King, *Roman Church*, page 168) has been adopted here.

Despite its Dutch origin, Adrien Ysenbrandt's *Mass of St. Gregory* appears to depict all these elements in a disposition compatible with the solutions adopted here: a subdeacon (?) kneels on the left, holding a torch in his left hand and raising the chasuble with his right; the deacon holds a torch in his left hand and swings the thurible with his right; a lesser minister (the thurifer?) rings the bell, kneeling at the south of the altar.

[63] Col 610: *confestim*. The Dominican celebrant is enjoined to pronounce the words of the first part of the Canon so slowly that he should not reach the elevation before the choir has concluded the *Sanctus*. See also Chapter VIII, note 51. He may take his time over the *Memento* of the quick.

[64] See Chapter XII, note 23.

[65] Rock IV.178. For the vexed question of the various bells, see Chapter II, notes 25 and 26. For the handbell at the *Sanctus* at High Mass, see Fortescue, *The Mass*, page 343.

[66] C 13.5. Against *Tracts*.79.

XIX

THE CANON TO THE COMMUNION

§1. THE CANON

For the entirety of the Canon, the celebrant proceeds as at Low Mass.¹ When they are not ministering elsewhere, the deacon, subdeacon and acolyte stand behind him on their steps. The deacon comes up to the left of the celebrant when the pages of the missal need to be turned.² Unless they hold torches, the taperers stand at their places in the choir.

The celebrant says the Canon a little more slowly than the rest of the Mass,³ but the singing of the *Sanctus* should not delay the Sacring.⁴ As he extends his hands at *ut placatus accipias*, the deacon steps to the right and the subdeacon comes up to stand on the deacon's step slightly to the left of the celebrant. The thurifer leaves the torchbearers on the step and goes to impose incense.

As the priest makes the sign of the cross over the offerings at *bene* ✠ *dictam*, the deacon and subdeacon kneel⁵ on the edge of the footpace, the deacon to the celebrant's

---

¹ As in the Roman Missal, most of the Sarum rubrics imply that the celebrant himself covers and uncovers the chalice (*discooperiat, cooperiat*). There, however, it is the deacon who does so. For Sarum ambiguity is removed by Col 619 (*sacerdos discooperiat*) and Col 620 (*cooperiat sacerdos*). If the greater corporal is used rather than the pall, moreover, it is safer for the priest to operate it. The deacon only assists, it seems, when the celebrant is holding the Host, at *Per ipsum*.
² OP.1068.
³ Col 649 (*Cautelae Missae*): *morosius*.
⁴ C 14.2 (*licet Sanctus finiatur ante elevacionem corporis Christi*) seems to contemplate the possibility that the *Sanctus* can sometimes be long enough to require being sung at least as far as the elevation, which evidently was not yet regarded as important enough to interrupt the *Sanctus*, as happens now in the Roman rite. *Tracts*.80 has the celebrant pronounce the Canon slowly enough not to reach the elevation before the choir has finished the *Sanctus*. To do otherwise nowadays might cause admiration.
⁵ Did the ministers kneel? *Tracts* (Plate I), taken from the Morris Missal (ca. 1320), shews the ministers standing. This, however, is not an accurate representation of the ceremonial at the time. It conforms to the instructions of neither Cons 39.27 nor C 66.27, since either the subdeacon or the acolyte is missing. As a further example of inaccuracy, none of the men appear to be wearing maniples. The picture, therefore, is an allusive composite that draws particular attention to two elevations: that of the Host and that of the paten. That the ministers are standing in the picture, therefore, need not be taken as evidence that they really stood at the elevation. Nor can it be deduced that the ministers did not kneel in the days before the celebrant genuflected, since in *Tracts*.80 the ministers kneel for the Consecration and the celebrant only bows. The Norfolk Ranworth Antiphoner (fol 107v) also shews the elevation of the Host with the ministers kneeling on either side of the celebrant holding up his chasuble. Therefore, since there seems to be no Sarum-related evidence to suggest that the

right, the subdeacon on the left. All in church except the thurifer kneel with them.[6] The acolyte kneels on the edge of the subdeacon's step. The thurifer comes up the south side to the deacon's step and delivers the thurible into the deacon's right hand. If the thurible's chains are too long for the deacon to swing it decently single-handedly, the thurifer should fold up the chains before giving it to the deacon, who should take it with the chains thus shortened. The thurifer descends the steps again and, having taken the handbell (if it is used),[7] kneels on the bottom step facing north. If, however, a larger bell operated from the sanctuary is used, he will kneel next to its rope.

The deacon swings the thurible continuously[8] during the Sacring. At the elevation, the ministers raise the back of the celebrant's chasuble slightly to relieve him of its weight.[9] The thurifer rings the bell continuously during the elevation.

As soon as the chalice is covered, the ministers and the acolyte rise. The thurifer leaves the bell, comes up the south side and takes back the thurible from the deacon. The deacon and subdeacon resume their places on their steps behind the celebrant. As the Canon continues, the thurifer and torchbearers return their instruments to the vestry.[10] Upon their return, the torchbearers and the thurifer take up their places in the choir.[11]

At *Supplices te rogamus*,[12] the taperers leave their places in the choir and come before the altar. There they bow and with the deacon and subdeacon go straight to the credence table or to the piscina, where they assist the sacred ministers to wash their hands.[13] When they have done so, the sacred ministers return and take up their usual

---

ministers stood, and there is late evidence (both English and Dominican) to suggest that ministers did kneel even before the celebrant's genuflection was introduced, it has been thought reasonable here to have the ministers kneel. The instruction of C 14.2 that they stand must be understood of the rest of the Canon.

[6] See Chapter XXII, note 58.
[7] See Chapter II, notes 25 and 26, and Chapter XVIII, note 65.
[8] So, apparently, the Dominicans (*Tracts*.80). Swinging the thurible seems to be an older form of using incense at the Consecration, rather than incensing the Sacrament at the elevation. King (*Roman Church*, page 168) reports that, at Laon in the thirteenth century, thuribles were swung from the *Sanctus* until the Communion. The Dominicans' *inceset continue* may well refer to swinging *in situ* rather than *ad Sacramentum*. Nowadays, the Dominican deacon incenses the Sacrament at each elevation (OP.1069). In practice, either method could be adopted.
[9] The excessive raising of the chasuble that one sees in churches nowadays is quite grotesque and should be avoided.
[10] *Tracts*.80 has the Dominicans' lights removed after the consecration of the chalice.
[11] OP.967–8.
[12] C 66.28.
[13] Writing of the Anglo-Saxon liturgy, Rock IV.41 has the deacons wash their hands at the altar with water brought to them by the acolytes. However, by the fifteenth century, the celebrant went to the piscina to wash his hands at the ablutions (see Chapter X, note 18), so it is likely that the ministers did likewise. Even when the celebrant later washed his hands at the south end of the altar, it is not unlikely that the ministers did so at the side, as they did earlier at the making of the chalice

C 66.28 appears to suggest that both sacred ministers washed their hands (*ad ministrandum diacono et subdiacono in manuum ablucione*). However, only the deacon will assist the celebrant with the elements at the end of the Canon, so there is little point in the subdeacon's hands being washed. For this reason, since Wells.37, Cons 39.28 and Cons 39.29 all imply that the taperers and the subdeacon assisted the deacon to wash his hands alone, it would not be unreasonable to omit the subdeacon's lavatory. At OPraem.IV.141–2, the deacon alone washes his hands, the subdeacon being occupied with the paten. It is strange that King, *Roman Church*, page 339, considers the reference of Amalarius to this lavatory unique.

positions. The taperers again assume their positions before the altar,[14] walking before the ministers and bowing with them in a line at the foot of the altar.

At *Sanctificas*, the deacon goes up to stand at the celebrant's right.[15] At *Per ipsum*, the celebrant and the deacon together discover the chalice. To do this, the celebrant places his right hand on the corporal and takes the upper left corner of the corporal as the deacon removes the upper right corner of the corporal with his right hand. Once the chalice is discovered, the deacon, using his left hand to keep his right sleeve from

---

[14] The books are silent on this point, but they are not bidden to return to the choir and there is no reason for them to stay by the credence table, which is their usual place in the Roman rite. The Dominican acolytes stay before the altar throughout the Canon. The taperers should be in the sanctuary for the Pax and to assist with the ablutions after Communion.

[15] The ritual that takes place here is a relic of the old elevation at the end of the Canon on which the Anglican ecclesiologists, anxious to deny transubstantiation at the Consecration, were so insistent. Although the barest trace of it may still be seen in the Roman rite, it has not survived at all in the Dominican rite or, apparently, in the Use of Hereford. It is described only cursorily (and unclearly) by the Sarum books (Col 619, C 66.29, Cons 39.29, and M.89). John of Avranches gives a few more details of the rite as it stood in the eleventh century, and the Cistercians have preserved it almost complete.

Although peripheral elements of the ceremony are mentioned (not all in all sources), the elevation itself is not mentioned at all in the Sarum books, and our task is to decide whether this omission is accidental or whether, on the contrary, the elevation had dropped out of the liturgy, leaving the deacon with nothing to do but assist with the corporal and kiss the altar and the celebrant's shoulder. It is by no means inconceivable that the rite should be so reduced. Other rituals (not least the reduction of the old Roman prayers of the faithful to a mere salutation and a neglected invitation to pray) have been reduced by time to no more than this. However, since the elevation itself is preserved in the Roman rite and rather more than this is preserved by the Cistercians, we have ventured (very tentatively) to presume the survival of the entire rite at Sarum, despite the silence of the books. It would be rash, however, to blame any celebrant who chose to omit this elevation.

The Sarum rite, as described by C 66.29, is as follows: the celebrant discovers the chalice with the assistance of the deacon, who, having washed his hands before this, his first ministration at the altar since the preface, comes to stand on the celebrant's right. After the celebrant has made the crosses in the course of the doxology, the deacon kisses the celebrant's right shoulder and descends. M.89 adds that the deacon kisses the altar before the celebrant's shoulder.

John of Avranches (*PL*.CXLVII.36) has the deacon come up at *Per quem haec omnia* and, taking the right corner of the corporal in his right hand, discover the chalice with the celebrant. After the crossings, both celebrant and deacon elevate the chalice, put it down again and cover it. The deacon then kisses the altar and the celebrant's right shoulder.

OPraem.IV.141–6 at *Per omnia saecula saeculorum* has the deacon place his hand under the chalice's foot and elevate it and then cover it together with the celebrant. At *Oremus*, the deacon kisses the celebrant's shoulder and withdraws. In the Præmonstratensian missal of 1578, the Host was elevated so as to be adored by all (*Tracts*.241).

At OCist.105, the deacon comes up at *Sanctificas*, kisses the altar and removes the right corner of the corporal with his right hand, while the priest removes the other corner with his left. Then the deacon, his left meanwhile holding his right sleeve out of the way, places the fingers of his right hand under the fingers of the celebrant's hand on the chalice's foot to make the chalice stable while the celebrant performs the crossings. As the celebrant begins to sing *Per omnia saecula saeculorum*, he and the deacon together raise the chalice until *Oremus* has been sung. They then place the chalice back on the corporal and together cover it in the same way as they discovered it. Finally, the deacon, bowing to the altar, recedes.

For the little elevation in continental uses, see *Tracts*.241–3.

The actions as described here are a composite of these three authorities.

The instruction to the deacon to help with the corporals is the clearest rubrical indication that, at High Mass at least, the greater corporal was in use. It would be absurd to have the celebrant cover and discover the chalice himself on other occasions but insist on his sharing this act with the deacon at this point, both tussling over the pall.

touching the corporal, places the fingers of his right hand[16] on the foot of the chalice in front, and the celebrant places the fingers of his left hand over those of the deacon's right to keep the chalice stable. The priest now makes the usual crossings with the Host. After *Spiritus Sancti*, the priest and deacon together elevate the chalice to the level of the eyes, the priest holding the Host and the bowl of the chalice with his right hand, as at Low Mass, and the knop with his left hand, while the deacon supports the foot with his right. Immediately, they lower the chalice and lay it anew on the corporal. As the priest says *Omnis honor et gloria*, they cover it in the same way as they discovered it earlier. With joined hands[17] the deacon kisses the altar straight in front of himself and then the celebrant's chasuble on its right shoulder. Bowing to the altar, the deacon returns to his step promptly so as to be in position for the ecphonesis.

§2. THE FRACTION AND THE *PRECES IN PROSTRATIONE*

As the priest sings the monition before the *Pater noster*, the subdeacon turns to the acolyte, receives the paten in the chalice veil from him[18] and turns back to hand it to the deacon, who takes it from him,[19] covered in the chalice veil,[20] once the celebrant has begun the *Pater noster*.[21]

At Masses at which the *Preces in prostratione* will not be said, if he will later take the Pax to the laity, the acolyte stays at the foot of the altar with the humeral veil hanging loose from his shoulders. When the *Preces* will be said, or if he will not take the Pax, the acolyte, aided by the first taperer,[22] removes and folds the humeral veil now. Leaving the veil on the credence table, he retires to his place in the choir. He will either receive the Pax there with the others or come back to put on the humeral veil and take up the pax-brede as necessary.

The deacon, meanwhile, going up to stand on the footpace at the celebrant's right, holds the paten in his right hand, his arm extended high above his head,[23] in such a way that his fingers hold its edge through the veil,[24] but the rest of the paten is exposed[25] and shines resplendent as a signal that the moment of Communion is approaching.[26]

---

[16] OCist.105. See Chapter XVIII, note 11.
[17] So the Roman deacon kisses the altar at the Pax.
[18] His function being over, perhaps the acolyte returned to his place. In other rites, the subdeacon remains at the foot of the altar and it would be more convenient for the acolyte to receive the Pax here. It is assumed here that the acolyte will remain at the foot of the altar.
[19] C 66.30.
[20] See Chapter XVIII, notes 12 and 54 for this suggestion.
[21] Cons 39.30.
[22] *Tracts*.82 has the Dominican subdeacon assisted by one acolyte (OP.1002 gives the more recent practice), but the Sarum acolyte, being of lesser dignity than the subdeacon, may be allowed to take the veil to the credence himself.
[23] Col 620; C 66.30.
[24] This is not specified, but it is not an unreasonable supposition. If the deacon did not receive the paten from the subdeacon enveloped in the veil, what would become of the veil? If the suggestion in the text is followed, the deacon can lay the veil on the altar, out of the way, once he has handed the paten to the celebrant. See note 18.
[25] Col 620; C 66.30.
[26] King, *Roman Church*, page 350.

At *Da propitius pacem*,[27] the deacon lowers the paten and hands it to the celebrant, kissing his hand. He then returns to the middle of his step.

When the *Preces in prostratione*[28] or equivalent prayers[29] are to be said, they take place before *Pax Domini*. The church bell is tolled.[30] All kneel, save for the celebrant, the deacon and the subdeacon, who remain standing in their places.[31] The *Preces* are said in a distinct voice,[32] not sung, until *Et ne nos inducas in tentationem*, which the celebrant sings, as he does the remaining versicles and the collects, the choir responding. He sings the collects in the ferial tone, reading them from the missal, with joined hands.[33]

As the choir replies to *Pax Domini*, the deacon and subdeacon come up to the footpace, the deacon to the right of the celebrant and the subdeacon to the right of the deacon.[34] There they say the *Agnus Dei* privately with the celebrant and return immediately to their places.[35]

§3. THE PAX

At the Pax,[36] as soon as he has finished the prayer *Domine sancte Pater*, the celebrant lays his hands on the corporal and then kisses the corporal at its right

[27] C 66.30.
[28] Rock IV.184 would have all parish churches say these prayers for the Holy Land, the bishop and the King, which are, in a way, equivalent to the Leonine prayers for the conversion of Russia. *Defensorium Directorii* [1] and [4], however, shortly after making a distinction between general and ceremonial rubrics, states categorically that the rubric concerning these *Preces in prostracione* is *tantum ceremonialis pro ecclesia Sarum. Nam clerici ecclesie Sarum. habent pro psalmis illis. xl. marchas annuales*. In similar fashion were said those prayers sought by private individuals in their wills, &c. See Wood-Legh *passim*. Wordsworth, *Tracts of Clement Maydeston*, page 206, reports an undertaking of the Sarum chapter, difficult to reconcile with the *Preces* printed in the Missal (Coll 631-4), to say certain different *preces* for Henry VII. At Sarum, these *preces* were said only from *Domine ne in ira* (the first Sunday after the Epiphany octave) to Maundy Thursday and from *Deus omnium* (the first Sunday after Trinity) to Christmas Eve, when on most days the choir was already kneeling (C 66.43). It would be reasonable to expect such penitential prayers to be omitted in festive seasons elsewhere also. For the bell commanded to be rung at the *Preces*, see Rock IV.185.

For those ceremonial parts of the Customary which Clement Maydeston asserts bind only the church of Sarum itself and for his reasoning, see his *Defensorium Directorii* [38]-[41].
[29] See Rock IV.185 and Wordsworth, *The Tracts of Clement Maydeston*, page 176, for other prayers said by engagement at this point.
[30] So Rock IV.185 on the authority of Wilkins.
[31] C 66.43. At Durham (Rock IV.185), the choir is said to be *prostratus*, but not so the celebrant and his ministers.
[32] *Rotunde et sine nota* (Wordsworth, *The Tracts of Clement Maydeston*, page 176).
[33] In the Roman rite, the celebrant sings the collects with joined hands at the *Asperges*, when the book is held before him by the ministers, as well as at the Litanies and in the Divine Office. The hands are only extended for prayers that form a proper part of the Mass. In the face of the silence of the Sarum books, it has seemed sensible to import this detail from the Roman.
[34] Col 623, with C 66.32 and the later ceremonial. This represents a change from Cons 39.23 and 23.32 and differs from both the Roman and Dominican rites.
[35] Where the ministers stand after the *Agnus Dei* is not explained, save for the detail that the deacon is at the celebrant's right when he receives the Pax (C 66.33) and that the subdeacon cannot be at the altar when the celebrant comes to the south horn for the ablutions (C 66.34). The Dominican ministers return to their steps behind the celebrant. The ornate standing aside of the ministers for the celebrant's Communion does not appear to be sanctioned by the books.
[36] None of the movements of the hands indicated here are mentioned in the rubrics but can be deduced from general principles.

side.[37] He uncovers the chalice. He takes both halves of the Host in his right hand, using the thumb and forefinger of his left to push the Host towards him if necessary. Steadying the foot of the chalice with his left hand, he touches the right rim of the chalice with the Host[38] and replaces it on the paten. Still steadying the foot of the chalice with his left and holding it by the knop with his right, he now kisses the right[39] rim of the chalice's bowl.[40] He does not cover the chalice again.[41] With joined hands he turns to the right to face the deacon, who has come back to stand at the celebrant's right,[42] on the footpace, to receive the Pax.[43] The deacon bows.

Taking care not to disjoin his thumbs and forefingers nor to touch him with them, bowing neither before nor afterwards, the priest places his hands on the deacon's shoulders as the deacon places his under the priest's arms. Standing thus, they place their heads on each other's left shoulders and their left cheeks close to each other.[44] As they do this, the celebrant says quietly but so that the deacon can hear, *Pax tibi et Ecclesiae Dei*. In the same voice, the deacon answers *Et cum spiritu tuo* and bows to the celebrant, who turns back to the altar and continues with the sacrifice.

Except for the celebrant, who does not bow before or after communicating the Pax, the rule is that only the person receiving the Pax bows beforehand, but both persons bow afterwards.

---

[37] Col 624; C 66.33.
[38] So B II.496 and M.92, in a rubric not found in the printed missals or most versions of the New Ordinal. It is possible that this rubric reflects French influence. King, *Roman Church*, page 363, refers to several French uses in which the Host itself was kissed at this point. Kissing the Host itself was forbidden in England (see King *loc. cit.*), but kissing the chalice touched by the Host is a mitigated form of the same phænomenon.

The rubric (*corpore Dominico prius tactam*) is expressed atypically. *Tactam* is a perfect passive participle. Most such participles found in the rubrics of the *Ordinarium* and *Canon Missae* are either in ablatives absolute or used adjectivally or semi-adjectivally (e.g. *conversus ad populum*). Only two are used in a purely temporal sense. The former (Col 617) instructs the celebrant to put down the Host *in modum crucis per eandem factae*. While a present participle might have been expected, the participle reflects the intimate connection between the main action (*reponat*) and the way in which the action is carried out (*in modum crucis*). The latter rubric, here, takes two actions of equal importance (touching and kissing) and demotes the former to little more than an adjective. Somehow, this does not ring true. Is it implausible that this rubric, found in French editions, is a printer's addition and does not really reflect genuine Sarum practice?

[39] *Tracts*.82 and OP.1294 go no further than instructing the celebrant to kiss the lip of the chalice but, in practice Dominican celebrants kiss the right edge, whereas the Carmelites, who have both hands round the chalice's bowl, kiss the rim at the front.

[40] Col 624 and C 66.33.

[41] Because kissing the chalice and kissing the deacon are part of a single action and so should not be interrupted. Moreover, as soon as he has given the Pax to the deacon, the priest will say the prayer *Deus Pater fons et origo*, holding the Host over the chalice.

[42] Col 624.

[43] The Sarum books give details of the formula and the order in which the Pax is handed down to the deacon, subdeacon and choir but say nothing about the ceremonial, nor about the other ministers and the congregation. Practice and precedence must have varied considerably from church to church, but the order recorded in Rock IV.186 is not in agreement with the rubrics of the Missal (Col 624). The indications given here are taken from Dominican, Carmelite and Roman practices combined with a good deal of guesswork.

[44] Neither the Sarum books nor *Tracts*.82–3 give the method whereby the Pax is to be communicated. The embrace or accolade is the most common in modern times and so has been adopted here. For other methods, possibly more likely to create wonder nowadays, see King, *Roman Church*, page 362.

The deacon comes down to the subdeacon's step and, turning north to face him, gives him the Pax⁴⁵ as he received it. The subdeacon gives the Pax to each of the taperers in turn as they approach him and then turns back to face the altar.⁴⁶

Having communicated the Pax to the subdeacon, the deacon goes to the choir step,⁴⁷ where he gives it to the representatives of the choir, first of the side of greater dignity and then of the other,⁴⁸ who take it to the choir in due order.⁴⁹ Returning to the sanctuary, the deacon goes up to his step to stand behind the celebrant.

If the congregation is to receive the Pax, the pax-brede⁵⁰ is employed. In this case, the ministers and clergy receive the Pax in the usual way, *per amplexum*. The acolyte⁵¹

---

⁴⁵ Col 624.

⁴⁶ So the Carmelites; cf. *Tracts*.82. The Sarum books make no mention of anybody other than the deacon giving the Pax to anyone. However, it strikes one as odd, and at variance with other rites, to have so august a figure as the deacon taking the Pax to the lowly taperers. The suggestions made here seek to reconcile the prescriptions of the Sarum books, meagre as they are, with the use of a single pax-brede. In practice, the only two practical procedures are either (1) to have the Pax given to the clergy alone without the pax-brede, or (2) to have the Pax given to the clergy without the pax-brede and to the congregation with it.

⁴⁷ Sarum is unusual in that it is the deacon (*ipse diaconus*, Col 624, against the mistaken C 66.33) who bears the Pax to the choir, whereas the Carmelites, Dominicans, early Præmonstratensians and the Roman Rite all presume that the subdeacon takes the Pax. (Only the Arundel Ordinal assigns this function to the subdeacon; see M.93.) This peculiarity makes reconstruction more difficult. The Roman books suppose that the Master of Ceremonies accompanies the subdeacon (who is the bearer of the Pax) to the choir and then is the first to receive the Pax, whereas the Carmelite Missal assumes that the thurifer accompanies the bearer. See Solans Part II, page 418. At Sarum, there is no indication that the deacon is accompanied on his way to the choir step, though it is choreographically neat for the laity's Pax to descend at the same time as the choir's. Moreover, in the other rites, the minister gives the Pax to the clergy in choir individually, whereas at Sarum, the deacon merely goes as far as the choir step, and it is the rulers of the choir who give the Pax to each of the clergy in choir (see Col 624: *et ipsi pacem choro portent uterque suae parti incipiens a majoribus*).

⁴⁸ In Sarum church itself, these were the dean's and the precentor's sides, respectively (C 66.33).

⁴⁹ C 66.33 and Col 624. See Chapter XXII.

⁵⁰ While in ordinary parishes, when Mass was celebrated without the attendance of sacred ministers, the Pax was kissed by the celebrant and passed to the congregation by the clerk (Cf. Duffy, *Stripping*, page 127, and Rock IV.187), the process of transmitting the Pax at High Mass is more obscure. Even in the well-regulated Roman rite, Solans, page 418, writing of Spain, where the use of the pax-brede has survived to the present day, gives three authorities (De Herdt, Carpo and Olalla) which make different recommendations. In light of this, perhaps it is legitimate to give one's own suggestion without fear of doing grave violence to the rite. Here we suppose that the deacon transmits the Pax *per amplexum* to the rulers of the choir, who can only really employ the *amplexus* if they are to transmit the Pax down either side of the choir simultaneously. At the Chrism Mass, when the Pax was taken by the single deacon of the Chrism to the choir, the vessel containing the Chrism took the place of the pax-brede (Cons 114). The deacon does not give the Pax individually to each of the clergy in choir (Col 624).

In the absence of detailed guidance from the Sarum books, we have followed De Herdt t. I. p. 2. n. 53 for the giving of the Pax to the laity.

⁵¹ The acolyte is the senior server and is perhaps to be identified with the parish clerk, one of whose duties was that of distributing holy water round the parish. Duffy, *Stripping*, page 127, mentions a famous incident in which the pax-brede was tendered to the laity by the holy-water clerk (*aquaebajulus*). The same anecdote makes it clear that the clerk offered the pax-brede to the congregation one by one; in other words, the pax-brede was not passed from layman to layman.

Edward VI's visitors at Doncaster in 1548 had the clerk bring the Pax and stand 'within the church door' (*Processions*.144). Becon, pages 261–2, states, though whether with accuracy or through invective is not clear, that 'the boy or Parish Clerke carryeth the Pax about'. Rock III.219 mentions an instance of a bearer of the pax-brede who was also in charge of ringing the sacring chimes, but at IV.227 he has the subdeacon present the pax-brede to the celebrant, though without providing any authority for this assertion.

puts on the humeral veil[52] at the credence table and comes to the altar during the prayer *Domine Sancte Pater*. He takes the pax-brede with its cloth and stands *in plano* to the south of the altar. While the deacon is embracing the subdeacon, the acolyte comes up to the celebrant, kneels to his right facing north[53] and with his left hand[54] offers it to the celebrant to kiss.[55] The celebrant says *Pax tibi et Ecclesiae Dei* and kisses it, the server replying *Et cum spiritu tuo*. Having wiped it with the cloth in his right hand, the acolyte kisses the pax-brede in his turn and then, having wiped it anew, goes to the chancel step or nave to administer the Pax to each layman[56] in turn, repeating *Pax tibi*, &c. to each and wiping the pax-brede between kisses, while the deacon, following the acolyte, goes as far as the choir step to pass the Pax to the rulers of the choir *per amplexum* as above. When the congregation has finished receiving the Pax, the acolyte replaces the pax-brede on the altar.[57] The Pax must be over before the celebrant sings *Dominus vobiscum* before the postcommon, and, if possible, before the ablutions.[58]

During the Pax, the celebrant continues with the Mass. The subdeacon remains on his step but may turn the pages of the missal if necessary until the deacon has returned from the choir step.

---

[52] Olalla.285.
[53] Goude, Plate XXVII, which describes the Roman rite as celebrated by the Observantine Friars Minor, *pace* the Roman *Caeremoniale Episcoporum*, which would deny the Pax to any who does not stand to receive it (Lib. I c. 24), and the silence of the Sarum books concerning kneeling. Nowadays, when the *amplexus* is employed instead of the pax-brede, the deacon stands to receive the Pax, but when it is given at Low Mass in the Roman rite the server receives it kneeling. See also Olalla.276–295.
[54] Rock IV.187.
[55] Olalla.283, quotes Gavanti: *Laicis vero datur [pax] per instrumentum osculatum ab eo, qui pacem a Celebrante accepit immediate*. See also Col 844* and Rock IV.186.
[56] Olalla.283 quotes Gavanti: *Ab Acolytho Laicis numquam vero a Diacono, alicui datur*. This agrees with English practice, as far as it is known. See the references provided by Duffy and Rock in note 50.
[57] Olalla.285.
[58] Olalla.286.

XX

FROM THE ABLUTIONS TO THE END OF MASS

After the celebrant has said the prayer *Gratias tibi ago*, the deacon comes up and stands at his left. Once he has gathered the crumbs into the chalice, the celebrant goes to the south corner as usual, followed by the deacon, who brings the purificator with him.[1] During the ablutions, the deacon administers the purificator to the celebrant, but otherwise the celebrant conducts the ablutions as at Low Mass.

At the south corner, the celebrant is met by the subdeacon (who has come round *in plano*), the acolyte and the taperers,[2] who take up the same positions as after the offertory. The first taperer brings the cruets; the second, the ewer and basin with the towel. As the celebrant approaches, the subdeacon and acolyte go up the steps to meet him, followed by the taperers. Standing on one of the steps, the subdeacon turns to receive the cruets. Both subdeacon and acolyte[3] bow to the celebrant, and the subdeacon administers the cruets for the ablutions as the clerk does at Low Mass.

After the ablution with water, the deacon goes back to the book, followed by the celebrant, who comes to the middle to invert the chalice over the paten. As the celebrant says the prayer *Adoremus crucis signaculum*, the deacon bows[4] with him.

After the prayer *Adoremus*, &c. is finished, the priest stands erect and turns slightly towards the deacon. The deacon takes the chalice from the paten and raises it to touch the celebrant's lips so that he may drain the last drop. As the celebrant returns to the south corner to wash his hands, the deacon stands in the middle of the altar and dresses the chalice with the purificator, the paten, the pall, the veil and the corporal,[5] which he inserts in the burse that has lain on the altar where the acolyte placed it earlier.[6] To

---

[1] This is nowhere mentioned, but it would both be helpful and give the deacon something to do.
[2] Unlike at the offertory, no mention is made of *alii ministri*, but their involvement seems fitting and not unlikely. That the acolyte should minister the water and the subdeacon the towel does not seem to contradict the rubric at M.95 (absent from the Missal and the Customary) *et subdiaconus ei ministret*. For the reasons behind this supposition, see Chapter XVIII, note 37.
[3] As is usual when two servers minister together.
[4] This action is invited by the plural *Adoremus*, but the rubrics remain silent on the matter.
[5] Some ordinals and the M.95 (which, however, corrects itself in a note) say that the corporals are placed under the chalice, and Chambers follows this quaint interpretation. Cons 39.34, C 66.34 and OP.1041 and other uses direct the corporals to be placed on top of the chalice, as is suggested here.
[6] See also Legg, *Ecclesiological Essays*, Plate I.

fold the corporal, he removes the chalice momentarily to the right.[7] Once the chalice is dressed, with the burse placed upon it, he replaces it in the middle of the altar.

At the south corner, the celebrant meets the subdeacon, who has returned the cruets to the first taperer and who has received the towel from the second taperer, and the acolyte, who has turned with the subdeacon to receive the ewer and basin from the second taperer. Both bow to the celebrant. As at the offertory, the acolyte pours water over the celebrant's hands. The subdeacon holds out the towel, which the celebrant returns after use. Bowing again to the celebrant, both return their instruments to the taperers, who go back to the credence table together with the acolyte and assist him to put on the humeral veil again so that he may collect the chalice presently.

Having washed his hands, the celebrant turns where he stands[8] to face the altar, while the subdeacon[9] goes round the front of the steps to bring the missal, as the server does at Low Mass.[10] Once he has replaced the missal at the south corner of the altar, he comes down to his step behind the celebrant and goes up to stand at the celebrant's left. As he does so, the deacon, who has left the dressed chalice in the middle of the altar, comes to his own step behind the celebrant and then goes up to the celebrant's right, where he stands facing somewhat north so as to read better[11] and finds the Communion antiphon. Standing thus, both ministers recite the Communion quietly with the celebrant.

On days when the ministers wear chasubles, the subdeacon, having transferred the book, stands on his step behind the celebrant and waits while the deacon goes behind the altar or to the credence table and there resumes his chasuble.[12] When the deacon returns, he goes straight to stand at the celebrant's right, and the subdeacon goes up to stand at the celebrant's left. So they read the Communion as usual.

While the celebrant and the ministers read the Communion, the taperers come to their usual places by their tapers, together with the acolyte, who, again wearing the humeral veil,[13] comes to stand at the foot of the altar in the middle.

After the Communion, the deacon and subdeacon take their places on their respective steps behind the celebrant. *Dominus vobiscum* and the postcommons follow with the same ceremonies as the collects did earlier.[14] During the first postcommon,[15] after *Oremus*, the deacon comes straight up to the middle of the altar and there takes

---

[7] *Et cum explicatur calix: reponatur super altare a dextris in loco mundo sequestratim et reverenter* (*Tracts*.83).

[8] The rubric *revertat se ad dextrum cornu altaris* found at M.96 may be a relic of the earlier practice of having the celebrant wash his hands at the sacrarium (M.95). In practice, the celebrant cannot move from the right corner between washing his hands and reading the Communion.

[9] C 66.34.

[10] See Chapter XII, note 17.

[11] See Goude, Plate V.

[12] It is not clear at what point the deacon resumes his chasuble. At Rome, he does so after moving the book; OPraem.VI.21–2, whence we have adopted our suggestion, has him do so before the first postcommon; the Carmelites and the Dominicans do not use chasubles. C 66.35 and M.96 say only that the deacon should have resumed his chasuble before singing *Benedicamus Domino*.

[13] OP.1041 explicitly proscribes the humeral veil. However, the words *ea solempnitate qua eum apportavit* (C 66.34) imply the contrary.

[14] Col 629; *Tracts*.83.

[15] Cons 39.34 and C 66.34, together with the implied practice of *Tracts*.83 (*interim*) and OP.1041 (which assumes that there will not be enough time during the last postcommon alone) against M.95.

the dressed chalice. During the conclusion, he turns by his right and hands it to the acolyte, who has come up the steps to receive it, and helps to wrap the folds of the humeral veil round it. At *Per omnia saecula saeculorum*,[16] the acolyte comes down the steps and, while the deacon returns to his place behind the celebrant, preceded by the taperers with their candles as far as the entrance of the sanctuary, takes the chalice back to the vestry[17] with the same solemnity as he used in bringing it in earlier.[18] The taperers go back to their usual places and put down their candles.[19] The acolyte returns immediately, in any case before the end of the last postcommon, and retires. If there be no time to take the chalice to the vestry before the end of the postcommons, it may be taken to the credence table without the assistance of the taperers.[20]

On days when the prayer over the people is to be said,[21] as soon as the choir has responded *Amen* to the last postcommon, the celebrant sings *Oremus* in the usual manner. The deacon turns to the people[22] and subjoins *Humiliate capita vestra Deo*. At these words, all, save the deacon, who is singing, incline their heads. As the deacon turns back, the celebrant sings the prayer in the usual way.

After the postcommons, or the prayer over the people, the celebrant crosses himself, turns and sings *Dominus vobiscum*. The deacon turns with him as usual and sings *Ite, missa est*.[23] On days when *Benedicamus Domino* is sung, however, both the celebrant and the deacon turn back towards the altar for this.[24]

As the choir sings *Deo gratias*,[25] the celebrant and the ministers go to the middle on their respective steps. There the celebrant, bowing before the altar, says the *Placeat*

---

[16] C 66.34.
[17] More accurately, he carries it back (*reportet*). Since a vestry is assumed, he will carry it back to the vestry. *Tracts*.83 does not make it clear whether the chalice is left in the vestry or by the piscina, but OP.1041 has it removed to the vestry. OPraem.IV.195 has the chalice put away (*recondat*) by the piscina.
[18] Cons 39.34 and C 66.34. An acolyte precedes the modern Dominican chalice (OP.1006).
No mention is made of the pyx and the other things that the taperers brought in earlier. *Tracts*.83 has the acolytes remove them to the vestry now. In any case, *ea solemnitate qua eum apportavit* suggests that the taperers should assist the acolyte with their tapers and that the humeral veil should be worn (see note 13). An alternative approach would be for the taperers to precede the acolyte to the vestry without candles, but carrying the vessels that they brought earlier.
[19] *Tracts*.83 would have them remove the cruets, basin and pyx to the vestry. Since the chalice is indeed removed according to Sarum Use, it is plausible that the other vessels should be taken also, but the books are silent on the matter. The question may remain open.
[20] This is a compromise between a strict observance of the rubric and OP.1041, which would have the chalice left on the altar in such a case.
[21] Col 138. The details of the ceremonial are taken from the Roman Missal (*Rubricae Generales* XI.3).
[22] So, sensibly, in the Roman rite, and by analogy with *Ite missa est*. OP.1073 omits all mention of the deacon's turning at these words.
[23] C 66.35.
[24] For the deacon, see C 66.35. For the celebrant, see *Tracts*.84.
The rubric at C 66.35 (*Et notandum quod in ea parte altaris qua missa incipiatur in eadem finiatur*) is noteworthy, forasmuch as it considers the Mass properly so called to begin with the Officium and to end with this *Deo gratias*, both said at the south corner. The accretions (the prayers, at any rate, rather than the ritual actions) before the former and after the latter were still considered semi-private devotions.
[25] The Mass now being ended (OP.813), the Dominican deacon receives the missal either during the *Placeat* (*Tracts*.83) or after the blessing (OP.1075); their subdeacon receives the book of the Gospels during the postcommon (*Tracts*.83) or after the blessing (OP.1042). Our suggestion here is sufficiently consonant with Dominican practice and is choreographically graceful.

prayer and signs himself as usual.[26] Meanwhile, the taperers go up to the altar and hand to the ministers the books with which they came.[27] The taperers, thurifer and acolyte now come to the middle in readiness for their withdrawal, the last carrying the cross again if he brought it in at the beginning of the Mass. As the celebrant stands erect, the ministers come down to the floor, to be followed by the celebrant. All bow to the altar. The celebrant and the ministers cover, and all, turning, withdraw to the vestry, preceded by a verger if customary.[28] They should bow to the choir as at the entrance.[29] If the celebrant and ministers are to wear caps, these should be brought to them by the thurifer before he takes up his position. As they go, the celebrant recites *In principio* silently. If None is to follow, it is begun immediately after the choir has sung *Deo gratias*.[30]

If a blessing, such as that of bread, is to follow Mass, the ministers do not receive their books until immediately before retiring. The celebrant says the Gospel *In principio* at the north corner, removes his chasuble and comes to the choir step to perform the blessing. After this all return to the altar, bow and retire as usual.

In the vestry, they bow to the cross and unvest. The ministers help the celebrant to unvest and then help each other to do so;[31] the taperers assist the ministers and the acolyte to unvest. The thanksgiving is now said.[32] Then, before unvesting themselves, the taperers return to the sanctuary, extinguish the candles, bring to the vestry the various instruments and books, and may replace the vesperal cloth on the altar.[33]

---

[26] C 66.35. OPraem.IV.197–8 makes the celebrant pray, bowed, alone, without the deacon.
[27] OP.1008, OP.1042 and OP.1075 all suppose that the ministers cover while holding their books, not an easy feat. In practice, they often stand beside the celebrant after *In principio* and cover with him before taking up the books from the altar themselves.
[28] So Durham.8.
[29] See Chapter XIII, note 29.
[30] Col 629. If the celebrant will say *In principio* at the altar, the choir still begins None and pays no attention to the Last Gospel (S.313).
[31] OP.1075.
[32] M.97.
[33] OP.1008.

XXI

THE SOLEMN ADMINISTRATION OF HOLY COMMUNION[1]

If Communion is to be administered outside Mass, the same rite is followed as after Low Mass, though the purification may be given by the ministers once they have removed dalmatic and tunicle.[2] However, if Communion is to be administered in its proper place, immediately after the celebrant's own Communion, the rite is more complex. The ceremonial will be different depending on whether the Sacrament is reserved at the altar where the Mass has been celebrated or elsewhere.

When Communion is to be administered at the altar of reservation or from hosts consecrated at the Mass, as soon as the celebrant has finished the prayer *Gratias tibi ago*, the deacon exposes the Sacrament, uncovers the ciborium,[3] turns by his left and without turning his back to the Sacrament returns to his step, standing a little to the south. There, in their respective places,[4] all kneel deeply bowed in adoration for a brief space, with the exceptions of the celebrant,[5] who bows profoundly, and of the taperers, who bring the houseling cloth from the credence table. The deacon begins the *Confiteor*, without note, and all join him. Turning by his right so as to stand a little to the north side of the corporal, the celebrant says *Misereatur* and *Absolutionem*.

If the sacred ministers are to receive Communion, they kneel on the footpace, leaving enough space before them for the celebrant and the houseling cloth, which

---

[1] As in the case of Communion administered without solemnity, the ceremonial described here owes much to the description of Dominican practice as reported in *Tracts*.84–7 and to the Gayton Thorpe and Great Glemham fonts. De Herdt has also been consulted extensively. See the notes to Chapter XI. For the reasons explained there, we presume here that at High Mass the Sacrament will be administered immediately after the celebrant's own Communion. For the Dominicans' general Communion on Maundy Thursday, see OP.1442–3.

[2] This by analogy with the removal of the celebrant's chasuble as illustrated in the Gayton Thorpe. Though unclear, the minister administering the purification in this font may be wearing an amice, which suggests the practice adopted here.

[3] OP.1317.

[4] The modern Dominicans, omitting this moment of silent adoration, have the celebrant kneel as the deacon approaches (OP.857), and the ministers then prostrate on the topmost step, facing each other (OP.1318). De Herdt seems to have the ministers kneel on the footpace at either side of the kneeling celebrant (t. I. p. 2. n. 54. cap. II). If the ministers are not to receive Communion, they may kneel on their respective steps, thus allowing the celebrant more space to turn for the absolution.

[5] *Tracts*.85 against OP.1325.

the taperers spread before them. Having received,[6] they go straight to the credence to drink the purification, after which the subdeacon returns to stand at the celebrant's left.[7] The deacon takes the vessel and napkin and takes his place on the south side of the sanctuary.[8] If the subdeacon is to administer a second chalice, he stands on the north side. The taperers spread the houseling cloth between them, as they take their places *in plano* at the ends of the altar, kneeling and facing each other across the sanctuary.[9]

Meanwhile, the acolyte and the thurifer come from the choir. If they are to communicate, they do so now, kneeling on the bottom step, the acolyte to the right of the thurifer. They rise and go to receive the purification from the deacon, after which they return to their places. If the taperers are to communicate, however, the acolyte and the thurifer hold the houseling cloth for them before going to drink their purification.[10] Other servers receive Communion in descending order of rank.[11] They are followed by the choir, who come up two and two in descending rank, and go to the deacon or the subdeacon for their purification, as is more convenient. They then return to their stalls and pray secretly. If any of the choir do not communicate, they remain kneeling and bowing profoundly in their stalls.[12]

When the clergy have been communicated, the taperers, having risen and abbreviated the houseling cloth somewhat, walk down to the chancel arch, where the laity will receive Communion. The celebrant follows them down the middle of the choir, with the deacon and subdeacon at his sides. All take up their positions again and the laity come to receive. Communicants may come two and two, as the choir did, or form a row across the church, as is more common nowadays. They kneel to receive and stand for the purification.

At the end, the celebrant places the pyx on the corporal. The deacon and subdeacon accompany him to the foot of the altar. There the taperers, having folded the houseling cloth and deposited it on the credence table, receive and remove the vessels and napkins. If there remain hosts to be reserved, the subdeacon kneels on his step, the deacon reserves the Sacrament and the Mass continues with the ablutions as usual.

If the Sacrament is reserved at a different altar, as soon as the celebrant has communicated, the deacon comes down to the foot of the altar. There he receives the humeral veil[13] on his shoulders from the taperers, who have brought it from the credence

---

[6] See John of Avranches (*PL* CXLVII.36) and Morse §236 for the ministers communicating from the celebrant's host.

[7] By analogy with the *Caeremoniale Episcoporum*, Lib. II, cap. xxix.3, if a communion plate is used in addition to the houseling cloth, the subdeacon may hold it under the communicants' chins as he stands at the celebrant's side.

[8] *Tracts*.86 and the *Caeremoniale Episcoporum*, Lib. II, cap. xxix.3, against OP.1322.

[9] OP.1442.

[10] OP.1320, which supposes that the purification is no longer taken other than on Maundy Thursday (OP.1319), would have the houseling cloth held by the sacred ministers while the acolytes are communicated.

[11] *Tracts*.85 would have the houseling cloth held by two brethren for the Communion of the servers at the altar and by the acolytes for that of the convent. The arrangements for communicating the servers and for holding the houseling cloth are not specified by the Sarum rubrics and will vary from Mass to Mass depending on who will communicate.

[12] *Stent super formas prostrati* (*Tracts*.86); *jaceant ... supra formas prostrati* (OP.1314). Du Cange explains *prosterni super formas* as *ad eas procumbere et curvari*.

[13] Unlike in the greater churches of the Roman rite, in England, the Sacrament generally was reserved at the High Altar, so the possibility contemplated here must have been rare. The use of the humeral

table and who now precede him, bearing their tapers, to the altar of reservation. All three return in the same fashion,[14] the pyx enveloped in the humeral veil.

As the deacon returns, all in choir kneel. The celebrant and subdeacon retire a little to the north on their steps to allow the deacon to come up to the altar, where he places the pyx on the corporal and opens it. Turning by his left and without turning his back to the Sacrament, he returns to his step, standing a little to the south. The celebrant returns to the middle and all adore as above. The taperers remove the humeral veil from the deacon and take it to the credence table when they fetch the houseling cloth.

After the Sacrament has been administered and the celebrant has placed the pyx on the corporal, once the taperers have removed the purification vessels to the credence table, the deacon receives the humeral veil at the foot of the altar, goes up, covers the pyx, envelops it in the humeral veil and comes down to reserve the Sacrament, preceded by the taperers. The choir kneels as before.[15] Upon their return, the taperers leave their candles in their places and the Mass continues with the ablutions as usual.

---

veil does not seem a reckless assumption and is in keeping with the genius of the rite, but see Chapter XXXVII, note 14, for a discussion of the pictorial evidence. OP.1751 dispenses with much of this solemnity.

[14] OP.1317.
[15] Tracts.86; OP.1321.

XXII

THE CHOIR AT HIGH MASS

§1. PRELIMINARY NOTIONS

The Sarum books understand by choir the clerical community of Salisbury cathedral assembled in its stalls west of the sanctuary. For a description of the disposition of the stalls, see pages 6-7.

Choir dress is only accidentally liturgical in character and so, for the most part, is subject to the general law in force and the particular norms of each church. In modern celebrations of the Sarum rite, therefore, it should be assumed that the clergy will wear their usual choir dress. In most cases, this will be cassock, surplice and biretta; canons and prelates will have their own choir dress. The exceptions to this rule are when the dress of the choir partakes of the character of sacred vestments. There are occasions on which some clergy in choir are required to wear albs in place of surplices or to put on copes over their usual habit. In addition to this, the upper and second forms of the choir wear copes over the surplice on those doubles that are celebrated with a procession.[1] The black *cappa choralis*, which at Sarum was worn at Mass over the surplice[2] throughout most of the year,[3] assumes a quasi-liturgical character in some functions, particularly during Holy Week, Easter and Whitsun.[4] For the sake of simplicity, and because it may serve as a guide to those modern clergy whose dress differs from the basic surplice, the use of this black *cappa choralis* is here assumed throughout in accordance with the norms in force before the schism.[5]

---

[1] C 46.1. The rubric does not specify the upper and second forms, but nobody of the first form (i.e. in minor orders) is ever said to wear a cope, whereas those of the other forms are frequently required to do so. The phrasing of P.11 is probably careless and does not intend to prescribe copes for the *pueri*.

[2] C 46.1. This black *cappa choralis* was common in cathedrals and some colleges but may not have been universal. St. George's, Windsor, prescribed them *ecclesiarum cathedralium more* (Wordsworth, *The Tracts of Clement Maydeston*, page 234). For a description of the garment, see Rock II.41-3.

[3] C 46.

[4] The norms formerly in force are given in C 46 and Cons 19. See also Frere, *Use of Sarum* I.263, and Rock II.41-59 and 69-75; much other interesting information is to be found elsewhere in chapter VI of the same work. *Processions*.109 also describes the choral habit of Sarum church. On certain doubles, silk copes were substituted for the black *cappa choralis*. For the significance of the *cappa choralis* during the Easter and Whitsun Vigils, see those chapters.

[5] At Lincoln I.391, this cloak is made *de panno qui vocatur deuxsauers et non de burneto siue aliquo alio tali panno excellenti*.

As well as the surplice and the black *cappa choralis*, the clerks of the upper form in the choir of Sarum, and they alone, wore a black almuce (Cons 19.3).

As well as the division by rank, the choir is also divided into the side that is 'on duty' on a particular day (*principalis pars chori* or simply *chorus*) and the other side (*pars chori altera*). The functions of these sides alternate according to schemata that vary from church to church.

The cathedral of Salisbury, like all churches, has customs, uses, and precedences that are proper to its own community. Here, only those ceremonies that can be presumed to be applicable to all churches following the same basic rite are studied. They must be allowed to yield to particular customaries.[6]

In Sarum church, choral functions may be divided into two classes: (1) those when the choir is presumed to be ruled (doubles, Sundays, most simples of nine lessons and certain simples of three lessons in Eastertide),[7] when the choir is placed under the guidance of two or four rulers (*rectores chori*), sometimes[8] under the direct supervision of the precentor; and (2) those on which the choir is not meant to be ruled, when the choir sings the chants undirected and these are intoned either by lesser cantors or by ordinary clergy from their stalls. Even in churches where there are no actual rulers,[9] this division of days affects the ceremonial of the rest of the choir, and references to the ruling of the choir are made below.

Since the rulers of the choir are taken from the upper or second forms,[10] it follows that they must be in major orders. In most churches nowadays, therefore, the choir will almost never be ruled.

§2. GENERAL DIRECTIONS FOR THE DEPORTMENT OF THE CHOIR

The Missal and those parts of the Processional with which this book is concerned assume that the choir is already in its stalls before the function begins.[11] Dispensing with the ceremonies proper to the choir of Salisbury cathedral and those associated with the choral office, we shall concentrate here on the ceremonies required for the choral celebration of Mass. The conduct of the choir in processions is dealt with in the appropriate chapters.

When entering or leaving the choir, clerks bow first to the altar, then to the senior person in choir.[12] When crossing from one side of the choir to the other, a bow to the altar is made in the middle.[13] When the choir enters processionally, they will do so in pairs or fours. On arriving at the choir step, each line bows to the altar, then to each

---

[6] This is the case even in the much more centralized Roman rite (De Herdt t. II. p. 4. n. 72. cap. I).
[7] The list is given at C 20 (also at Cons 20) but will vary somewhat depending on the calendar adopted.
[8] C 5.
[9] All parish churches were bound to possess a *capa chori* (see Chapter IV, note 1), though whether this was meant for the celebrant at Matins and Evensong or for a ruler of the choir is not clear.
[10] C 19.2.
[11] Since, unlike in the Roman rite, the Officium of the Mass is begun before the celebrant enters the sanctuary, it is necessary that the choir should be in its stalls in advance (C 66.2 and C 66.36).
[12] C 2.
[13] C 3.

other and then retires to the stalls. When departing processionally, each man goes to the step, bows to the altar and to his colleague, and departs.[14]

It is presumed that those who may cover their heads do so while sitting but discover when standing.[15]

From time to time, the rubrics require that permission should be sought for certain actions.[16] Permission should probably be sought by bowing to the person from whom it is sought; it should be granted by bowing in return. The bow of the person seeking permission should be lower than that of the person granting it.

When it is necessary to bow at a word or phrase, the choir does so while singing. However, cantors and rulers at the step or lectern bow when they have finished the verse in question.[17]

§3. THE CHOIR AT MASS

The choir stands to face the altar for the intonation of the Officium. As they take up the antiphon, they turn back to face across the church. This is their normal posture during Mass. For the verse *Gloria Patri*[18] only they turn to face the altar. At Masses of St. Mary and when the choir is ruled (except in Passiontide),[19] the Officium is sung after this manner:[20] first, the antiphon is intoned by the cantors or rulers and then sung straight through by the whole choir; then, the psalm verse is intoned and completed as the antiphon was; then, the antiphon is repeated by the whole choir; then, *Gloria Patri* is intoned and then, with *Sicut erat*, completed by the whole choir; finally, the antiphon is sung through by all for a third time. In Passiontide, at Masses of the season, the antiphon is sung straight through, then the verse and finally the antiphon is repeated. At all other Masses throughout the year, the antiphon is not repeated between the verse and *Gloria Patri*. On days when the choir is presumed to be ruled, the celebrant will enter the sanctuary as the choir sings *Gloria Patri*; on other days, as the Officium is intoned.[21] The choir returns the celebrant's greeting by bowing to him.

The clergy in choir stand in their usual position during the sung *Kyrie*,[22] which is intoned as the Officium was,[23] whether farsed or not, and alternated.[24] The farses are given in the Missal[25] and the Gradual.[26] The ordinary chants given in the Gradual are to be observed according to the class of feast and without mixing.[27]

---

[14] OP.751 (1).
[15] See Chapter III, note 18.
[16] E.g. at C 36.2.
[17] OP.761.
[18] C 13.2, describing conduct in the divine service.
[19] See page 209.
[20] Coll 581–82; C17.4; Cons 23.2.
[21] C 66.2; C 66.36.
[22] C 66.7 prescribes sitting for the celebrant and the ministers, but C 12.3 seems to exclude sitting for the choir.
[23] C 17.4.
[24] OP.690.
[25] Col 928*–933*.
[26] Gradual Plates 1+-9+.
[27] C 66.7.

Once intoned by the celebrant, the *Gloria in excelsis* is sung straight through by both sides of the choir without alternation.[28] At the words *Gloria in excelsis Deo, Adoramus te, Suscipe deprecationem nostram* and *Jesu Christe*, they turn to the altar and bow.[29] From *Jesu Christe* to the *Amen* after the last collect, they remain facing the altar.[30] At *In gloria Dei Patris*, they bow to the altar and sign themselves.[31] They sit for the prophecies, the epistle, the gradual and the tract.[32] However, those who are actually singing always stand to do so.[33] For the Alleluya (but not its verse), they stand but only on doubles.[34] These chants and the sequence are intoned by cantors or the rulers[35] and then continued by the choir.

The gradual is sung in this manner.[36] The cantors intone the chant's incipit and then the entire respond is sung through by the whole choir, repeating the incipit. The cantors then sing the verse on their own and the choir repeats the entire respond. However, on most doubles and certain other days when there is a tract and when there is a lesson before the epistle, the respond is not repeated.

The Alleluya is sung by having the cantors sing *Alleluya* without its jubilus. The choir repeats *Alleluya* and continues to the end of the jubilus. The cantors sing the verse, the final pneuma of which is concluded by the whole choir. *Alleluya* is repeated by the whole choir, without its pneuma when a sequence follows, and with it if there is no sequence.[37]

The tract[38] should normally be sung by four cantors, two from each side of the choir. All four intone the first verse, which is completed by the cantors from the principal side; the subsequent verses are alternated between the cantors of each side, the other side singing the second verse. The last verse is sung by all four cantors together. On certain days, indicated in the Missal, the verses of the tract are alternated by the whole choir, that side standing which is singing while the other sits.

For *Dominus vobiscum* before the Gospel, they stand. At *Gloria tibi Domine*, they turn to the altar, bow and sign themselves.[39] They then face the reader throughout the Gospel.[40]

At the intonation of the creed, which is sung straight through with no alternation,[41] they turn to the altar as for *Gloria in excelsis*. Likewise at *Et incarnatus est* they turn to the altar. Standing thus,[42] they bow thrice, at *Et incarnatus est de Spiritu Sancto*

---

[28] C 66.7.
[29] C 13.5. Graduale PL 11+-12+: *inclinando*. OP.759 prescribes a deep bow (*inclinatio usque ad genua*).
[30] C 13.5.
[31] C 13.5.
[32] C 12.3.
[33] C 12.3.
[34] This is the implication of C 12.3. Cf. OP.693-8.
[35] C 17.4. It would be reasonable to assume that the choir retains for the sequence its position at the Alleluya, since that is an emanation from this.
[36] C 22.2; Coll 8 and 9; C 66.16 (which also gives further exceptions applicable only to the cathedral).
[37] Coll 9-10. See OP.694 and OP.700 for the Dominican way of singing the sequence, which by its nature requires alternation.
[38] C 66.18; Col 12; Cons 40.2. The tract is omitted on feasts when the choir is not ruled, the gradual then being repeated (Coll 684 and 694).
[39] C 13.5.
[40] C 13.5.
[41] C 66.22.
[42] C 13.5: *in una conversione*.

ex Maria Virgine, at *Et homo factus est* and at *Crucifixus etiam pro nobis sub Pontio Pilato*. They then turn back. They are incensed and kiss the Text while facing across the church. They face the altar and bow at *Et vitam venturi saeculi. Amen*, signing themselves as before.[43]

They remain facing the altar until the Offertory has been intoned.[44] Continuing the chant, they face across the church. A motet may follow.[45] If it is to be incensed after the offertory, the choir observes the same ceremonies as during the creed.

The *Sanctus* is intoned and continued as was the *Kyrie*.[46] As they sing *Benedictus*, they turn to face the altar, bow and sign themselves as before.[47] They remain facing the altar until *Deo gratias* has been sung at the end of Mass.[48] Generally, they stand but, in all ferial Masses celebrated outside the season from Easter to *Deus omnium*[49] the choir kneels prostrate, facing the altar,[50] from the end of the sung *Sanctus*, rising again only for *Pax Domini*.[51] At all Masses, however, irrespective of their rank and season, they kneel erect for the Sacrings and elevations.[52] They raise their eyes to the Host at the elevation and then make a prostration over their forms until the *Pater noster*, when they stand facing the altar until the *Agnus Dei*,[53] unless the *Preces in prostratione* are to be said. The choir always kneels prostrate for these even at festal Masses.[54] The *Agnus Dei* is intoned and continued like the other chants.[55]

When the choir is not ruled, the easternmost clerks of the second forms receive the Pax from the deacon at the choir step. Each then transmits it to each clerk of his side's upper form in descending order of rank and then to the first clerk of the second form and to the first clerk of the first form, who pass it down their respective forms.[56] The ritual when the choir is ruled is given below.

---

[43] Col 587 et seq. See Chapter VIII, notes 11 and 12.
[44] C 17.4. The word *offerenda* can refer to the offertory antiphon, to the act of oblation at the altar, to the people's offerings and to the entire offertory rite. At C 13.5, by analogy with OP.703-4, in its first occurrence the word has been understood in the first meaning and in the second occurrence in the last. See Missal.xi.
[45] To the lollards' distress (Wordsworth, *The Tracts of Clement Maydeston*, page xvii).
[46] C 17.4. OP.759 prescribes a deep bow at *Gratias agamus* before the preface, but the Sarum books make no mention of this.
[47] C 13.5. OP.704 and F.85 have the choir alter their posture at *Per omnia saecula saeculorum*, but Blunt, page 330, suggests that the choir turns to the altar at *Benedictus*.
[48] C 13.5: *quousque totum servicium misse impleatur*. Elsewhere (e.g. C 66.35), *Deo gratias* seems to be understood as the end of Mass in the same way that the Officium is considered its beginning.
[49] Eastertide finishes at *Deus Omnium*: Col 631.
[50] C 14.2. OP.705 has the choir make a prostration facing across the church.
[51] C 14.2; C 66.42; Cons 18.2. The implication is that on other days the choir must remain standing.
[52] In the Sarum books, there is no indication that the choir knelt for the Consecration outside the times when a prostration was made until *Pax Domini*. This should not be as surprising as it seems: OPraem.XI.44 allows the choir to sit for the Canon. However, at Wells.4 and 74-5 the choir and congregation are told to kneel, and prostrate at that (*cum omni humiliatione provolutis*) *in elevatione corporis et sanguinis Christi*, and this seems both plausible and less likely to cause scandal in a modern congregation. To allow the choir to look at the elevated Host, we follow here the rule of the Constitutions of Lincoln (1212) (Wilkins I.535), against the Dominicans.
[53] C 14.2 does not say what posture the choir should adopt when the prostration is not prescribed, and these details have been taken from OP.705.
[54] Col 631; C 66.43.
[55] C 17.4.
[56] C 66.33; Cons 45.3; Tracts.82.

When all in choir have received the Pax, if it is a day when copes have been worn and there is no general Communion, these are removed[57] and the black *cappae chorales* resumed.[58] On days when a general Communion is held, however, they should be retained until the ministers at the altar have commenced the ablutions. Boys from the first form collect the copes from the clerks of the other forms and extend them in a pile on the floor in the middle of the choir[59] or remove them to the vestry.

The Communion is intoned and continued as were the other chants[60] while the celebrant communicates himself.[61] During the *Placeat*, the choir is presumed to begin None.[62] If this is not the case, it should face across the church until the celebrant departs, bowing in response to the celebrant's greeting.

At Low Mass,[63] the choir kneels throughout, prostrate at the requisite places according to the rite of the Mass, except for the Gospel, to which they attend with the same ceremonies as at High Mass.

§4. CANTORS

In lesser churches, the Mass will be sung by the choir, one or two members of which will act as cantors and intone the chants from their places. Indeed, in the absence of a larger choir, a single surpliced cantor can sing all the chants on his own. However, it is possible for the cantors to observe some of the ceremonial associated with these chants, variable according to the rank of the day and the season. Most of this ceremonial affects the gradual, the Alleluya and the tract.

When the choir is ruled, the gradual is intoned from the choir lectern.[64] On doubles, the cantors (who should be three clerks from the second form, two from the principal side of the choir and one from the other) go to the choir step, bow to the altar and retire to the vestry[65] during the epistle and put on copes. Returning to the choir step and bowing again, they go down the middle of the choir to the pulpitum where, facing east, they intone the gradual and sing its verse. At its end, they return to the choir step,[66] bow and go to the vestry to remove their copes, before resuming their places in choir. On

---

[57] C 46.1. Presumably, the idea is that, since None (at which copes are not worn) will follow immediately after Mass, the choir should be made ready in good time. The rubric does not contemplate the effect of a general Communion (and so has the copes removed before the Communion antiphon is begun), but it is reasonable to assume that the bustle involved in the removal of the copes should not interfere with the administration of the Sacrament. Even at Masses at which there is no general Communion, if the subsequent hour is not to follow in choir, it might be admissible to keep the copes until the end of the Mass. This is likely to be the case in modern celebrations.

[58] Lincoln I.391.

[59] Whence they are supposed to have been taken before the procession and the Mass: P.11 and Rock II.40.

[60] C 17.4.

[61] Col 237.

[62] Col 629.

[63] These directions are taken completely from OP.707.

[64] C 66.13. A more plausible interpretation of *pulpitum* here.

[65] So the cantors of the Alleluya at C 66.15.

[66] C 66.16 has *ad gradum altaris*, but this seems unlikely and does not agree with the bow after the Alleluya (C 66.17).

other days when the choir is ruled, the gradual is sung from the lectern by two boys in surplices (i.e. with no black *cappae chorales*). They bow at the choir step before going down the middle of the choir to the lectern.[67] At the end, they return to the choir step, bow and go to their places.[68]

Outside Advent, when the choir is not ruled the gradual is sung by a single boy from the principal side in an alb at the choir step.[69] This may be one of the taperers, if he is not occupied preparing the lectern for the Gospel.[70] However, when the invitatory at Matins is meant to have been sung by two cantors,[71] the gradual is sung from the choir step by two surpliced cantors also.[72] On Advent ferias, the cantor wears a surplice.[73] The cantor comes to the step towards the end of the epistle, bows and intones the gradual. Whenever cantors must occupy the choir step while the subdeacon is singing the epistle there, they will stand and perform their ceremonial actions behind him.

The Alleluya follows the gradual immediately and is always sung from the same place as this.[74] On days when the gradual has been sung by first-form boys and on certain days in Eastertide,[75] the Alleluya is sung by two upper-form clerks in copes of the colour of the Mass, which they put on in the vestry while the gradual is being sung and remove in the same place after the Alleluya,[76] observing the same ceremonies as the cantors who sang the gradual. Within octaves when the choir is ruled, however, the Alleluya is sung by the rulers of the choir.[77] When the choir is not ruled, the Alleluya is sung by two second-form clerks in copes at the choir step,[78] except in Advent, when it is sung there by a single surpliced boy.[79] The cantors bow to the altar at the choir step before and after accomplishing their duty.[80]

The tract[81] is sung from the choir step[82] by four upper-form clerks in copes, two from either side. All four stand at the choir step to intone the first verse, which is concluded by the two cantors from the choir side. Meanwhile, the other two retire to sit in the easternmost stalls of their side's first form. They return to sing the second verse entire, during which the other two cantors retire to their equivalent stalls. So they alternate the verses, bowing to the altar upon reaching and leaving the choir step. The

---

[67] Cons 39.12.
[68] Cons 39.16.
[69] C 66.37. Cons 113 prescribes a surplice for this boy.
[70] C 66.37 calls this boy *uno solo puero ceroferario*. This peculiar description and the wearing of the alb suggest the possibility that he might be one of the taperers of the Mass. At C 66.14, only one taperer is assumed to cover the eagle, assisted by another boy from the choir.
[71] C 45 and Cons 112 give lists of these days. Certain exceptions concerning the cathedral are given in Cons 111.
[72] Col 9.
[73] Cons 45.2.
[74] Col 10; C 66.15.
[75] C 39.2.
[76] Cons 39.15. Col 10 and C 66.37 give special details for when the verse of the Alleluya is *Laudate pueri*. This rubric is unlikely to be of general obligation.
[77] C 66.15.
[78] C 66.37.
[79] Cons 45.2.
[80] Col 10; C 66.17; and by analogy with what was done at the gradual.
[81] C 66.18; Col 12; Cons 40.2.
[82] Or from the lectern (OP.699).

final verse, however, is concluded by all four cantors at the choir step. During the tract, the rest of the choir sits. On those days when the verses of the tract are alternated by the whole choir, the side which is singing stands while the other sits.

§5. THE RULING OF THE CHOIR

The days when the choir is ruled can themselves be divided into four classes: doubles, Sundays, simple feasts of nine lessons when the choir is ruled by two rulers from the second form only, and certain simples of three lessons in Eastertide. On doubles, the choir is ruled by two principal and two secondary rulers taken from the upper or second form according to the custom of the church;[83] on the other days, two rulers from the second form suffice.[84] The ceremonial differs but slightly depending on whether there are four or two rulers.

The function of the rulers is to regulate the singing, in particular the pitch,[85] to pre-intone and intone some of the chants and to govern the behaviour of the boys, none of whom may leave the choir without their permission.[86] They also carry out certain additional ceremonies. They wear copes over their surplices,[87] carry staves[88] in their left hands[89] and occupy places in the middle of the choir, in front of the first form, facing each other across the church.[90] At the beginning of all the chants, whether intoned by them or not, they turn to the altar.[91] When not occupied about their business, they stand and sit with the rest of the choir.[92]

The rulers of the choir are presumed to be in place before the beginning of Mass. Ideally, they put on their copes at the end of the preceding hour and take up their places in the middle of the choir with the customary bows.[93] Each of the secondary rulers sits on one side of the choir facing the other, immediately east[94] of the principal rulers, each of whom also sits likewise on one side of the choir. In this way, they can easily advance in a line when required to do so. The principal ruler of each class will be that on whose side the choir is that day.

In the cathedral,[95] the principal ruler asks the precentor[96] (or the succentor in his absence)[97] for the tone and pitch of certain chants. To do this, the principal ruler

---

[83] C 19.2; C 70.1.
[84] C 19.3.
[85] By delegation from the precentor, if this is the meaning of *chorum in cantuum elevacione et depressione regere* (Cons 3).
[86] Cons 24.
[87] C 46.3.
[88] See Chapter II, note 33.
[89] Chambers, page 98.
[90] If they did not face each other, they would not be described as turning to the altar at certain moments, e.g. C 12.3.
[91] C 12.3.
[92] C 12.3.
[93] C 2.
[94] This position works well choreographically but is also supported by the fact that it is the secondary rulers who go to the step to receive the Pax from the deacon (C 66.33).
[95] C 17.4; C 18.
[96] The precentor is expected to be present in choir (or send the succentor in his place) on all doubles (C 5.2).
[97] C 10.

approaches the precentor in his stall, bows to him and waits for the instruction. This will normally be a quiet pre-intonation of the chant's incipit. Bowing again, the ruler retires, returns to his fellow (or fellows), who turn to face him and bow, and, standing in the middle of the choir, repeats the instruction to them. The other rulers bow in acknowledgement. Going to the appointed place they then intone or pre-intone the chant. When there is no precentor or succentor in choir, this ceremony is omitted. The principal ruler gives the tone to the others and all go to pre-intone or intone the chant straight away.

At the beginning of the Mass, the principal ruler asks the precentor for the Officium.[98] All the rulers then go to the choir step,[99] the secondary rulers preceding the principal. At the step, they form a line, the principal rulers in the middle and the secondaries at the sides, bow to the altar and intone the antiphon. When the choir has finished the antiphon, the rulers sing the first half of the verse and in due course *Gloria Patri* as the cantors do when the choir is not ruled.

While the choir sings through the antiphon for the last time, the rulers bow again to the altar and return to their places in the middle of the choir. The principal ruler at once returns to the precentor and asks for the *Kyrie*, which the rulers intone together at the choir step as they intoned the Officium earlier. The chant intoned, the rulers return to their places. The same ceremonies are observed at beginning the sequence, Offertory, *Sanctus*, *Agnus Dei* and Communion.[100]

On doubles only,[101] the principal ruler asks the precentor for the *Gloria in excelsis* and goes alone to the foot of the altar,[102] from which he pre-intones it to the celebrant.

The gradual, Alleluya and tract are intoned by cantors from the choir, either at the choir step or the choir lectern according to the norms given earlier. However, for the incipit of each of these, the rulers stand and turn to face the altar. They always stand facing across the church for the Alleluya (but not its verse)[103] except within octaves, when they themselves sing the Alleluya from the lectern.[104] At the sequence, they observe the same ceremonies as for the Officium.

They have no special function during the creed,[105] but they begin the Offertory as they did the Officium.

---

[98] C 17.4.
[99] At least, the intonation takes place at the choir step during Vespers (C 22.2, whence the ceremonial described here is taken). More recently, in many continental churches, the rulers clustered round the great choir lectern (cf. OP.691: *nisi aliqui ad librum stare voluerint*). This is what Rock IV.156–9 presumes would free them from having to juggle their staves and a book. See Pérès, pages 175–6.
[100] C 17.4.
[101] C 18.2.
[102] With Rock IV.216, a much more sensible place for a quiet pre-intonation than the choir step. C. 18.2 does not specify a place.
[103] C 12.3.
[104] C 66.15.
[105] At least the books mention none. Since there is only one tone to which the creed is intoned, this is perhaps not surprising. The celebrant will need to pitch his intonation carefully. At Pontifical Masses, C 5.2 has the precentor pre-intone *omnes cantus ab episcopo incipiendos*, which presumably include the creed. In light of this, it might not be unreasonable to have the principal ruler pre-intone the creed to a presbyter celebrant as he did the *Gloria in excelsis*.

They receive incense before the rest of the choir,[106] first the principal ruler from the principal side, then his fellow from the other side, then the secondary ruler from the principal side, then his fellow from the other. To receive the incense, the rulers turn somewhat towards the east and face the acolyte, who stands in the middle of the choir, facing west. The principal rulers bow to each other. Then the principal ruler from the principal side bows to the acolyte and receives the incense and the Text, bowing to the subdeacon afterwards. In this way, both principal rulers are incensed. The secondary rulers then bow to each other and are incensed likewise.

At the Pax,[107] when there are two rulers, these should come to the choir step to receive the Pax from the deacon, first that from the dean's side and then that from the precentor's. Each then gives the Pax individually to each clerk of his side's upper form in descending order of rank, and then to the first clerk of the second form and to the first clerk of the first form, who pass it down their respective forms. When there are four rulers, the two secondary rulers receive the Pax from the deacon at the choir step as above and take it, each to his side's principal ruler in the middle of the choir. If there is a precentor (or a succentor) who is ruling the choir personally that day, they give the Pax to him[108] before visiting the principal rulers. The four rulers now go to communicate the Pax to each of the clerks of their side's upper form, the principal rulers beginning at the west end of the form and the secondary rulers at the east. They then give the Pax to the uttermost clerks of the second form to pass on in their own form. Finally, the secondary rulers give the Pax to the easternmost clerk of the first form to do likewise.

Having returned to their places after the Pax, once the celebrant has communicated from the chalice, the rulers intone the Communion with the same ceremonies as the Officium. For the remainder of the Mass, the rulers carry themselves like the rest of the choir.

As usual, if the full complement of clerks in major orders may not be had, the choir may be ruled by a smaller number of rulers or even by one if he will be audible when intoning the chants. If, however, a single clerk rules the choir and he is assisted by another cantor when intoning the chants, the cope must not be worn; instead, the ruler appears in the same attire as his colleague.[109] A single ruler takes the Pax to both sides of the choir, beginning with that of greater dignity.

In the cathedral on solemn occasions,[110] the precentor rules the choir personally. In this case, a fifth seat is prepared for him in the middle of the choir,[111] a little west of those of the principal rulers, facing the altar. He gives the tone of the chants to the

---

[106] C 66.24. The books give no details beyond *incipiens a rectoribus chori*. The ceremonies suggested here are taken from modern Roman practice, common liturgical courtesy and reasonable guesswork.
[107] C 66.33.
[108] The precentor will be the ranking parson in choir, since on the days when he is bound to be present (doubles: C 5.2) the dean will be celebrating (C 4).
[109] C 18.2; Cons 23.7.
[110] On greater doubles (C 5.2).
[111] C 66.24.

others unbidden and follows them to the choir step, where he stands between them, to intone the chants.[112] He receives incense and the Pax before the other rulers.[113]

---

[112] Cons 114 explicitly has the precentor intone the *Agnus Dei* at the Chrism Mass. Cons 70.3 has the precentor pre-intone the *Gloria in excelsis* to the celebrant on Holy Saturday. This is not surprising: the celebrant is supposed to be either the Dean or the Bishop. It is inconceivable that in his own cathedral, the Precentor of Sarum should pre-intone anything to anyone whom he outranked.

[113] C 66.24; C 66.33.

BOOK V

SPECIAL FORMS OF MASS

XXIII

MASS FOR THE DEAD[1]

The complete funeral rite is given in the Manual[2] and lies outside the scope of this book. Here only the special ceremonies of the Requiem Mass are considered.

When the body is present, the hearse is erected, with its foot to the east, either in the middle of the choir (in the case of a canon or a king or peer) or in the nave (in all other cases).[3] The hearse is covered by at least one pall[4] and surrounded by candles and, if suitable, banners or other insignia. If there are only two candles, they should be placed at the head and foot of the coffin.[5] There may be many more.[6] It must be possible to walk all round the hearse. On anniversaries[7] of people buried in the church, the tomb may be furnished in this way and the relevant ceremonies carried out there.

---

[1] Some differences between ordinary Masses and those for the dead are indicated clearly by the Sarum books themselves. Other differences are mentioned here only when comparison with other rites suggest them, but restraint has been applied when admitting these. So, e.g., it is presumed that the chalice is brought in as usual, even though this is the case neither in the Dominican (OP.1997, where the usual practice of ferias is followed) nor Roman rites (where the humeral veil is not used: F.133).

[2] M.118–62. The full rite consists of the preparation of the body (M.118–23); its bringing to the church (M.123–4 and P.167–8, although with textual variants; Cons 116); the commendation of the soul (M.142–4) sung in church over the body, during which the priest goes to mark the grave (M.125) and the digging of the same is begun; the office of the dead (M.132–42); the Requiem Mass (M.143); responsories over the body (M.152–4) and the ceremonies surrounding the burial (M.154–62). For the form of apostolic absolution in use before the schism, see M.105–6. The arrangement of the rites in the Manual is made more confusing by its conflation of the obsequies on the day of burial with the prayers said for the dead in the choir of Sarum. With the details given in the Manual, confer B.i.xliv–li, B.ii.271–83 and Wells.35.

The Douay editions of 1604–11 prescribe that, when the body is brought to the church after Vespers, it is to remain there until the morning and the obsequies completed then (M.124–5). However, the body may not be present while the day Mass is said (M.91). The procession to the house and back to the church is ordered like that of an ordinary Sunday. The choir carries candles and wears its ordinary *cappae chorales* (C 46.3 and M.123; not copes, which are probably a misunderstanding of the Douay editions). At no point of the function does the celebrant wear the cope (M.123; M.125; M.152-3, contradicted, however, by the Bodleian Library's MS. Auct. D. Inf. 2. 11. (fol. 188v)). A helpful and well-documented description is given in Rock II.377–418.

[3] M.124 (*canonici vel alterius magnatis*) and Rock II.380.

[4] Palls will often be black but other colours are possible (HA.117 and Rock II.377–419 *passim*).

[5] MS Gough Liturg 3, fol. 72v, *apud* Rock II.394.

[6] See e.g. Rock II.404.

[7] Rock III.73.

The vestments are black.[8] When the body is present and on All Souls' Day, the deacon and subdeacon wear dalmatic and tunicle. On other days, they wear neither these nor chasubles.[9] The organ is silent throughout.[10]

At the foot of the altar, the celebrant omits *Habete osculum pacis* and its accompanying kisses.[11]

At Masses when the body is present and at certain anniversary Masses,[12] after he has incensed the celebrant,[13] the deacon, accompanied by the thurifer, both having bowed to the altar, goes to incense the coffin or tomb. Beginning at the head, he incenses the left side of the body[14] until he reaches the foot, swinging the thurible constantly. He returns to the head and repeats the operation on the other side. He returns the thurible to the thurifer and takes up his usual position.

At the Officium, the antiphon is repeated once after the verse[15] and *Gloria Patri* is omitted.[16] There is no *Gloria in excelsis*. The epistle is sung from the choir step and the Gospel from next to the altar.[17]

At all Masses when the body is present, the gradual is sung by three clerks of the second form in choir dress at the head of the coffin; likewise at all masses for bishops, even if absent, at the choir step.[18] At all other Requiem Masses (except on All Souls' Day),[19] the gradual responsory is sung sitting by the whole choir, but its verse is sung by three clerks either at the head of the body or at the choir step.

The tract *Sicut cervus* is sung from the same place as the gradual by four clerks of the upper form in choir dress standing at the head of the body if present or at the choir step otherwise. The verses are then alternated as explained in the Missal[20] while the choir sits. When the tract is *De profundis*, it is alternated by the whole choir sitting throughout, except on All Souls' Day.[21]

There is no sequence.[22] At the making of the chalice, the water is blessed neither by sign nor by word.[23]

---

[8] C 66.42. But see Chapter IV, note 57.
[9] C 66.42; Col 860*; Cons 45.4. In Sarum church, dalmatic and tunicle are worn also on bishops' anniversaries. Presumably the same may be observed in other cathedrals of their own bishops and in other churches of their founders, &c.
[10] OP.1197.
[11] C 66.4.
[12] Col 861*; M.149.
[13] Col 861* gives *postquam executor officii in inceptione Missae altare thurificaverit*, but, since in the Roman rite the celebrant will be incensed after the altar at the offertory, it seems reasonable to assume that at Sarum too the incensations of the altar and of the celebrant were regarded almost as a single rite.
[14] F.422.
[15] Such is the implication of Col 18 note *, which appears to refer to the absence of *Gloria Patri*.
[16] OP.1994.
[17] Wells.48.
[18] Col 863*.
[19] Col 863*.
[20] Col 864*; OP.1998.
[21] Col 865*.
[22] A sequence (*Dies irae*) is provided as an optional addition at Col 884*. Since the sequence is a development from the *jubilus* of the Alleluya, its presence at a Requiem Mass is incongruous. On the other hand, such incongruity is not altogether exceptional and can be found on Candlemas and Lady Day (Coll 704 and 727).
[23] OP.1011; OP.1217; OP.1994.

At the Gospel, if he has done so at the Officium, the deacon, once he has incensed the middle of the altar, incenses the body or the tomb again in the same way as before.[24] *Dominus sit in corde meo*[25] is omitted. The taperers and thurifer attend as usual but the cross is not carried.[26] At the end of the Gospel, the book is not kissed[27] and the celebrant is not incensed.[28] There is no creed.[29]

At the offertory,[30] on days when the body or tomb has been incensed earlier,[31] the deacon repeats the ceremony as soon as he has incensed the altar[32] without imposing new incense.[33] While he does so, the celebrant waits in the middle of the altar. He should not go for the lavatory until the body or tomb has been incensed.[34]

At the oblation of the people, all kisses are omitted.[35]

In all Masses when the body is present, and in all anniversary Masses and during trentals,[36] but then only,[37] immediately after the lavatory (at Low Mass as soon as the server has returned from leaving the cruet, bowl and towel at the aumbry), the priest, standing in the middle of the altar with hands joined[38] without turning round, sings *Hostias et preces tibi Domine offerimus*.[39] Then, bowing, he says *In spiritu humilitatis* as usual while the choir (or the clerk) replies, *Tu suscipe*.[40] Turning round, he says *Orate, fratres et sorores, pro fidelibus defunctis* in a low voice.[41] Turning back, the priest continues as usual, while the choir or clerk replies, *Requiem aeternam*, &c. and *Quam olim*, &c.[42]

Except on All Souls' Day,[43] the paten is left partly under the corporal by the deacon[44] and not handed to the acolyte,[45] who therefore does not come to the foot of the altar after the offertory. The common preface is said. The deacon does not hold up the paten

---

[24] Col 861*.
[25] O.P.1229.
[26] Col 958, which is contradicted (presumably for All Souls' Day, when the Gospel is sung from the pulpitum) in the note taken from the Gradual; O.P.1997.
[27] *Tracts*.77; O.P.1231; O.P.1994.
[28] F.134. This omission matches that of the kiss.
[29] Col 15, which implies that the creed is not said even on Sundays, rather than that it is said on other days.
[30] The notation of the Offertory *O pie Deus* is printed clearly in the Appendix III of Collins's edition of the Manual.
[31] Col 861*.
[32] Col 961* says *postquam sacerdos sacrificium … loco suo dispositum thurificaverit*, but it is unlikely that the body should be incensed before the altar, and there is no parallel in the Roman and Dominican rites for omitting the incensation of the altar.
[33] The imposition of new incense is not mentioned on the other two occasions when this ceremony is carried out, and there seems no need to impose new incense if the choir and congregation are not to be incensed as well.
[34] Col 861*: *ante lotionem*.
[35] Olalla.206.
[36] Col 596. This is not done in other Requiem Masses, even on All Souls' Day.
[37] Coll 596 and 868*; C 66.25.
[38] Col 595. G.233, has *Sacerdos tenens calicem in manibus*.
[39] Col 595; C 66.25.
[40] Coll 596 and 867*; C 66.26.
[41] Col 596.
[42] Coll 596 and 868*; C 66.26. The chant is given in Appendix IV of Collins's edition of the Manual.
[43] C 66.27.
[44] F.134.
[45] C 66.27.

before Communion but he takes it from the altar and hands it to the priest in the normal way.[46] The *Agnus Dei* has a special form.[47] The Pax is not given,[48] nor does the celebrant receive it from the altar or from the chalice.[49] *Requiescant in pace* is said, facing the altar, instead of *Ite Missa est*.[50]

---

[46] OP.1070. Traditionally, at Requiem Masses, general Communions have not been held. The canonical discipline is more relaxed now; see also OP.1331 for a distinction drawn by the Roman curia in 1741 between the administration of Communion as sacrifice and as sacrament.

[47] Col 623.

[48] Col 623, note b; *Tracts*. 28 (Langforde's *Meditations*): 'Allso know that in the masse of *Requiem* ther ys no pax gewyn to the people.'

[49] *Crede Michi* [33]); OP.1994.

[50] Col 529. If a blessing is usually given (see Chapter X, note 34), it should probably be omitted at Masses for the dead: see *Tracts*.172 (Burckard).

XXIV

WEDDINGS AND THE NUPTIAL MASS

§1. PRELIMINARY NOTIONS AND REMOTE PREPARATIONS

More than in other areas, the liturgy of the Church concerning marriage is bound up with her canon law. Sacramental validity is related to (though not identical with) contractual validity, and both priests and spouses are cautioned to act with prudence lest aspects of sixteenth-century canon law be confused with the norms now in force, since grave harm could follow from this. The relation between the spiritual and the secular arms should also be borne in mind.

The Missal gives the traditional times when it is forbidden to celebrate weddings with full solemnity.[1] Assuming that pious churchmen will wish to respect *devotionis causa* what they are no longer bound to observe *jure canonico*, it is presumed here that the forbidden times are observed. The consent, that is to say, the celebration of marriage without solemnity (by which is meant that part of the function that takes place before the Mass, with the exception of the giving away of the bride),[2] may still be exchanged during the forbidden times.[3] In this case, the nuptial Mass and blessing should be celebrated once the forbidden time has passed.[4] The spouses should go to Confession and receive Communion at least three days before the wedding.[5]

§2. PROXIMATE PREPARATIONS

On the day of the wedding itself, the usual requisites for Mass are prepared and also the following: a book with the words of the service (a missal or a manual), including the parts that are read in the vulgar tongue; if the rings are not to be placed on the book

---

[1] Col 829*. The canons now in force are more permissive. See M.45 for some of the reasons for this prohibition.
[2] M.45.
[3] Col 829*.
[4] Col 829*. This was the custom in England under the Pio-Benedictine Code of Canon Law and agrees with the rubric *carnalis copula non est facienda ante benedictionem super nubentibus*, by which carnal relations after marriage and before the reception of the nuptial blessing (rather than merely fornication) are forbidden.
[5] Council of Trent, session 24, cap. I *apud* M.44n.

(this latter being the preferred option),[6] a plate is prepared in a suitable place; the holy water and stoup; if it is to be used,[7] the canopy or care-cloth[8] (not of a funereal colour) to be held over the spouses and surplices for the servers who will hold it; candles for the spouses if these are to be held during the Mass; bread and wine to be blessed after the Mass. On the south side of the presbytery, west of the sedilia and facing north, are prepared seats for the contracting parties. In smaller churches, where there is no presbytery, these seats will be between the altar and the choir. In any case, they should be in the chancel. The man is responsible for bringing the ring and the *arrhæ*, which will usually take the form of coins of gold and silver.[9] If the woman is a widow, her right hand at least should be gloved;[10] otherwise, her right hand should be bare. It is likely that the woman should be veiled, at least for the marriage itself and probably until the end of the nuptial blessing.[11] The priest will vest as for Mass, but he will not put on the chasuble until the Mass itself.[12] If the function will be sung, he may wear a cope for the marriage itself.[13] If the declarations demanded by the Crown are to be made in the vestry between the marriage and the Mass, the priest will put on the chasuble there immediately before the Mass. Otherwise, the chasuble may be laid on the altar.[14]

If the marriage is to be celebrated solemnly, as presumed here, the priest will be assisted as at the Sunday procession; otherwise, a single server will assist and stand in the deacon's place. Even in this case, four surpliced servers will be needed to hold the care-cloth over the spouses.[15]

§3. THE SACRAMENT OF MATRIMONY

The clergy's procession advances to the area outside the church door, where the function will begin. If necessary, this may take place in the nave. Generally, the man will arrive

---

[6] The plate is contemplated at Col 832* but not mentioned at all at 833*.
[7] Col 839* gives the occasions when it is omitted. The care-cloth is used whenever the nuptial blessing is given.
[8] Rock IV.201.
[9] Col 832*; F.407.
[10] Col 831*.
[11] M.47 suggests that the woman should be veiled from the beginning of the function. This veil should not be confused with the woman's usual headcovering. The books themselves do not mention the nuptial veil, but its presence goes back to pagan Rome and is associated with the nuptial Mass as early as the Leonine sacramentary, where the nuptial blessing is called *velatio nuptialis*. For the use of a circlet, see Rock IV.201–2.
[12] Great Witchingham font, which shews the priest in green vestments (see also Chapter IV, note 58); Hereford.437: *coram presbytero amictu, alba, fanone, et stola revestito*; also Rock I.344, the sixteenth-century *Manuale ecclesie Toletane* and note 43.
[13] A detail taken from the *Rituale Romanum cum appendice Toletano* of 1950 (Appendix, page 42) but consistent with most solemn functions. HA.158 notes 'a Cope with white Rosys called the weddyng Cope' at High Wycombe in 1518–19.
[14] Whether the chasuble be taken from the altar or assumed in the vestry is of little importance and practice probably varied depending on the custom and appointments of the church. Col 343+ has the chasuble taken from the altar on Holy Saturday. For a discussion of this point, see Chapter XXVI, note 41, Chapter XXVII, note 2, and Chapter XXIX, note 36.
[15] Col 839*. In small parishes, it is probably licit to permit laymen in secular garb to hold the care-cloth in case of necessity.

first and the woman will be escorted by her father or friend who will give her away. The clergy form a crescent in a station with the church door behind them. The celebrant will stand in the middle; to his right, the deacon, and to his left, the subdeacon; the other servers stand on either side or behind the celebrant in processional order. Facing the priest stand the spouses, the man to the right of the woman. One of the witnesses will stand on the man's right. The other, who is presumed to be the woman's father, will stand at her left.

Reading from the book before him,[16] the priest reads the introductory admonition, *Ecce convenimus*, in the vulgar tongue.[17] At *hujus viri et hujus mulieris*, he looks at the man and then at the woman. At *admoneo vos omnes*, he should look straight at the congregation.

The priest should now make a similar admonition to the spouses,[18] in a somewhat lower voice, since it is addressed to them and not to the congregation. Before continuing, the priest should ask whether the *arrhæ* have been brought.[19]

Continuing in the vulgar tongue, the priest addresses the man by his Christian name only,[20] *N. vis habere*, &c. He should speak so as to be heard by all,[21] as should the man in reply. The woman's consent is sought likewise.

The woman's father takes her right hand and places it in the man's right hand;[22] or he may lay her hand in the priest's to place in the man's.[23] Saying each phrase after the priest, the man plights to the woman his troth and withdraws his hand.[24] The spouses join hands again and the woman plights her troth to the man in the same way, withdrawing her hand at the end.[25]

The man now places the ring and the *arrhæ* on the priest's book or on the plate held by the server or one of the ministers. The priest should enquire whether the ring has been blessed previously.[26] If it has not,[27] the priest blesses it now, saying the prayers with joined hands if possible and making the sign of the cross as indicated in the book. At the end, he sprinkles holy water on the ring. If the ring has indeed been blessed previously, the blessing is omitted and the ring is given to the man as soon as it has been placed on the book.

---

[16] The font at Great Glemham shews the book held by a surpliced book-boy, but the priest must hold it himself if necessary.

[17] M.45 gives sources for this form in English.

[18] Col 830*. An English form is given in Ebor.24. In the Protestant Book of Common Prayer, this is reflected by the charge *I require*.

[19] M.45 so interprets the words *interroget sacerdos dotem mulieris* of Col 830*.

[20] F.407.

[21] M.47.

[22] Hereford.438.

[23] This seems to be the practice encouraged by the Book of Common Prayer and is that of the *Manuale ecclesie Toletane*.

[24] Col 831*; F.407.

[25] Col 832*, unlike in the Roman rite.

[26] M.48.

[27] The ring only is blessed and becomes a sacramental that should not be repeated. According to Sarum use, the *arrhæ* are not blessed, as is clear from the wording of the prayers.

  The distinction between the dowry, the *arrhæ* and coins given to the poor is not clear from the books, and different customs were probably observed across the country. Missals CA.413 clearly disagree with our Missal and M (since they have the woman handed over later in the service). Missal B agrees with these in order but includes additional details: the handing over of the dowry

The priest now takes the ring in his right hand and delivers it up to the man, who receives it into his left palm.[28] Picking it up with the thumb and first two fingers of his own right hand, and taking the woman's right[29] hand with his left, he repeats each phrase of *With thys ryng*, &c. after the priest. Then, putting the ring lightly on her thumb, he says *In nomine Patris*. He removes the ring and, putting it on her forefinger, says *et Filii*; putting it on her middle finger, he says *et Spiritus Sancti*. Placing it firmly on her ring finger, he says *Amen*. He now takes the coins and drops them into the hands of the woman, who puts them away or hands them to another person to look after. The spouses bow their heads[30] to the priest as he says *Benedicti sitis*, &c. and reply *Amen*. They remain bowing until the conclusion of the prayer *Benedicat vos Deus Pater*, which the priest says as he did the blessing of the ring before.

The procession of the clergy is marshalled as before and enters the church, followed by the spouses, side by side.[31] On the way, the clergy say the psalm, *Beati omnes*, without note, and *Kyrie eleison, Christe eleison, Kyrie eleison*. The witnesses and lay attendants walk behind the spouses according to custom.

(for the meaning of *per cultellum*, see Du Cange s.v. 'investitura') and the placing of coins on the book with the ring (and by implication their tradition at a point after this). In this detail, Missal B is supported by Missal C.414 (*Hic accipiat sponsus anulum et incipiens a pollice sponse dicat dicente presbitero.* In nomine patris. *ad secundum digitum:* Et filii. *Ad tercium:* Et spiritus sancti amen. *Ibique dimittatur. Postea dicat sponsus. De isto annulo te sponso. Tunc det ei aurum dicens.* Et de isto auro te honoro.) Ebor.27 has the priest inquire after the dowry once the ring has been put on the woman's finger, suggesting that this is the moment when the *arrhæ* might be handed over. This also was the moment when in the older form of the Sarum ritual the woman kissed the man's foot (Ebor.20*n). Ebor.164* gives a form from the thirteenth-century parish missal of Hanley Castle which (agreeing substantially with Missal C.414) has the ring imposed with *In nomine Patris*, &c. and then the form *De isto annulo te sponso et de isto auro te honoro* as the man gives the gold to the woman. Elsewhere, especially in those places linked to Spain, the *arrhæ*, which have been placed on the book to be blessed with their own prayer (see *Manuale ecclesie Toletane*), are received by the man from the priest after the imposition of the rings and immediately dropped slowly between the bridegroom's hands into the woman's cupped hands (see García, page 14). It is to the jingle of the coins as it is deposited in the woman's hands that the Missal may allude when referring to *sonoritate argenti* (Col 833*). But the British Museum's fifteenth-century Harleian MS 2860 (Ebor.166*) has the gold (possibly not the *arrhæ*) distributed to the clergy or paupers before the ring is blessed. The Anglicans regard them as 'the accustomed duty to the Priest and Clerk' (Dearmer, page 412, and 'The Solemnization of Matrimony' in the Book of Common Prayer) and they are handed by the priest to the clerk as soon as they are laid on the book. The English form of the Roman rite has the man hand over the *arrhæ* to the woman at the words 'This gold and silver I thee give' (F.407).

The balance of evidence, therefore, inclines slightly towards the implied practice of Missal C. Because the Sarum rubric excludes the modern English practice (since the man is holding the woman's hand as he speaks the words), the handing over of the *arrhæ* after the ring is suggested here. If monies are to be given to the clergy or the poor, they may be delivered up immediately before the blessing of the ring.

[28] M.48: *vir accipiat manu sua dextera cum tribus principalibus digitis a manu sua sinistra: tenens dexteram sponse.* The rubric is punctuated more convincingly here than at Col 833*.

[29] Col 833*; M.48. This remained the custom among English Catholics until the eighteenth century (*The Catholic Encycopedia* s.v. 'Marriage, Ritual of'). The left hand was prescribed by the 1549 Book of Common Prayer (Gibson and Ratcliff, page 254).

[30] The implication is that they remain standing, against F.407.

[31] The books do not give the manner in which they enter. The *Manuale ecclesie Toletane* has: *Tunc episcopus vel sacerdos apprehendens manum dexteram viri: et dexteram femine mittat eos in ecclesiam dicens psalmum ut sequitur. ps.* Beati omnes.

At the chancel arch,[32] a further station is made, the clergy once again facing west,[33] the spouses between the witnesses kneeling or lying prostrate[34] before the priest. So the priest says *Pater noster* and the verses and prayers that follow, as he did before, singing[35] from the book held before him.

The wedding itself is now concluded. During the forbidden times, all further ceremonies should be omitted.[36]

If the civil declarations are to follow,[37] the procession retires to the vestry, followed by the spouses and the civil witnesses only. If the priest is to take the part of the civil registrar, he will remove his stole[38] before beginning the civil process. The civil witnesses retire to their places in the nave: they play no further part in the function.

§4. THE NUPTIAL MASS

If permitted, the nuptial Mass follows.[39] It is that of the Holy Trinity[40] and is celebrated with the rite of a double.

---

[32] Col 834* and M.49 have *ad gradum altaris*, but Col Col 841* supposes a blessing *in introitu chori*, and at Col 836* the spouses are said to be *introducti in presbyterium*, which implies entry from the laity's nave rather than from the clergy's High Altar. Missal A.414 has the spouses make a prostration *in medio ecclesie* and Missal C.416 has them then led *in chorum ecclesie* for the Mass. The entrance of the choir will also be more convenient if the civil declarations are to be made in the vestry.

[33] F.407; Hereford.440: *Sacerdos stans super gradum Altaris verso vultu ad eos.*

[34] Col 834* and M.49: *prostratis*; Missal A.414: *prosternant se in medio ecclesie*. Hereford appears to distinguish between *tunc genuflectant* here (page 440) and *prosternant se in oratione extenso pallio super eos* later (page 441) but expects the spouses to hold their candles *prosternentes* (page 441). The question remains as moot as ever.

[35] Col 834* prescribes that *Beati omnes* is to be said *sine nota*, but is silent on the tone used for *Kyrie eleison* and the rest. Generally, singing is presumed.

[36] Unless the entry to the church and everything from *Beati omnes* onwards should also be excluded. The Missal is not clear. On the forbidden times, see note 1.

Naturally, the Sarum books do not contemplate the possibility of mixed marriages. These, exceptional, weddings should be conducted in line with the conditions imposed by the Ordinary if he agrees to dispense from the impediment.

[37] The practicalities of reconciling the requirements of the canonical and civil forums in these days of heresy and schism are complex. Much will depend on how accommodating individual parish priests and civil registrars are willing to be.

In Mary's Dowry, there was no need to go to the vestry and the function continued seemlessly. Presumably, the clergy advanced to the altar as usual, the cope was exchanged for the chasuble and the Mass was begun, while the spouses walked behind the clergy and took their places in the presbyterium. The *Manuale ecclesie Toletane* (*deinde episcopus vel sacerdos faciat confessionem et celebret missam*) certainly supposes something similar, though there the spouses kneel *juxta cancellos*. Ebor.167* gives the rubric from the British Museum's fifteenth-century Harleian MS 2860: *Tunc aspergat aqua benedicta eos et thurificet. Postea praecipiat intrare Ecclesiam. Tunc Sacerdos, induta casula, dicto* Confiteor, *incipiat Missam.*

[38] F.407, a most necessary if minor protest against the usurped jurisdiction of the secular arm over Christians' marriage.

[39] Col 836*.

[40] The Douay manuals of 1604-11 permit the Mass *pro Sponso et Sponsa* from the Roman Missal in place of this (M.50 n40).

The spouses are led[41] to the presbyterium, between the choir step and the altar.[42] There places will have been prepared for them on the south side so that they face north. The woman's place should be to the right (east) of the man's, an inversion of their positions earlier. They may hold lighted candles.[43]

The *Kyrie* is farsed. The *Gloria in excelsis* follows. Special prayers are said under the same conclusions with the usual prayers of the Mass. The gradual is not repeated after its verse.[44] There is a creed. The spouses are incensed first of the laity with unblessed incense.[45]

At the end of the sung *Sanctus*,[46] the spouses come before the altar steps and lie prostrate[47] or kneel on the floor, the woman again to the left of the man.[48] If it is to be used,[49] the four servers bring the care-cloth and hold it by its four corners over the spouses.[50] They kneel while doing so.[51] The care-cloth is held in place until after the *Agnus Dei*, when it is withdrawn.

Immediately before he sings *Pax Domini*,[52] the celebrant leaves the Host in three parts on the paten, covers the chalice,[53] rubs his fingers over the chalice to dispel any crumbs, covers the chalice and turns to the spouses,[54] who kneel erect[55] under the care-cloth[56] at the foot of the altar. The ministers stand on the footpace on either side of the priest, the subdeacon to the celebrant's left, and the deacon, who holds the missal before him, to his right. The acolyte should retire somewhat to the north end of his step

---

[41] Col 836* has *introductis*, but by whom is not said. They may be taken by a verger or, by analogy with the manner in which they may have been brought to the chancel earlier, the celebrant may lead them by the hands as he goes up to the altar.

[42] Col 836*. This will be the only time when trousers will be worn openly in the chancel or (even in nuns' convents) a woman will be present east of the choir. There can be few ways in which the dignity of the sacrament of marriage can be displayed more clearly or movingly.

[43] Hereford.441.

[44] M.51.

[45] Col 838*.

[46] *Post Sanctus* (Col 839*). This is when the choir at High Mass kneels.

[47] Col 839*: *prosternant se*. The, rather earlier, Magdalen College Pontifical (Ebor.160*) has *simul prostrati ante altare jaceant*. This seems to have been the common practice of French churches (*The Catholic Encyclopedia* s.v. 'Marriage, Ritual of').

[48] So at the beginning of the function, when the parties are presumed to be facing east: Col 830* and M.44 (where, however, see note). When facing north the bride is placed to the right of the bridegroom (Col 836*) but it will be more convenient for the man to receive the Pax at the celebrant's right.

[49] The care-cloth is used whenever the nuptial blessing is given within Mass. It is omitted, therefore, when either of the spouses has received the nuptial blessing previously (Col 839*). Somewhat prosaically, the *Codex Iuris Canonici* of 1983 (canon 1139) no longer requires that bastard children be placed under the care-cloth for legitimization (Rock IV.201).

[50] It is not clear whether this pall is held over the spouses or laid on them. That the clerks are told to hold it (*teneant*, Col 839*) and that they are expected to kneel erect under it for the *Propitiare* might suggest the former, *pace* M.53 (*extenso super eos pallio*). The pall is laid on nuns at their profession and the Spanish veil is laid on the spouses' head and shoulders from the *Pater noster* until the blessing at the end of the Mass: see *The Catholic Encyclopedia*, s.v. 'Ritual of Marriage' and *Rituale Romanum cum Appendice Toletano* (Appendix), pages 46–47.

[51] This is the natural position of servers during the Canon except when engaged in other duties.

[52] Col 839*.

[53] Ebor.35.

[54] In the Roman rite, at the middle of the altar and after genuflecting (F.408). At Toledo, the priest stands at the south corner of the altar.

[55] M.53: *illis interim genuflectentibus*.

[56] Col 839*; M.53.

and face south. Using the special tone provided in the Missal,[57] with joined hands[58] or extending his right hand over the spouses,[59] the left placed on his breast, without separating his thumbs and forefingers except when making the sign of the cross, the celebrant sings *Dominus vobiscum* and the prayers *Propitiare* and *Deus qui potestate virtutis tuae* as in the Missal. The clause *Deus qui tam excellenti mysterio*, &c. is omitted when it has been said over either of the spouses[60] previously.[61] At *Ea benedictione donatur*, he makes the sign of the cross over the woman. At *Respice propitius*, he should raise his eyes to the woman.[62] Turning back to the altar,[63] the celebrant and ministers continue with the Mass as usual.

When the celebrant has said the *Agnus Dei* secretly,[64] the servers remove the canopy and withdraw. The spouses stand. The man goes up to the deacon's step, a little to the right of the celebrant, and there receives immediately[65] from him the Pax. It will be easiest if he does so *per amplexum*, and in any case before the deacon or clerk.[66] While the clergy proceed as usual, the man comes back to his place and communicates the Pax to the woman, kissing her.[67] Neither spouse communicates the Pax to anybody else.[68] Mass continues to its conclusion as usual.

After Mass, the celebrant removes his chasuble[69] and blesses bread and wine or some other good drink[70] with the same ceremonies as on Sundays. A special formula is provided.[71] The spouses should taste of both the bread and wine. The procession and the spouses withdraw.

The Missal contains also the blessings to be imparted by the priest on the wedding night.[72] For these, the priest should probably wear a surplice and stole. A server with the holy water stoup should assist. The ceremonies are explained clearly in the Missal.

---

[57] Col 588.
[58] F.408.
[59] Hereford.442.
[60] Col 842*.
[61] M.53. The question being unclear and belonging to the juridical realm, no final interpretation can be given except by competent authority.
[62] This seems to be the interpretation of the rubric *respice* at M.59, which is identical with that here (M.54). Ebor.37: *Hic respiciat Sacerdos mulierem*.
[63] F.408 prescribes a genuflection.
[64] The rubric at Col 844* must refer to the celebrant's and not the choir's *Agnus Dei*, since the care-cloth must have been removed before the Pax.
[65] Col 844*: *a sacerdote*.
[66] Col 844* seems to imply that the clerk should receive the Pax from the celebrant immediately after the bride has received it from her spouse.
[67] Col 844*: *ferat sponsae, osculans eam*; on the cheek (Rock IV.202); *per osculum oris* (*The Catholic Encyclopedia* s.v. 'Marriage, Ritual of'). In any case, it must be remembered that this kiss conveys the peace of Christ and all hint of lasciviousness is to be avoided.
[68] Col 844*.
[69] Ebor.39.
[70] Col 844*. Rock IV.203 reports that at the wedding of Princess Margaret, daughter of Henry VII, to James IV of Scotland, 'all the ceremonyes accomlysched, ther was brought by the lordes bred and wyn in ryche potts and ryche cuppes', while at the nuptials of Queen Mary and King Philip, 'wyne and sopes were hallowed and delivered unto them'.
[71] The cup itself (*vasculum*, Col 844*) is blessed. Since, as a general rule, sacramentals are not to be repeated, it is likely that this vessel is to be given to the couple and a new cup used and blessed on each occasion.
[72] Coll 844*–845*.

The first blessing is imparted on the bridal chamber; the second over the empty bed; the last three blessings are imparted over the spouses after they have got into bed. Finally, the priest sprinkles the spouses with holy water and withdraws, leaving them in peace.[73]

---

[73] Col 845*: *et sic discedat et dimittat eos in pace.*

XXV

MISSA CANTATA

There will be occasions when the solemnity of a High Mass will be greatly desirable and yet for want of ministers or of singers its celebration will not be possible. The Missal itself provides for such an eventuality.[1] Although the guiding principle should be that as much solemnity as possible should be observed,[2] most celebrations will fall into two principal categories: (1) Masses that follow the ceremonial of a Low Mass with music and additions; and (2) Masses that approximate to the ceremonial of a High Mass with neither deacon nor subdeacon nor acolyte. Other, less probable, circumstances are also considered.

§1. THE SOLEMN FORM

The greatest impediment to the celebration of a High Mass will generally be the lack of ordained ministers, so the most common form of Sung Mass will be that in which there is a sufficient number of lay servers and singers but no deacon, subdeacon and acolyte to assist the celebrant. In case of necessity, a single chanter may take the place of the choir. This chanter may occupy a place in choir or sing from elsewhere in the church. In the latter case, no notice is taken of him during the function.

The celebrant will be assisted by two taperers, a thurifer and, if convenient, a crucifer. There may be additional torchbearers. The altar is prepared as for High Mass but there will be no Texts or lectionaries. The missal stands in its place, open at the Officium.

---

[1] Coll 12 and 589. However, ceremonial details are sparse in the extreme, and those offered here are the fruit of much conjecture. That Masses without a full complement of sacred ministers had a long history in England is shewn by the description in Rock IV.171 of such a Mass in the twelfth century. An anecdote from Gerald of Wales (Thurston (ed.), *Life of St. Hugh*, pages 234–5) shews that in the twelfth century a spoken Mass could be turned into a sung Mass by a single singer, again suggesting that the distinction between High and Low Mass was not strict. The mediæval Dominicans also sang Mass without sacred ministers with as much solemnity as was possible in the circumstances, which presumably varied from case to case (*Tracts*.84).

[2] See Rock IV.171 (mentioned in note 7) for an application of this principle, and OP.1299. This approach contrasts with that of the post-Tridentine Roman rite, which has sought to curtail the solemnity of such Masses by limiting traditional observances (see, e.g., Solans §§612–13 and notes). The vagueness of this principle makes it very difficult to prescribe ceremonial norms, and even within the Roman rite there is much variation. In writing this section, OP.1012, OP.1300, De Herdt t. I. p. 2. n. 35, Solans (§§609–33), Olalla.310–26 and F.36–143 have all been consulted.

If an ordained lector is to read the epistle, the book is prepared in a suitable place. The celebrant may sit at the sedilia for part of the function. In the vestry, the usual preparations are made, the humeral veil and the covering for the Gospel lectern alone omitted. If the taperers are to hold torches, these must be prepared in the sanctuary, as for Low Mass.[3]

The clergy advance to the altar in the usual order: the crucifer (if present) in an alb and no tunicle; the two taperers; the thurifer; finally, the celebrant, who brings the chalice with him.[4]

At the altar, the celebrant unfolds the corporal and sets the dressed chalice on it. He comes down to the topmost step and says the preparatory prayers as usual, assisted by the taperers, who face each other for the *Confiteor*. *Habete osculum pacis*, &c. is omitted. As the celebrant goes up to the altar, the taperers put down their candles. The thurifer offers incense on the spoon and, once the celebrant has blessed it, imposes it in the thurible, which he delivers up to the celebrant, kissing his hand as he does so.[5] The thurifer may accompany the celebrant while incensing the altar. In this case, the senior taperer may remove the missal. The thurifer incenses the celebrant and retires. The celebrant alternates the *Kyrie* with the taperers. He may sit for the sung *Kyrie*. Meanwhile, the taperers bring their vessels as usual. The *Gloria in excelsis* and collects follow, the taperers standing at their tapers.

An ordained lector may sing the epistle from the usual place.[6] In this case, the celebrant retires to the sedilia as usual. Otherwise he sings the lesson at the missal and goes to the sedilia for the gradual and the other chants.[7] The thurifer holds the missal before him. But if the sung chants are to be very brief, it will be more seemly for the celebrant to read them at the altar.

When the celebrant has finished reading the last chant secretly, the thurifer returns the missal to the altar, flits the book[8] and goes to prepare the thurible. The celebrant returns to the altar and unveils the chalice. The taperers come to the south corner, the senior (standing to the right of the other) bringing the pyx, the second with the cruets. The celebrant comes to the south corner with the paten, takes a host from the pyx and returns to place the paten on the corporal. He then makes and veils the chalice as at Low Mass,[9] leaving the purificator on the altar.

The chalice made, the celebrant waits at the middle. The taperers stand at the foot of the altar with their tapers, awaiting the thurifer. On doubles, the crucifer may

---

[3] To leave the celebrant alone in the sanctuary while the thurifer and the taperers went to the vestry would be unseemly.
[4] OP.1300.
[5] OP.955
[6] This detail, borrowed from the Roman Missal ('Rubricae Generales', Tit IV. no. 8), raises the same question as the acolyte (see Chapter XVI, note 5). By analogy, it may be presumed that an instituted lector in the new mode will suffice. *Pace* Rock IV.172, it would be altogether contrary to the nature of the rite to allow any other layman to sing the epistle.
[7] Against the Dominicans (OP.1300) who seem here to violate their general rule of observing as many of the ceremonies of High Mass as possible (OP.1299).
[8] The book must be transferred before the making of the chalice to allow space at the south end of the altar. See also S.205.
[9] So commonly the Dominicans.

assist. The thurifer comes up, assists at the blessing and imposition of the incense[10] and comes down again while the celebrant incenses the corporal on either side of the chalice. Collecting the thurible, the thurifer comes down and stands in front of the taperers while the celebrant says *Jube, Domine, benedicere*, &c. As the choir finishes the last chant, the celebrant goes to the missal at the north corner.[11] The thurifer goes to the bottom step of the altar on the south side and stands there, facing the celebrant and swinging the thurible gently.[12] The taperers and the crucifer go round *in plano* to the north of the altar, where they stand, facing south.[13] There the celebrant sings the Gospel. At its conclusion, he goes with the missal to the middle. If it is to be said, the celebrant intones the creed now, turns, is incensed by the thurifer, who has come to the middle before the bottom step, turns back, kisses the book and continues the creed quietly while the thurifer descends alone to incense the choir. On other days, he sings *Dominus vobiscum* and *Oremus*, kisses the book and continues with the offertory as at Low Mass.[14]

The thurifer assists with the thurible and with the chasuble at the incensing of the sacrifice and the corporal, but he does not touch the chalice. A taperer removes the missal. The thurifer incenses the celebrant as at the Officium. Taking back the thurible, the celebrant incenses the altar as before.[15]

At the offering of the people, the celebrant is assisted by the taperers and the thurifer. The bidding of the bedes and the sermon may follow, as at Low Mass.

The taperers assist at the lavatory while the thurifer, if *Credo* has not been said, goes to incense the choir, the taperers and the congregation. The thurifer and torchbearers retire to the vestry. At *Orate fratres*, the taperers reply *Spiritus Sancti gratia*.

During the Canon, the taperers do not go down to the choir but remain by their tapers. They hold up the chasuble at the Sacring. They may also hold torches. The thurifer imposes incense and swings the thurible by its shortened chains during the Sacring, kneeling on the bottom step facing north or by the bellrope. At the elevation, he rings the bell.

As soon as the chalice is covered, all rise. The thurifer and the torchbearers retire with their instruments. The taperers go to their places by their tapers. At the *Preces in prostratione*, all save the celebrant kneel. Except for the singing, all now continues as at Low Mass. The Pax is communicated by the thurifer, who comes up from the choir to receive it. The taperers assist at the ablutions, one of them flitting the book. At the

---

[10] This is an inversion of the order of the ceremonies at High Mass. It is advocated here to reduce the gap between the imposition of the incense and its use, created by the need to make the chalice at the altar.

[11] Col 589; C 66.9.

[12] By analogy with the days when at High Mass the Gospel is sung from the altar steps (C 66.41).

[13] When the Gospel is sung at the altar itself, the taperers cannot stand on either side of the celebrant facing him. Facing south will look neater than forming a scrum round the book.

[14] We have attempted not to separate excessively the incensation of the celebrant and the kissing of the book from the singing of the Gospel while maintaining as closely as possible the sequence of ceremonies observed at High Mass.

[15] The cause of much of the complex choreography when the deacon incenses the altar is removed by having the ceremony performed by the celebrant. It is not inconceivable, however, that, in the absence of the deacon, the incensation of the altar should be omitted altogether.

end, the celebrant takes the chalice with him and, preceded by the taperers with their tapers, returns to the vestry.

If there is to be a general Communion, this is administered as at Low Mass.

§2. THE SIMPLE FORM

The priest celebrates as he would a Low Mass except that he sings all the parts that the celebrant, deacon, subdeacon and acolyte would sing at a High Mass. He may make the chalice either at the beginning of the Mass or at the altar before the Gospel.[16] The chants may be sung by a choir or, if necessary, by a single chanter.

There may be two servers. In this case, they share their duties. They may carry tapers, which they hold at the beginning, put down after the *Confiteor*, hold before the celebrant at the Gospel and carry back to the vestry at the end of the Mass. If one of the taperers has been ordained lector, he may sing the epistle, the celebrant waiting at the altar and the other taperer (who should be the junior) remaining in his place. At the elevation, both may hold torches. When not engaged otherwise, they stand at their tapers, except from the *Sanctus* to the priest's Communion, when they kneel as at Low Mass. If there are two taperers, it is better for the celebrant to make the chalice after he has finished reading the sequence.

A single server conducts himself as at Low Mass. The celebrant may make the chalice either at the beginning or after the sequence.

In the absence of a chanter, the celebrant may sing the chants himself, assisted by the server,[17] who may join in with the choral parts and should sing the responses. This requires the celebrant to use a noted missal[18] and implies considerable modification in the server's ceremonial. The preparatory prayers are said aloud as usual. When the celebrant goes up to the altar, the server goes round to the missal. There he sings the Officium, *Kyrie* and *Gloria in excelsis* with the celebrant, who intones the chants. The server returns to his place to stand for the collects and the epistle but returns to the missal to sing the gradual, Alleluya, tract and sequence with the celebrant. He flits the book and assists at the Gospel. He stands in his place to sing the *Credo*.[19] It is assumed that the server will know the music of this and the other ordinary chants from memory. After *Oremus*, he goes round to stand at the celebrant's left, where he joins in with the Offertory. At its conclusion, he comes down and goes to the credence table. He stands in his place for the preface and the *Sanctus*. The celebrant may sing the *Sanctus* with the server (who bows and signs himself at *Benedictus*) or embark at once upon the Canon.[20] The server occupies himself with the bell and torch as usual. He kneels in

---

[16] OP.1300.
[17] Rock IV.171 relates an episode from the life of St. Bartholomew of Farne (A.D. 1182) in which a celebrant and a single server sing the Officium after the *Confiteor*.
[18] Such as that of St. Denis in the Victoria and Albert Museum (MSL/1891/1346).
[19] The usual rule is that whoever is singing does so standing (C 12.13). The briefest responses may be allowed as exceptions to this rule.
[20] For the repeated (and failed) efforts to prevent the celebrant from embarking upon the Canon while the choir sings the *Sanctus*, see King, *Roman Church*, page 302.

his usual place but stands to sing the *Agnus Dei*. He goes to the missal as before to join the celebrant in singing the Communion and returns to his place where he stands for the rest of the Mass. When the celebrant and server are to sing the chants before the Gospel, it will be better for the making of the chalice to take place at the beginning of the Mass.

§3. SUNG MASS WITH ONE OR MORE ORDAINED ASSISTANTS

Here are considered some of the possible combinations but it is inevitable that much will have to be left to the ingenuity of a liturgically sympathetic master of ceremonies. Knowledge of the ceremonial of High Mass and of the solemn form of Sung Mass is presumed.

(a) When the celebrant is assisted by deacon and subdeacon but no acolyte

When the acolyte only is absent, his functions are divided up between the subdeacon and the thurifer. Most of the ceremonies of High Mass can then be observed.

The processional cross may be omitted altogether or it may be carried by a supplementary server vested in an alb to whom is assigned the acolyte's place in the choir.

If there is a prophecy, this may be read from the usual place by an ordained lector or, if necessary, by the subdeacon.

At the end of the epistle, the subdeacon replaces the book on the altar himself and goes to the vestry to fetch the chalice enveloped in the humeral veil.[21] This he leaves covered on the credence table and brings the corporal to the altar. He kisses the altar, comes down to the middle, bows with the taperers and goes to the sedilia. The thurifer now comes up and brings the missal to the sedilia for the celebrant and ministers to read the chants. He then assists the ministers at the credence table and at the making of the chalice.

The choir is incensed by the thurifer, whether during the creed or after the offertory.

After reading the Offertory, the subdeacon goes to the credence table, puts on the humeral veil and brings up the veiled chalice to the altar. The taperers follow him to remove and fold the humeral veil before returning to their places. At the lavatory, the subdeacon handles both the ewer and the basin.

At *Orate fratres*, the subdeacon goes to the credence table and returns to his step wearing the humeral veil, through which he receives from the deacon the veiled paten. At the *Sanctus*, he goes up to the footpace as usual, still holding the paten, but he remains on his step thereafter until the *Pater noster*, kneeling there for the Sacring. He does not go to the piscina at *Supplices te rogamus*. At *Pater noster*, he gives the paten to the deacon and returns to his step. The taperers remove and fold the humeral veil.

---

[21] The subdeacon holds the chalice through the humeral veil at High Mass when preparing it at the credence table.

If the Pax is to be given to the congregation, it is conveyed by the thurifer, who wears the humeral veil for this purpose. The subdeacon and taperers assist at the ablutions.

During the first postcommon, the subdeacon goes to the credence, puts on the humeral veil with the assistance of the taperers, comes up the middle, receives the chalice from the deacon and conveys it to the vestry. He should return to his place behind the deacon before the end of the last postcommon.

(b) When the celebrant is assisted by deacon and acolyte but no subdeacon

In this form of the Mass, most of the subdeacon's functions are carried out by the acolyte.[22]

The acolyte may wear the tunicle[23] when the deacon wears the dalmatic, but neither the maniple nor the chasuble.[24] When the ministers stand on their steps behind the celebrant, the acolyte does so on his own step, not the subdeacon's.[25] He may sit in the subdeacon's sedile,[26] or he may have his own place in the choir.

He sings the epistle as well as the prophecy and brings the chalice as the subdeacon does when there is no acolyte. When bringing the corporal, he kisses the altar, brings the missal down to the middle, bows and goes to hold the missal before the celebrant and the deacon for the gradual and the other chants.[27] This done, he replaces the missal and goes to the credence table.

At the washing of hands and the making of the chalice, the acolyte carries out his normal duties. The part of the subdeacon is discharged by the deacon, who washes his hands before making the chalice only, not before unfolding the corporal. Having unveiled the chalice, the deacon, wearing the humeral veil,[28] takes the paten with the host, covered with the pall if used, to the celebrant. Having shewn him the host, he returns to the credence table, collects the chalice and, with the acolyte, returns to the celebrant to make the chalice there. Having redressed the chalice, the deacon goes to unfold the corporal before returning to his seat. On days when he wears the chasuble, the deacon removes this and puts it over his stole before washing his hands.

---

[22] The case is similar to that in the Roman rite. The conjectures made here are informed by the provisions of the Roman Congregation of Rites and its competent successor (O'Connell, *Celebration of Mass*, III.14; Fortescue, O'Connell and Reid, page 133).

[23] Since the Roman substitute subdeacon is allowed the tunicle, it is reasonable to posit it for the Sarum substitute also, particularly since the tunicle is, at least on some days, a proper vestment of the Sarum acolyte.

[24] It must be acknowledged that there is no authority for this restriction, but the wearing of the chasuble by a clerk in minor orders seems a step too far. Likewise the Roman substitute subdeacon does not wear the maniple.

[25] Whereas the Roman rite employs an extraneous substitute for the subdeacon, the Sarum acolyte has his own proper status and function, which should not be wholly subsumed into those of the subdeacon whose place he is taking.

[26] As the Roman substitute does.

[27] Although this function could be allocated to the thurifer, it seems better to allow the acolyte to perform as many of his proper duties as is possible. The acolyte is not bound ordinarily to read the chants privately (see Chapter XV, note 21).

[28] The sacred vessels should never be carried unveiled. This is the case even when the priest carries the chalice himself at Low Mass.

At the Gospel, the acolyte flits the book. If a Text is to be used, the acolyte takes the part of the subdeacon. An additional server may carry the cross or this may be omitted altogether. If there is no Text, the acolyte carries out his own part. After the Gospel, the acolyte will remove the cross before assisting at the incensation of the priest and the kissing of the book.

Whether during the creed or after the offertory, the acolyte takes the part of the subdeacon, leaving his own to the thurifer, when going to incense the choir and present the Text.

After reading the Offertory, the acolyte goes to the credence table. He puts on the humeral veil and brings the chalice to the deacon, who executes the part of the subdeacon as well as his own. Having returned the humeral veil to the credence table, the acolyte goes to the celebrant's left and assists with the incensations, the Text and at the lavatory.

At *Orate fratres*, the acolyte receives the humeral veil at the credence table and returns to his step behind the celebrant. At *Per omnia saecula saeculorum*, he goes up to receive the paten and comes down again to his place. He may go up to recite the *Sanctus* with the celebrant,[29] but otherwise he plays his usual part until the *Pater noster*.

At the *Pater noster*, the acolyte hands the paten to the deacon, returns to his step and gives up the humeral veil to the taperers. He does not kneel for the *Preces in prostratione*. He receives the Pax from the deacon and gives it to the taperers. The congregation receives it from the thurifer, who has it immediately from the celebrant, wearing the humeral veil.

The acolyte assists at the ablutions and flits the book. During the first postcommon, he goes to put on the humeral veil and comes up the middle to collect and remove the chalice. Before the end of the last postcommon, he should return to stand on his step behind the deacon. At the end, he may take the place of the subdeacon when bowing to the altar and returning to the vestry.

(c) When the celebrant is assisted by a deacon with neither subdeacon nor acolyte

Other than when a priest sings a Mass with no ordained assistants, this is the most likely form of Missa Cantata to occur in ordinary churches.

For the most part, the functions of the subdeacon are divided up between the deacon and the thurifer, who also carries out those of the acolyte. An additional server may be employed as crucifer or the cross may be omitted. The humeral veil is not used.[30] There is no Text. An ordained lector may sing the prophecy and the epistle or the deacon may do so from the customary place.

---

[29] As in the Roman rite.
[30] The humeral veil's purpose is to protect profane hands from handling the chalice. The deacon is entitled by virtue of his order to touch the sacred vessels (e.g. at *Per quem haec omnia* and at the ablutions). When the celebrant brings the chalice with him, e.g. at Low Mass, he does not use the humeral veil.

For the preparatory prayers, the deacon stands on the celebrant's right. Nobody takes the place of the subdeacon on the celebrant's left. The prayers, including *Habete osculum pacis*, remain in the plural. The thurifer may walk on the celebrant's left when incensing the altar at the Officium. In this case, one of the taperers removes the missal. At *Dominus vobiscum*, the celebrant's chasuble is not held. On days when he wears a chasuble, if he will sing the lessons, the deacon removes this and puts it over his stole at the end of the collects, not resuming it until the Communion. If another is to sing the epistle, the deacon will not remove his chasuble until he goes to wash his hands and make the chalice.

After the epistle (or before its conclusion if it is sung by another), the deacon goes to the vestry and returns with the veiled chalice. He does not wear the humeral veil. He leaves the chalice on the credence table and takes the corporal to the altar with the usual ceremonies. Retiring to the sedilia, he reads the chants with the celebrant from the missal, held by the thurifer. This done, the thurifer returns the missal and goes to the credence table to assist the deacon, who washes his hands, takes the paten to the celebrant and makes the chalice as when there is an acolyte but no subdeacon.[31] Having veiled the chalice anew, he unfolds the corporal and returns to the sedilia.

Before the Gospel, the thurifer flits the book. The preparations for the Gospel take place as usual, except that there is neither subdeacon nor acolyte. The deacon holds the Gospel-book when being blessed and when going to the lectern. At the conclusion of the Gospel, the deacon kisses the book and the procession returns to the altar. The taperers go to their places and put down their tapers. The deacon, with the thurifer on his right, advances to the altar step. The junior taperer (or the substitute crucifer) comes to stand at his left. The deacon hands him the book, incenses the celebrant, takes the book back and presents it to the celebrant. As the deacon replaces the book in its place on the altar, the thurifer and the taperer withdraw. Whether during *Credo* or after the offertory, the choir is incensed by the thurifer alone.

After reading the Offertory, the deacon comes down the middle and brings the veiled chalice (without the humeral veil) up the south steps and assists the celebrant with the offertory. The paten remains on the altar. The incensations take place as usual. At the lavatory, the taperers assist unaided, one handling the water and the other the towel. All perform their duties as normal until *Pater noster*. Then the deacon takes up the paten and holds it up until *Da propitius pacem*. The deacon takes the Pax to the choir, transmitting it to the taperers only on his return.[32] The thurifer conveys the Pax to the congregation. At the ablutions, the taperers take the place of the subdeacon and acolyte. The deacon takes the dressed chalice to the vestry during the first postcommon, returning in time for the conclusion of the last.

---

[31] See note 34.
[32] The Sarum books suppose that in the choir sit the cathedral's great parsons. If, however, the taperers are of higher rank, if only by virtue of their function, than those in choir (e.g. if these be lay singers), then it would be more seemly for the deacon to convey the Pax to the former before going down to the choir step.

(d) When the celebrant is assisted by a subdeacon and an acolyte but by no deacon

The absence of the deacon brings with it the loss or modification of many of the ceremonies of High Mass. Many of his most important functions are performed by the celebrant and most of the others are assigned to the subdeacon, some of whose duties are in turn transferred to the acolyte.

The Text, Gospel-book, Gospel lectern and its cloth are omitted. It will be convenient if a place is prepared near the north corner of the altar to put the cross when not in use, since after the Gospel the acolyte will need to remove the cross and assist at the book in quick succession. The missal may lie open on the altar or the subdeacon may bring it with him. The subdeacon will occupy the deacon's place at the sedilia; the acolyte may sit in the subdeacon's sedile or he may have his usual seat in the choir. He may retain his proper vestments or he may wear the tunicle (but not the maniple) when the subdeacon does so.[33]

The procession to the altar will be formed by the acolyte (with the cross on doubles), the taperers, the subdeacon with the missal and the celebrant.

At the altar, the acolyte puts away the cross. He may now stand at the celebrant's left. If he does so, the subdeacon will stand on the right. There the preparatory prayers are said. At *Habete osculum pacis*, the celebrant kisses first the subdeacon and then the acolyte. Incense is imposed with the assistance of the subdeacon and the thurifer. The celebrant incenses the altar, assisted by the subdeacon on his right and the acolyte on his left, and is then incensed by the subdeacon. At the Officium, *Kyrie, Gloria in excelsis* and collects, the part of the deacon is taken by the subdeacon (except that he stands on his own step and does not turn round at *Dominus vobiscum*) and that of the subdeacon by the acolyte, who holds the celebrant's chasuble and then stands on his own step. The acolyte reads the prophecy; the subdeacon, the epistle.

At the epistle, the acolyte brings the chalice to the credence table, takes the corporals to the altar and holds the missal before the celebrant for the gradual, &c. The subdeacon washes his hands as usual. Wearing the humeral veil, he places the host on the paten and takes them (covered with the pall) to shew to the celebrant. He goes back to the credence table, leaves the paten there and goes to make the chalice before the celebrant in the usual way. Finally, he returns to the sedilia. There he imposes incense.

Escorted by the subdeacon, the celebrant goes up to the altar and unfolds the corporal. Meanwhile, the subdeacon flits the book and comes down to stand facing south on the uppermost step below the footpace on the north side of the altar. The thurifer comes up and the celebrant incenses the middle of the altar as the taperers and the acolyte take up their usual positions. Having returned the thurible, the celebrant says *Jube, Domine, benedicere*, &c. and goes to the north corner to sing the Gospel.[34] The thurifer goes to stand at the bottom step of the altar on the south side. There he faces the celebrant and swings the thurible gently for the duration of the Gospel. The taperers (and the acolyte on doubles) go round *in plano* to the north end of the

---

[33] The former may be considered preferable, since here the acolyte is not a substitute subdeacon.
[34] See Figure IV.

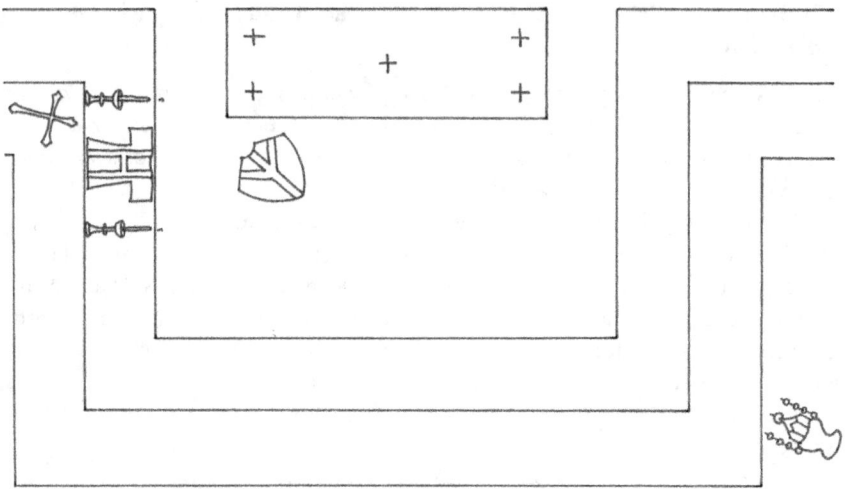

Figure IV. Sung Mass: The Gospel sung from the altar

altar. The taperers stand behind the subdeacon on either side of him, facing south. The acolyte stands behind the eastern taperer, facing the celebrant. The celebrant sings the Gospel (Figure IV).

At the end of the Gospel, the celebrant goes to the middle. The subdeacon picks up the missal from its desk and comes down to the middle as the other servers do so *in plano*, the thurifer to stand on the right of the subdeacon, the acolyte, having removed the cross, to his left. The taperers go to their usual places. The celebrant should wait in the middle until he perceives that all the assistants are in place. He then intones the creed, if it is to be said, and turns round. The subdeacon hands the missal to the acolyte and incenses the celebrant, then takes the missal up for the celebrant to kiss. As the celebrant turns back to the altar, the subdeacon replaces the missal on its stand and brings both closer to the corporal. He then crosses to the celebrant's right and both say the creed quietly while the acolyte and the thurifer go to incense the choir. If the creed is not said, the celebrant is not incensed. The subdeacon comes up to offer the missal to be kissed, the servers retire and the offertory takes place as usual.

The subdeacon reads the Offertory with the celebrant, standing at his right side. Meanwhile, the taperers impose the humeral veil on the acolyte, who brings up the chalice. The subdeacon receives the chalice and places it, still veiled, to the right of the corporal. The celebrant unveils the chalice and proceeds as at Low Mass. The subdeacon may fold the chalice veil and lay it on the altar to the right of the corporal.

Having removed the humeral veil, the acolyte comes up to the celebrant's left. Incense is imposed as at the Officium and the celebrant incenses the sacrifice and the altar, attended by the subdeacon and the acolyte, as at a Sung Mass without ministers.

At the offering of the people, the subdeacon takes the place of the deacon, his own being taken by the acolyte. The lavatory takes place as at High Mass. If the creed has not been said, the acolyte and the thurifer go to incense the choir. The subdeacon makes the reply to *Orate fratres* and assists at the missal. The paten remains on the altar.[35]

After the incensation of the choir, the acolyte has no further function until the Pax. He may retire to his place, therefore, as at High Mass for the dead. However, he may remain at the foot of the altar, recite the *Sanctus* at the celebrant's left and hold up the celebrant's chasuble at the consecration to the left of the subdeacon *solemnitatis tantum causa*.

The subdeacon says the *Sanctus* standing at the celebrant's right and turns the pages as the deacon does, returning to his own step each time. At the Sacring, he kneels behind the celebrant to his right, holding the chasuble and swinging the thurible. He does not wash his hands at *Supplices te rogamus*. The taperers remain in the choir. If they will not be required until the ablutions, they may receive the Pax with the choir. However, if a general Communion is to be administered within Mass, they may come up to receive the Pax in the usual way and remain there to hold the houseling cloth.

The subdeacon does not assist the celebrant with the chalice at *Per quem haec omnia*, nor does he hold up the paten. He remains standing for the *Preces in prostratione*. He stands to the celebrant's right to say the *Agnus Dei* privately. If the acolyte has remained in the sanctuary, he will stand at the subdeacon's right to recite it. The subdeacon receives the Pax as the deacon does and conveys it to the taperers (if they are in the sanctuary) and to the choir, returning immediately to his step; the acolyte conveys the Pax to the congregation.

The celebrant conducts the ablutions and dresses the chalice as at Low Mass, assisted by the subdeacon, the acolyte and the taperers as at High Mass. During the first postcommon, the acolyte comes up to the middle and takes away the chalice in the humeral veil.[36] He returns and Mass concludes as usual, *mutatis mutandis*.

(e) When the priest is assisted by a subdeacon but by neither deacon nor acolyte

The Text, the Gospel lectern, its cover and the Gospel-book are not used. The processional cross may be omitted.

The celebrant advances to the altar preceded by the subdeacon with the missal, by the thurifer and by the taperers. An additional server in an alb may act as crucifer.

At the altar, the subdeacon stands on the celebrant's right for the preparatory prayers. He receives the kiss of peace in the usual form in the plural. He imposes incense at the Officium, escorts the celebrant when incensing the altar and incenses the celebrant thereafter. If the thurifer accompanies the celebrant on the left, one of the taperers may remove the missal.

---

[35] Only the deacon may pick up the paten from the altar.
[36] In the complete rite, the acolyte does not take the chalice himself but receives it from the deacon, who may ordinarily handle the sacred vessels. Nevertheless, since the acolyte takes the chalice himself (through the humeral veil) in the vestry and from the credence table at the offertory, he may be permitted to do so now.

The subdeacon stands on his own step behind the celebrant for the Officium and the Kyries. If the celebrant goes to sit, the subdeacon may occupy the deacon's place at the sedilia. The subdeacon stands at the celebrant's right to recite the *Gloria in excelsis*. At *Dominus vobiscum*, the subdeacon holds the chasuble and then comes down to his own step for the collects. An ordained lector may sing the prophecy or the subdeacon may do so. The subdeacon sings the epistle. On days when he wears the chasuble, the subdeacon removes it immediately before singing his first lesson.

After the epistle, the subdeacon replaces the book on the altar and brings the chalice in the humeral veil to the credence table. Thence he conveys the corporal to the altar and comes to the sedilia, where he reads the chants with the celebrant from the missal held before them by the thurifer.

Assisted by the thurifer, the subdeacon washes his hands, presents the paten to the celebrant and makes the chalice. He imposes incense at the sedilia.

Before the Gospel, the celebrant goes up to the altar and unfolds the corporal while the subdeacon flits the book. The celebrant incenses the middle of the altar and goes to the north corner to sing the Gospel. The others adopt their positions as when the celebrant sings Mass assisted by subdeacon and acolyte but no deacon. A crucifer may take the place of the acolyte or the missal may be held after the Gospel by the junior taperer. The choir is incensed by the thurifer alone, whether now or after the offertory.

The subdeacon reads the Offertory with the celebrant, standing on the right, and then goes to the credence table to bring the chalice in the humeral veil. Leaving the chalice on the altar to the right of the corporal, he receives the veil from the celebrant and folds it, leaving it on the altar. He does not touch the paten or the chalice. The taperers remove the humeral veil or the subdeacon may return to the credence table to do this. He must be in place to impose incense and assist the celebrant at the incensation of the sacrifice and the altar.

The paten remains on the altar. The subdeacon stands on the celebrant's right to say the *Sanctus*. For the rest of the time, he stands on his own step, turning the pages of the missal as required. He kneels to the right of the celebrant and behind him for the Sacring, swinging the thurible. He does not wash his hands at *Supplices te rogamus*, nor does he come up to the altar at *Per quem haec omnia*. He stands on his step for the *Preces in prostratione* and comes to the celebrant's right for the *Agnus Dei*. He conveys the Pax to the choir and the taperers. The thurifer receives the Pax from the celebrant and takes it to the congregation.

At the ablutions, the celebrant is assisted by the subdeacon and the taperers. The subdeacon, wearing the humeral veil, removes the chalice during the first postcommon. The Mass is concluded as usual.

(f) When the priest is assisted by an acolyte but by no sacred ministers

With the exceptions noted below, the ceremonies are the same as when the celebrant is assisted by neither deacon nor acolyte. The acolyte carries out the duties that fall then to the subdeacon, but, though he alternates the *Kyrie*, he does not go up to recite the other chants privately with the celebrant.[37] He may wear the tunicle on the days when the subdeacon would do so but may not wear the maniple.

The celebrant advances to the altar preceded by the acolyte with the missal, the thurifer and the taperers. An additional server in an alb may act as crucifer.

When standing before the altar, the acolyte stands on his own step, not the subdeacon's. If there are several prophecies, he may occupy the deacon's place at the sedilia or he may retire to his own place in the choir.

He sings the prophecy and the epistle,[38] returning the book to the altar after the latter.

While the celebrant reads the gradual and the other chants from the missal held before him by the thurifer, the acolyte goes to the vestry and brings the chalice in the humeral veil to the credence table. He takes the corporal to the altar as usual and goes to the sedilia. Thence he escorts the celebrant to the altar and flits the book as the celebrant unfolds the corporal. The acolyte goes to the credence, puts on the humeral veil and brings up the chalice to the altar, leaving it to the right of the corporal. The taperers follow him, the senior with the pyx, the junior with the cruets. The acolyte, retaining the humeral veil over his shoulders but not over his hands,[39] receives the pyx and holds it out to the celebrant, who selects a host and lays it on the paten, returning to the middle to lay the paten on the corporal. He then makes the chalice as at Low Mass, receiving the cruets in turn from the acolyte. As he dresses and veils the chalice anew, the taperers remove the humeral veil to the credence table, whither they will already have taken the pyx and the cruets.

The taperers and the thurifer now go to the foot of the altar. The acolyte assists at the blessing and imposition of the incense. At the Gospel, the acolyte takes the place of the subdeacon. A crucifer may assist on doubles or the missal may be held after the Gospel by the junior taperer.

As the celebrant reads the Offertory, the acolyte stands on his step in the middle. He goes up to assist with the incensations.

The paten remains on the altar. The acolyte remains standing on his step throughout the Canon. He does not turn the pages of the missal. He kneels behind the celebrant on his right and holds the chasuble and the thurible during the Sacring. He stands for the *Preces in prostratione*.

---

[37] Unlike the Roman substitute subdeacon, the acolyte here is acting as himself and not for another. Although he takes on many of the duties of the subdeacon, he should probably not be bound to recite these texts when he is not substituting for the subdeacon and complementing the part of the deacon. For the obligation of reciting the choral texts secretly, see Chapter XV, note 21.

[38] Inasmuch as he acts for the subdeacon, he should read the epistle, but he should not neglect his own function by relegating the singing of the first prophecy to another lector.

[39] So the Roman subdeacon.

BOOK VI

PROCESSIONS AND BLESSINGS

XXVI

PROCESSIONS

For our purposes, processions[1] are of four kinds: (1) those associated with another function, such as the blessing of candles or palms, or with certain feasts or seasons; (2) those that are held on ordinary Sundays; (3) those that are held on doubles; and (4) occasional processions. The first kind is dealt with in the chapters on the ritual year; here the ceremonial of the other three kinds is considered.

§1. THE *ASPERGES* AND THE SUNDAY PROCESSION

The ordinary Sunday procession is held on Sundays below the rank of double, whether the service be festal or of the season; it takes place before Terce[2] and is associated with the *Asperges*;[3] but, in churches where the hours are not sung publicly, it may be followed immediately by the Mass, the clergy retiring to the sacristy to finish vesting for Mass.[4]

The following preparations are made. In the vestry, the vestments are laid out: amices, albs and cinctures for the celebrant, the deacon, the subdeacon, the acolyte,

---

[1] P includes the texts to be sung in processions and indicates the ceremonial to be followed. P.1 seq. gives the model for the ordinary Sunday procession; the Christmas procession (P.11–15) presents the model for processions on double feasts. Henderson's edition may be considered standard but is here supplemented by *Processions*. Both these editions include woodcuts, taken from sixteenth-century editions of the Processional. Transcriptions in figured notation of many of the chants are provided by Bailey.

[2] *post capitulum* (P.1). There appears to be no connection on ordinary Sundays between the Procession, which forms its own service, and the High Mass, celebrated after either Terce or Sext. (But see Cons 123.7.) Only this morning procession, and not the procession at Evensong, is dealt with here.
M.1 gives details of the bells to be rung for the *Asperges*.

[3] P.1–8; *Processions*.18–32; OP.1017, OP.1049, OP.1275; F.88.

[4] Becon, pages 283–4:

> Hee saw also a fellow with a shaven crowne going up and downe in the church, and casting water in the peoples teeth, and afterward having a iolly coat upon his backe he saw him goe about the church-yard, after an Image, all the people following him. After all these things hee saw that shaveling cast off the gay-coat againe, and put on other game plaiers garments, & so to addres himselfe unto an altar covered with white linnen cloathes, wherupon was set, as hee thought, meate, and drinke.

the two taperers and the thurifer; for the water-boy and the book-boy, surplices; the deacon will also wear a stole; the celebrant, a stole and (if the church possesses one) a cope.[5] The ministers do not wear dalmatic and tunicle. The celebrant and the sacred ministers may wear maniples if it is the custom of the church.[6] The thurible with its boat, a salver with salt, the holy-water stoup with its sprinkler, the taperers' tapers and the processional cross are also prepared. The subdeacon will carry a Text, if the church possesses one.

The procession sets out from the vestry in the following order. A surpliced[7] verger may precede it, carrying his verge. First comes the water-boy,[8] bearing the holy water in his right hand and the salver with the salt in his left; then the acolyte with the processional cross; then the taperers, side by side, with their tapers; then the thurifer; then the book-boy,[9] who carries the Processional, held through the sleeves of his surplice;[10] then the subdeacon, carrying the Text;[11] then the deacon; finally the celebrant.

The acolyte advances into the presbyterium and the other servers and ministers follow him,[12] except for the water-boy and the book-boy, who stand aside to take up their places, the latter to the north of the former.[13] The celebrant, standing behind the deacon,[14] stops east of the choir step,[15] the water- and book-boys standing in front of

---

[5] Col 29**: *cum aliis vestibus sacerdotalibus*. M.1 requires a red cope but probably assumes the ordinary Sunday procession. Within Eastertide and on other feasts, it would be reasonable to adopt the colour of the day. Rock I.344 describes an illumination that omits the cope. All parishes were bound to have at least one *capa chori* (see Chapter III, note 16). However, since the sacred ministers are commanded to be *albis cum amictibus indutis*, the question remains as unclear as ever. See Chapter III, note 4.

[6] O.P.541 and Morse §105.

[7] *Processions*.72.

[8] P.5.

[9] The position of the book-boy is not clear, but this is the usual position for additional participants in processions: between the front of the procession (water-boy, acolyte, taperers and thurifer) and the subdeacon. So on Palm Sunday, &c. When actually ministering, the book-boy stands close by the priest (P.2: *ad manus in libro tenendo eidem sacerdoti*). The woodcut at P.1 would have him in front of the celebrant, but it seems unlikely that he should walk between the celebrant and the deacon, and the picture may represent a conflation of the order of the procession when advancing and of the celebrant's assistants when the water is blessed. C 27.4 and P.94 have the water-boy walk immediately in front of the celebrant and after the deacons of the holy oils in the procession to the font after the second Vespers of Easter, but then there are no sacred ministers. When sacred ministers are present, on the way to the font on Holy Saturday, the book-boy walks behind the thurifer (P.84).

[10] Rock II.9.

[11] P.1.

[12] The position of the servers is by no means clear. The woodcuts for Candlemas (P.140) and Ash Wednesday (P.45) and F.348 suggest that they should stand on the north side facing across the church, while the rubric at P.4 (*ministros ordinatim incipiendo ab accolito qui crucem defert*) could mean that the acolyte should stand east of the thurifer while the taperers remained at the choir step, but P.1 (*omnibus albis cum amictibus indutis et in medio presbyterii ad altare conversis*) with its woodcut and Cons 33 support the solution adopted here.

[13] It will be more convenient to have the water-boy on the south side so that the celebrant does not have to look over his shoulder at the book while blessing the water. *Pace* the woodcut at P.1, which has the water-boy stand on the north side, the directions given in the editions of 1523 and 1528 (*Processions*.18) are followed here. *Tracts*.73 has the acolytes stand to the left of the ministers, but there the water is not blessed immediately before its sprinkling.

[14] Woodcut at P.1 and *Tracts*.73.

[15] Col 30**; P.2.

him. All bow and remain facing the altar. The book- and water-boys turn round to assist the celebrant. Addressing the salt held out to him by the water-boy, the celebrant, with joined hands, says *Exorcizo te, creatura salis*, &c. and sings the following collect. At *benedicere* and *sanctificare*,[16] he makes the sign of the cross over the salt, holding his left hand on his breast. With the same ceremonies, he exorcises and blesses the water, after which he takes the salver of salt and pours all[17] its contents into the water in the form of a cross, saying secretly *Commixtio salis et aquae*, &c. With joined hands, he sings *Dominus vobiscum* and the blessing that follows.

A cantor[18] intones *Asperges me* or *Vidi aquam* and the choir continues it. Likewise, the cantor intones the verses of the psalm and, after each verse, the antiphon on his own.[19] For the verse *Gloria Patri*, the choir turns to face the altar.[20] Meanwhile, the celebrant, accompanied by the water-boy alone,[21] who walks at his right, approaches the altar. In his absence, the deacon and the subdeacon change places. At the foot of the altar, the water-boy dips the sprinkler in the water stoup and hands it to the celebrant,[22] who, while standing still,[23] sprinkles the altar three times, in the middle, its north and its south.[24] The celebrant then touches his own forehead with holy water. The celebrant returns the sprinkler to the water-boy, who replaces it in the water stoup. Both now bow to the altar[25] and return to the choir step. As they approach the acolyte, the celebrant receives the sprinkler again and sprinkles first the acolyte and then the other servers in order. Finally, he sprinkles the deacon and the subdeacon.[26] As each man is sprinkled, he bows. At the choir step, the celebrant, facing west with the deacon standing to his right and the subdeacon to his left, awaits the members of the choir, who approach him to be sprinkled in order of seniority.

When the choir has been sprinkled, the celebrant with the water-boy descends to the laity and sprinkles them according to the custom of the church.[27]

The celebrant returns to the choir step and stands there, facing east. There, with the ministers on either side as before and assisted by the book-boy, the celebrant sings the verses and the collect with joined hands. The thurifer now approaches. Incense is blessed and imposed as at Mass. When there are two thuribles, the celebrant blesses incense twice. The procession is reformed in the same order as before. The choir

---

[16] *Processions*.19, confirmed by the Processional of 1517 (P.2).
[17] No sacramental salt should be kept for another occasion. For the Church's reluctance to repeat blessings, see Chapter XVII, note 2.
[18] This will be the precentor or the senior rulers of the choir (Cons 34).
[19] Cons 34.
[20] C 13.2.
[21] Against the Dominicans (OP.1274, OP.1048, OP.1017, OP.983) and the Roman rite, whose deacons and subdeacons accompany the celebrant; but they do not carry Texts.
[22] OP.1049.
[23] P.4: *stando*.
[24] P.4 gives *circunquaque*, not *circueundo*.
[25] OP.1275.
[26] It seems extraordinary for the acolyte to be sprinkled before the sacred ministers. Nevertheless, the rubric at P.4 is unambiguous: *in redeundo imprimis aspergat ministros ordinatim incipiendo ab accolito qui crucem defert*.
[27] F.89. Becon, pages 283–4, has the priest 'going up and downe in the church, and casting water in the peoples teeth'.

follows arranged thus: first walk the rulers of the choir, if there be any[28], two abreast, the secondary before the principal,[29] or the cantors;[30] then come the boys of the first form and the clergy of the second form in the order that they occupy in choir, forming four lines in total: two inner lines consisting of the lowest form and two outer lines consisting of the second form.[31] These four lines are followed by the clergy of the upper step advancing two by two in order (in Sarum church that which they keep when sitting in the chapter house), the dignitaries bringing up the rear.[32] The water-boy may sprinkle the ground before him as he goes.[33] As the procession reaches each side altar, it pauses and stands aside to allow the celebrant and the ministers, with the water-boy, to approach and sprinkle the altar.[34] During the procession, the chants prescribed in the Processional are sung.

The route to be followed will depend on the architecture of the church.[35] The basic principle is that the procession should move clockwise and end by moving eastwards through the choir. In churches with an ambulatory, this is visited first in a clockwise direction; then the procession goes down the south side of the nave, turning at the west end and returning up the middle of the nave to the Rood. In smaller churches, the procession may come straight to the west doors, turn right and come up the north side of the nave, cross at the chancel arch to the south side and move west again, coming up the middle and ending at the Rood.

When the front of the procession[36] reaches the Rood, all make a station. Unless the bedes are to be bidden after the offertory,[37] they are said here. The station over, the responsory is begun and the procession advances as far as the choir step. On certain days mentioned in the Processional, a verse is sung from the pulpitum facing west.

When the station is to be lengthy, the crucifer halts and turns to face west. The taperers and the other clergy remain facing east. If cantors are to sing a verse, they come up to stand behind the taperers and turn westwards. The choir comes up to stand on either side of the clergy, facing each other. In the last place, standing between the choirs, is the celebrant, facing east.[38] The station concluded, the procession reforms and enters the choir.

When the procession has reached the choir step and the choir, having greeted the altar, has returned to its stalls, the celebrant, minsters and servers stand in a straight line.[39] The book-boy comes before the celebrant, who sings the verse and collect standing at the choir step. If fasts or feasts are to be declared, or any other

---

[28] P.128. Also the woodcuts at P.96 and P.129.
[29] P.94.
[30] P.128, n+.
[31] P.5: *non bini*, Cons 37 notwithstanding.
[32] *Processions*.21.
[33] OP.1725; Lincoln I.375; Durham.11.
[34] P.6.
[35] The route proper to Sarum church is given at P.5–6. For the route on doubles, see P.11.
[36] Cons 37.
[37] P.8.
[38] This arrangement is adopted from OP.1552.
[39] OP.950 has the cross put away, but if this is to be borne at the entrance to Mass, it will be convenient to have it return to the vestry with the other clergy.

announcements to be made, this is the time to do so.[40] Finally, the procession reforms and departs for the vestry.[41]

If the *Asperges* is to take place but the procession to be omitted, the celebrant may omit the cope.[42] The clergy all return to the vestry as they came and vest for Mass.[43]

§2. FESTAL PROCESSIONS

On all doubles[44] that fall on a Sunday, and on Palm Sunday, salt and water are blessed privately at a side altar[45] after Prime and the *Asperges* takes place immediately before the procession, which goes forth after Terce or Sext.[46] The procession does not pause to sprinkle the side altars.[47] The choir wear copes. Three acolytes carry processional crosses (two only on minor doubles).[48] However, in ordinary churches it will be rare to find more than one processional cross. In the cathedral, two vergers and two thurifers are presumed. The deacon and subdeacon (but not the acolytes, except on greater doubles) wear dalmatic and tunicle and each carry a Text.[49] The choir advances *excellentioribus subsequentibus*. On greater doubles and above,[50] the three acolytes wear tunicles. On certain days, as explained in the Processional, banners and relics are carried in the procession. On these days, the processional cross is generally omitted.[51] Local custom may suggest additional ornament and solemnity, such as the carrying of decorated candles.[52]

On days when a prose is to be sung, the cantors sing the first verse in the middle of the choir. The choir repeats this standing. Only as the cantors begin the second verse does the procession set out.[53]

---

[40] Cons 123.7.
[41] P.8 and Cons 37 have the celebrant go with his ministers to sprinkle the canons' cemetery. Becon, pages 283–4, supposes likewise (see note 12). OP.1276, Lincoln I.376 and OPraem.XIII.57–8 (where Mass follows the procession immediately) have the celebrant return to the sacristy to vest. C 40.3 has the celebrant at Vespers go to the vestry to put on a cope, suggesting that retiring to the vestry during a function (and so also between functions) is not repugnant to the genius of the rite.
[42] Rock I.344.
[43] OP.1017, OP.1049, OP.1275.
[44] For many of these details, see P.11.
[45] P.3: *ante aliquod altare* (writing of parish churches). In churches where there is an altar in the vestry, the water should be blessed there (P.59: *in vestibulo ante altare*).
[46] P.3–4. The procession on doubles was moved from after Terce to after Sext in the early sixteenth century (P.xi, P.3 and the references there to Frere), presumably when the Mass also was moved. Since on these days an association is created between the procession and the Mass, it would not be unreasonable for the Mass to begin at once without a return to the vestry, the chasuble being assumed in the sanctuary. No authority can be quoted for this, however. See Chapter XXX, note 2.
[47] P.6.
[48] P.11. Rock I.331 has all three acolytes wear tunicles but seems to misquote P.11. However, later in the same note, he has the paten borne at Mass by one only of these acolytes 'vested in a tunic as well as alb and amice', implying that tunicles were not worn for the procession.
[49] OP.11.
[50] P.14. It is reasonable to assume no lesser solemnity on principal doubles than on greater doubles.
[51] *Crede Michi* [87].
[52] Rock II.342–4.
[53] *Crede Michi* [86].

Occasional processions, such as those to ask for rain, are conducted after the manner of those in Rogation Week, with the exceptions explained in the Processional.[54]

§3. THE RECEPTION OF MAJOR PERSONAGES[55]

By major personage, the Processional understands the metropolitan of the place, the Ordinary, a Papal Legate, a cardinal, the Sovereign and the Queen consort.[56] In these times, the solemn reception of the last two will not occur.[57] The ceremonial details of the public reception of a greater ecclesiastic into a town do not belong in this work. However, from the perspective of the church that receives such a personage, the following should be observed.

The principal clerk of the church is the celebrant, accompanied at his side by the clerk next in rank. Both wear copes. The procession is conducted as on Christmas Day, the choir following *majoribus praecedentibus*. It goes down the middle of the choir and leaves the church by its principal door and goes to the city gate or other place where the personage is to be received. The two principal clerks of the church conduct the ceremony.

At the appointed place, the celebrant meets the visitor and presents to him incense to bless. The incense imposed in the usual way, the celebrant incenses the visitor. Surrendering the thurible, he presents the sprinkler to the visitor, who takes holy water and then sprinkles those before him. The sprinkler is returned to the water-boy and the procession reforms, the visitor being conducted to the church by the celebrant and his fellow, who walk on either side of him, the principal on the right.[58] The choir follows as before. As they set out, the responsory, *Summae Trinitati*, is sung. At the altar step, the visitor makes a prostration[59] and prays silently. The celebrant, standing, says *Kyrie eleison*, &c. without note, and then sings *Et ne nos inducas*, &c. The visitor rises and all proceed to their next business.

---

[54] P.164–7.
[55] Cons 115 and P.169, supplemented by Wells.34–5 and the *Caeremoniale Episcoporum* (Lib. I. Cap. II. §5), which sources fail to agree on the ceremonies. P.169 has the visitor offered incense, holy water and an escort back to the church. Wells.34–5 offers incense, a Text to kiss and an escort. The *Caeremoniale Episcoporum* would have the prelate offer a cross (not a Text) at the city gates and then, at the church door, holy water and incense. Cf. OP.1780–9.
[56] This list interprets *archiepiscopum, proprium episcopum, legatum vel cardinalem, regem vel reginam* (P.169). This understanding of *reginam* is consistent with the sacramental treatment given to the queens consort of England at their coronation. Presumably, a queen regnant's consort would not be received with the same solemnity on account of his marriage alone.
[57] The English Act of Settlement (1701) precludes the possibility of a Catholic Sovereign or royal consort. See Chapter IX, note 3 on naming the Sovereign in the Canon.
[58] *Caeremoniale Episcoporum loc. cit.* has this priest stand at the south of the altar step later.
[59] P.169: *cum prosternant se*.

XXVII

THE BLESSING OF BREAD ON SUNDAYS

If bread is to be blessed and distributed after the principal Mass on Sundays,[1] it is brought up at the people's offertory and set aside with the other offerings until the end of Mass, when it is to be blessed.

After Mass, the priest, instead of saying the Gospel *In principio* on his way to the vestry, says it at the north end of the altar, as he did the first Gospel. Removing his chasuble,[2] which may be left on the altar, he comes to the choir step.[3] He is assisted by the deacon on his right and the subdeacon on his left. The water-boy hands the sprinkler to the deacon as required. The book is held by the book-boy. The loaf, most suitably on a plate, is held by the server who will distribute it to the congregation later.

According to custom, the bread may be distributed by the server or received by the people from the hand of the celebrant. It may be consumed in church or taken home to the sick. In either case, it should be treated with the respect due to a sacramental.

---

[1] This blessing is given with slightly different wording at Coll 35**and 849*, M.4 and M.67. The bread is the Latin equivalent of the Greek ἀντίδωρον and may be given to any Catholic who has not been excommunicated, whether eligible to receive Communion or not. See *The Catholic Encyclopedia* s.v. 'Bread, Liturgical Use of' and Duffy, *Stripping*, page 125. Pascal Dagnan-Bouveret's *Le Pain Bénit* depicts its distribution in nineteenth-century France, by a server to seated congregants. In England, the holy bread seems to have been received from the priest's hands and taken home for those who had been unable to attend the Mass (S.336). At Lyons III.307, the bread is blessed at the offertory. The loaf is of ordinary leavened bread. The churchwardens' accounts of Stanford-in-the-Vale, to which Duffy refers, after listing the houses from which the bread came, give the following:

> Thus endythe geuyng of the breade to make holy bredde of Throwgh the whole Towne both wher yt begyneth & endyth The wholl valure of The cargs [sc. charge] cumyth to ii*d* ob [sc. ½ d] and yt ys Thus devided. The offer to the curats hand Too peny worth of bread with a halfepeny candull or a halfepeny for the candull putte in to a Taper & browght uppe to the preste at the highe altr. of the Too penyworthe of bredde they Resyrve a halfepeny lofe wholl for to be delyvered to The next that shal geve the holy loofe for a knowledge to prepare agaynst the sooneday folloyng. And thus I make an ende of this matter. (Haines, p. 71)

[2] Ebor.39 has the chasuble removed for the blessing after the nuptial Mass. The chasuble may be removed after the Last Gospel or before it, as at Coutances (*Tracts*.67).

[3] The water at the *Asperges* and the spouses after the exchange of consent are blessed at the choir step. It is less clear whether he should face east or west. East seems more plausible.

BOOK VII

THE RITUAL YEAR

XXVIII

ADVENT AND CHRISTMAS

§1. THE SEASON OF ADVENT

At all Masses, whether of the season or not,[1] the *Gloria in excelsis* is omitted, and *Benedicamus Domino* takes the place of *Ite missa est*.[2] The acolyte leaves off his tunicle and vests in amice, alb and cincture.[3] He uses the humeral veil in the usual fashion.[4] At Masses of the season and votive Masses other than those of the Cross and *Salus populi*,[5] the deacon and subdeacon wear chasubles instead of dalmatic and tunicle. On vigils now and throughout the year, unless otherwise specified, the ministers wear neither chasubles nor dalmatic and tunicle,[6] but on Christmas Eve,[7] if it falls on a Sunday, the ministers wear dalmatic and tunicle, and then the acolyte reads the prophecy from the pulpit and not from the choir step.[8] Mid-Advent has no special colour or ceremonies.

§2. THE EMBER DAYS

The Ember Days are held in the third week of Advent, the first full week of Lent, Whit Week and in September.[9] The Masses for these last may be found in the Missal after the last Sunday after Trinity. All are celebrated on the lines of those in Advent, with very few differences. Except in Whit Week, the ministers wear neither chasubles nor dalmatic and tunicle.[10] Likewise, the acolyte does not use the tunicle.

On Wednesday and Friday, there are no significant variations from the usual ceremonial. Saturday is more complicated.[11] The prayers are sung at the south corner of

---

[1] Col 3; Col 659; Missal C.233.
[2] Col 2.
[3] The rule is that the acolyte wears the tunicle only when *Gloria in excelsis* is said: Cons 55.
[4] C 66.12 has the humeral veil worn in Advent.
[5] For this Mass, see Coll 1, 19 and 740–741*. The rubrics at Coll 1 and 19 are probably merely ceremonial (see *Defensorium Directorii* [1]).
[6] Coll 1 and 676.
[7] Col 1.
[8] Col 45.
[9] The rule for determining the dates of the Ember Days is given at C 56.
[10] Coll 1 and 676.
[11] As usual, the Sarum rubrics are sparse. They are here supplemented from OP.1530-1 (which deal with Holy Saturday) and De Herdt, t. I. p. 2. n. 42. cap. II (for the ceremonial surrounding *Flectamus*

the altar, attended by the ministers as for the collect. They are not preceded by *Dominus vobiscum*. In Lent, *Oremus* is preceded by *Flectamus genua* and *Levate*. The deacon, as he sings *Flectamus genua*, kneels,[12] followed at once by all except the celebrant.[13] Likewise, the subdeacon rises as he sings *Levate*. All follow him, kissing the forms.[14] For the prophecies and chants, the celebrant and ministers sit, returning to the altar for each prayer. The lessons are read in ordinary choir dress from the choir step,[15] the first by an acolyte (who may be the acolyte of the Mass in his vestments)[16] and the others by clerks in ascending order of rank.[17] On Ember Saturdays, the lessons are read by readers taken alternately from the two sides of the choir.[18] The first four chants are sung at the choir step by a single different surpliced cantor,[19] the last by two of a higher rank in choir dress.[20] The tract of the Mass is sung straight through by two second-form clerks in choir dress at the choir step. Meanwhile, the choir sits.[21] At Low Mass, the celebrant remains at the missal after the *Kyrie*. He kneels whenever he says *Flectamus genua*.[22] All kneel with the celebrant. The server replies *Levate*. The celebrant reads all the lessons and chants himself.

§3. CHRISTMAS AND EPIPHANY

The Processional makes Christmas the model for all processions on principal doubles. The Missal[23] includes three Masses for Christmas: *in gallicantu* (with four rulers), *in aurora* (with two rulers) and *in die* (with four rulers).[24] The usual rules concerning bination apply. The Missal presumes that the first Mass follows on immediately from Matins, the Officium being intoned as soon as *Te Deum* is finished.[25] In this case, the

---

genua). The Roman rite has the celebrant stand at the altar for the lessons, as it does for the epistle at Mass, though even he is allowed to sit on Holy Saturday after he has read each prophecy at the altar until the lector has finished chanting it (F.326).

[12] De Herdt reports that some authorities prescribe kneeling on both knees, though he himself recommends genuflecting on one knee only. OP.775 prescribes kneeling.

[13] OP.1281.

[14] Col 135.

[15] C 66.39. Col 543 (September) has the lessons and chants run through the choir as in Advent. Col 34 (Advent) gives no such directions. Neither does Col 164 (Lent). Although Whit Week may be an unreliable guide, it is the order given there (Col 444) that has been adopted here.

[16] For this supposition, see Chapter XV, note 1.

[17] In the cathedral, the first four lessons are sung by surpliced clerks of the second form and the fifth by a priest of the upper form.

[18] Coll 543 and 546 say this of the Ember Days in Advent, Whit Week and September, so it is reasonable to assume that the same order was followed in Lent.

[19] C 66.39: *singuli pueri*.

[20] Two clerks of the second form are appointed: C 66.40; Coll 37, 167, 449 (where the black *cappa choralis* is naturally omitted) and 546 (also without *cappae*).

[21] C 66.40.

[22] See Chapter V, note 21.

[23] Col 47 includes the additional Gospel sung immediately before *Te Deum* at Matins. Since this is inseparable from the choral office, which is beyond the scope of this book, we omit the ceremonies with which it is sung.

[24] Cons 47 gives the number of rulers for the first two Masses; of the third (*ad magnam Missam*), Cons 59 has *simili modo ut primam*.

[25] Col 50.

celebrant, ministers and servers will leave the choir during *Te Deum* in order to vest.[26] In this Mass, when it is sung, the prophecy is farsed by two clerks of the second form in copes from the pulpitum[27] to a special tone.[28] At Low Mass, the prophecy is said, without farsing, in the usual way.[29] In the second and third Masses, the prophecy is sung in the usual manner from the pulpitum, if possible not by the acolyte of the Mass but by a surpliced clerk, chosen from the second form for the dawn Mass and from the upper form for the day Mass.[30] At the end of the third Mass, if None is to follow immediately in the choir, before leaving the altar, the priest sings the verse *Verbum caro factum est*.[31] On Epiphany Eve, the deacon and subdeacon wear dalmatic and tunicle.[32] On the day itself, the verse *Balaam*, &c. in the sequence is sung thrice.[33]

---

[26] OP.1355.
[27] M.5.
[28] M.5 and its Appendix I.
[29] Col 51.
[30] Coll 55 and 58; Cons 56.
[31] Frere, *Use of Sarum* II.31. When the Bishop celebrates the Mass, the verse is sung by the officiant of None from his stall.
[32] Col 80.
[33] Col 85.

XXIX

CANDLEMAS[1]

§1. PREPARATIONS

The function takes place after Sext.[2] In addition to the usual preparations for Mass, the following are made.

In the vestry are laid out a cope for the celebrant, which he will wear over alb, stole and maniple;[3] amices, albs, cinctures and tunicles will be required for the acolyte-crucifers. In greater churches, there may be three of these.[4] The ministers wear their Mass vestments, including dalmatic and tunicle.[5] An additional surplice is prepared for the sacristan who will carry the candle destined for use during the Easter Vigil.[6] If another server will help with the distribution of candles, a surplice is laid out for him also. Two thurifers with thuribles are supposed.[7] Three processional crosses are prepared, as are the holy-water stoup and sprinkler.

The choir should assist in copes.[8] These may be prepared in the vestry, but if the function is to follow Sext immediately, six boys[9] will bring them into the middle of the choir and spread them on the floor for the clergy to don them as soon as Sext is finished.[10]

Next to the south horn of the altar,[11] an easily portable table is prepared, decently apparelled, on which are laid the candles that will be blessed. Alternatively, the candles

---

[1] Neither OP.1620-4 nor the Sarum books (P.139 seq.; Coll 696–706; Cons 58–59 and the Customary) give complete instructions, so this paragraph owes much to F.257 seq.
[2] Col 696. The earlier practice (Cons 58) was to bless the candles after Terce.
[3] Col 696: *cum aliis indumentis sacerdotalibus*. But the maniple may be omitted: see OP.546 and Chapter III, note 4.
[4] P.11.
[5] Unlike in the Roman rite, but like OP.1620, the function is entirely festal and so the sacred ministers wear dalmatic and tunicle (a detail deduced from Col 1).
[6] P.143.
[7] P.140.
[8] C 46.1.
[9] P.11 describes these boys as *ad ministrandum vestiti*, i.e., either in surplices (for attending the choir) or in albs (as servers in the sanctuary).
[10] P.11; Rock II.40.
[11] Col 695; P.140. The woodcut at P.140 is interpreted at *Processions*.99). The celebrant will have to stand *super supremum gradum altaris converso ad orientem* (P.139) or *ad summum gradum altaris* (Col 695).
   The Missal, P and the woodcut at P.140 give mutually exclusive directions, possibly reflecting local differences. If the book is to be held before the celebrant while he blesses the candles (as

may be piled up on the floor.[12] Among these will be the candle which will be used at the blessing of the font on Holy Saturday.[13] It will be convenient if the candles for distribution among the choir and congregation are placed in baskets. On the altar itself are placed the Texts (if used) and the open missal on its stand.[14]

§2. THE BLESSING AND DISTRIBUTION OF CANDLES

The celebrant makes his entrance as for a procession on a major double, save that the surpliced sacristan (with an assistant server, if present, to his left) walks behind the thurifers and in front of the subdeacon and that the sacred ministers do not carry Texts.[15] If the feast falls on a Sunday, the *Asperges* follows using the water blessed earlier.[16] If the *Asperges* is to be omitted, the water-boy does not bring the salt and the book-boy may be dispensed with.

At the choir step, the acolytes (and the second thurifer) stand aside, on the north side of the sanctuary, facing east.[17] The taperers remain at the choir step. The ministers stand aside to let the celebrant and the book-boy pass. Preceded by the water-boy (and the book-boy, if he be present),[18] the deacon at his right and the subdeacon at his left, the celebrant advances to the foot of the altar. There he goes to the missal at the south corner of the altar and faces east.[19] The ministers stand on either side of him. The deacon must take care not to stand between the celebrant and the candles.[20] The (first) thurifer and the water-boy stand to the right of the deacon, facing north. With joined hands,[21] the celebrant sings *Dominus vobiscum* and the prayers of blessing. When making the sign of the cross over the candles, he lays his left hand on the altar.[22] During these prayers, all in choir stand facing the altar.[23] The preface is sung with joined hands.[24] At the spoken end of the preface, the thurifer approaches the deacon. Incense is blessed

---

indicated by the woodcut at P.140), the celebrant cannot stand on the footpace. If he is to stand *super supremum gradum altaris converso ad orientem* (P.139), he will need to read the blessings from the missal lying on its desk on the altar, as we suppose here.

[12] *Super gradus presbyterii* (OP.1620). This will be more practical if all the candles that the church will consume over the course of the following year are to be blessed.

[13] In Sarum church, this was the candle presented by the Bishop and weighed 6 lb (*Processions*.100). This candle should not be confused with the Paschal Candle itself.

[14] The ministers will not carry books (see note 23) and the missal will be needed by the celebrant when blessing the candles.

[15] If they are to carry candles later (P.143: *omnes clerici*).

[16] OP.1620; F.87 and 258.

[17] Woodcut at P.140.

[18] Woodcut at P.140.

[19] This position (P.139 but see note there, P.140 (woodcut), Col 696) is disputed: *Defensorium Directorii* [21] and *Crede Michi* [134].

[20] Col 695 (*cereos et candelas sub manu sua dextera jacentes*) does not require the celebrant to touch the candles, but the crosses must be made over the candles.

[21] See Chapter XIX, note 33.

[22] But if he reads the prayers from a book held by a book-boy, he will lay his left hand on his breast.

[23] OP.1379.

[24] By analogy with the blessing of the font on Holy Saturday in the Roman rite (F.329).

and imposed as at Mass. The thurifer withdraws.[25] The water-boy now approaches. The deacon takes the sprinkler and hands it to the celebrant, who sprinkles the candles. He returns the sprinkler to the deacon, who replaces it in the stoup. The water-boy steps back. The thurifer passes the thurible to the deacon, who hands it to the celebrant. The celebrant incenses the candles with three swings and returns the thurible to the deacon, who hands it back to the thurifer. The sacristan approaches and, having lit that candle which will be the celebrant's,[26] holds it up to the celebrant,[27] who in the same way as before sings *Dominus vobiscum* and the next two prayers.

During these prayers, the senior ruler of the choir,[28] being ordinarily the priest highest in rank present, comes up to the candles and, the prayers finished, receives the celebrant's candle from the sacristan. The celebrant and ministers return to the middle of the altar where they turn west, so that the deacon stands on the celebrant's left and the subdeacon on the right. There the celebrant receives his lit candle, standing, from the senior ruler of the choir, who immediately returns to the choir,[29] which at once begins *Lumen*[30] and the *Nunc dimittis*, repeating it if necessary until all the candles have been lit and distributed. If there is no suitable priest, the celebrant takes his own candle from the altar, where the sacristan will have placed it.[31]

Meanwhile, the sacristan hands lit candles to the ministers[32] who, with the celebrant, retire to the sedilia[33] until the distribution of the candles is complete. The sacristan, assisted as necessary, now distributes candles to the choir, beginning with the upper form on the senior side.[34] If laymen are to be given candles, they receive them after the clergy and at the chancel step or in the nave. During the distribution, the servers assemble for the procession in the same order as before.

§3. THE PROCESSION AND THE MASS

When the distribution is over, the celebrant and ministers come back to the choir step. The sacristan brings the candle for the blessing of the font. Incense is now blessed and imposed at the choir step, the thurifers holding the boats, and the procession sets out

---

[25] In funerals of the Roman rite, at the absolution the celebrant blesses the incense, then sprinkles and lastly incenses the catafalque (F.422).
[26] Rock IV.69 supposes that from this candle all the others will be lit.
[27] P.142.
[28] OP.1621.
[29] The implication of OP.1621.
[30] OP.1621 has the cantor intone *Lumen* as he gives the celebrant his candle.
[31] F.258.
[32] OP.1621.
[33] Cons 58; P.143. The rubric mentioning the Bishop is unclear; by analogy with the Roman rite, it is possible that the Bishop distributed the candles from the throne (Ahearne and Lane, page 147), but it appears that a presbyter celebrant did not distribute the candles personally at all. At Wells, he certainly did not (Wells.30). It is unlikely that the celebrant distributed the candles from his stall in choir and that *stallo* is used at Cons 58 to signify the sedilia.
[34] OP.1621; OPraem.XXVIII.19. Neither the Sarum nor the Dominican books mention kneeling to receive the candles. P.143 does not state who lights the candles. The rubric suggests that the candles are lit and then distributed, but this would take a long time and it may be more practical, as in the Roman rite, to take *accendantur candelae et distribuantur* as a hysteron-proteron.

as on principal doubles. All who are able to do so carry candles.³⁵ As the procession sets out, the choir begins *Ave gratia plena*. At the station before the Rood, three senior clerks from the choir turn west and sing the verse *Hodie*. After the collect *Exaudi*, the procession retires to the vestry as usual.³⁶ The celebrant should wash his hands. Mass follows.

The Mass has its own peculiarities.³⁷ The table used for the blessing of the candles is removed. The sacristan takes his previous place in the entrance procession. He will occupy a place in the sanctuary near the credence table. Those in choir hold their candles lit constantly until the oblation, when they present them as their offering.³⁸ The celebrant, deacon and subdeacon bring their lit candles with them as they enter and give them up to the sacristan at the foot of the altar. They are then kept on the credence table. Before Septuagesima, the gradual *Suscepimus Deus* is sung, followed by *Alleluya Adorabo* and the sequence *Hac clara die*, during which the verse *Ave Maria gratia Dei plena per saecula* is sung thrice. After Septuagesima, the Alleluya and its verse are omitted but the sequence is sung as usual. However, at the sedilia, the celebrant and the ministers read the tract *Nunc dimittis* in place of the sequence.³⁹ If the celebrant is to hold his lit candle for the Gospel,⁴⁰ the sacristan brings it up to him after he has signed himself at *Gloria tibi Domine* and receives it back before the celebrant intones the creed. After the altar has been incensed at the offertory, the celebrant and ministers come down to the foot of the altar as usual for the people's offering. There a taperer brings them their candles, lit. The deacon is given the celebrant's candle to pass on and then his own; the subdeacon is given his from the left. The celebrant and ministers come to the choir step, where they extinguish their candles and, in order, deliver them to the sacristan.⁴¹ The choir,⁴² having extinguished their candles, then come up as usual and offer their candles, the subdeacon passing them to the sacristan.

---

³⁵ Wells.52.
³⁶ On Holy Saturday, the celebrant takes his chasuble from the altar (Coll 343+ and 352) but the circumstances are different. Then the chasuble is assumed in mid-service for the prophecies. Likewise, on Maundy Thursday, after the reconciliation of the penitents, a presbyteral celebrant takes up the chasuble from the altar (P.58), but the very fact that this detail is mentioned suggests that it was a rubrical peculiarity of this day. Even on such days, there appears to have existed a certain latitude of praxis. On Good Friday, Col 328 (note d) assumes that the chasuble is left at the sedilia, but P.69 has it left on the altar. It does not seem to be anywhere suggested that on Sundays the chasuble is taken from the altar after the procession. Rather, it is implied that the clergy come from the vestry. However, on Sundays, the Mass does not necessarily follow the procession immediately, whereas on Candlemas both procession and Mass take place after Sext (Col 696). Like the Dominicans on Holy Saturday (OP.1529) and Candlemas (OP.1623), a return to the vestry is contemplated here, but room may be allowed for legitimate variation.
³⁷ OP.1623.
³⁸ OP.1624.
³⁹ Col 705. One can see here an evolution of the rite: Cons 59 has: *sacerdos vero et ministri eius ad altare privatim dicant tractum* Nunc dimittis.
⁴⁰ F.260. Neither the Sarum nor the Dominican books mention this, but Wells.52 has the somewhat garbled *praeterea eodem die [sc. purificationis] candela de lib: tenend' sacerdot in celebracione misse*.
⁴¹ OP.1624.
⁴² OP.1623. OPraem.XXVIII.29-33 has the choir offer their candles immediately after the procession and laymen theirs at the offertory. The candles are delivered up lit and removed to be extinguished.

§4. THE SIMPLE FORM OF THE RITE

In the absence of sacred ministers, the celebrant supplies their part. It is unlikely that there will be a choir composed of clergy. The celebrant imposes and then blesses incense himself. He will receive his candle from another priest if one is present; otherwise, he will receive it from the sacristan. He does not hold his candle while he sings the Gospel.

If necessary, the function may be carried out with the celebrant and two servers only: a thurifer, who will double as crucifer and water-boy; and another, who will assist with the candles. The celebrant may sing or recite the chants himself.

XXX

SEPTUAGESIMA AND LENT

§1. VEILS

Before Matins of the first Monday of Lent all the crosses, images[1] and reliquaries are veiled until Easter morning. The tabernacle or other place of reservation of the Blessed Sacrament is also concealed with a veil.[2]

In addition to these veils, from the first Monday[3] of Lent until Spy Wednesday, a great veil hangs over the presbyterium, between the choir and the altar.[4] This is raised to reveal the altar and lowered to conceal it. It remains lowered throughout Lent but is raised during ferial Masses at the beginning of the Gospel. It is lowered immediately before[5] *Orate fratres* but raised from the Sacring to the elevation, after which it is lowered immediately.[6] It is raised again for *Humiliate capita vestra Deo* and so until the end of the Mass,[7] when it is lowered again. However, on Sundays and during the week when the office is not of the feria, the veil remains raised throughout the day from before first Vespers to before the next ferial Matins; but if on these days a ferial Mass is also said (after None),[8] the veil is lowered from the beginning of this until the Gospel and is then raised for the rest of the day.[9] On Lenten ferias, the epistles are read at the choir step,[10] between the choir and the veil, except for those taken from the prophetical books, which are read in the presbyterium, between the veil and the altar.

---

[1] C 60.1 makes an exception of the principal image of St. Mary on Lady Day, either on account of the solemnity of the day or because she is the cathedral's titular saint.
[2] C 60.1. No colour is specified. Lenten array would be suitable.
[3] Not the preceding Saturday as at Cons 64.2.
[4] C 60.2. For the positioning of this veil, see Chapter I, note 10.
[5] The ambiguity of C 60.2 is removed by Cons 64.2: *et post sacerdos dicat* Orate fratres.
[6] C 60.2, C 60.3. This was an innovation not contemplated by Cons 64.2.
[7] Cons 64.2.
[8] Col 730. On these days, the choir prostrates after the *Sanctus* only at the ferial Mass. See Chapter XXII, note 57.
[9] C 60.3.
[10] Cons 64.3 says *in presbyterio inter chorum et velum*, which does not seem materially different from the choir step.

§2. THE FERIAL PROCESSION

On Wednesdays and Fridays in Lent unimpeded by feasts of nine lessons, a special procession is held after None and before the ferial Mass.[11] Those who take part are the taperers with their tapers, the subdeacon, the deacon and the celebrant.[12] A book-boy may take part, or the book may be held by one of the ministers. There is no cross.[13] The clergy wear albs. The deacon and the celebrant wear their stoles.[14] The choir follows in choir dress. The procession leaves from the choir step and goes directly to a different side altar on each day, taking them in order and beginning on the north side. On arrival at the day's side altar, the taperers place their tapers on the altar and come to stand on either side of the ministers. The celebrant stands in the middle, with the deacon on his right and the subdeacon on his left. The choir stands behind them in processional order.[15] When the responsory is finished, all make a prostration.[16] The celebrant begins *Kyrie eleison* and *Pater noster* without note. *Et ne nos inducas* and the following verses are sung to the usual tone. The psalm, *Miserere*, is said without note but with *Gloria Patri* and *Sicut erat*, after which the celebrant alone rises and sings *Exurge Domine*, the other verses and the collect. As the priest sings *Per Christum Dominum nostrum*, all kiss the ground and rise. Two clerks of the second form begin the litany. After *Sancta Maria* has been sung, the procession turns and departs.[17] As far as possible, the procession should move clockwise to the west door of the choir,[18] singing the section of the litany appointed for that day. If there is time, more than one section may be sung. There is no station at the Rood. When the celebrant reaches the choir step, the verses *Omnes sanctae virgines* and *Omnes sancti* are sung. The choir having occupied the stalls to begin the Officium, the celebrant and his ministers return to the vestry[19] to vest. Mass follows immediately.

§3. RITUAL PECULIARITIES

From Septuagesima and throughout Lent, at all Masses, whether of the season or not,[20] the *Gloria in excelsis* is omitted and *Benedicamus Domino* takes the place of *Ite missa est*. On ferias, the gradual is not repeated when a tract is sung.[21] The gradual is repeated on feasts of three lessons from Septuagesima to Ash Wednesday.[22] On Sundays and

---

[11] P.32–41.
[12] There is no need for water-boy and thurifer, though the Processional is silent on the matter.
[13] The rubric specifies that there is no cross. See also Cons 65.
[14] Maniples are worn at these processions if they are used normally in processions. See Chapter III, note 4.
[15] P.32. Cons 65 says *quo ordine in choro ordinantur*.
[16] P.32: *prostrationem faciant*.
[17] This is the general rule when the litany is said in procession (C 55).
[18] In Sarum church, the procession left the choir by the north presbytery door, went to the first altar on the north side and then went round the ambulatory to the west door of the choir.
[19] P.41: *sacerdos cum suis ministris abscedat*.
[20] Col 108 (also implied at Coll 3 and 674).
[21] Coll 109, and 139; Cons 46.1. For the days when the tract is omitted, see Col 111.
[22] Cons 46.1. The same rule applies to the commemoration of St. Mary in those churches that celebrate it.

feasts of nine lessons, the tract is sung by four upper-form clerks.[23] On the first Sunday in Lent, and on all ferial Mondays, Wednesdays and Fridays until Spy Wednesday,[24] the verses of the tract are alternated by the two sides of the whole choir, that side standing which is singing while the other sits.[25]

From the second Sunday in Lent until the Triduum, at functions of the season, whether dominical or ferial, and then only, the ordinary processional cross is laid aside and in its place is used the red-painted wooden cross without a crucifix.[26] On other occasions when the processional cross would normally be borne, the ordinary crucifix is used.

As in Advent, at Masses of the season and votive Masses other than those of the Cross and *Salus populi*, the deacon and subdeacon wear chasubles instead of dalmatic and tunicle. The acolyte leaves off his tunicle but uses the humeral veil as usual. Dalmatic and tunicle are worn for festal Masses.[27]

The tracts are sung alternately by the choir.[28] In the tract *Domine non secundum* no genuflexion is made.[29]

On the Ember Days and on vigils, the ministers wear neither chasubles nor dalmatic and tunicle.[30] On Ember Saturday, the Tract *Benedictus* is sung by two surpliced clerks of the second form at the choir step, alternating with the choir,[31] but the Tract *Laudate* is sung straight through by two clerks of the second form in *cappae chorales*;[32] on this day, the prayer over the people is omitted at the ordination Mass.[33]

If Lady Day falls before Easter, the choir sing the gradual and then the sequence *Ave mundi spes*, but the celebrant and the ministers at the sedilia read secretly the Tract *Ave Maria* in place of the sequence.[34]

Mid-Lent Sunday has no special colour or ceremonies.

At Masses of the season from Passion Sunday until Maundy Thursday, the *Gloria Patri* is omitted in the Officium.[35]

On the ferias of Holy Week, Mass is celebrated as on other Lenten ferias in Passiontide. On Tuesday and Wednesday, the Passions and Gospels are read with the same ceremonies as on Palm Sunday, introduced with *Dominus vobiscum* and the title. On Spy Wednesday, the Lenten veil remains lowered during the Passion until the words *Velum templi scissum est*, when it is suddenly dropped to the ground altogether and not used again.[36]

The functions on Ash Wednesday, Palm Sunday and the Sacred Triduum merit special treatment.

---

[23] Col 109.
[24] Cons 46.1; Col 288.
[25] C 66.18.
[26] C 58 (for Sundays) and P.41 (for ferias). This cross is not used at functions at which the processional cross would not normally be carried.
[27] Cons 60. In greater churches, the festal Mass is said in the morning and that of the feria after None.
[28] See Coll 136 and 288 and C 66.18 for the way to do this.
[29] Coll 137, 142 and 205.
[30] Coll 1 and 676.
[31] Col 167.
[32] Col 169.
[33] Col 170.
[34] Col 728.
[35] Coll 2 and 235. For the manner of singing the Officium in Passiontide, see page 147.
[36] Col 294; C 60.4.

XXXI

ASH WEDNESDAY

The function takes place after Sext, though it may be preceded immediately by a sermon.[1] The colour is red.[2] In addition to the usual preparations for Mass, the following preparations are made.

In the vestry are prepared a cope for the celebrant; surplices for the book-boy and water-boy; chasubles for the sacred ministers;[3] the holy-water stoup and sprinkler; and the penitential banner,[4] which, however, may well be omitted if there are no penitents to expel. The choir, which is presumed to be already in its stalls, will assist in ordinary choir dress. Of its number should be the priest who will impose the ashes on the celebrant. For this purpose, he should wear a stole.

The altar is prepared as for Mass on a Lenten feria. To the right of the open missal in silver plates are placed the ashes.[5]

If the expulsion of penitents is to follow the imposition of ashes, at the credence table or the piscina should be a vessel with water and a basin, a towel and a plate with bread for the celebrant to wash his hands after distributing the ashes. More generally, the celebrant will wash his hands in the vestry before beginning the Mass.

The clergy make their entrance in the usual order, the acolyte with the banner and the celebrant in cope. The ministers do not put on their chasubles until the Mass. The water-boy does not bring salt. The celebrant and the ministers go as far as the altar step, where they kneel prostrate,[6] the deacon on the right and the subdeacon on the left. The celebrant begins the antiphon *Ne reminiscaris* in a clear spoken voice. As he does so, all make a prostration with them, except the acolyte, who stands east of the choir step on the north side of the sanctuary, holding the banner.[7]

---

[1] Col 123; P.26. Missal B.51 has a sermon preached after the ashes have been blessed and before they are imposed.
[2] Col 123.
[3] Col 1.
[4] Called the *vexillum cilicinum*, so presumably made of goat's hair (du Cange s.v. *cilicium*). The woodcut at P.30 illustrates it.
[5] P. 28.
[6] Col 123: *in prostratione*. The usual ambiguity of this term makes it possible that the celebrant and ministers lay prostrate on the floor, as the Dominicans do both today (OP.1376) and on Maundy Thursday (OP.1438).
[7] Col 131.

All, including the celebrant and the ministers,[8] recite the seven penitential psalms in the same voice, the choir alternating as usual.[9] During the silent *Pater noster*, the celebrant and ministers,[10] together with the book-boy, rise. Facing east,[11] from the book held by the book-boy,[12] the priest sings *Et ne nos inducas in tentationem* and the following verses.[13] With joined hands,[14] the celebrant chants the prayers[15] under a single *Dominus vobiscum* but repeating *Oremus* at the beginning of each. He does not turn for *Dominus vobiscum*.[16] After the last prayer, which is *Deus cujus indulgentia*, the celebrant turns by his right and, reading from the book held by the book-boy, who has come round before him, extending his right hand over the people, keeping his left on his breast, pronounces in a clear spoken voice[17] the absolution, *Absolvimus vos*. As the celebrant says the conclusion, *Qui vivit*, &c. all rise from their prostration, kissing the forms or the ground.[18] Turning east again, the celebrant goes up to the missal with the ministers, who stand on either side of him. There, with neither *Dominus vobiscum* nor *Oremus*, the priest says the prayer of blessing, *Omnipotens sempiterne Deus qui misereris*, making the sign of the cross over the ashes at *bene* ✠ *dicere et sancti* ✠ *ficare*. During this prayer, the choir stands facing the altar.[19]

As this prayer comes to an end, the water-boy comes from the choir step to stand at the right of the deacon, to whom he hands the sprinkler. Receiving this from the deacon, the celebrant sprinkles the ashes[20] and returns the sprinkler to the deacon, who passes it to the water-boy. The water-boy retires. Meanwhile, facing the missal, the celebrant says *Dominus vobiscum*, *Oremus* and the prayer *Deus qui non mortem*, as before. At the conclusion of this prayer, the choir begins singing the antiphon *Exaudi* and the chants that follow it.

The priest should receive the ashes from another priest, the senior clerk present. The deacon bringing the ashes,[21] the celebrant and ministers go to the middle of the altar and come down to the presbytery or altar step, the deacon and subdeacon changing places behind the celebrant so that they stand either side of him, the

---

[8] Coll 123, 130. It is presumed that the psalms are recited from memory. In case of necessity, a server may bring a book to the deacon who, together with the subdeacon, holds it open before the celebrant.
[9] OP.1377.
[10] Col 131, against *Crede Michi* [72].
[11] *Defensorium Directorii* [21], against OP.1378.
[12] P.26.
[13] F.269.
[14] F.269.
[15] The tone is not clear. Col 131 has: *omnes orationes dicuntur cum* Oremus, *et finiantur more lectionis*. C 66.38 (Frere, *Use of Sarum* I.272) gives a drop of a fourth after the last accented syllable for a *punctus* in the lesson tone, which corresponds to the end of the ferial tone in the Roman rite. However, the fall at the end of the lesson is given as a semitone only.
[16] The implication of Col 131; so also F.269.
[17] Col 132.
[18] Col 133.
[19] OP.1379.
[20] Col 133; P.28. Apparently the ashes are sprinkled in silence. There is no mention of incense, which the Dominicans also omit (OP.1380).
[21] So in the Roman rite.

deacon on his right and the subdeacon on his left to the south. At the step, they stand facing west. The priest who will impose ashes on the celebrant now comes up from the choir, in surplice and stole.[22] The celebrant kneels on the step facing east and receives ashes from the senior priest. Ashes are imposed by making an ashen cross on the head of the recipient with the thumb and forefinger of the right hand while pronouncing the form *Memento homo*, &c.[23] The celebrant and the senior priest exchange places and the celebrant imposes ashes on the latter, who retires immediately.

If no other priest is present to impose ashes on the celebrant, the priest kneels on the footpace before the middle of the altar and puts the ashes on himself, saying nothing.[24] The ministers kneel on the step behind him. Rising, the celebrant and ministers go down to the presbytery step as above.

Handing the plate with the ashes to the subdeacon, the deacon kneels before the celebrant and receives ashes on his own head. Taking the plate back, he assists the celebrant as he imposes ashes on the subdeacon. The clergy now come in descending order of rank[25] to receive ashes, kneeling,[26] from the celebrant. After the servers have received the ashes, going down to the chancel arch, the celebrant, still assisted by the ministers, imposes ashes on the laity.

The celebrant, accompanied by the deacon on his right and the subdeacon on his left, returns to the choir step, where he is met by the book-boy. There, facing east as before, he sings *Dominus vobiscum*, *Oremus* and the prayers *Deus qui juste irasceris* and *Concede nobis*.

The expulsion of penitents will hardly ever occur. If it is to be omitted, then the clergy assemble at the choir step after the prayer *Concede nobis* and return to the vestry.[27] There the celebrant washes his hands and puts on the chasuble. The ministers also put on their chasubles. Mass follows as usual. The collect is preceded by *Flectamus genua*[28] and *Levate*. The tract is alternated by the whole choir, the side that is singing standing while the other sits.[29]

The ceremonies may be carried out by a priest and one server only, who will supply the part played by the ministers. Any servers will prostrate themselves on either side

---

[22] OP.1376 has the hebdomadary and prior come in the procession, the latter wearing a surplice and stole, but at Sarum the relationship between the two priests is different. Since at Candlemas the celebrant receives his candle from the senior ruler coming up from the choir (OP.1621), an analogous priest in choir is supposed here. P.29 has the clerks who assist the Bishop to impose incense wear stoles.
[23] Col 134.
[24] F.269.
[25] Col 134.
[26] OP.1383.
[27] See Chapter XXIX, note 36, for why the clergy should return to the vestry before Mass. However, P.31 (*non dicatur versus neque oratio, sed statim incipiatur missa a cantore*) leaves open the possibility of beginning the Mass immediately after the procession has returned from expelling the penitents. The celebrant will then need to clean his hands, either at the piscina or at the altar, as in the Roman rite, before the prayer *Deus qui juste irasceris*. In the latter case, perhaps he may be permitted to say the final prayers at the altar instead of at the choir step. The celebrant and ministers will then put on their chasubles at the sedilia.
[28] Col 135 has: *omnes genu flectant*. Missal C.52, gives *omnes genua flectant*.
[29] Coll 12 and 136.

of the celebrant for the penitential psalms. The following verses and prayers, the absolution and the blessing of ashes may all take place at the missal. The server will administer the sprinkler. The celebrant will take the ashes from the altar and then read the antiphons at the distribution from the missal before imposing ashes on the server at the step.[30] The final prayers may be said at the missal. Low Mass follows.

---

[30] F.271.

XXXII

PALM SUNDAY

§1. PREPARATIONS

The function consists of three parts:[1] (1) the blessing and distribution of the palms; (2) the processions with the four solemn stations; and (3) the Mass, at which the Passion is read. The colour is red.

The following take part in the function:[2] the celebrant; the deacon of the Mass; the subdeacon of the Mass; the acolyte; the thurifer; the two taperers; the water-boy; the book-boy; the torchbearers, if desired; the three deacons of the Passion; a second crucifer for the Sacrament procession; a bearer of the lantern; two banner-bearers; two clerks in major orders[3] to carry the feretrum; canopy bearers in surplices;[4] if possible, a further clerk (deacon or presbyter) to place the Sacrament in the feretrum and reserve it later; the prophet; three cantors to sing at the first and third stations;[5] seven boys to sing at the second station; the choir; the vergers; and a sacristan.

In addition to the usual preparations for the Sunday procession and Mass, the following preparations are made.

In the vestry are prepared the Lenten processional cross and the ordinary[6] processional cross for the Sacrament procession; two processional banners;[7] the chest with the relics; a lantern to precede the Blessed Sacrament; the canopy to carry over the feretrum; vestments for the three deacons who will sing the Passion; clothing for the prophet; and surplices for the banner-bearers and for the sacristan who will assist with the palms and the unveiling of the crosses. The crosses should not be decorated with palms or flowers.[8]

---

[1] For the manner of performing the details of many of these ceremonies, see the description of Candlemas.
[2] Cons 26 gives the *tabula* for Palm Sunday.
[3] In the cathedral, of the second form (P.49).
[4] Bailey, page 16, numbers among the participants in this procession 'one clerk holding a canopy over the feretory on one side, and another in front, carrying a lighted lantern – both in surplices', but he does not give the Latin of his source (a manuscript processional, Bodley, Ms Rawl. Lit.d.4). On Corpus Christi, four bearers are required and we presume this here.
[5] In the cathedral, there should be three cantors of the second form to sing at the first station (P.50) and a further three priests of the upper step to sing at the third station (P.53).
[6] P.51. It need not be of silver as in Sarum church.
[7] No description of these banners is given.
[8] *Crede Michi* [79].

On the altar are placed the palms or fronds[9] for the clergy, that is to say, for the celebrant, the ministers and the choir. They should lie somewhat towards the south end of the altar so that they may be blessed with the same sign of the cross as those of the laity, which should be laid on the south steps of the altar.[10] The missal lies on its desk at the credence table unless the deacon will bring it with him at the beginning of the Mass. If used, a Gospel lectern is set up next to the north steps of the altar.[11]

§2. THE BLESSING AND DISTRIBUTION OF THE PALMS

The salt and water for the *Asperges* are blessed privately in advance, as on doubles.[12] The celebrant in cope, with the ministers in albs and amices without dalmatic and tunicle or chasubles,[13] with the servers, come to the sanctuary for the *Asperges*. After the prayer *Exaudi* is concluded, the celebrant and ministers repair to the sedilia. The taperers go to their positions as at Mass and lay down their candles. The acolyte, vested in an alb, takes the lesson book and reads the lesson *Venerunt*, standing at the south end of the altar step, facing east. At its conclusion, he returns the book to its place.

All now take up their positions as for the Gospel at ferial Masses.[14] Incense is blessed and imposed as usual.[15] The celebrant and ministers go to the altar, which is not incensed,[16] and the deacon is blessed.[17] The deacon sings the Gospel next to the altar as on ferias, but facing east,[18] with *Dominus vobiscum* and *Gloria tibi Domine* as usual. The cross is not carried. After the Gospel, the celebrant kisses the book as usual but is not incensed.[19]

The celebrant comes down and stands at the south end of the altar on the subdeacon's step[20] between the ministers.[21] There, facing east,[22] he reads from the book held before him by the book-boy the exorcism and the prayers from the missal with joined hands,

---

[9] Cons 38.2. They may be of yew, willow or box (Rock.IV124 and IV.265) and may include flowers (*Crede Michi* [79]).

[10] Col 255 and the woodcut at P.45, *pace* the rubric on the same page. See also *Crede Michi* [79].

[11] C 66.41.

[12] P.1.

[13] P.44.

[14] *Crede Michi* [79]. See OP.1409 for details of the Dominicans' practice.

[15] Its omission is nowhere mentioned and all the other normal ceremonies are presumed. The Roman rite uses incense (F.274).

[16] The incensation of the middle of the altar is probably connected with the corporal and so should be omitted here.

[17] Col 254.

[18] Col 254; M.12; *Crede Michi* [79] and the 1517 edition of the Processional say that this Gospel is read facing east, against P.44, which has it read facing north.

[19] C 66.41. OP.1410.

[20] The woodcut at P.45 supposes that the book is held by the book-boy. The celebrant is to stand *in gradu tertio* (P.45), *super gradum tertium altaris* (Col 255), where the Cross on Good Friday will be laid (*super gradum tertium ab altari*, Col 330). The footpace elsewhere is the *supremus gradus* (P.139, Col 695), so it appears that the altar steps are to be counted in descending order.

[21] Woodcut P.45.

[22] *Crede Michi* [79]; *Defensorium Directorii* [21]. See also M.13.

the former in a clear spoken voice[23] and the latter in the ferial tone.[24] The book-boy should stand a little to the celebrant's left so as not to stand between him and the clergy's palms on the altar. The choir stands facing the altar during these prayers[25] and remains so until the distribution begins. The celebrant should make the crosses large enough to cover the palms of both the clergy and the laity. The thurifer and the water-boy stand to the right of the deacon facing north. After the prayer *Deus qui dispersa*, incense is blessed and imposed as at Mass. The deacon assists the celebrant as he sprinkles and then incenses the palms. *Dominus vobiscum*, *Oremus* and the prayer *Domine Jesu Christe mundi conditor* now follow.

At the conclusion of the last prayer of blessing, the choir sings the two antiphons beginning *Pueri Hebraeorum*, and the palms are distributed as were the candles at Candlemas.[26]

The senior priest present, who will ordinarily be the first ruler of the choir,[27] comes up to the middle of the altar, takes from it the celebrant's palm and descends. The celebrant and ministers come to the middle of the altar. The celebrant receives his palm from the ruler and immediately hands it to the subdeacon to place again on the altar. If there is no suitable priest, however, the celebrant takes his own palm from the altar, kneeling to do so.[28] The ruler withdraws.

The sacristan gives palms to the deacon and to the subdeacon,[29] who with the celebrant retire to the sedilia until the distribution is complete. The palms are distributed to the choir and to the congregation as at Candlemas.

§3. THE PROCESSIONS[30]

The distribution complete, the first procession assembles. Once incense has been imposed and blessed as usual, the procession sets out in the following order: first, the vergers; second, the water-boy; third, the acolyte with the Lenten cross; fourth, the taperers; fifth, the thurifer; sixth, the subdeacon, without the Text;[31] seventh, the deacon; eighth, the celebrant; ninth, the book-boy, carrying the Processional; and finally, the choir with its rulers, *juniores priores*, carrying their palms,[32] save for those

---

[23] As is normal for exorcisms. So also the absolution on Ash Wednesday (Col 132).
[24] So on Ash Wednesday (Col 131).
[25] OP.1379.
[26] The Sarum books themselves give no details of how this distribution is to be made. What follows is taken from OP.1407, from the Roman rite and from the ceremonies suggested above for Candlemas and Ash Wednesday.
[27] OP.1406.
[28] F.274.
[29] If the chapter is present, Fortescue has the canons receive their palms before the ministers, unless these themselves are canons also.
[30] Coll 258–62; P.47–54. For a clear exposition of the procession and its relation to other rites, see Bishop, *Liturgica Historica*, pages 276–93.
[31] This may be a far-fetched interpretation of the exception made for Palm Sunday at P.1, but it seems more likely that palms should be carried today. It is also likely that the ministers should kneel with the celebrant at the first station, and this would be difficult for the subdeacon if he were carrying a precious text.
[32] Bailey, page 116, by analogy with Candlemas.

who will form the second procession, the prophet and the boys who will sing at the second station. The celebrant and the ministers carry their palms, brought to them by the sacristan after the incense has been imposed.[33] As the procession advances, the choir sings the antiphon *Prima autem*, intoned by the rulers[34] at setting out, and the others provided in the Processional.

The procession is presumed to go out of the church by the great west door and go round the church by its south side until it reaches the north-east angle of the churchyard,[35] where the first station is made. In smaller churches, the route and the locations of the stations will be subject to congruent adaptation. All who are able to do so carry palms.[36]

At the place of the first station, the procession halts. It is assumed that the procession is facing west at this point. The deacon is blessed by the priest with the usual form and moves slightly away from him.[37] There, assisted as at Mass on a simple (i.e. without the cross), facing north,[38] he sings the Gospel *Cum appropinquasset* with *Dominus vobiscum* and *Gloria tibi Domine*. The book is held by the subdeacon, whose palm is held by the book-boy.

Meanwhile, as soon as this procession has set out, the sacristan removes any remaining palms from the sanctuary and choir, and places the missal-stand on the altar. At the same time, the second procession of clergy in choir dress is formed at the choir step, in the following order:[39] first, two processional banners,[40] borne by clerks in surplices;[41] second, the ordinary processional cross, unveiled;[42] third, the lit lantern; and finally, the chest of relics (feretrum)[43] containing also the Blessed Sacrament,

---

[33] OP.1416.
[34] P.48: *cantor*. This might mean the precentor in the cathedral (cf. Wells.29: *precentore*).
[35] Col 261; P.47–8. At Sarum, there was a great cross here, close to which the first station was held.

The route of this procession at Salisbury cathedral has been much disputed, and many of the details given in the books have been omitted here. See Frost, page 146, and Davison for recent theories and a review of old ones. For our purposes, the only significant factors are: (1) that the first procession (possibly representing the people of Jerusalem as Davison suggests) should leave through the west door of the choir and thence the church; (2) that it should circumambulate the church in an anticlockwise direction; (3) that at the first station, the procession be met by the Sacrament procession, reminiscent of Our Lord's approach with his disciples; (4) that the two processions return over the route of the first procession, escorting Our Lord back towards the city, walking clockwise; (5) that the second station should take place somewhere between the place of the first station and the principal door of the church; and (6) that the third station should take place at the principal door, by which the processions enter the church.

[36] OP.1416. The Sarum books themselves make no mention of this, but it is a universal tradition elsewhere and attested earlier in England (Rock IV.79-82).
[37] Col 261: *parumper secus*.
[38] Col 261 and P.49.
[39] P.48–9.
[40] P.48 does not explain clearly whether the banners or the cross should come first. However, *Processions*.73, 91–2 and 93 implies strongly that banners usually precede the cross, and a variant reading of *Crede Michi* [79] is explicit on this point. In Cons 38, the banners precede the first procession.
[41] Wells.43, of the Chrism Mass.
[42] This seems to befit the triumphal cross as opposed to the wooden, penitential cross.
[43] This feretrum was in origin a chest of relics and included the Blessed Sacrament only when the rite was modified. See Bishop, chapter XII. It may sometimes have taken the form of those floats still in use on the continent for the Corpus Christi procession, with arches from which the pyx hung and with reliquaries surrounding it or with the chest of relics sitting under the pyx. A rather different feretrum for carrying the Blessed Sacrament is described at *Processions*.163. Since it is later held *ex*

borne by two clerks of the second form.[44] A canopy is borne over the feretrum by surpliced clerks.[45] The feretrum will have been brought into the sanctuary during the distribution of palms[46] and a priest or deacon in a stole will have placed a Host from the reserved Sacrament in a pyx and hung it,[47] veiled, inside the feretrum. If no other clerk is available for this, the deacon of the Mass may place the Sacrament in the feretrum during the distribution of the palms, returning immediately to the sedilia. This, second, procession sets out when the first has left the church and goes by the shortest route[48] to meet the first head on, so that it should come into sight of the first as the deacon sings the words *Benedictus qui venit in nomine Domini* in the Gospel *Cum appropinquasset*.[49] At this moment, the banners move aside to allow the feretrum to advance, which they escort on either side.[50] The procession advances slowly, pausing if necessary, to allow the first procession to greet it as follows.

When the Gospel has been concluded, the first procession forms an arc, with the celebrant in the middle, facing west, the deacon at his right and the subdeacon at his left. To the deacon's right stand the book-boy, the thurifer, the first taperer and the first verger. To the subdeacon's left stand the water-boy, the acolyte, the second taperer and the second verger. The book-boy will go to stand in front of the deacon only when assisting at the book. Behind this arc is another, formed by the choir. Three clerks of the second form who have been walking in the first procession go to stand immediately west of the churchyard cross and face the people.[51] So the first procession welcomes the Blessed Sacrament.

A junior clerk, dressed as a prophet, stands in an elevated place.[52] The prophet sings *Hierusalem*, &c. in the lesson tone[53] and is answered by the three clerks singing *En rex venit* in unison. The celebrant, facing the Blessed Sacrament approaching from the west,[54] intones *Salve quem Jesum* and then, together with the ministers and the choir,

---

transverso for the procession to pass under it (P.53, Col 262), it may have had rods extending before and after it.

[44] Col 258; P.48–9. These clerks of the second form should be at least deacons. To have anybody else carry the Blessed Sacrament would surely stir admiration in the people.

[45] At York, the Sacrament went under a canopy held by two deacons and two acolytes (Ebor.149).

[46] Col 258.

[47] *dependeat* (P.48, P.49; Col 258).

[48] In the cathedral, it would leave through the small north door in the western transept or by the Porta Speciosa. The latter would allow time for the threefold adoration to take place without the procession having to halt.

[49] P.49

[50] This is how they will be later, after the two processions have joined up (P.51), but it is not indicated when the banners are moved. Doing so now would allow the celebrant and choir to behold the feretrum more clearly when greeting the Sacrament. See Figure V.

[51] P.50 presumes the assistance of the people and would have the three clerks face this way. This is part of the drama, since the clerks' first chant is addressed to Israel.

[52] P.50. This may be on the steps of the churchyard cross, an elevated place in the church building or on a scaffold erected for the occasion.

[53] So *lectionem propheticam* (P.50) implies.

[54] Despite the prophet's wording, *Hierusalem, respice ad orientem*, there can be no doubt but that the Sacrament procession comes from the west. The first procession has come round the church from the south-east, and the second procession is said not to follow it but to come to meet it (*non tamen processionem sequendo, sed ad locum primae stationis obviam veniendo*, P.48), presumably along the north side of the church.

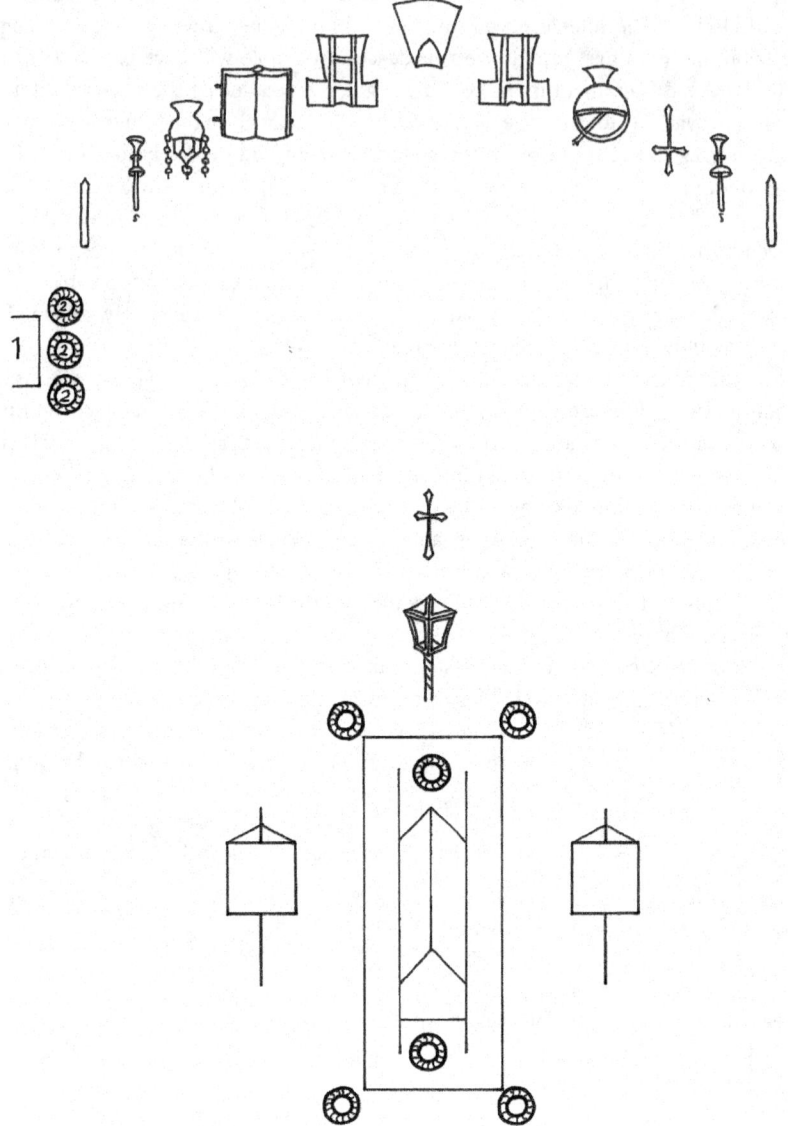

Figure V. Palm Sunday: The first station. (1) Churchyard cross and prophet. (2) Cantors.

kneels and kisses the ground. Rising immediately, the choir continues *Testatur*, &c. The same ritual is followed with *Ecce salvator, Hic est qui de Edom* and *Salve rex mundi*; and again, for the third time, with *Ecce appropinquabit, Hic est ille* and *Salve nostra salus*. As soon as he has chanted *Ecce appropinquabit*, &c. the prophet withdraws.[55]

The Sacrament procession continues on its way. As it reaches the acolyte, the crucifers exchange crosses.[56] The second crucifer retires with the Lenten cross. The first procession turns round and heads back round the apse of the church, preceded by the banners in their usual position,[57] the Sacrament with its lantern incorporating itself to it between the thurifer and the subdeacon.[58] In this manner, the joint procession advances to the second station, as the antiphons *Dignus es* and *Occurrunt turbae* are intoned and sung as above. To these may be added *Dominus Jesus* and *Cogitaverunt*.

The second station is presumed to be about halfway along the south side of the church.[59] As the procession comes to a halt, seven boys from an elevated place[60] sing *Gloria laus* and its verses, the antiphon being repeated by the choir after each verse. The chant concluded, the procession advances straight along the south side of the church to the west door, singing the antiphon *Collegerunt*.

At the west door, which is closed against it,[61] the procession halts. The celebrant and ministers, and the choir, form arcs as at the first station.[62] Before the celebrant stands the feretrum, with a banner on either side and the lantern before it. Three clerks from the upper form come up to the door itself and, turning to face the people, sing the verse *Unus autem*. At its conclusion, they stand aside, one and two, to allow the feretrum to be carried up to the door. The clerks carrying the feretrum raise it high above their heads and hold it across the doorway,[63] standing on either side of the door. To the west of these two clerks stand the banner-bearers. To the west of one of these stand the lantern-bearer and one of the three cantors who have sung *Unus autem*; to the west of the other stand the other two cantors. All face each other across the doorway. As they stand thus, *Ingrediente Domino* is begun, the sacristan opens the doors from within[64]

---

[55] The rubric at P.51, *evanescat*, conjures up a vivid image which would be difficult to reproduce.
[56] P.51.
[57] Banners usually precede the procession and they certainly do so at Cons 38.
[58] P.51.
[59] In the cathedral, the second station may have been made just outside the door leading to the cloister from the canons' cemetery. The procession then perhaps proceeded along the north walk of the cloister to the third station. See Bishop, page 291, and P.52 (*fiat secunda statio ex parte ecclesiae australi*) pace Frost, page 146.
[60] See note 52 on the first station for a discussion of possible elevated places. Davison (pp. 12–13), supported by the rubric, suggests the roof of the cloister; Blum (note 10), supported by the architecture but against the rubrical consensus subsequent to the building of the cathedral, posits that, in the new cathedral, the second and third stations were fused into one at the west door and *Gloria laus* was sung from the western gallery.
[61] *Crede Michi* [79]; OP.1413.
[62] The distance from the canons' door of the cloister at Sarum to the west door of the cathedral church is not long enough to permit a seemly approach of the procession so as to allow it to face the door for the station. The arcs, though nowhere mentioned in the books, do not seem improbable, therefore. In the Roman rite, the clergy form an arc at the equivalent point in the function. For similar, though not identical, arrangements, see the first station on this day and P.86 (at the font on Holy Saturday).
[63] Col 262; P.53.
[64] *Crede Michi* [79]: *erubescant sacerdotes parrochiales qui percutiunt ostium cum cruce in introitu ecclesie expresse contra Ordinale*. Tradition was to outlive the rubric.

and the procession enters the church, walking under the feretrum, the three clerks resuming their places in due course.

The feretrum plays no further part in the function. Its procession, with no crucifer, is reformed, the feretrum once more following the banners. It returns discreetly by another route and the Sacrament is reserved.[65]

The procession advances straight up the nave to the Rood, where the fourth station is held.

At the fourth station,[66] standing before the Rood, as soon as this is unveiled,[67] the celebrant intones the antiphon *Ave* in a low note. The celebrant, ministers and choir kneel and kiss the ground.[68] All rise and the choir replies, *Rex noster*. The celebrant sings *Ave* for a second time, on a higher note than before. All kneel and kiss the ground again. All rise and the choir replies, *Rex noster*. The ceremony is repeated a third time, on a higher note still, but this time the choir continues its reply to the end of the antiphon, standing still. While this antiphon is sung, the cross on the High Altar and all other crosses in the church are unveiled. They remain unveiled until after Compline.[69]

The responsory *Circumdederunt me* is now intoned and the procession advances as far as the choir step. The verse *Eripe me* and the prayer *Omnipotens sempiterne Deus qui humano generi* are sung after the usual fashion. The celebrant and his attendants retire to the vestry to prepare for Mass.[70] The celebrant should wash his hands.

§4. THE MASS

The Mass follows the usual rules for the season. The ministers wear chasubles.[71] The ordinary processional cross is carried, not the Lenten cross.[72] Palms are carried until the offertory, when they may be offered.[73] The tract is alternated by the whole choir,

---

[65] The presence of the Blessed Sacrament, a late addition to the rite, would distract from the fourth station, as indeed it did at Rouen (see Bishop, page 287). At Sarum, the feretrum may have retired via the cloister, but nowhere is this withdrawal of the Sacrament procession (if indeed it took place) described.

[66] P.53; Col 262.

[67] Col 262, Missal CA.96 and G.85, with Wells.29, have the celebrant sing *Ave* after the Rood is unveiled; P.53 punctuates differently and implies that the Cross is unveiled after the celebrant has sung *Ave* but before the choir replies *Rex noster*. At York, the celebrant himself unveiled the Cross, pulling its veil towards him (Ebor.151).

[68] Col 262: *una cum choro fiat genuflexio*. The Dominicans do otherwise (OP.1412).

[69] Missal A.96 insists that the altar cross should be unveiled before the procession enters the choir. Col 262 and P.54 would have all the crosses unveiled until after Vespers. C 60 and Cons 38.2, with Wells.29 (assuming *cooperta* to be a *lapsus calami*) mention only that the cross on the High Altar is unveiled but would have this and the principal Cross remain unveiled for the rest of that day only. OP.1415 has the Cross remain unveiled until Compline.

[70] See Chapter XXX, note 2.

[71] C 66.2.

[72] C 58, in giving rules for the Lenten cross, deals only with the Sunday procession. Although at Mass the processional cross is prescribed only on doubles (C 66.19), and Palm Sunday is not a double, Col 271 would have the Gospel sung *more duplicis festi*. In the light of the triumphal character of the procession and the unveiling of the crosses, it seems more suitable to carry the ordinary cross on this day.

[73] The Dominicans lay aside their palms after the procession (OP.1416), but Rock IV.79–82 gives Anglo-Saxon evidence for their retention and offering.

Palm Sunday 223

the side that is singing standing while the other sits.[74] Only the reading of the Passion presents unusual features.

The Passion is sung from the pulpitum not by the deacon of the Mass but by three additional deacons. They sit in choir and go to the sacristy to vest in albs, maniples and stoles[75] during the singing of the tract. While they do so, if lecterns are to be used, the taperers set these up on the pulpitum side by side, facing north, before retiring to their places in the choir, whence they will listen to the Passion, unless they are to hold the books. Neither incense nor tapers attend the singing of the Passion.[76] The Passion should not be read from the eagle.[77] The three deacons, each carrying a book (unless they will sing from a single book) come to the choir step,[78] bow to the altar and, the blessing omitted, go down the choir to the pulpitum. There they sing the Passion to its peculiar tone, the narrator singing *Dominus vobiscum* and the title. *Gloria tibi Domine* and the accompanying sign of the cross are omitted.[79] While the Passion is sung the celebrant and the ministers stand at the sedilia.[80] All turn to face the deacons.[81] At *emisit spiritum*, the deacons turn to the east and kneel,[82] saying privately *Pater noster*, *Ave Maria* and *In manus tuas*. The celebrant, ministers and servers do likewise, but the choir makes a prostration over the forms, one side facing the other. The celebrant rises first and all with him.[83] The deacons continue the Passion up to *sedentes contra sepulchrum*. They then return to the choir step and retire to the vestry. They resume choir dress and return to their stalls.

In case of necessity, the ministers of the Mass (if both have been ordained to the diaconate) may assist in singing the Passion. To do so, they wear albs, maniples and stoles only. If there is no third deacon, the celebrant may supply the part of Christ, singing from the missal at the north corner of the altar.[84] In this case, it would be better for the two deacons to sing their parts from lecterns placed next to the north steps of the altar.

At the conclusion of the Passion, the Gospel is read by the deacon of the Mass with the ceremonies usual on doubles.[85] The acolyte carries the processional cross. Incense is used but the taperers do not hold their tapers. At its conclusion, the sign of the cross is not made and the book is not kissed.[86]

---

[74] C 66.18.
[75] OP.1418.
[76] OP.1419.
[77] It seems best to reserve this for the Gospel itself.
[78] As do the cantors at the gradual.
[79] Col 272. Cf. OPraem.XXXIII.58–60.
[80] At Rome and among the Dominicans, the celebrant and ministers stand at the altar, but in those rites the Passion is read privately at the altar.
[81] F.279.
[82] Col 271 has *inclinet se diaconus vel prosternet* but Coll 284 and 294 have *genuflexio*.
[83] OP.1420.
[84] OP.1418.
[85] *more duplicis festi* (Col 272). Unlike at Hereford.91, there is nothing to suggest the omission of lights, but, by analogy with other rites, it is presumed here. Similarly, no grounds are given for the omission of the deacon's blessing by the celebrant.
[86] OP.1486.

§5. THE SIMPLE FORM OF THE RITE

The function in its full form as described above supposes what nowadays would be an exceptionally large number of clergy. However, it is possible to simplify the ceremonies somewhat.

If two deacons may not be had for bearing the Blessed Sacrament, the relics only may be carried. In this case, the part of the prophet and the greeting of the Sacrament at the first station are omitted. Or the second procession may be omitted in its entirety and the first station reduced to the reading of the Gospel *Cum appropinquasset*.

If it is not possible to conduct the procession outside the church, the first two stations may be held at suitable locations inside the church. The third station is held most aptly at the west end of the nave. The fourth station should be held at the entrance to the choir.

If there are not enough ordained ministers to sing the Passion, the celebrant himself may read this without note at the north corner of the altar, as at Low Mass.[87] He will then sing the Gospel as he would at a Sung Mass.

The function may be celebrated by a priest with as few assistants as two servers and a sacristan. In this case, he is preceded to the altar by the first server carrying the cross and the second server carrying the holy water. At the altar, the celebrant reads the lesson, *Venerunt*, from the missal at the south corner. The first server moves the missal to the north corner, where the celebrant reads the Gospel, *Turba multa*. Missal and celebrant having returned to the south corner, the celebrant says the exorcism and the following prayers. The first server assists at the thurible; the second, at the sprinkler. The servers kneel on the footpace and receive their palms, which they immediately remove to the credence table. They then assist the celebrant at the distribution of palms to the laity, standing on either side of him. The sacristan removes the laity's palms to the chancel. The procession is formed of the first server, carrying the cross; the second server, who will act as book-boy at the first station; and the celebrant, who recites the antiphons from the Processional. The procession makes the four stations. At the first station, the second server holds the book before the celebrant, who faces north to read the Gospel, *Cum appropinquasset*. As soon as this Gospel is finished, they turn back on their way to the second station. At the fourth station, the sacristan unveils the Rood. He then unveils the altar cross as well. At the conclusion of the procession, the second server may hold the book when the celebrant says the prayer *Omnipotens sempiterne Deus* at the choir step. Low Mass follows. The celebrant reads the Passion himself at the north corner. At *emisit spiritum*, he kneels in his place.[88] After *sedentes contra sepulchrum*, he says *Jube Domine benedicere* in the middle and then reads the Gospel as usual.

The Missal makes no special provision for private Masses. Therefore, although the introductory lessons, the blessing of palms and the procession may be omitted, the Passion should be read in its entirety.

---

[87] F.278. It would seem impractical to expect the celebrant to sing the entirety of the Passion on his own as well as all his other proper chants.
[88] OP.1420.

XXXIII

MAUNDY THURSDAY

The Missal gives the form of five functions held on this day: the reconciliation of penitents; the Mass, incorporating Vespers; the washing of the altars; the Maundy; and the *potus caritatis*. The first will hardly ever occur.[1] The last two are really no more than peculiar features of the life of the cathedral clerical community and so are omitted here.[2] With the Chrism Mass we are not concerned.[3]

§1. MASS AND VESPERS

A pyx must be prepared for the Sacrament that is to be reserved.[4] This may be the ordinary ciborium from the dove or tabernacle. In the vestry, the place of reservation,[5] most fittingly a secure tabernacle, is prepared. This should be clean, neat and honorably adorned.[6] A light will burn before it all the time that the Sacrament is enclosed within it.[7]

At a presbyter's Mass, the choir is not ruled.[8] The bells are rung as usual to summon the faithful to this Mass and thereafter are not rung again until the *Gloria in excelsis* on Holy Saturday.[9] For the bells is substituted the sound of wooden clappers or rattles.[10] The vestments are red.[11] Three hosts are consecrated, which the subdeacon must place

---

[1] Col 295. The reconciliation of penitents is presumed to be inseparable from the Mass. Its ceremonial is easily understood from the rubrics in the Missal and the Processional (P.54).
[2] It is worth bearing in mind that even the boys of the first form would have been tonsured clerks (see Orme, *Medieval Schools*, page 135). The Maundy and the *potus caritatis* do not take place in the church but in the chapter house and do not concern ordinary laymen, whose sole involvement is that they may have been present at a sermon. Even this is described as a *sermo ad populum* in the Processional only (P.64); the Missal gives merely *deinde dicitur sermo*, to which the Gradual there quoted adds *si placuerit* (Col 311). For these two functions, see also P.63–9 and *Processions*.79–81.
[3] For this, see P.58–9 and *Processions*.72–3.
[4] OPraem.XXXIV.91–5 has the Sacrament in its normal pyx. Col 332 assumes that on Good Friday the Sacrament is in the pyx.
[5] P.72: *ad vestibulum*. The place of reservation varies from rite to rite and has changed over time.
[6] OPraem XXXIV.93: *in pulcro et honesto scrinio*.
[7] OPraem.XXXIV.94–5.
[8] P.58.
[9] B I.dcclxxi; Cons 64.4.
[10] Missal A.104.
[11] Col 583; C 66.3

on the paten at the making of the chalice.[12] The ministers wear dalmatic and tunicle. *Habete osculum pacis* and its corresponding kisses are omitted. There is no *Gloria Patri* at the Officium. The *Kyrie*[13] is not farsed. There is no *Gloria in excelsis*.[14] *Flectamus genua* is not said before the collect. The epistle and Gospel are sung from the pulpitum as on ordinary, non-double, Sundays, and the gradual, sung from the pulpitum by two surpliced boys,[15] is repeated after its verse. There is no creed. The *Communicantes*, *Hanc igitur* and *Qui pridie* are proper. The *Agnus Dei* and the Pax are omitted.[16] There may be a general Communion.[17] *Benedicamus Domino* is said at the end.

A shortened form of Evensong is joined to the Mass.[18] This begins as soon as the Communion antiphon has been sung.[19] The choir is not ruled and stands throughout.[20]

The first antiphon is intoned by the most junior clerk of the upper grade, who sits eastmost of that grade on the choir, or side of greater dignity.[21] He faces across the choir to do so.[22] When he has intoned the antiphon, he waits until the last word of the first verse has been sung.[23] Thereupon he turns to the altar, bows his head[24] towards it and then faces the choir once more. The choir faces the altar as the first antiphon is intoned and then across the church for the psalm.[25] *Gloria Patri* is omitted.[26] The other antiphons are intoned without turning to the altar. The second antiphon is intoned by the most junior upper-grade clerk on the other side. The third antiphon is intoned by the most junior clerk of the second form on the first side and the fourth antiphon by his opposite number. The fifth antiphon is sung by the second-most junior second-form clerk on the first side.[27] At the end of the fifth psalm, the choir turns to the altar for the antiphon and then resumes its previous position.[28] The antiphon on the *Magnificat* is intoned by the senior upper-form clerk[29] on the side of greater dignity.[30] It is not doubled and must not be intoned until the celebrant has finished reading Vespers quietly and the deacon has gone to the middle of the altar. The *Magnificat* follows as

---

[12] Most of this Mass's peculiarities are given at Coll 300–8.
[13] Col 300 and P.58 prescribe *Kyrie Conditor* (i.e. the tone) without verses.
[14] When the Bishop celebrates, *Gloria Patri* is sung in the Officium (Col 235), *Gloria in excelsis* (Col 108) and *Agnus Dei* are said (P.59), the Pax is given with the vessel of the chrism (P.59) and the Mass ends with *Ite missa est* (Col 308). The dalmatic and tunicle are worn whether the Bishop be present or not (Col 308).
[15] C 66.13.
[16] OPraem.XXXIV.76–7 has the previously reserved Sacrament consumed at this Mass.
[17] OP.1331 would allow a general Communion only within the Mass itself.
[18] Col 304 directs that these Vespers should be celebrated *festivae sine regimine chori*. The special directions for these are given at C 44.4. As often, the directions are far from complete and need to be supplemented from elsewhere: see further the notes below.
[19] Col 304.
[20] C 12.1.
[21] Col 304 and C 44.6.
[22] C 13.1.
[23] C 13.1. The text is less than clear.
[24] C 13.1.
[25] C 13.1.
[26] Col 304.
[27] C 44.6.
[28] C 13.3. Ordinarily the choir turns back for the responsory or chapter, which today are omitted.
[29] B I.dcclxxii, speaking of Vespers on Spy Wednesday, which seem to be a form of first Vespers of Maundy Thursday, says that at the *Magnificat* the antiphon is intoned in the upper form.
[30] An inference from C 32.1.

usual. Incense is not used.³¹ At its conclusion, the choir turns to face the altar³² and remains so to the conclusion of the function.³³

While Vespers are sung in the choir, the Sacrament is reserved.³⁴ As the celebrant communicates himself, the choir sings the Communion, *Dominus Jesus*.³⁵ The first antiphon of Vespers, *Calicem salutaris* is intoned immediately.³⁶ If there is to be a general Communion, this is administered during the psalms of Vespers.³⁷ The second and third hosts, together with any others kept for the sick, are enclosed in a pyx or ciborium. The ablutions take place³⁸ but the corporal is not folded. On it are placed the dressed chalice and, behind it, the pyx containing the Sacrament, which the deacon covers with a silk veil.³⁹ The celebrant and ministers go to read the Communion antiphon,⁴⁰ after which the acolyte comes up to receive the chalice from the deacon and remove it.⁴¹ If it will be used later, he must remember to carry back the humeral veil for the deacon to wear when reserving the Sacrament. At the missal, the celebrant now reads Vespers up to the end of the *Magnificat* and its antiphon in a quiet voice, the ministers standing on either side of him and alternating the verses with him.⁴²

When they have finished the *Magnificat* with its antiphon, but not before the choir has finished the antiphon *Considerabam*,⁴³ the subdeacon returns to his step behind the celebrant and the deacon goes to the middle and receives the humeral veil from the taperers. Taking the Sacrament enveloped in the veil, the deacon⁴⁴ comes down and

---

31 C 44.4.
32 C 13.2.
33 As ordinarily at Mass (C13.5).
34 The ceremonies with which this reservation takes place have evolved considerably over time. The Sarum books give very few details and it is likely that, with the development of Eucharistic devotion during the period when the rite grew and flourished, the practice of Sarum changed materially. Since the Missals are altogether silent and the Processional does no more than imply that the Sacrament was reserved in the vestry (P.72), the directions given here are the fruit of reasonable deduction informed by the early evidence of John of Avranches (PL.CXLVII.50), of the early Præmonstratensians (OPraem.XXXIV.80–95) and the Carmelites (King, *Religious Orders*, page 266), and of OP.
35 OPraem.XXXIV.81–2.
36 Col 304.
37 The implication of OPraem.XXXIV.
38 De Herdt, t. III. p. 5. n. 16. cap. IX, writing of Holy Saturday.
39 OP.1441: *serico Velo albi coloris super eum expanso*. This may be an especially rich humeral veil which the deacon will wear to reserve the Sacrament, or a smaller veil.
40 OP.1445–6.
41 OP.1445.
42 This seems to be the meaning of the rubric at Col 332. Since the celebrant and the ministers are bound to the Breviary, it is reasonable that they should recite Vespers here, as they do with the choral parts of the Mass.
43 The moment of reservation has been subject to variation. John of Avranches is not specific (PL CXLVII.50); OPraem.XXXIV.91–5 and the Carmelites, who have been followed here, reserve the Sacrament during the *Magnificat* (OCarm.164); OP.1446 allows the moment after Communion or at the end of the Mass depending on local custom; OP.1447, perhaps following later (and Roman) practice, presumes the end of Mass, but OP.1450 restricts this possibility to celebrations in which Vespers are separated from the Mass.
44 Some rites have the celebrant reserve the Sacrament; others, the deacon. When the reservation takes place before the end of Mass, it may be more reasonable not to have the celebrant leave the sanctuary, though the early Præmonstratensians seem to have done this (OPraem.XXXIV.91). The early Carmelites, who appear to have preserved an earlier form of the rite than the Dominicans, have

goes to the vestry, where the Sacrament will be reserved. The deacon is preceded by the taperers and torchbearers,[45] who have remained before the altar since the Canon or have left the choir during the psalms with the same ceremonies as at the offertory. As they depart, the celebrant and subdeacon turn to face them and remain facing them until they have left the sanctuary, when they turn back to the altar. The deacon returns, leaving the humeral veil in the vestry, and goes up to stand behind the celebrant. When the choir has finished singing the antiphon after the *Magnificat*, *Dominus vobiscum* and the postcommon follow as at Mass.[46] Mass concludes as usual.

If the public celebration of Vespers is to be separated from the Mass,[47] the Sacrament is reserved at the end of the function. The chalice is removed before the postcommon, as above. Mass concludes as before the Sacrament exposed, that is to say, all must take care not to turn their backs to the Sacrament.[48] After *Placeat*, &c. the celebrant himself receives the humeral veil from the deacon[49] and reserves the Sacrament in the vestry, preceded by the ministers and servers. In the vestry, he may fittingly incense the Sacrament before enclosing it in the tabernacle, all the others kneeling round him.[50]

The celebration of the function without solemnity does not present any difficulties. The celebrant will sing or say Vespers from the missal, assisted as well as possible, with no ceremonies. The Sacrament will be reserved at the conclusion of Mass.

§2. THE WASHING OF THE ALTARS

The washing of the altars[51] takes place after luncheon.[52] The choir is presumed to be in its stalls. Water is blessed privately at a side chapel or in the vestry with the formula

---

been followed here. It may be relevant to bear in mind that, on Good Friday at Sarum, the Sacrament is not brought to the altar by the celebrant (P.72).

[45] OCarm.164. The Sacrament will be accompanied by the taperers on Good Friday (P.72). There is no indication in the Sarum books that either today or on Good Friday the canopy of OP.1448 was carried over the Sacrament as it was over the chrism (Cons 114), but different churches may have developed their own customs.

[46] That the postcommon is said as at Mass and not as at Vespers is shewn by B I.dcclxxxv, which prescribes the Mass ceremonial: *dicat Sacerdos ad populum conversus, Dominus vobiscum, et Oremus: deinde postcommunionem*. The direction at C 24.2, although it explicitly includes Maundy Thursday in its provisions, omits all mention of the sacred ministers. It should probably be taken to refer either to Vespers separated from the Mass or to a mere recognition of Maundy Thursday's semifestal character (Col 304: *festivae sine regimine chori*). The Dominican celebrant, who sits for the psalms, comes to the altar for the postcommunion (OP.1451-2).

[47] The Sarum books do not contemplate this possibility, and the survival of Vespers attached to the Mass is a distinct feature of Sarum Use which it would be undesirable to lose. OP.1450, however, provides for this separation.

[48] OP.1444.

[49] OP.1447.

[50] OP.1448-9.

[51] Coll 308-10, P.59-63, Processions.73-9 and OP.1454-62. The washing of the altars presumes their stripping, which is nowhere mentioned. It is possible that the altars were stripped by the sacristans without ceremony, (cf. OP.1436) and then washed ritually. This washing, which has died out in the Roman rite, was originally the part of the function to which greater mystical significance was attached. See *The Catholic Encyclopedia* s.v. 'Stripping of an Altar'.

[52] Col 308: *post prandium*.

used on Sundays.[53] The clergy set out for the High Altar as follows:[54] first, the priest;[55] second, the deacon, carrying the book; third, the subdeacon, carrying a bunch of box branches or hyssop and a linen towel with which to scrub and dry the surface of the altars; fourth, two taperers walking side by side and carrying lighted tapers; and finally, two further boys walking side by side, one carrying a vessel with wine and the other the water in a stoup or bucket.[56] Additional servers may be present if needed to expedite the stripping of the sanctuary and remove furnishings to the vestry. All wear amices and albs with no apparels.[57] The celebrant and the deacon may wear stoles and maniples; the subdeacon, the maniple. On arrival, they perform the usual bows. The taperers set down their tapers. The deacon and subdeacon deposit their burdens on the step and go up with the priest. If the altar has not already been stripped,[58] they do so now. They take off the altar cloths, hand them to the taperers and descend. There they wait while the taperers, leaving the altar cloths at the credence table or other suitable place (whence the sacristan will collect them later), return to remove the frontal, altar cross, candlesticks, carpet and any other furnishings of the altar, of which they dispose in similar fashion.

The priest and the ministers now go up to the altar again, the subdeacon now carrying the broom. The boys with the wine and water assist at the south side. The deacon receives the wine from the boy and hands it to the celebrant, who pours a little over each of the five consecration crosses on the surface of the altar, beginning with that in the middle. Returning the wine to the deacon, he receives the water and does the same with this. The deacon pours a moderately generous quantity of water over the middle of the surface of the altar and returns the stoup to the boy. Taking the broom from the subdeacon, the celebrant scrubs the surface of the mensa. Meanwhile, the choir sings the responsory *In monte Oliveti*. Returning the broom to the subdeacon, the celebrant takes the towel and dries the altar. He returns the towel to the subdeacon and comes down again with the ministers. At the conclusion of the responsory, the celebrant reads without note the verse and collect appointed from the book held by the deacon, the choir answering. The collect will be that of the saint in whose honour the altar is dedicated. Finally, the priest goes up to the altar and kisses it in the middle. All the other clergy do the same,[59] two by two, in descending order of rank. If there are lay servers, they do not kiss the altar.[60] Assembling again as they came in, they leave the sanctuary with the usual bows.

[53] Col 308; P.59; *Processions*.73.
[54] P.59: *majoribus praecedentibus*, a singularly peculiar direction omitted from the Missal (Col 310) and not observed by the Dominicans (OP.1455).
[55] The books suppose two priests (the same who will perform the Maundy), up to two deacons and two subdeacons, two taperers and two additional boys, but there is considerable variation and there is no reason why a single priest could not wash all the altars in a small church.
[56] OP.1454: *situlam*.
[57] P.59; Rock I.367.
[58] The Dominicans strip all the side altars before None and leave but a single altar cloth on the High Altar until the end of Mass. This is removed during Vespers (OP.1436, OP.1451).
[59] This rubric is omitted in some editions of the Processional (P.60). Nevertheless, it is a touching detail, whereby, in anticipation of Good Friday, the disciples wash and kiss the body of our blessed Lord, represented by the altar.
[60] The rubric speaks of *alii clerici*. Even taken in a broad sense, it would be at least mildly scandalous to allow a layman to kiss the altar.

The ceremony is repeated at every altar in the church. The choir sings the responsories from Matins in turn, repeating the cycle if necessary, but in such a way that the last responsory, *Circumdederunt*, is always sung last. The responsories must not be begun before the priest has arrived at the altar. The altars are visited in the same order as during the procession on Sundays.[61] The side altars remain bare until after Sext on Holy Saturday;[62] the High Altar is vested for the Mass of the Presanctified and then again for the Easter Vigil.

In small churches, there will be no choir. The celebrant removes the altar cloths and washes the altar himself. At least one server will be needed to minister wine, water and box, and to remove the furnishings. The priest reads the responsory, verse and collect after washing the altar, immediately before departing.

---

[61] P.5–6; *Processions*.74–9. In the cathedral, the clergy left the choir by its north door, went clockwise round the church, beginning at the north of the eastern transept and ending at the south of the north-western transept.

[62] P.60 gives *altaria nuda usque ad Sabbatum Paschae conserventur praeter principale altare*. That this must be interpreted as Holy Saturday, however, is made clear by Cons 69.1.

XXXIV

GOOD FRIDAY

§1. PREPARATIONS

The function consists of six parts: (1) an office of lessons and chants culminating in the Passion; (2) solemn collects; (3) the worship of the Cross; (4) Mass of the Presanctified; (5) Vespers; and (6) the deposition in the Sepulchre. The liturgical colour is red.[1] All bows to persons may be omitted today.[2]

The clergy who take part will be the celebrant, the deacon, the subdeacon, the acolyte, the two taperers, the thurifer and the choir as for Mass as usual. There should also be three deacons to read the Passion, of whom two may also sing *Agyos*, and two senior priests[3] to hold the Cross and bring the Sacrament. Two surpliced clerks from the choir will be needed to tear the additional cloths from the altar, one of whom may act as second thurifer.

The following preparations are made.

In the vestry, vestments are laid out as for Mass, except that dalmatic and tunicles are omitted and today apparels are not worn.[4] Only the celebrant wears a chasuble.[5] Amices, albs, cinctures, maniples (if they were worn on Palm Sunday) and stoles are laid out also for the deacons who will sing the Passion; and plain albs and amices, together with stoles[6] and maniples, for the two presbyters who will hold the Cross. These will also require surplices later, as will the two boys who will tear the cloths from the altar. Also ready should be two thuribles and the taperer's candles, although these will not be required until later in the function.[7] If they are to be used, lecterns as on Palm Sunday for the Passion are erected on the pulpitum or they may be brought out at the time. A chalice dressed with a purificator, paten and veil,[8] and two humeral veils, one for the Sacrament and another for the chalice, are prepared. The latter may also be used to carry the Cross to the Sepulchre.[9] The Blessed Sacrament is reserved privately in the

---

[1] Col 316.
[2] F.303.
[3] Col 328: *de superiori gradu*.
[4] P.69. OP.1483 prescribes maniples.
[5] Coll 316 and 328.
[6] Ebor.156.
[7] OP.1483.
[8] Missal A.114. Cf. also OP.1504.
[9] See note 123.

vestry. The two hosts consecrated on the previous day will be in a veiled pyx; any hosts reserved for communicating the sick will be in a separate ciborium. For reservation in the Sepulchre, the Sacrament may be held in a special pyx or monstrance.[10] This should then be prepared in the vestry and taken up to the altar after Communion.

The Sanctuary remains stripped from the previous night. All the lights about the altar should be extinguished. There may be a single carpet laid from the altar to the choir.[11] During None,[12] the altar is covered with a single altar cloth,[13] which should be folded so as not to hang over the edges of the mensa. The altar cloth will be unfolded later by the taperers. The candles are not lit until the Mass of the Presanctified.[14] The cross is veiled.[15] This cross is that which will be worshipped later. It should be big enough to be carried decently between two priests[16] but small enough to be susceptible of being buried in the Sepulchre later. It will probably not be the ordinary altar cross.[17] The missal may lie on its stand on the altar[18] or it may be brought from the credence later, just before the prayer *Deus a quo*. On top of the altar cloth, but not underneath the missal, are laid two additional altar cloths, lying in such a way that when placed contiguously they appear to form a single altar cloth.[19]

At the credence are the cruets and the basin for the lavatory, the corporals in their burse[20] and two books: that of lessons and that containing the responsories that are to be intoned at the Sepulchre. In a suitable place, the carpet on which the Cross will be placed later is prepared; likewise, a cloth for wiping the feet of the Crucified if it is to be used. The veiled ordinary processional cross,[21] which will be required for the Gospel, should be placed in a convenient place. If portable lecterns are to be employed for

[10] Feasey, pages 164–5; Durham.10.
[11] Ebor.156.
[12] In other words, immediately before the function (OP.1482).
[13] OP.1482 has more than the single altar cloth of the Roman rite and two lit candles throughout but Missal A.109 prescribes a single altar cloth and candles that should not be lit *nisi ante corpus domini*. On this occasion, Sarum is closer to the Roman curia than to St. Dominic: the altar cloth should be unfolded over the edge of the mensa by the taperers immediately before the acolyte takes the corporal to the altar. Cf. *Caeremoniale Episcoporum*, lib. 2, cap. 25, n. 28.
[14] Missal A.109: *Candele non accendantur circa altare. nisi ante corpus domini*. However, this could be construed of lights round the altar, which should be kept extinguished (see above) except before the place of reservation.
[15] OP.1490 as well as the clear implication of P.69 and Col 328.
[16] Col 328.
[17] At Durham, this cross was taken from an image of Our Lady of Bolton and was of gold (Durham.26).
[18] In the Roman rite, the missal is brought from the credence table to the altar at the beginning of the function together with the altar cloth. The Dominican ceremonial is silent on the matter, but the missal must be on the altar for the prayer *Deus a quo* (OP.1484), so it is not unreasonable that the missal is placed on the altar before the function, when the cloths are laid on it. See Missal A.114.
[19] The sense of Col 323 is made clearer by Hereford.91: *sindones duas super altare prius ibi positas, hinc indeque sibi invicem cohaerentes*. These two cloths may be lightly stitched together as they were at York (Rock IV.281).
[20] F.302.
[21] The Gospel is to be sung as on double feasts, on which the ordinary cross is carried, and C 58 states only that the Lenten cross is carried at the Sunday procession. On Palm Sunday, the ordinary cross should probably be carried unveiled at the Gospel. On Good Friday, however, which does not partake of the same triumphal nature, the question is less clear. The solution proposed here is no worse than any other, viz. that the ordinary cross, veiled, should be carried at the Gospel, which is sung before *Ecce lignum Crucis*.

singing the Passion, these may be set out before the function or, which is more fitting, brought out at the time.

The Easter Sepulchre[22] should be erected in a suitable place on the north of the presbytery or elsewhere. It should be richly lined within so as to be a fitting receptacle for the Blessed Sacrament and covered with equally rich hangings. If the Cross and the pyx are to be shrouded in linen,[23] this shroud should lie extended within. About the Sepulchre should stand many unlit lights,[24] but access to and about it should not be impeded before the end of the function. Until the Cross and the pyx are included therein, the Sepulchre should remain open.

§2. THE LESSONS AND THE SOLEMN COLLECTS

The function takes place after None. In silence, the clergy proceed to the altar as for Mass, except that the taperers do not carry their tapers[25] and the processional cross is not borne.[26] The celebrant says *Pater noster* secretly on his way.[27]

As soon as they have bowed to the altar,[28] the celebrant retires with the ministers to sit at the sedilia and the acolyte goes at once[29] to the choir step, where he will read the first prophecy as soon as the celebrant has sat down. The first two lessons, their chants (which the whole choir sings, standing alternately)[30] and the collect *Deus a quo et Judas* are sung as on Ember Days, the first lesson by the acolyte and the second by the subdeacon, both at the choir step, without titles and to the lesson, not epistle, tone.[31] The celebrant reads the tracts privately at the seat as usual. The choir sits and stands with the celebrant.

The Passion is read from the pulpitum as on Palm Sunday, except that *Dominus vobiscum* and the title are omitted.[32] At *Partiti sunt vestimenta mea sibi*, two surpliced clerks, having come up from the choir and taken up positions each at one horn of the altar,[33] whip the additional cloths off the altar and, taking them away with them, return to the choir.[34] At *Tradidit spiritum*, all kneel and say privately *Pater noster, Ave*

---

[22] For an introduction to the Easter Sepulchre and its significance, see Duffy, *Stripping*, pages 29–37. For its design and ornament, see Bond, pages 220–41.

[23] That the pyx and the Cross should be enveloped in a linen shroud is eminently reasonable. Less so is the misinterpretation found sometimes of the rubric *linteo tergatur* in Hereford.95, confusing *tergere* with *tegere*. Scrubbing with linen is prescribed in some rituals when the Host has fallen on clothes.

[24] One light at least is prescribed by the rubric (Col 333).

[25] OP.1483. The tapers will not be needed until the Mass of the Presanctified.

[26] OP.1483. OP.1504 prescribes the processional cross for the Mass of the Presanctified, but the Dominicans return to the vestry after the worship of the Cross and hold a procession to and from the Monument. It will be required for the Gospel.

[27] Missal A.109.

[28] OP.1483. At Rome and Hereford.90, the celebrant tarries awhile in prayer before the altar and then kisses this. In a significant omission, supported by OP.1483, neither ceremony is mentioned in the Sarum books.

[29] Col 316: *statim*.

[30] Col 318, Col 12, C 66.18, OP.1483 and OCarm.167.

[31] Missal.109. OP.1484. Coll 316–17 has *lectionem*; OCarm.167 has *per modum leccionis, non epistolae*.

[32] Coll 272 and 319.

[33] Col 323.

[34] Hereford.91: *in modum furantis distrahant, et secum auferant*.

Maria and *In manus tuas* as on Palm Sunday. The deacons continue the Passion up to *Videbunt in quem transfixerunt*. The Gospel *Post haec autem* is read by the deacon of the Mass with the same ceremonial as on Palm Sunday.[35]

The solemn collects follow, sung at the south corner of the altar as are the prayers on the Lenten Ember Days and each preceded by the celebrant's summons to pray.[36] During these prayers, the choir faces the altar.[37] They kneel and rise in accordance with the ministers' instructions. The eighth prayer, that for the Jews, is preceded by *Oremus* as the others are, but *Flectamus genua* and *Levate* are omitted.[38]

§3. THE WORSHIP OF THE CROSS

Towards the end of the collects, the taperers take the carpet and lay it on the bottom altar step in readiness to receive the Cross.[39] They then retire to their places in the choir until the time comes to assist the celebrant to remove his shoes.

After the last collect, the celebrant and the ministers retire to the sedilia. There they remove the chasuble,[40] which is placed next to the sedilia,[41] ready to be resumed later. Meanwhile, the choir sits. All stand[42] while two presbyters of the upper form, who during the collects have bared their feet and vested in unapparelled albs, crossed stoles and maniples,[43] come from the vestry, go behind the altar and bring thence the veiled altar cross between them, each holding it by one of its arms.[44] These priests should stand at the south end of the altar, facing west over its surface,[45] but if the altar is fixed to the wall, they should stand to the right of the altar.[46] There they sing the verse *Popule meus*. A server (most conveniently the thurifer) brings the missal from the altar and holds it before them.[47] The reply, *Agyos*, &c., is sung from the choir step by

---

[35] Col 272: [*Evangelia*] *etiam in die Parasceves, alta voce legantur, more duplicis festi.*
[36] Whether the fourth prayer, for the King, should be omitted at present is considered in Chapter IX, note 3.
[37] OP.1486.
[38] Coll 324 and 327.
[39] OP.1498 (*ad gradus Pesbyterii super tapetem ibidem stratum*). OCarm.168 gives *ad gradus presbyterii super tapetum mappa honesta coopertum*. OPraem.XXXV.41–3 also has the carpet laid out now, by a sacristan.
[40] OP.1489 supposes that the maniple is retained.
[41] If it may be done without risk of damage to the vestment, the chasuble may be laid on the seat itself. For a treatment of where the chasuble should be left, see Chapter XXX, note 2. Since the chasuble will be removed when the Sacrament is brought to the altar it has seemed better to follow Col 328 and not OP.1489, which has the chasuble removed to the vestry.
   From this point onwards, P.69–73 supplements the Missal.
[42] The rubric does not state that they stand, but the Dominicans do so (OP.1489), albeit not at the sedilia, and it seems more fitting than sitting throughout the unveiling of the Cross. The Dominican celebrant and his ministers do not kneel with the choir (OP.1493).
[43] Col 328 and P.69 specify that the albs should be unapparelled but make no mention of other vestments. OP.1488, however, prescribes crossed stoles and maniples for these presbyters, against OPraem.XXXV.43–4. Ebor.156 prescribes crossed stoles but makes no mention of maniples.
[44] Col 328; P.69; OP.1490.
[45] P.69 against OP.1490.
[46] Missal A.112: *a dextris altaris*.
[47] Among the Carmelites, who do not mention the thurifer as a full-time server, the book is held by one of the acolytes (OCarm.168). F.304 gives this duty to an acolyte also.

two deacons of the second form in choir dress.[48] The choir kneels in its stalls and sings *Sanctus*. Having kissed the forms, all rise and sing *Deus*. Kneeling again, they again sing *Sanctus*, kiss the forms or the floor[49] and rise to sing *fortis*. Kneeling a third time, they sing *Sanctus* once more. Kissing the forms, they rise and sing *et immortalis, miserere nobis*. Neither the celebrant nor the sacred ministers nor the presbyters holding the Cross nor the deacons at the choir step kneel.[50] These actions are repeated[51] at *Quia eduxi te* and *Quid ultra* with their replies, the two presbyters still standing in the same place.[52] Coming round to stand next to the south-east corner of the altar,[53] they remove the veil from the Cross in one movement[54] as they sing *Ecce lignum Crucis*, holding the Cross aloft by its vertical to display it.[55] A server takes the veil and lays it on the carpet. The choir[56] kneels, kisses the floor or the forms and sings the antiphon *Crucem tuam* with the psalm *Deus misereatur*, repeating the antiphon, kneeling,[57] after each verse of the psalm. The two presbyters carry the Cross down to the bottom step[58] in the middle, where they lay it down on the cloth and then sit on the step themselves, each on one side of the Cross, touching it with the closer hand.[59] As *Crucem tuam* and the psalm are sung, the celebrant and the ministers sit at the sedilia and bare their feet[60] with the help of the acolyte[61] and the taperers. The servers do not discalce themselves until shortly before they creep to the Cross.[62] The other crosses in the church remain veiled.[63]

The worship of the Cross now takes place.[64] The ministers stand at the sedilia.[65] As the sitting presbyters and the standing choir sing *Crux fidelis* and *Pange lingua*,

---

[48] They are presumed to wear their black *cappae chorales* (Missal.112). These deacons are described as *sparsim stantes*: should they not stand too close to each other? At P.70, this term is explained as a corruption of *semper sint*, an explanation which is less convincing at P.69. *Crede Michi* [82] confirms that they should stand while singing.
  Ebor.157 has these deacons barefoot, but this seems not to have been the case at Sarum.
[49] P.70.
[50] Col 329; OP.1492.
[51] OP.1494.
[52] Against OP.1494 and Missal.113, Col 329 and P.70 make it clear that the two presbyters do not move before singing *Quia eduxi*.
[53] P.70.
[54] The rubric at Col 329 (*deinde sacerdotes discooperientes crucem juxta altare in dextera parte, canant*) and P.70 (*deinde sacerdotes stantes juxta altare ex dextera parte discooperientes crucem simul cantent*) may lead some to wonder whether only the right arm of the Cross should be unveiled now. However, there is no mention of a later unveiling of the rest of the Cross, and the Gradual is much less ambiguous: *tunc sacerdotes discooperientes crucem canant* (page 102). The Dominicans also unveil the Cross all at once (OP.1496).
[55] OP.1498.
[56] OP.1497 has the priests, ministers and deacons kneel also but the implication of Col 330 is that the celebrant and the ministers do not kneel until they worship the Cross later.
[57] Missal.113.
[58] Col 330: *super tertium gradum ab altari*.
[59] OP.1498. The Dominican priests recline on their sides (*ibidem*), and at Durham.10 they sit kneeling, but P.71 and Col 330 have *sedeant*. The English 'sit' is used elsewhere of kneeling, but this meaning is not given to *sedere*. *Crede Michi* [82] suggests that 'sit' means 'sit'.
[60] *nudatis* (Col 330) seems to imply more than merely shoes. So OP.1499: *nudatis omnino plantis*.
[61] At Rome, this is done by the Master of Ceremonies (F.305).
[62] Col 330 implies that all the clergy worship the Cross barefoot.
[63] C 60.1.
[64] The Sarum books give no details of the ceremonial to be followed beyond saying that the clergy do so barefoot and in descending order of rank (Col 330). The details given here are taken from OP.1499–1501, supplemented from F.305-7.
[65] F.305.

the celebrant, alone, comes to stand in the middle some considerable distance before the Cross.[66] There he kneels and bows. Rising, he advances half the distance, walking gravely, and again kneels and bows. He rises and goes as far as the Cross. There he kneels and prostrates himself with his whole body, laying his hands on the floor before him or embracing the Cross lovingly. He kisses the feet of the Crucified once only.[67] Rising forthwith, he bows profoundly and steps to the right of the Cross, where he stands, taking the place of that side's presbyter.[68] The presbyter now comes the full distance from the Cross and creeps thereto in his turn. Stepping to the left side of the Cross he takes the place of the second presbyter who now creeps to the Cross in his turn. Upon his return to his place, the first presbyter passes between the altar and the Cross to resume his own place and the celebrant returns to the sedilia *per breviorem* where he sits and is assisted to put on his shoes. Considerable skill will be required to ensure that the worship of the Cross does not interfere with the presbyters' singing.

The others creep to the Cross in the same way, retiring to their places and resuming their shoes as soon as they have bowed to the Cross. The order to be followed is this. First, the celebrant; then the two presbyters, the one holding the right arm of the Cross going before his companion; then the deacon; after him the two deacons who sang *Agyos* earlier, one after the other; after these, the subdeacon; next, the choir,[69] barefoot, in descending order of rank, approaching two and two;[70] after the choir come the servers in order, one by one: the acolyte, the taperers and the thurifer. On returning to their places, all resume their shoes.

The clergy advancing towards the Cross should do so in seemly fashion, so that there should be three persons before the Cross at all times. As the first prostrates himself, the next will kneel at half the distance and the third will kneel at full distance. They should all rise and advance simultaneously, a fourth person taking the place of the third as the second does of the first.

When the clergy have concluded their worship, the two presbyters take up the Cross and come down the middle of the choir to the chancel step,[71] preceded by the taperers bringing the cloth,[72] where they lay down the Cross for the people's worship. The congregation creeps to the Cross as did the clergy, kneeling or genuflecting every

---

[66] OP.1499 seems to presume a distance of about 15 yards (*quindecim circiter passuum*) but makes allowances for smaller churches.

[67] Missal B.113 gives what must be presumed to be a private prayer to be said by the priest while worshipping the Cross:

> Domine Jesu Christe gloriosissime conditor mundi qui cum sis coaequali Patri sanctoque Spiritui carnem immaculatam assumere dignatus es et gloriosissimas tuas sanctas palmas crucis patibulo permisisti configi. ut claustra dissipares inferni. et humanum genus liberares de morte. miserere miserere facinoribus oppressi. ac labe nequitiarum sordidati non me digneris Domine gloriose derelinquere. sed indulge malum quod egi. exaudi me prostratum ad adorandam tuam sanctam crucem ac praesta ut in sacris solemnibus diebus tibi merear assistere mundus.

[68] The directions for the presbyters' worship of the Cross are taken from OP.1499.

[69] F.306, in an order that seems more plausible for seculars than that prescribed at OP.1500.

[70] With Fortescue and against the Dominicans.

[71] Col 331 has *ante aliquod altare*. In the cathedral, this would presumably be that of the Holy Cross (16 in the diagram in *Processions*.72). In other churches, a side altar or the chancel step could be used. No provision appears to be made for the laity to worship a different cross, as is seen sometimes in the Roman rite and is prescribed in OPraem.XXXV.66–9.

[72] P.72. There is no mention of the taperers' candles or the cloth, but it will be convenient to have these two servers spread the cloth in the new place.

three paces. It may be desirable for the feet of the Crucified to be wiped after each layman's kiss with a cloth brought to one of the priests. The customary collection or offering may take place. Meanwhile, the choir, sitting, sings *Dum fabricator mundi*[73] and the celebrant and ministers read all the responsories, sitting at the sedilia,[74] from the missal held before them by the acolyte, as at Mass. While they do so, the taperers unfold the altar cloth so that it hangs a little over the front edge of the altar[75] and light the altar candles.[76] The acolyte brings the corporal to the altar.[77]

§4. MASS OF THE PRESANCTIFIED AND VESPERS

The worship of the Cross concluded,[78] the two presbyters, preceded by the taperers, return up the middle of the choir with the same reverence as before to the altar and replace the Cross in its usual place, aided if necessary by a sacristan.[79] As they pass up to the altar, all in the choir and the sanctuary, including the celebrant, kneel.[80] The presbyters come to the middle and follow the taperers to the sacristy, where the Sacrament has been reserved since the previous day. There they remove their vestments

---

[73] Col 331 and P.72 seem to assume that this responsory will be sung, not only while the laity worships the Cross, but also while the Cross is replaced on the altar and the presbyters retire to the vestry. See also the translation of the Rawlinson manuscript Processional provided in Bailey, page 21.
[74] OP.1501.
[75] *Caeremoniale Episcoporum*, lib. 2, cap. 25, n. 28.
[76] OP.1482 has the candles lit from the beginning of the function; F.307 has the candles lit just before the corporal is taken to the altar. Missal A.109 gives *candele non accendantur circa altare. nisi ante corpus domini.* These words do not exclude the possibility that the candles may be present but unlit from the beginning, and, if taken *latissimo sensu*, the words *ante corpus domini* could be taken to refer to the whole of the Mass of the Presanctified from its preparation onwards. See notes 21 and 22.
[77] In the Roman rite, the corporal is brought by the usual minister, the deacon. The Sarum books do not mention the corporal, but its omission is unthinkable. The ceremonial suggested here departs as little as possible from the usual ritual of High Mass.
[78] Col 331 and P.72 give somewhat different directions. The approach suggested here (informed by Missal.114, OP.1501-11, OCarm.169 and F.307-10) seeks to reconcile these differences so as to result in a reasonably graceful service.
The rubric at Missal A.114, inasmuch as it might explain some of the rite's presuppositions and presents an easier ceremonial than that of Col 331, is worth quoting in full:

> *et accedens ad altare dicat confessionem. Interim dum ipse sacerdos se preparet quidam alius sacerdos intret in sacrarium ubi priori die repositum fuit corpus domini ponens illud in patenam. et subdiaconus eat ante illum calicem portans et ipse sacerdos sequens deferat sic corpus domini super altare cantando secreto communionem. Hoc corpus. Cumque altari appropinquauerint: adorent omnes cum genuflexione corpus domini. quod executor officii a sacerdote incipiens more solito componat. et uini et aque infusione in calicem a diacono facta. et sacrificio super altare more solito deposito. et incensato: inclinans se ante altare dicat cum humilitate. In spiritu humilitatis Et cum erexerit se: dicat humili uoce. Oremus. Preceptis salutaribus. Cum oracione dominica Respondente choro. Set libera nos. Deinde dicat solito more* Libera nos quesumus. *In qua oracione dum dicat* Per eundem. *et cetera: frangat hostiam sicut solet ceteris diebus et dicendo interim modesta uoce.* Per omnia secula. *Et respondente choro* Amen *dimittat in calicem sicut solet partem hostie nec dicatur.* Pax domini. *sit nec* Agnus dei *neque pax detur. set statim postquam communicauerit se sacerdos: dicant priuatim hostias* † *quas in cena domini alta uoce dixerant. Post vesperas. dicat sacerdos postcommunionem hoc modo incipiens.* Respice quesumus domine. *Require. in quarta feria precedente super populum sine.* Qui tecum.

[79] OP.1504.
[80] F.307.

and, still unshod, resume their surplices. They should wear no other choir dress over these,[81] but the Sacrament should be held through a humeral veil.[82]

As soon as the presbyters and the taperers have removed themselves to the vestry, the clergy in choir come up to the sanctuary[83] and draw themselves up on either side of the altar, where they stand as if forming a guard of honour for the Sacrament.[84] It will be most convenient if they divide as they do for the Sunday procession. They should take care not to impede the route that the celebrant will follow from the sedilia to the altar. In smaller churches, it may be necessary for the choir to remain in its stalls. The thurifer goes to prepare the thurible. The celebrant, assisted by the ministers, dons his chasuble again at the sedilia.

All three[85] come to the foot of the altar, bow[86] and say the preparatory prayers, beginning with the *Confiteor*.[87] They omit the kiss of peace and *Habete osculum pacis*. They go up to the altar. After the celebrant has said *Aufer a nobis*, kissed the altar and signed himself,[88] he stands a little to the north while the deacon unfolds the corporal[89] and the subdeacon transfers the missal to the position it usually occupies for the offertory. The subdeacon should time his arrival so as to ensure that the celebrant is back in the middle of the altar.[90]

The two presbyters return now, preceded by the taperers with lighted candles. The former carries the dressed empty chalice.[91] Behind him walks the other, bearing the veiled pyx containing the two hosts consecrated on the previous day.[92] He should carry the pyx somewhat elevated before his breast.[93] As the Sacrament passes, the choir

---

[81] P.72: *in superpelliceis discalceati sine almico*.

[82] It would appear contrary to ordinary Eucharistic devotion not to hold the pyx through a veil. At High Mass, the acolyte ordinarily brings the empty chalice in a humeral veil, but his order does not permit him to handle the sacred vessels directly. Lincoln I.378 has the chalice and corporals brought in at Mass by the primary and secondary subdeacons, respectively, each wearing a humeral veil. The Roman subdeacon also holds the chalice through a veil at the offertory. However, at Low Mass, the Sarum priest brings the chalice with no humeral veil because it is proper to the presbyterate to handle the chalice. For a discussion of the pictorial evidence, see Chapter XXXVII, note 14.

[83] Col 331 and Missal.114 imply that the choir does not come up to the sanctuary after the Mass of the Presanctified has begun. The Dominican choir comes up much later, probably because it attends the procession to the Monument.

[84] There is no mention of candles held by the choir, quite possibly because the choir does not take part in the procession from the Monument (OP.1505; F.308). If it be desired that candles should be held, they should be lit from the time that the presbyters bring the Sacrament until the Sepulchre is closed and the choir disperses.

[85] Col 331.

[86] OP.1504.

[87] The preparatory prayers as a whole are sometimes called the *Confessio* (e.g. C 66.4). That he is to begin here with the *Confiteor* itself is deduced from the choice of the latter term over the former (Col 331).

[88] Col 331 gives no details after *Aufer a nobis*, but the point indicated here seems the most natural at which to interrupt the usual ritual.

[89] OP.1504.

[90] In the Roman rite, which omits the prayers at the foot of the altar, the missal is transferred when the corporal is extended (*Caeremoniale Episcoporum*, lib 2, cap. 25, n. 28).

[91] Missal A.114 has the chalice carried by the subdeacon. P.72, in garbled Latin, has the Sacrament borne by two presbyters. Bailey's (page 21) translation of the Bodleian Library's Rawlinson manuscript processional has the taperers precede a single presbyter with the Sacrament, who appears not to be one of the two presbyters of the Cross. Although we are bound by the rubric as it stands at P.72, it would be neater (and more congruent with the rite elsewhere) for the Sacrament to be brought by a single presbyter and the chalice to be carried by the subdeacon or the acolyte, as at High Mass.

[92] Missal A.114 enjoins this presbyter to say quietly the Communion antiphon *Hoc corpus*.

[93] OP.1508.

kneels prostrated and remains in this position until after Communion.[94] The presbyters come to the foot of the altar, he who holds the pyx standing in the middle, the other at his right. The celebrant and ministers turn to receive the Sacrament. The celebrant[95] takes the pyx and places it on the corporal. With the ministers and the presbyters he may kneel briefly in silent worship.[96] The subdeacon passes to stand at the right of the deacon and receives the chalice from the second presbyter. Both presbyters now withdraw, resume their shoes and join the choir. The taperers put down their candles and adopt their usual stations.

The ceremonies of the offertory follow, subject to certain modifications. All kisses are omitted.[97] The acolyte brings up the cruets, which he passes to the subdeacon. Having unveiled the chalice as usual and handed the paten to the celebrant, the deacon[98] receives the wine and then the water from the subdeacon and makes the chalice. The water is not blessed.[99] The acolyte retires with the cruets and the subdeacon takes up his usual station at the celebrant's left. The celebrant disposes the chalice and the paten as usual, then slides one of the hosts from the pyx onto this, taking care not to touch it. He places the veiled pyx to the right of the chalice and a little behind it, as he would a ciborium. He now slides the Host onto the corporal and sets the paten to his right, on the corporal.[100] He covers the chalice but omits the sign of the cross.[101] The sacrifice is incensed with unblessed incense[102] in the usual manner but the corporal's, altar's and all other incensations are omitted.[103] The thurible will not be used again until after Vespers. The lavatory and *In spiritu humilitatis* with their usual ceremonies follow. At *Orate fratres*, since he should not turn his back fully to the Sacrament, the priest turns by his right on the north side and turns back the same way, without completing the circle.[104] Until after the Communion, the acolyte and the taperers comport themselves as at Mass, *mutatis mutandis*.

The celebrant now says *Oremus. Praeceptis salutaribus moniti*, &c. and the *Pater noster*, in a spoken voice, low but loud enough for the choir to hear,[105] holding his hands as at Mass. *Libera nos*, &c. and the fraction follow as usual. He speaks *Per omnia saecula saeculorum* without note in the same voice as before.[106] There is no elevation,[107] but the commingling follows in silence, *Pax Domini*, *Agnus Dei* and the sign of the

---

[94] Missal A.114; OP.1510; OCarm.169.
[95] Missal A.114. The Dominican celebrant also places the Sacrament on the corporal himself (OP.1511), unlike in the Roman rite.
[96] OP.1511 and the Roman rite. This kneeling is mentioned neither by the Carmelite nor the Sarum books (unless *omnes* in Missal A is to be understood of the celebrant and his ministers) and may be a later addition to the rite.
[97] F.310.
[98] Missal A.114. However, in light of the confusion at C 66.18, it could hardly be wrong to have the chalice made by the subdeacon as normal.
[99] OP.1511.
[100] F.309. The reason for this is that, unlike at a normal Mass, the paten may have consecrated crumbs on it.
[101] The Roman rite's omission of the cross (F.310) is presumed here because the accompanying words are not said.
[102] F.310 and the implication by omission of OP.1511.
[103] OP.1511.
[104] F.310. This interpretation reconciles Col 331 and *Crede Michi* [83].
[105] Col 331: *humili voce sine nota*. The choir needs to hear if it is to respond.
[106] Col 332: *modesta voce*.
[107] OP.1513 prescribes the elevation but Col 331 makes no mention of it. Although the argument from silence is often perilous, it seems unlikely that such an important rite should not be mentioned if observed.

cross being omitted;[108] nor is the Pax given today. The priest's Communion follows at once, its preparatory prayers being omitted. To receive the Host, the priest says only *Corpus Domini*, &c. and makes the usual sign of the cross.[109] He takes the chalice and drains the wine with the particle, saying *Corpus et Sanguis Domini nostri Jesu Christi custodiat nos in vitam aeternam. Amen.* The ablutions follow. The subdeacon transfers the missal. The celebrant and the subdeacon go to their steps at the south of the altar. The chalice is dressed but the corporal, which still holds the veiled pyx as on the previous day, is not folded. If a special monstrance is used, the Sacrament is inserted in this and the pyx is removed. The acolyte comes to receive the chalice from the deacon, who should not turn his back to the Sacrament. The deacon arranges the pyx in the middle of the corporal and goes to stand on his step behind the celebrant.

A shortened form of Vespers now follows. They are not chanted but said standing[110] in a low voice by the choir in pairs, as the *Confiteor* is alternated by the choir in the Roman rite. The ministers come to stand on either side of the celebrant at the altar, as they do ordinarily for the Communion verse, and alternate with him. At the end of the psalm *Miserere*, the celebrant says, aloud, but without note, *Dominus vobiscum*, *Oremus* or conclusion, the postcommon *Respice*. So ends the Mass of the Presanctified.

§5. THE DEPOSITION IN THE SEPULCHRE[111]

Returning to the sedilia, and assisted by the sacred ministers, the celebrant removes his chasuble[112] and bares his feet.[113] All three return to the foot of the altar, from which one[114] of the aforementioned presbyters, also barefoot,[115] removes the Cross.

---

[108] OP.1514.
[109] So in the Roman rite.
[110] Col 332, in a contested reading (*stando*), suggests that the psalms are said kneeling and that the choir rises for *Pater noster*, which seems unlikely.
[111] The visit to the Sepulchre in Sarum Use presents some very unusual features. The inclusion of the Blessed Sacrament in the Sepulchre, quite probably a later addition to the rite (Bishop, page 295), makes the working out of the ceremonial very tricky. Furthermore, as so often, the Sarum books do not give full details of the ceremony. Consequently, we are reduced to applying first principles and drawing analogies. Accordingly, since it is unlikely that the Sacrament should not be attended by lights, the presence of the taperers is presumed. Likewise, since both priests will incense the Sepulchre (P.73), two thurifers are assumed, this being the case when two priests incense the altar during Divine Service (C 23). It would also be strange for the ministers not to attend the celebrant, especially if the choir is expected to do so. Remembering that much modern Eucharistic piety is post-mediæval, we have not neglected to observe that the two priests are treated by the rubric on terms of equality (P.72: *socio*). The closest parallel with this procession among the Dominicans and the Carmelites is to be found in the reservation of the Sacrament on Maundy Thursday, and so it is there, according to our usual analogical method, that we have sought inspiration. Hereford.95–7, although its use is significantly different from Sarum's in its origin (Bishop, page 295), came to adopt the Sarum practice of reserving the Sacrament in the Sepulchre and so may be used with caution as a guide to the practice at Salisbury. Despite this combined approach, it necessarily remains the case that the suggestions presented here consist of guesswork to a considerable degree.
[112] Col 332.
[113] Col 332.
[114] P.72. At Durham.10, two monks carry the Cross.
[115] Nothing suggests that this priest wore a humeral veil, but both the importance of the Cross and the priest's equality with the celebrant would be shewn more clearly if he did so. The question may be

Good Friday

From the vestry, whither they should have repaired towards the end of Vespers, come the thurifer, accompanied by another boy, both wearing albs and each carrying a lit thurible. At the foot of the altar, they form a single line with the taperers, who hold their tapers, behind the celebrant. In the middle stands the acolyte, holding the humeral veil.

The celebrant and the ministers kneel, as do the taperers and the thurifers.[116] Before he also kneels, the acolyte[117] imposes the humeral veil on the celebrant as the deacon goes up to the altar and takes the pyx, which he delivers into the kneeling celebrant's left hand[118] and wraps in the ends of the humeral veil.[119]

The procession to the Sepulchre is formed in the following order.[120] First goes the acolyte bearing the processional cross; then the taperers with burning tapers; then the two thurifers with their thuribles; then the choir, *junioribus prioribus*; then the subdeacon, followed by the deacon carrying the book;[121] then the presbyter, surpliced and barefoot, carrying the Cross; lastly, the celebrant, also barefoot, carrying the Sacrament.[122]

At the Sepulchre, the servers and the choir divide as they did earlier in the sanctuary.[123] The deacon[124] stands to the right of the celebrant, to whose left stands the presbyter, with the subdeacon at his left. All, except the acolyte, the presbyter and the celebrant, kneel. The presbyter lays the Cross in the Sepulchre and stands aside as the celebrant does likewise with the pyx. If the body of Christ is to be enveloped in a shroud, this is done now by the two priests. Both kneel and the celebrant intones the responsory *Aestimatus sum*. They rise immediately as the choir, still kneeling, continues the responsory. During this responsory, the ministers and the thurifers also

---

allowed to remain open. It is worth considering that when the two priests brought in the chalice and the pyx (see note 90), their use of humeral veils was also conjectured from first principles and not from any specific rubric. But see Chapter XXXVII, note 14.

[116] OP.1447.
[117] *Pace* OP.1447, since the Dominicans do not have this acolyte. The processional cross borne by the Dominicans on Maundy Thursday is omitted here.
[118] F.308.
[119] OP.1447.
[120] This is the order of the Sunday procession and also that followed by the Dominicans on Good Friday (OP.1506 and 1509), except that the Dominicans have the thurifer immediately precede the Sacrament and in the Sarum Sunday procession the choir follows the celebrant. Since it is escorting the Sacrament and the Cross, rather than merely walking in procession, this position for the choir seems more suitable.
[121] OP.1725 has the subdeacon carry the book in ordinary processions. However, on this occasion, it is more fitting for the deacon to carry it, since he will assist at the celebrant's side when the responsories will be intoned.
[122] Hereford.95-6 implies that, in the later rite, when the Sacrament also was enclosed in the Sepulchre, the Cross was taken first and the Sacrament somewhat later. This may justify the Sarum celebrant following his fellow priest rather than walking beside him. There is no mention of a canopy of any kind (see Chapter XXXIV, note 45).
[123] The choir accompanies the procession to the Sepulchre in other rites.
[124] The positions taken by the various clergy and the parts played by the ministers and the thurifers are plausible suppositions more than deductions from the rubrics. When incensing the altar at Vespers, the senior priest (here supposed to be the celebrant) stands to the right of his fellow. The ceremonial suggested here for the incensation of the Sepulchre is based on that used when incensing the altar during the *Magnificat* at Vespers (C 23).

rise. The deacon assists at the imposition of incense in both thuribles, but the celebrant does not bless the incense.[125]

The Sepulchre is now incensed by both priests. To do this, the celebrant stands somewhat to the right of the centre of the Sepulchre with the deacon on his right and the first thurifer on his left. The surpliced presbyter stands to the left of the Sepulchre's centre, flanked by the subdeacon and the second thurifer. The priests swing the thurible three times, once straight ahead, the second time towards the ends of the Sepulchre, and the third towards its middle. They then walk as far round the Sepulchre as they can, the celebrant towards the right and the presbyter towards the left, censing as they go. At the ends of the Sepulchre, they face each other across it and swing the thurible again. Coming back to the middle, they return the thuribles to the ministers, who give them to the thurifers. These retire to join the other kneeling servers. The two priests lock the Sepulchre and come back to their place before it, where, both kneeling, the celebrant intones the responsory *Sepulto Domino*. They remain kneeling throughout this and the three following antiphons, *In pace in idipsum*, *In pace factus est* and *Caro mea*, which the celebrant intones.

All spend some time kneeling before the Sepulchre and praying privately.[126] Then, as the choir departs in no particular order, the celebrant, ministers and servers rise and return in order to the sanctuary. There being no need for the taperers' candles, these may fittingly be left before the Sepulchre. If the taperers are to take them back, however, they should be extinguished before setting out from the Sepulchre.[127] The celebrant, having removed the humeral veil, resumes his shoes and chasuble at the sedilia, comes to bow before the altar, and all return to the vestry in the usual order.[128]

A light[129] should burn constantly before the Sepulchre from this moment to that when the Sacrament is removed on Sunday morning. It is extinguished from the beginning of the *Benedictus* to the end of the service at Tenebræ on Holy Saturday and from the beginning of the Easter Vigil until the Paschal Candle is lit.[130] Constant watch should be kept over the Sepulchre until the procession on Easter morn.

§6. THE SIMPLE FORM OF THE RITE

In most churches, it will be impossible to hold the function in its full form. The celebrant and the ministers may read the Passion as on Palm Sunday. The taperers will remove the cloths from the altar at *Partiti sunt*. If there is no other priest, the celebrant unveils the Cross with the deacon, and *Agyos* is sung by the subdeacon, accompanied

---

[125] This was proposed earlier at the Mass of the Presanctified (see note 102).
[126] Col 333. At Durham.10, they pray a great space.
[127] OP.1450.
[128] Col 333: *dictis orationibus ad placitum secrete ab omnibus cum genuflexione, omnibus aliis ad libitum recedentibus, ordine non servato, reinduat sacerdos casulam, et eodem ordine quo accessit in principio servitii cum diacono et subdiacono et caeteris ministris altaris abscedat.*
[129] Cons 5.1 has two lights on Good Friday and then one light only from the night of Good Friday until the early morning procession on Easter Day. For the parish church of St. Edmund, Sarum, see Bond, page 224. At Durham.10, two lights burn until Easter morning.
[130] Col 333; P.73; C 59.

by a senior cantor from the choir.[131] After unfolding the corporal, the deacon brings the Sacrament,[132] shod[133] and wearing the humeral veil over his vestments. This is taken from him after he has delivered up the pyx to the celebrant. The chalice is brought by the subdeacon[134] or by an acolyte. At the end, the Cross is taken to the Sepulchre by the deacon. The subdeacon assists at the imposition of incense. The celebrant alone incenses the Sepulchre, flanked by the ministers. There is no second thurifer.

Further simplification is possible if there are no ministers. It is highly desirable that the celebrant should be attended at least by two taperers and a thurifer in albs and a further clerk in surplice who will carry the Cross to the Sepulchre. The dressed chalice, with its corporal in the burse, is prepared on the credence table, together with the cruets and the basin. Nearby should be the carpet. At the Sepulchre, the book for intoning the responsories is put in a suitable place. In the vestry are prepared the celebrant's vestments, the humeral veils, the taperers' candles and the thurible.

The taperers lead the thurifer and the celebrant to the altar. The clerk in surplice sits in the choir until he is required. The celebrant reads the lessons and tracts at the south corner of the altar. He may sit for the tracts if they are sung. He reads the Passion and the Gospel from the north nook of the altar, as on Palm Sunday. At *Partiti sunt*, the taperers come to snatch away the cloths.

The solemn collects follow at the south corner. The taperers may occupy their usual places before the altar. At the conclusion of the collects, the celebrant goes to the sedilia, where he removes the chasuble and bares his feet. Towards the end of the collects, the taperers lay out the carpet from the Cross and go to the sedilia to assist the celebrant.

The celebrant unveils the Cross on his own.[135] *Agyos* is sung from the choir. If there is no choir and no one to make the responses, the celebrant reads them himself from the book held before him while all kneel. He then worships the Cross alone[136] as the servers go to remove their shoes. After they have worshipped the Cross and shod themselves anew, the taperers take the cloth to the chancel step, followed by the celebrant, who, still unshod, brings the Cross and then returns to the sedilia, where he sits to put on his shoes and read *Dum fabricator mundi* aloud (if there is no choir), assisted by the taperers. It is fitting that the thurifer should remain with the Cross. If there is an additional clerk, he may take the Cross to the step, barefoot, and attend it. After the people have finished their worship, he will bring it to the altar and retire. If there is no such clerk, the celebrant brings the Cross to the altar himself. In this case, he does not put on his shoes until he has returned the Cross to the altar.

After *Dum fabricator mundi* has been read, the taperers unfold the altar cloth and light the candles. At the apt moment, they escort the Cross back to the altar.

---

[131] OCarm.169. The Carmelites suppose that the subdeacon's associate is vested, but additional subdeacons are not to be had easily, and at Sarum, *Agyos* is sung by deacons in choir dress. OP.1503 gives the Dominican alternative, which presumes an additional priest and an additional deacon.

[132] OCarm.169. This probably represents the more primitive practice and is more in accord with the genius of the rite, which has the Sacrament brought to the altar by persons other than the celebrant, whereas the modern Dominicans (OP.1506–10) have the celebrant bring the Sacrament.

[133] He will need to minister immediately upon arrival.

[134] Missal A.114.

[135] OP.1503 allows the celebrant to unveil the Cross with one assistant presbyter.

[136] F.313–14.

The celebrant puts on his chasuble, takes the chalice from the credence table and goes to the foot of the altar, as he would for Low Mass. He goes up, unfolds the corporal and places the veiled chalice on it, leaving enough space for the pyx later. Coming down to the topmost step, he says the abbreviated preparatory prayers. At *Aufer a nobis*, a server transfers the missal. Coming down to the middle, the celebrant follows the taperers and the thurifer to the vestry, from which they return, the taperers with their candles, the thurifer with the thurible and the celebrant with the pyx in the humeral veil. The celebrant places the pyx on the corporal. All may kneel briefly. Rising, the taperers leave their candles in their usual places, one of them taking the celebrant's humeral veil to the credence.

The taperers bring up the cruets and hand them to the celebrant, who makes the chalice as at Low Mass, omitting the blessing of the water. He imposes unblessed incense in the thurible brought up by the thurifer and incenses the offerings. Everything now follows as when the function is celebrated with solemnity. After Communion, the celebrant dresses the chalice, which remains on the corporal. A taperer transfers the missal and the celebrant goes to the south corner to read Vespers and the postcommon aloud.

The celebrant goes to the sedilia, removes his chasuble and shoes, and returns to the altar. There one of the taperers imposes the humeral veil on him before returning to pick up his candle. If there is an additional clerk, the removal to the Sepulchre takes place as normal, the taperers and the single thurifer leading the way. If there is no other clerk, the celebrant takes the Cross to the Sepulchre unaccompanied and then[137] returns to bring the Sacrament with the usual procession.[138] The celebrant lays the pyx in the Sepulchre, intones the responsory *Aestimatus sum*, imposes incense and incenses the Sepulchre on his own, first on the right and then on the left. If there is no choir, the Sepulchre is incensed after the celebrant has read the responsory out loud. *Sepulto Domino* and the three antiphons follow. The function is concluded as in the solemn form.

---

[137] The burial of the Sacrament being an addition to the rite, it is reasonable to look to a use in which this addition was made later than at Sarum in an attempt to ascertain how a single priest can carry out both elements of the ceremony. Hereford.95–6 has the Cross brought to the Sepulchre before the Sacrament.

[138] Feasey, page 166.

XXXV

HOLY SATURDAY

§1. PREPARATIONS

The function consists of four parts: (1) the new Fire and the Paschal Candle; (2) the Lessons; (3) the ceremonies at the Font; and (4) Mass with Vespers.

None is celebrated later than usual, so that the Vigil Mass may begin at dusk.[1] The function begins after None, during which all vest[2] and at the conclusion of which all the lights in the church are extinguished.[3]

The following clergy are presumed to take part:[4] the celebrant; the principal deacon; the principal subdeacon; an acolyte, who will carry the triple candle and later the processional cross;[5] a server in a surplice to bear the second candle, used in blessing the font;[6] two taperers; a thurifer; a water-boy; and a book-boy. Clergy in choir will also attend, of whom two juniors in major orders[7] will sing *Inventor rutili*, four senior priests[8] will read the lessons, seven boys will sing the sevenfold litany,[9] five deacons[10] will sing the fivefold litany, a further[11] two deacons will carry the holy oils and three senior priests[12] will sing the third litany. A sacristan, or one of the servers, will light the Paschal Candle. If catechumens are to be made during the lessons, a priest other than the celebrant will need to carry out this office. He may be one of the priests from the choir.

The following preparations are made.

In the vestry, everything is prepared as for Mass, except for the celebrant's chasuble, which lies on the altar.[13] He will wear a red cope. For the Mass, the best vestments are

---

[1] Cons 69.1.
[2] F.320.
[3] OP.1523.
[4] Col 334.
[5] Col 334: *quidam [etiam] de prima forma*. P.74 adds *scilicet accolitus in superpelliceo*. Since there is no need for two acolytes at the same time, only one is necessary.
[6] Col 343+ and P.83 call him a *minister*. Col 350 calls him a *puer*.
[7] Col 337+: *de secunda forma*.
[8] *Dignioribus personis* (Col 343+).
[9] Col 348. The Gradual quoted at Col 347 has these be surpliced deacons.
[10] Of the second form (Col 350).
[11] These two deacons will carry the oils while the other five are still singing the litany: Col 350; P.88.
[12] *De superiori gradu* (P.90).
[13] Col 343+. Cons 69.1 contemplates the celebrant changing his chasuble but makes no mention of other vestments. These, therefore, could conform to either colour. Our preference is for that of the

worn.[14] If the neophytes are to communicate, hosts are prepared for them in the pyx, but otherwise a general Communion is not presumed. The ministers[15] will wear dalmatic and tunicles, either red or of transversed stripes. The acolyte[16] will wear a surplice until the lessons and a red tunicle over an alb for the blessing of the font. The deacons who will carry the holy oils will wear amices, albs, cinctures, red stoles and humeral veils.[17] If the assistant presbyters wore maniples on Good Friday, these deacons may do so now.[18] Either in the vestry or near the font are prepared one white and two red copes for the priests who will sing the threefold litany. The four senior priests who will sing the lessons will wear albs, as will all those who sing at the choir step.[19] Surplices are prepared for the server of the second candle, for the water-boy and the book-boy,[20] for the two clerks who will sing *Inventor rutili*, for the seven boys who will sing the sevenfold litany and for the five deacons who will sing the fivefold litany. If another priest will make the catechumens, he will do so in surplice and red stole.[21] The choir attends in choir dress. In addition to the vestments, the following are prepared: the triple candle;[22] the second candle, being the same which was blessed at Candlemas;[23] the ordinary processional cross, veiled;[24] the holy-water stoup and sprinkler; the book for the various blessings; and the chrism and the oil of the catechumens.

The church is decorated festally after Sext, all the altars being dressed as for feasts,[25] but the crosses and images remain veiled until Easter morning.[26]

In the sanctuary, the altar is prepared as for Mass with the missal on its desk.[27] The altar cross remains veiled.[28] The candles are not lit until the Mass. Two chasubles lie on

---

Vigil since the genius of the rite seems to consider the Easter festivities to begin properly on Sunday. The striped dalmatic and tunicle mentioned in CCC (C47) may have combined the colours of the Vigil and the Mass.

[14] Cons 69.
[15] Col 1; Cons 69.2; Col 334.
[16] Cons 55.
[17] At least, veils are worn at the Chrism Mass on Maundy Thursday (*Processions*.72–3). The stole is nowhere mentioned (P.84), and the humeral veils are sufficient to distinguish these deacons from lesser servers.
[18] See Chapter XXXIV, note 51.
[19] Cons 69.1. The reason is that the angels who appeared at the Holy Sepulchre also wore albs.
[20] They wear surplices for the ordinary Sunday procession (P.2). P.84 also has the book-boy wear a surplice on the way to the font.
[21] The Manual does not mention the colour of the stole but, if the celebrant were to carry out this duty, he would do so in a red cope, the colour of the Vigil and the blessing of the font. The font at Great Witchingham shews the priest in surplice and red stole.
[22] See Chapter II, note 40.
[23] P.143. This may be carried in a candlestick if so wished (woodcut at P.80).
[24] C 58 ordains the Lenten cross for Sundays in Lent (excepting the first) only. Since the cross is not borne at the Mass (Col 355), it would seem better not to use the Paschal, beryl, cross.

The Sarum books do not make it clear whether the processional cross should be veiled or not. C 60.1 would have all crosses veiled until Sunday morning and, since on the strength of this rubric we have presumed that the altar cross remains veiled, we have followed the same reasoning in the case of the processional cross.

[25] Cons 69.1.
[26] C.60.1; P.92.
[27] Unlike among the Dominicans, who bless the fire in the sanctuary (OP.1523), the ministers will not be able to bring books with them.
[28] Since the Cross is still in the Sepulchre, it is possible that for this function there should be no altar cross at all. This, however, seems unlikely, not least because on Sunday morning the Cross from the

the altar, the red chasuble used at the Vigil on top of the chasuble used for the Mass.[29] At the credence table, as well as those things ordinarily prepared for Mass, the book of lessons[30] is prepared. In a suitable place, if it is to be used, a lectern for the lessons is prepared. At the north end of the presbytery step,[31] the Paschal Candle[32] is set up but not lit. On either side of this, east and west, is a large standard candlestick with an unlit candle.[33] If these will be used, a ladder and taper are prepared to light the Paschal Candle. Throughout the church, all lights are prepared and extinguished, including those before the Sepulchre.[34]

At its appointed place[35] is prepared a fire. For this, if within the church, a brazier will be necessary. Nearby, most suitably on an occasional credence table,[36] are prepared charcoal and tongs for the thurible, flint[37] to light the fire, a taper or spill with which to light the triple candle (if needed) and a salver with ten[38] grains of incense to be inserted into the two candles. The fire is lit immediately before the function is to begin.

The font, which should have been emptied and cleaned, is filled with clear water. Near the font should be a towel for the second candle and for the celebrant's hands. If baptism is to be celebrated, the usual things for this are prepared, together with bread and cotton wool for the priest's hands.[39] The holy oils are brought by their deacons. There may be a taper to transfer the light from the second candle to those of the

---

Sepulchre is not placed on the High Altar at all. Here it is presumed that the ordinary cross, veiled, is on the altar.

[29] Col 343+ has the chasuble assumed from the altar after the *Exultet*. Coll 351-2 has the chasuble assumed from the altar at the beginning of the Mass. Cons 69.1 presumes cheaper vestments for the Vigil if baptisms are to be celebrated and precious vestments thereafter but precious vestments throughout if there be no baptisms. This schema conforms to a division of vestments by quality rather than by colour. Presuming a difference in colour, as we have throughout this work for the most part, it has seemed reasonable to posit a red chasuble for the Vigil and a white one for the Mass.

[30] Or this may be placed on the altar as usual.

[31] Col 337+.

[32] In the cathedral, this candle was 36 feet in height (Col 333) and was probably placed in a very tall candlestick, since Col 341+ permits the grains of incense to be fixed on this rather than in the candle itself. It is impossible to tell whether the height of 36 feet refers to the candle itself or to the candle inserted in its candlestick. If to the former, a candlestick of about 8 feet may be presumed. The floor of the triforium is about 42 feet above the floor of the nave (Sloper). Allowing for the presbytery to be somewhat elevated above the nave's level, a combined height of 44 feet for candle and stick would make it reasonably easy for a sacristan (Cons 69.3) to light the candle from the triforium if placed reasonably close to the north wall of the sanctuary.

[33] Cons 69.3. The later books make no mention of these candles or of the ceremony associated with them in the same way that the Consuetudinary makes no mention of a triple candle on the *hasta* (Cons 69.2). It is not impossible that the ceremony of dividing the light was transferred from the two standard candles to the triple candle on the *hasta*. If this interpretation be followed, the two standard candlesticks are omitted and only one wick of the triple candle should be lit at the fire, the other two being lit during the *Exultet*. An alternative explanation of the triple candle is that it reduces the risk of the light being extinguished prematurely.

[34] Col 333; P.73; C 58.

[35] At Sarum, the fire was lit in a brazier (woodcuts at P.76 and *Processions*.82) between the second and third pillars from the West that separate the nave from the south aisle, opposite the font (Col 334).

[36] In the cathedral, because the fire was lit near the font, the same table could serve as credence for both blessings.

[37] The traditional practice is that this fire should be altogether new and lit from flint.

[38] The number of grains is not mentioned, but five are used for one candle in the Roman rite and Col 341+ directs the grains to be inserted *in modum crucis*.

[39] F.331.

neophytes. After its part in the function has been concluded, the font is covered with a cloth.[40]

§2. THE NEW FIRE AND THE PASCHAL CANDLE

The choir is presumed to be in its stalls. The clergy come from the vestry to the altar in this order:[41] first, the surpliced water-boy with the stoup and sprinkler; second, the principal acolyte, in a surplice and carrying the triple candle on its shaft;[42] third, the taperers, carrying their tapers extinguished, going on either side of the surpliced clerk with the candle for the blessing of the font; fourth, the thurifer with the empty thurible; fifth, the surpliced book-boy, carrying the Processional; sixth, the subdeacon; seventh, the deacon; last, the celebrant in cope. There is no cross. Having bowed to the altar, they go in the same order down the middle of the choir to the place where the new fire has been lit. The choir follows, *excellentioribus praecedentibus*.[43] On the way, all alternate the psalm, *Dominus illuminatio mea*, omitting the *Gloria Patri*, without note.

At the fire, a station is made (Figure VI).[44] To the left of the fire and facing east stands the celebrant. To his left stands the deacon. The subdeacon stands to the left of the deacon. To the left of the subdeacon stands the clerk with the candle for blessing the font.[45] Before the celebrant stands one of the taperers. Between them, a little to the celebrant's left, stands the book-boy. Behind the celebrant stands the other taperer. Between them and a little to the celebrant's right stands the water-boy. The acolyte with the triple candle stands behind the second taperer. The thurifer stands to the right of the fire. The choir stands in an arc to the north of the subdeacon. All face the celebrant.

There the celebrant sings *Dominus vobiscum* and the prayer, *Domine, Deus noster*, with joined hands in the lesson tone.[46] At the places indicated, he makes the sign of the cross over the fire to his right. At the end of this prayer, he takes the sprinkler from the water-boy and sprinkles the fire. In similar fashion, he sings the prayers *Domine, sancte Pater* and *Coelesti lumine*. As soon as the celebrant has sprinkled the fire, the water-boy removes the stoup and sprinkler to the little table, from which he brings the salver with the grains of incense. Standing now in front of the celebrant and a little to his right, he holds out the salver as the celebrant exorcises and blesses the grains of incense. During these prayers, the thurifer places the charcoal in the holy fire. The last blessing completed, the thurifer brings the thurible, now containing the charcoal, and substitutes the water-boy, who returns to his previous place, behind the celebrant.

---

[40] M.35; Missal B.123.
[41] Col 334. Missal A.115 describes a significantly different procession. Since the procession goes to the fire down the middle of the choir, it appears that they go to the sanctuary first.
[42] Cons 69: *precedente processioni post aque latorem*. Missal.115 confirms that the acolyte bears the candle at the head of the procession but has him follow the water-boy and precede a crucifer.
[43] P.74.
[44] The woodcut at P.76 contradicts the rubrics at both P.75 and Col 334.
[45] Mention of this server is omitted except when he actually ministers. This seems the best place for him here.
[46] Col 335.

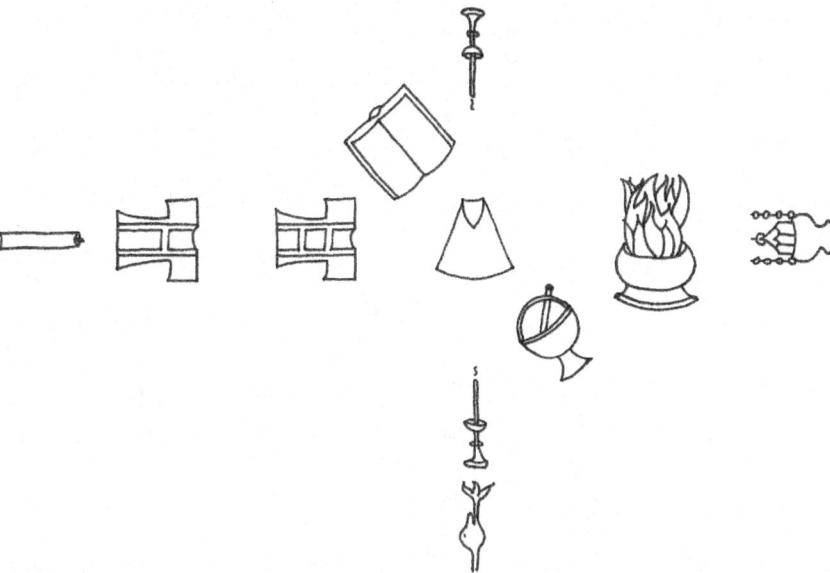

Figure VI. Holy Saturday: The blessing of the fire

Incense is imposed as usual and the celebrant fumes the new fire. The triple candle is lit[47] from the fire by the acolyte who carries it; likewise the candle for blessing the font.[48]

The procession to the sanctuary is now reformed in the same order as before, except that the two clerks who sing *Inventor rutili* walk, side by side, immediately behind the celebrant, and the water-boy carries the salver with the incense grains.[49] As the two clerks sing the first verse, the procession stands still, setting out only when the choir begins to repeat it. The two clerks sing the verses alone, the choir repeating *Inventor rutili* after each of these. The procession walks up into the choir. There the choir returns to its stalls, and the others go up to the presbytery step. They bow to the altar. *Inventor rutili* should last until the beginning of the *Exultet*.[50]

The book-boy surrenders the book to the deacon and retires. The celebrant goes up to the altar and then to the south corner as before the Gospel at Mass.[51] He does not kiss the altar.[52] He is followed by the deacon who, bowing to him at the middle with the book in his hands, is blessed by the celebrant with the sign of the cross and *In nomine Patris*, &c.[53]

---

[47] Unlike in the Roman rite, the triple candle is not said to be lit otherwise than in a single act. OP.1524 also has the candle lit at once, but it is not the triple reed.
[48] Cons 69.2.
[49] The water-boy generally precedes processions because he carries the stoup. On this occasion, however, it seems more fitting that he should go immediately before the reed. We can adduce no authority for this suggestion.
[50] Cons 69.3.
[51] The celebrant blesses the deacon (P.79) and in both the Roman and Dominican (OP.1525) rites the celebrant acts as at the Gospel and listens to the *Exultet* from the altar.
[52] Only some Roman authors prescribe this kiss (F.323), but Col 343+ has the celebrant kiss the altar when he has assumed the chasuble after the *Exultet*, so we presume that he does not do so here.
[53] P.79: *accepta prius benedictione ab exsecutore officii*. For the form of this blessing, see OP.1525.

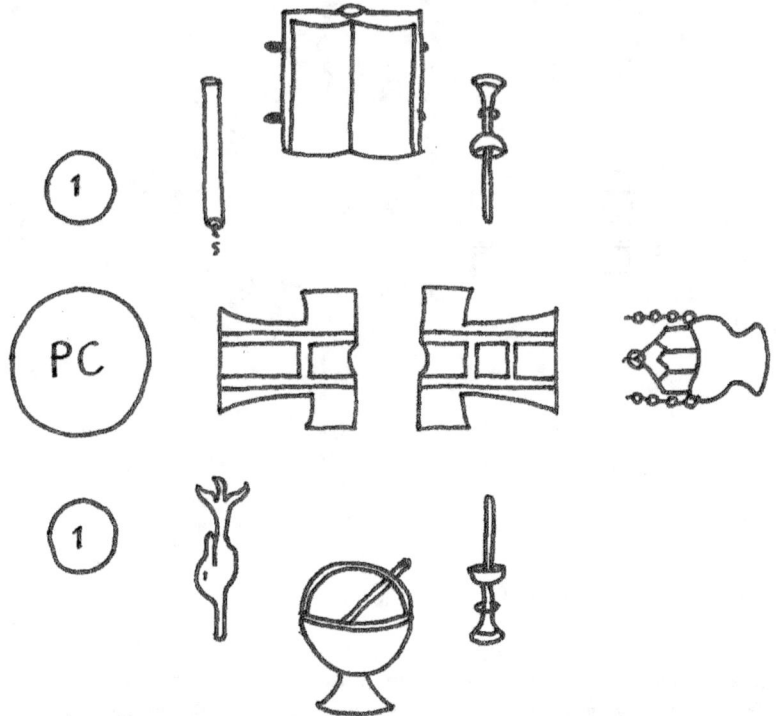

Figure VII. Holy Saturday: The blessing of the Paschal Candle

(1) Standard candles.

The procession to the Paschal Candle is now formed: first, the acolyte with the triple candle; then the taperers with extinguished tapers on either side of the server with the font's candle; then the thurifer; then the subdeacon; finally, the deacon. At the Candle, they make a station (Figure VII).[54]

The deacon stands opposite the Paschal Candle, facing north. On either side of him stand the taperers, turned towards him. Opposite the deacon, between him and the Candle, stands the subdeacon, who holds the book for the deacon to read from it. To the subdeacon's right stands the acolyte with the triple candle and on his left the server with the candle for blessing the font. These candles should be the only lights to burn in the church.[55] Both face the subdeacon. Behind the deacon stands the thurifer with the smoking thurible.[56] As well as these,[57] the water-boy stands between the triple candle and the taperer, a little to the west of them, facing east. Opposite him, a little east of the server with the font candle and the other taperer, stands the book-boy or

[54] Coll 337+-338; P.79–80, with a very unclear woodcut. This represents a development from the rite outlined at Cons 69.3. Pearson's diagram (page 160) appears misdesigned. See Figure VII.
[55] Missal A.118 and Cons 69.2.
[56] Cons 69.3: *cum thuribulo fumigante*. Is this insistence on *fumigante* because the thurible was swung as we suppose in Chapter XVII, note 26?
[57] These last two servers appear to have been forgotten by the rubricist, who, nonetheless, presumes their presence later (Cons 693; Col 341+).

the sacristan who will light the Paschal Candle, turned to face the water-boy. Everyone else, including the celebrant standing at the south corner of the altar,[58] turns to face the Paschal Candle.[59]

The deacon now sings the *Exultet* to the tone in the Missal. At *Incensi hujus sacrificium vespertinum*, he pauses, turns by his right, imposes incense, receives the thurible and incenses the Paschal Candle and the grains of incense held before him by the water-boy.[60] He returns the thurible to the thurifer, who returns to his place and swings the thurible.[61] The subdeacon stands aside as the deacon and the water-boy come to the candlestick. The deacon takes five grains of incense and fixes them in the Paschal Candle or, if this is not possible, in its candlestick,[62] in the form of a cross.[63] The bearer of the second candle now approaches and the deacon repeats the operation on this candle. He should not insert the grains of incense so low on this candle that they will be moistened by the water in the font later. All resume their positions and the deacon continues.

At *Rutilans ignis accendit*, the deacon pauses once more. The sacristan (or the book-boy) goes to light the Paschal Candle, taking the flame from the triple candle, either by holding up the *hasta* or by means of a separate taper.[64] The deacon should not resume his singing until this is done.[65] As he sings *Qui licet divisus in partes*, the sacristan or book-boy lights the standard candles placed either side of the Paschal Candle and then, assisted by the taperers, all the lights in the church.[66] They should begin with the lamps about the Sepulchre[67] and the High Altar and go round the church in order.[68] The taperers' candles are also lit.[69] If the King is habitually named in the Canon of the Mass, he is named in the *Exultet*.[70]

As soon as the *Exultet* is ended, the sacristan or book-boy extinguishes the standard candles.[71] The book-boy receives the closed book from the subdeacon and all return to the altar. The ministers go up the middle of the altar, where they assist the celebrant to remove his cope and put on the chasuble, which he takes from the altar.[72] The acolyte removes

---

[58] Cons 69.3 has the Bishop alone sit in his throne during the *Exultet*.
[59] Cons 69.3: *omnibus ceteris astantibus ad tam sacri luminis confeccionem intendentibus*.
[60] At Cons 69.3, five grains are presumed because the second candle has not yet acquired its later importance.
[61] Cons 69.3.
[62] Col 341+.
[63] O.P.1526 has the server offer the grains to the deacon one at a time. Either method could be followed.
[64] O.P.1526 has the second candle used for this, but among the Dominicans, this candle has retained its primitive function of merely guaranteeing that the flame from the holy fire is not lost. The same candle is used to light the taperers' tapers and the church lights. At 6 pounds (*Processions*.100), the Sarum candle was no mere taper.
[65] F.326 permits the choir to sit while the lights are lit and has them rise only when the deacon begins once more to sing.
[66] Col 342 has the taperers light their own candles, but this is not confirmed by P.82, and the taperers later have extinguished tapers at the Gospel (Col 355). It will be better if the taperers leave their tapers on the ground now and assist the sacristan, since there will be many lights to be kindled.
[67] Col 333.
[68] Cons 69.3: *per circuitum*.
[69] Cf. O.P.1530.
[70] See Chapter IX, note 3.
[71] Cons 69.5.
[72] Col 343+. Cons 69.5 has *cum diacono et subdiacono revestitis*. This last word could mean no more than 'in vestments' or (which is less easily explained) 'in a new suit of vestments'. In any case,

the triple candle.[73] The server with the candle for blessing the font goes to stand at the north end of the bottom step of the altar, facing south. He remains there until the end of the sevenfold litany.[74] The taperers put down their tapers in their usual Mass places[75] and come to the altar to remove the cope which they receive from the ministers. The book-boy and water-boy retire to their places in the choir.

§3. THE LESSONS

The celebrant[76] stands on the altar step below the footpace between the ministers, bows to the altar[77] and says *Pater noster* silently. He goes up to the altar, kisses it in the middle and goes at once with the ministers to the sedilia.

The lessons are read without titles at the choir step by senior clerks from the choir, in albs and amices.[78] As on Ember Days, the celebrant and the ministers sit at the sedilia to listen to the lessons and read the tracts privately, going to the altar for the collects,[79] which are said with hands extended and of which the last two are sung under a single conclusion. *Flectamus genua* is not said.[80] The choir alternates the tracts.[81]

During the tract, *Sicut cervus*, the acolyte goes to the vestry, whence he returns, vested in alb and red tunicle, carrying the cross, as the sevenfold litany is sung. With him go the two deacons who, having put on their vestments, bring the holy oils.

§4. THE LITANIES AND THE BLESSING OF THE FONT WITH BAPTISM

Seven boys in surplices come into the middle of the choir and, facing the altar,[82] start singing the first, sevenfold, litany,[83] during which the choir faces the altar.[84] As they do so, the celebrant and the ministers come back to the altar as usual and go up to the middle. There the ministers assist the celebrant to remove his red chasuble and lay it on

---

the ceremonial has changed from Cons 69.5 to Col 343+ and P.83, since the later form does not contemplate a visit to the vestry at this point.

[73] Col 343+: *abscedat*, which is more probable than *accedat* (P.83) and could represent a later development of the ceremony of extinguishing the two standard candles (Cons 69.5).
[74] Col 343+.
[75] OP.1530.
[76] Col 343+.
[77] OP.1530.
[78] Col 343; Cons 69.1. The order of the lectors is not stated. F.327 has the Roman prophecies sung in increasing order of rank.
[79] OP.1531.
[80] Col 344+.
[81] Col 345.
[82] Cons 69.5.
[83] The manner of singing this litany is not explained. In the Roman rite, it is doubled, that is to say, the cantors sing each petition straight through and the choir responds by singing the whole petition again (F.331).
[84] OP.1532.

the altar, where it was before. Receiving the cope from the thurifer,[85] they put it on the celebrant. They hand the red chasuble to the thurifer to remove. It will not be needed again.[86] All three come down the steps and remain standing, facing the altar.[87] While the litany is being sung, the procession is formed.

Towards the end of the sevenfold litany, the five surpliced deacons who will sing the fivefold litany come to the middle of the choir so that they may take the boys' place as soon as the first litany is finished. They begin the second litany at once.[88]

As soon as the petition *Sancta Maria, Ora pro nobis* has been sung, the procession sets out for the font in this order.[89] First goes the acolyte with the cross; second, the two taperers with their extinguished tapers; third, the thurifer without the thurible;[90] fourth, the book-boy (with the Processional) and the server carrying the candle for blessing the font, the latter to the right of the former, both in surplices; fifth, the two deacons of the holy oils, he who carries the chrism to the right of the other; sixth, the subdeacon; seventh, the deacon; and finally, the celebrant. The choir follows the procession, *dignioribus prioribus*, the deacons who sing the litany taking their places behind the celebrant.[91]

At the font, a station is made.[92] The procession, from the acolyte to the deacon, passes the font and halts, all facing east. The celebrant stands west of the font, facing east over it. Behind him, side by side in a row, stand the five deacons who are singing the litany.

The first part of baptism, up to *Ingredere in templum Dei*, should have been conducted by another priest in surplice and stole[93] during the singing of the lessons. If there is no other priest, the celebrant will do so now, after the fivefold litany and before the blessing of the font,[94] the procession making a station at the church door to do so before advancing to the font. In this case, the catechumens and their godparents incorporate themselves to the procession behind the celebrant, who leads them into the church.

---

[85] The thurifer is the most indicated server to do this, since he will be able to remove the cope later, at the beginning of the Mass.
[86] See note 37.
[87] That the celebrant stands during the sevenfold litany is peculiar, but it is the most probable explanation of P.83 (*et interim exuat sacerdos casulam, et super altare reponat, et sumat capam rubeam adhuc stando ante altare, donec cantetur letania*) and is confirmed by P.84, which has the Bishop also stand (*stet in sede sua*). The Dominican celebrant sits at the sedilia (OP.1532).
[88] P.84: *statim*.
[89] P.84.
[90] Incense will not be used at the font and the thurifer will be needed to minister the towel.
[91] In the cathedral, they leave by the south presbytery door and go down the south side of the nave to the font (Col 350; Wells.31), which they approach from the west. Cons 70.1 has the procession (in a different order) go out of the south presbytery door.
  Cons 70.1 seems to have the deacons who sing the fivefold litany walk ahead of the rest of the choir. Col 350 and P.85 are no more clear: *in medio clericorum de secunda forma post executorem officii*.
[92] P.86; Cons 70.2. OP, being written for convents of friars rather than for secular parish churches, omits the blessing of the font entirely.
[93] M.25.
[94] F.327 and 230. This separation of the making of a catechumen from the baptism itself is historically unobjectionable and liturgically neater, since the celebrant and assistants do not have to abandon the font to conduct a different function at the church door. The Processional, the Manual and Legg's Missal, while preserving in their layout what may have been a more primitive practice, do not seem to contemplate the clergy going to the door of the church but rather presume that the procession goes from the choir to the font. Nevertheless, it is possible for the complete ceremony to be performed by the celebrant.

Figure VIII. Holy Saturday: The blessing of the font
(K) The oil of the catechumens. (X) The chrism.

As soon as the litany is over, the ministers and servers turn and take up new positions (Figure VIII).[95] The deacon comes to stand to the right of the celebrant with the deacon of the chrism to his right. The subdeacon stands on the celebrant's left with the deacon of the oil of the catechumens on his own left. All these face east. Opposite the celebrant, beyond the font, stands the acolyte with the cross. The taperers stand on either side of him, one so placed as to look between the deacons and the other so as to look between the subdeacon and the deacon of the oil of the catechumens. In front of the former taperer stands the server with the candle; in front of the latter, the book-boy. Both of these should be close enough to the celebrant to be able to assist him. All these face west. The thurifer goes to fetch the towel and then to stand behind and between the principal deacon and the deacon of the chrism.[96] The choir and the people stand in a circle round the font.[97]

[95] Neither the woodcut at P.87 nor Pearson's diagram (page 167) accord with the rubric. See Figure VIII.
[96] The rubric has the thurifer walk in the procession but neglects to mention where he makes his station. *Processions*.87 seems to suggest that he, together with an unexplained additional taperer, should stand in front of the principal taperers, but the inclusion of this additional taperer, which makes no sense, might indicate some corruption. Assuming that a towel was in use, the suggestion made here employs him usefully.
[97] Hereford.461, quoting the Hereford Ordinal. In the Sarum books, the choir is mentioned nowhere. Otherwise, by analogy with the blessing of the fire earlier, the choir could form an arc behind the celebrant, facing east. F.328 would have the choir stand in two lines north and south of the font.

The celebrant sings *Dominus vobiscum*, the collect and the preface[98] with joined hands[99] from the book held before him by the book-boy. At *Qui hanc aquam*, he makes the sign of the cross in, not over, the water. He dries his hand on the towel given to him by the deacon, who has received it from the thurifer. The thurifer takes the towel back from the deacon and remains in his place.

The celebrant continues the preface. At *Unde bene* ✠ *dico te, per* ✠ *Deum vivum, per* ✠ *Deum verum* and *per* ✠ *Deum sanctum*, he makes the sign of the cross over the water, not touching it. At *rigare praecepit*, he casts a little water with his extended hand to the four points of the compass, east, west, north and south,[100] turning in his place to do so and drying his hand as before. At *Bene* ✠ *dico te*, and at *Pa* ✠ *tris et Filii* ✠ *et Spiri* ✠ *tus Sancti*, he makes the sign of the cross over the water, not touching it, as before. On one note, as if singing a lesson, he continues *Haec nobis praecepta*.[101] When he has sung *tu benignus aspira*, he breathes thrice over the water in the form of a cross. He continues with *Tu has simplices aquas* in the preface tone. As he sings *Descendat in hanc plenitudinem fontis*, he takes the candle from the deacon, who has received it from the server, and lets fall five drops of liquid wax therefrom into the water in the shape of a cross. At *fecundet effectu*, he lowers the base of the candle into the water with both hands, tracing a cross with it in the water, as he sings *Hic omnium peccatorum maculae deleantur*. He does not raise the candle out of the water until he has sung *cunctis vetustatis squaloribus emundetur*. He returns the candle to the deacon, who holds it as the thurifer dries it with the towel, which is now returned to the table, and then gives it back to the server as the celebrant continues the preface. At *Per Dominum*, the celebrant changes to the lesson tone and so ends the preface, the choir replying *Amen* in the same tone.[102]

The deacons of the holy oils now approach the celebrant,[103] who receives the oil of the catechumens directly from its deacon. He pours a little into the font in the form of a cross as he says *Conjunctio olei unctionis et aquae baptismatis. In nomine Patris et Filii et Spiritus Sancti. Amen*. He returns the vessel to its deacon and repeats the ceremony with the chrism, saying *Fecundetur et sanctificetur fons iste hoc salutifero chrismate salutis. In nomine Patris*, &c. Taking both vessels, he now pours from both at once, making a single sign of the cross[104] as he says *Conjunctio chrismatis sanctificationis et olei unctionis et aquae baptismatis. In nomine Patris*, &c.

The catechumens and their godparents are now conducted to the font, boy catechumens to the celebrant's right and girls to his left.[105] The second part of the

---

[98] Neither Dickinson's Missal nor Henderson's Processional give the tone for this preface. A tone can be found in Hereford.106–12.
[99] F.329.
[100] Missal C.129; F.329.
[101] Missal C.129.
[102] M.35, correcting the omission of P.89.
[103] At this point, both the Missal and the Processional fail us and recourse must be had to Missal C.129 and M.35. P.89 presumes that baptism will not follow and preserves merely a vestigial rubric to the effect that the oils are poured into the font only if baptisms will actually follow.
[104] There is no mention of the Roman rite's triple cross.
[105] M.25. In the cathedral, they would approach the font from the Porta Speciosa and face west. After their baptism, they would turn to face east and go up towards the Rood for their first Mass (Frost, pages 170–1).

baptismal service, beginning with *N. Abrenuntias sathanae*, takes place now in the usual way,[106] save that the ministers hand to the celebrant what he needs[107] and the optional Gospels are better omitted today. The neophytes' candles are lit from the candle used for blessing the font.[108] After the baptisms, the celebrant should wash his hands, assisted by servers.[109] The neophytes should receive Communion at the Mass.[110]

When that part of the function which is conducted at the font has been concluded, the font is covered with its cloth. This water must on no account be used to sprinkle the people.[111] The procession to the altar is now formed in the order in which it came. The five deacons return to their usual places among the clergy of the second form. Three priests of the upper form, who during the baptisms or the blessing of the font have assumed copes, follow the celebrant at the head of the choir.[112] They walk abreast, that in the middle in a white cope, the other two in red copes. Before the procession sets out, these three priests sing the verse *Rex sanctorum angelorum*. The whole litany, as it is called, is alternated between these three priests and the choir as the procession advances back to the choir in the same way that *Inventor rutili* was sung before.[113]

§5. MASS WITH VESPERS

At the altar, the celebrant and the ministers bow. The acolyte, the book-boy, the server with the candle and the deacons of the holy oils retire. The taperers lay down their tapers and light the altar candles but not their own tapers, which they resume for the preparatory prayers. The priests who have sung *Rex sanctorum angelorum* also retire to doff their copes and then return to their stalls in choir dress. The clergy in choir wear black *cappae chorales* over their surplices as usual in winter.[114]

The Mass is celebrated without rulers.[115] When the choir has returned to the stalls and *Rex sanctorum angelorum* has been finished, the cantor begins the *Kyrie*, which is not farsed. The celebrant and the ministers go straight up. There[116] the ministers take the cope from the celebrant and hand it to the thurifer, who removes it and goes to prepare the thurible. The festal chasuble is put on.[117] All three come down to the step and say the abbreviated preparatory prayers, beginning with the *Confiteor*, the taperers

---

[106] M.35–8; Missal C.130–1.
[107] F.331.
[108] Cf. F.331.
[109] F.331.
[110] If the Bishop is present, the neophytes should be confirmed immediately after they have received the lighted candle (M.37).
[111] M.31, M.41.
[112] P.90 has them walk *in medio processionis*. The rulers of the choir walk immediately behind the celebrant in the procession to the font at Vespers on Easter Day (P.94).
[113] P.79.
[114] C 46; Cons 19; see also Chapter XXII.
[115] Col 348.
[116] This reflects what was done before the prophecies and during the sevenfold litany (P.83).
[117] Cons 70.3, which relates an earlier form of the rite (see note 80), has the ministers vest festally as well. This would probably require a visit to the vestry.

holding their tapers as usual. *Habete osculum pacis* and its kiss are omitted, as on Good Friday. The altar is incensed and the *Kyrie* is said secretly as usual. When the *Gloria in excelsis* has been intoned, the choir kneels or genuflects for a moment, removing their black *cappae chorales*, and rise at once, clad in surplices.[118] A clashing peal[119] is rung on the church bells as the rest of the hymn is sung. The sanctuary bell may be rung also.[120] But other than in the cathedral, the church bells are not to be rung before the bells of the mother church of the city or town have been rung, though handbells may be employed within the church.[121] The bells are not rung again until the first Compline of Easter.[122] Mass is celebrated as usual until Communion, with the following provisos. The epistle and Gospel are sung from the pulpitum, as on Sundays.[123] The Alleluya is sung from the pulpit by three clerks of the upper form in copes. The tract is sung straight through by two second-form clerks in choir dress (with black *cappae chorales*) at the choir step, the choir sitting throughout.[124] At the Gospel, the cross is not carried and the taperers attend with extinguished tapers,[125] but incense is carried as usual.[126] There is no creed. The Offertory antiphon, *Agnus Dei*, the Pax and the Communion antiphon are omitted. The Preface, *Communicantes* and *Hanc igitur* have special forms. If the neophytes are ready to communicate,[127] they should communicate and a general Communion may be held, but the Sacrament should be consumed. There is no reservation until Easter morning.[128]

When the choir has sung the reply to *Pax Domini*, after a short interval,[129] Vespers are sung with the same ceremonies as on Maundy Thursday. A clerk of the upper form intones the antiphon, which is not doubled. After the antiphon on the psalm has been repeated, that on the *Magnificat* is intoned by the most senior clerk after the celebrant,[130] but not doubled. Incense is not used.[131] The celebrant and the ministers say Vespers as on Maundy Thursday. The postcommon follows and the Mass concludes with the usual ceremonies. *Ite missa est* has a special tone.[132]

---

[118] The rubric does not state whether the black *cappae chorales* are resumed later. At Hereford.112, they are removed for *Alleluya* after the epistle and resumed as soon as this is finished.
[119] Col 353: *classicum*. The melodious ringing associated with English bells nowadays was not introduced until the seventeenth century. Cons 70.3 (*dum* Gloria in excelsis *canitur*) implies that the bells are rung throughout the entire hymn.
  Cons 70.3 also has the bells rung for Vespers at the *Sanctus* and another clashing peal at *Per omnia saecula saeculorum* after *Pater noster* (but see note 130).
[120] F.333.
[121] *Caeremoniale Episcoporum*, Lib. II, cap. xxvii.23; OP.1533.
[122] B I.dcclxxi; Col 356.
[123] Col 354; C 66.11.
[124] Col 355, against Cons 70.3.
[125] Col 355.
[126] Missal.133; Cons 70.3.
[127] That is to say, according to the canons in force at the time when the rubrics were drawn up, if they have reached the age of reason and have been confirmed (M.37; Missal.131). The canonical position now is different.
[128] The Sacrament is brought from the Sepulchre to the altar as part of the ceremonies in the morning.
[129] Frere, *Use of Sarum* II.69; Missal C.133.
[130] In the cathedral, the Dean is bound to celebrate today (C 4).
[131] Col 357.
[132] Col 637.

§6. THE SIMPLE FORM OF THE RITE

As a general rule, this, the most complex function in the Church's year, will need to be celebrated in a simplified form, with more or less solemnity as the church's establishment will permit.

A solemn celebration is possible with no more than the clergy usual at a Sunday High or Sung Mass supplemented by an additional server to carry the font candle. If there is no acolyte, his place may be taken by an ordinary server. He will wear a surplice for the first part of the Vigil and put on an alb afterwards. One or two cantors from the choir may sing the three litanies and the four lessons. The deacon may carry the holy oils. He will put on a humeral veil for this purpose. The subdeacon will then minister to the celebrant at the font.

At a low celebration, the celebrant will be assisted by five servers: one to carry the triple candle, a second for the font candle, a thurifer, a water-boy and a book-boy. These five servers will assist the celebrant when vesting at the altar and perform other services for him as required. At the font, they stand round the celebrant and minister to him. The holy oils are prepared by the font as for an ordinary christening. The celebrant himself will sing the *Exultet* at the candle and read the lessons at the south corner of the altar. Vespers may be read at the same place.

When there are no catechumens to be baptized, the oils are not poured into the font.[133] However, the deacons still bear the oils.[134] If the church possesses a font in regular use, however, this should be consecrated.[135] In churches where there is no font, Mass begins immediately after the sevenfold litany.[136] The celebrant may put on the cope for the litany and then assume the chasuble, or he may change directly into the festal chasuble.

---

[133] P.89.
[134] The oils are carried in the procession to the font before Vespers on Easter Day, when they are never used (P.94). Their presence, however, is a reminder of baptism.
[135] *Crede Michi* [22].
[136] This seems to be the practice of the Dominicans (OP.1532–3).

XXXVI

EASTERTIDE

§1. THE SEASON OF EASTER

Eastertide runs from the Easter Vigil to the Saturday after Trinity.[1] Except for the feast of the Invention of the Holy Cross (3 May), the colour at all Masses of the day is white. Votive Masses keep their usual colour.[2]

On Sundays from Easter to Ascension not otherwise impeded, the Mass is that of Easter Day (except for the gradual, sequence, *Communicantes* and *Hanc igitur*), the proper Sunday Mass being relegated to ferias during the week.[3] On Sundays from Easter to Trinity, *Asperges me* at the blessing of the water is replaced by *Vidi aquam*.[4] On ferias during Eastertide, the *Gloria in excelsis* and *Ite missa est* are not said.[5]

From Easter Saturday onwards at Mass (other than at the vigils of Ascension and Whitsun, and at the Rogation Masses that follow the procession[6] and at those of Requiem), the Great Alleluya replaces the gradual and Lesser Alleluya. The Great Alleluya takes this form: *Alleluya* is sung once with no jubilus and repeated once with its jubilus. The verse follows, after which *Alleluya* is sung to a second tone (with its jubilus). After the second verse, this *Alleluya* is repeated, without its jubilus if a sequence is to follow; otherwise with it.[7] The rules for choosing the second verse are given in the Missal.[8]

On Easter Saturday and all ferias, the first Alleluya is sung by two surpliced boys at the choir step and the second by another two surpliced boys also at the choir step; but on feasts when the choir is not ruled, the first Alleluya is sung by two surpliced boys at the choir step and the second by two surpliced second-form clerks at the choir step.[9]

---

[1] Col 631.
[2] See Chapter IV, note 26.
[3] Col 391.
[4] P.4–5.
[5] Col 385.
[6] Col 386.
[7] Coll 9–10 and 379–80.
[8] Coll 386, 390 and 731–2;
[9] C 66.37 gives some confusing directions and differs from Cons 46.4, which has the first Alleluya sung by a single surpliced boy from the principal side and the second by another such from the other side, and from Cons 92, which has the second Alleluya sung by two similar boys.

The Paschal Candle,[10] lit at the Easter Vigil, burns continually until Compline on Easter Day. From Easter Monday to Low Sunday, it burns at Matins, Mass, Vespers and Compline, except that on Thursday and Friday it is not lit for Compline. On Lady Day (if it falls after Easter), on the Invention of the Holy Cross and on Ascension Day, it is lit as on Easter Monday. However, on the vigil of the Ascension it is lit for Vespers and Compline only. On Sundays, and on the feasts of Ss. Philip and James and of St. Mark,[11] it is lit for Mass only. The Paschal Candle is removed on the Friday after Ascension before Mass.[12]

The font remains covered with the cloth placed over it at the Easter Vigil until the end of Eastertide.[13] Its water must not be used at the sprinkling of the people.[14]

On Easter Friday before Mass, the Sepulchre is removed.[15]

Until the Ascension, the ordinary processional cross may be replaced by that of beryl.[16]

The black *cappa choralis* is omitted at Mass throughout the Easter octave and on all double feasts until Michaelmas.[17]

§2. EASTER DAY

In places where the Cross was laid in the Sepulchre on Good Friday,[18] there is a procession on the morning of Easter Day.[19] This should not be confused with the ordinary procession at the sprinkling of the holy water.

All the lights in the church are lit. A corporal[20] should be unfolded on the High Altar, which is presumed to be that of reservation. The altar candles should be lit.[21] At a side altar, a cushion or carpet is prepared for the Cross. This altar's candles should be lit unless the taperers will leave their tapers on it.[22]

---

[10] C 62.

[11] So C 62.2. Cons 69.2 would have the candle lit at Mass *omnibus festivis diebus*, where perhaps *festivis* should be understood as holidays rather than merely liturgical *festa*.

[12] C 59, a change from Cons 69.4. A constitution of William de Bleys, bishop of Worcester, (1219) ordained that after Trinity, the Paschal Candle should be made into lesser candles for use at paupers' funerals (Wilkins I.571), a laudable custom worthy of revival. See also *The Catholic Encyclopedia* s.v. 'Paschal Candle'.

[13] Cons 70.2.

[14] M.31, M.41.

[15] C 59.

[16] See Chapter II, note 38.

[17] C 46.2.

[18] As a general rule, only those processions associated with functions included in the Missal are described in this work. An exception is made in this case, since this procession is the complement of the deposition of the Cross in the Sepulchre during the function on Good Friday.

[19] P.91: *ante matutinas et ante campanarum pulsationem*. The procession should certainly take place before Mass. The rubrics of P.91-2 are interpreted helpfully by Rock IV.287-90. For an earlier (or alternative) form of this procession, see Rock II.345.

[20] This corporal is not mentioned in the rubrics but may be presumed, since it would be unique to place the Sacrament on the altar other than on a corporal.

[21] On the double principle that they should be lit for a function involving the altar and that lights should burn when the Blessed Sacrament is exposed. P.32 has the taperers place their lit candles on stational side altars during the Lenten processions.

[22] As they do during the Lenten ferial processions (P.32). Otherwise, they may leave them on either side of the Cross.

The clergy come from the vestry in the following order:[23] first, one or two thurifers[24] with thuribles and incense; then two taperers with lighted tapers; then the two most senior priests in surplices.[25] The choir follows in choir dress, *excellentioribus praecedentibus*.[26] They go straight to the Sepulchre, where they stand as on Good Friday. The priests kneel[27] and so incense the Sepulchre. Rising, they take the Blessed Sacrament and bear it to the High Altar, preceded by the servers as before.[28] Placing the Sacrament on the corporal, they and all the others kneel in adoration as the sacristan[29] reserves the Sacrament. If there is no ordained sacristan, the second priest will reserve the Sacrament, or, in places where there is only one priest, the celebrant will do this. As soon as the Sacrament has been reserved, the bells are rung in a jangling peal,[30] during which the clergy rise and return to the Sepulchre.

From the Sepulchre, the two priests extract the Cross, and, holding it with his fellow, the senior priest intones the antiphon *Christus resurgens*, which the choir takes up. The procession, in the same order as before, goes to the side altar where the creeping to the Cross will take place.[31] There the taperers leave their tapers, either on the altar, or either side of the Cross,[32] which is now laid before the altar. The senior priest sings the versicle, *Surrexit Dominus*, and its collect. He, then his fellow, and then all in descending order of rank kneel joyfully before the Cross and kiss it in worship.[33] As each has done so, he retires individually, not in procession, either to the choir for Matins or elsewhither. The crosses and images throughout the church are unveiled now.

---

[23] For the order on Good Friday, see Chapter XXXIV, note 128.
[24] P.91: *thuribulariis*. Cons 71: *cum thuribulario*.
[25] Cons 71. On Good Friday, they wore albs and stoles. A humeral veil may be added. Frere, *Use of Sarum* II.70, seems to presume that the Bishop or Dean will conduct this function with other clergy merely assisting. A single principal officiant would make the ceremonial much easier to execute.
   In what comes across as a neater ceremony, Wells.32 has:

   > omnes Clerici in superpelliciis accedant ad altare et duo excellentiores presbyteri in superpelliciis et in capis sericis prius incensato sepulchro cum magna veneratione corpus dominicum et crucem inde tollant, et super altare deponant excellentiore presbytero inchoante antiphonam, et finita antiphona, et processio solito modo dicat excellentior sacerdos versum deinde orationem. Qua finita incensent corpus, et altare, et sic recedant, deinde inchoentur matutine post campanarum pulsationem.

   In other words, the Cross and Sacrament were returned to the High Altar, from which they were taken on Good Friday. At Sarum, however, the rite is different and the Cross is taken to a side altar, making two visits to the Sepulchre more likely.
[26] P.92, against *Crede Michi* [85].
[27] Rock IV.287, reporting the custom at Durham (see Durham.10). Does this convey the meaning of *cum magna veneratione*? *Genuflectendo* seems rather to qualify *deponant*.
[28] P.91 has the Sacrament taken to the altar *privatim*. Presumably this means with no ceremony, but it is implausible that the servers should remain at their places instead of escorting the Sacrament, and the adverb is taken here to mean that the choir remains at the Sepulchre and that no singing accompanies the reservation itself.
[29] P.92 entrusts this function to the *subthesaurarius*, who is the vice-sacristan.
[30] A *classicum* (P.92).
[31] In the cathedral, the procession went from the Sepulchre to the south door of the presbytery, down the south to the pulpitum, up through the choir and out of the north door of the presbytery to St. Martin's altar at the north of the north-eastern transept (P.91–2; Cons 71).
[32] Since there is no return procession, the tapers will not be required further.
[33] Rock IV.287, after Piers Ploughman ('And creop on kneos to þe cryos and cusse hit') has the worshippers creep to the Cross as on Good Friday.

At the ordinary procession before Mass, which follows the pattern of a procession on a double, after the *Vidi aquam* and before the procession sets out,[34] three senior clerks in copes[35] begin *Salve festa dies* in the middle of the choir. The procession should leave the church by its principal door and go round the churchyard in a clockwise direction before returning by the same door as it left.[36] Everything else is done as set out in the Processional.

§3. THE LITANIES

On the three days before Ascension (which are known as Rogation, Gang or Cross Days) and on the feast of St. Mark, the Mass of the day is said after Sext. If the Pie permits that year, a procession,[37] which concludes with its own Mass, is held after None. But on Rogation Monday, if not impeded by a feast when the choir is ruled, the Gang Mass is celebrated as the principal Mass, after Sext.[38]

The procession should depart from the principal church and go to another church in the city or suburbs,[39] where a stational Mass is celebrated before the return to the home church. In case of necessity, however, the procession may return to its own church and the stational Mass celebrated there. It is even possible for the procession to be held entirely within its home church.[40] The ceremonial is similar on all four days, though there are significant variations, which are detailed below. On these days, abstinence is no longer obligatory.[41]

In the principal church, everything is prepared as for the Sunday procession. The Draco,[42] Leo and lesser banners should be carried by surpliced clerks.[43]

---

[34] P.13.
[35] P.122 describing the Ascension Day procession, said to be modelled on that of Easter.
[36] P.93 (*circueundo ecclesiam et claustrum*), made clearer by P.121 (*circumeundo extrinsecus totam ecclesiam et atrium, intrando per portam juxta cimiterium canonicorum circumeundo claustrum*), describing the Ascension Day procession, which is modelled on that of Easter Day.
[37] Coll 407, 409, 739; P.103-21. The Gang Days attracted several paraliturgical practices, which often varied from place to place. Among these are the beating of boys as well as of the parish bounds, the ringing of bells and the singing of particular Gospel passages at certain stations. For treatments of some of these, see Ebor.183-5; *The Catholic Encyclopedia*, s.v. 'Processions'; Rock III.297-8; Durandus (VI. cap. 10); F.348; Duffy, *Stripping*, Index s.v. 'Rogationtide procession'.
[38] Col 407.
[39] P.104; P.146. Frost discusses the routes at Old Sarum and in Salisbury. The idea seems to be that the bounds of the city should be beaten over the period from Monday to Wednesday (not all the perimeter each day) and those of the cathedral close on Ascension Day (Frost, pages 221 and 231).
[40] F.347. In these days of heresy and schism, this necessity is likely to arise.
[41] Durham.87. The traditional abstinence does not seem to have prevented participants in the procession from having 'good chere after' (Rock III.182).
[42] *Processions*.93 calls it *draconis vexillum*, but the woodcuts there suggest something more three-dimensional. In some places, the Draco was made of leather and was inflatable (Frost, page 50) or filled with chaff. *Processions*.93 refers to Jacobus de Voragine's *Golden Legend* for a symbolical explanation of the part that Draco plays in these processions.
[43] The woodcut at P.122 shews them carried by tonsured clerks. See also Wells.43, of the Chrism Mass, and F.357, writing of the banner-bearer on Corpus Christi. If the water-boy (see note 56) wears his black *cappa choralis*, it would be reasonable for these clerks to do likewise.

At the stational church, everything is prepared for High Mass, except most of the vestments, which the clergy will already be wearing. The chasuble and the books are on the altar.[44] The maniples are placed on the sedilia.[45]

The procession will assemble as on Sundays[46] and proceed in the following order. Behind the vergers[47] go three red banners, borne by surpliced clerks; then the Draco; then the Leo; then the other banners; then the ordinary procession as usual, with the addition of the chest of relics. That is to say, first the surpliced[48] water-boy with stoup and sprinkler, who may sprinkle the ground before him as he goes; then follow the acolyte in alb alone[49] with the processional cross,[50] the taperers in albs and the thurifer; then two deacons of the second form in choir dress carrying the chest of relics; then the subdeacon in an alb with neither tunicle nor chasuble; then the deacon in alb and stole with neither dalmatic nor chasuble; then the celebrant in alb and stole with no cope.[51] The choir follows in the order usual at the Sunday procession. The book-boy will attend as usual. One or more surpliced servers may ring handbells on the way.[52]

The clergy gather at the choir step as usual. The cantors intone *Exurge Domine*, and the responsory is sung throughout. The cantors now[53] intone *Surgite sancti*, and the procession turns and moves down the church through the choir and out the principal door of the church.[54] The celebrant carries his own book. *Surgite sancti*, *De Hierusalem* and *Memento* are sung as the procession advances. The antiphons set forth for rain, good weather and in time of war are sung if opportune. Otherwise they are omitted. *Ne reminiscaris* and the seven penitential psalms follow without note if there is time. At last the litany of the saints is said, also without note. Up to *Peccatores Te rogamus audi nos* inclusive, the litanies are doubled,[55] that is to say, the celebrant reads out both parts of each petition and both parts are repeated by the choir in their entirety. From *Ut pacem nobis dones* to *Fili Dei*, however, the celebrant reads the first half of the petition and the choir responds with *Te rogamus*. Thereafter up to the end of the *Agnus Dei*, the

---

[44] F.348 has the celebrant vest at the sedilia. It would not be unreasonable, however, for the celebrant to vest in the sacristy. See Chapter XXX, note 2.
[45] See Chapter III, note 4.
[46] OP.1566.
[47] The dragon, the lion and the banners precede the cross (P.121).
[48] The surplice is presumed because it is his usual attire. Some processionals (P.103) require him to wear his black *cappa choralis*, a sensible measure for a lengthy procession outdoors in April.
[49] If at the Mass that follows the *Gloria in excelsis* is not to be said. See note 72.
[50] P.103, against *Crede Michi* [87].
[51] This penitential tone could be taken further. At the translation of the see from Old Sarum (28 April 1220, Rogation Tuesday), the Bishop retained the traditional practice of walking barefoot. The practice may well have survived into the sixteenth century, as it has among confraternities in the south of Europe during Holy Week processions (Frost, page 154).

In contrast with the penitential nature of the Sarum rogations, among the early Præmonstratensians the tone was festive: festive copes were worn and feet were not bared (OPraem.XLII).
[52] Rock II.373.
[53] This interpretation assumes that *his dictis* (P.105) refers to the repetition of *Exurge Domine* and not to all the antiphons that follow, viz. *De Hierusalem* and *Memento*.
[54] P.104: *per ostium ecclesiae occidentale*. Cons 93 of the church at Old Sarum has *per ostium ecclesiae australe*.
[55] P.107.

petitions are doubled once more. *Kyrie eleison* and the verses that follow should not be begun until the procession has arrived at the altar of the church where this is to end.[56]

The procession may make brief stations at churches on its way. In this case, the chants are interrupted and the antiphon of the church's patron is begun at the lychgate.[57] There the church's clergy receive the procession; its senior priest may offer holy water to the celebrant.[58] The procession goes straight to the church, not circling the churchyard, and advances to the choir. The choir may occupy the stalls or remain in the middle of the choir behind the celebrant. In this case, it must make way for the celebrant and his ministers when these go out later. The Draco, Leo and the banners retire. The celebrant and servers stand before the altar as at the beginning of Mass. The taperers place their tapers on the altar.[59] All greet the High Altar, and the celebrant sings the patron saint's verse and collect. Bowing again, the procession continues on its way, the chants being resumed at once.

At its destination, the procession is received as at the other stations. The choir should occupy the stalls. When the celebrant has sung the verse and collect, all kneel[60] for *Kyrie eleison* and *Pater noster*, which are also said without note. *Et ne nos inducas* and the verses that follow are sung in the usual form, all still kneeling. The celebrant alone rises to sing *Dominus vobiscum*[61] and the collects. At *Per eundem Christum Dominum nostrum*, all the others kiss the floor or the forms and rise.[62]

The Mass now follows, at which the deacon and subdeacon wear neither chasubles nor dalmatic and tunicle.[63] A server brings two maniples to the deacon and one to the subdeacon. The deacon gives the celebrant his maniple and all three put the maniples on. They then go up to the altar where the celebrant is assisted to put on the chasuble. They come down to the step and begin the Mass. The *Gloria in excelsis* is not said.[64] The second collect is of the titular saint and the third of All Hallows. A sermon may be preached.[65]

After Mass, the procession returns to its home church. The chasuble is laid on the altar and the maniples are returned to the sedilia. The procession assembles at the choir step. From their places in the procession, three upper-form clerks in choir dress (on doubles) or two clerks similarly attired (on non-doubles) sing one of the special

---

[56] F.349.
[57] *Ad januas cimiterii* (P.112).
[58] F.349.
[59] P.32, which sets out the rules for stations during penitential processions.
[60] *Preces in prostratione* (P.112); *prostrationem faciant* (P.32). For the meaning of *prostratio*, see pages 34–5.
[61] It is certain that the celebrant is standing for *Dominus vobiscum* (P.33; F.349), but the moment when he stands is not clear. At the ferial Lenten stations, he rises after the psalm and so sings the last three verses before *Dominus vobiscum*. Neither the psalm not these verses are sung at the Rogations. In the Roman rite, the celebrant rises for *Dominus vobiscum*.
[62] P.33.
[63] Col 1.
[64] The Mass is *de jejunio* (P.113), so it is presumed that the usual rules for penitential Masses are observed. If it be objected that the *Gloria in excelsis* is said on the Whitsun Ember Days, it may be replied that the Rogation Masses are not those of the day but rather in the nature of penitential votive Masses associated with the processions. The Sarum books appear to include no comprehensive rubric listing the days when the *Gloria in excelsis* is to be said.
[65] Col 408.

litanies given in the Processional.[66] When the Pie permits the procession to be held on St. Mark's Day, the first litany is sung then and the second is sung on Rogation Monday. Each of the other two litanies is sung on Rogation Tuesday and Ascension Eve.[67]

The litanies are begun facing east at the choir step. After the cantors have sung *Sancta Maria*, the procession sets out.[68] The procession enters the choir of the home church by the west door.[69] At the choir step[70] of the home church, the litany, if it has not been finished, is interrupted[71] and the appropriate verse and collect as given in the Processional[72] are sung. The clergy retire to the vestry.

On Monday and Tuesday in Rogation week, the procession takes place as described above. On Ascension Eve, the Draco[73] goes behind the banners and before the water-boy.[74] On St. Mark's Day, if it falls on a Sunday, the usual procession is held before the principal Mass, as given in the Processional, and the penitential procession is omitted altogether.[75] If the feast falls on a weekday, the penitential procession is held after None[76] as on Rogation Monday, except that the Leo and the Draco are omitted. In the return procession, the first litany is sung.[77]

§4. ASCENSION

On the day itself, the procession[78] is held in the same form as the principal procession on Easter Day, except that processional banners, borne by surpliced clerks,[79] go at the front of the procession, behind the vergers. If the church possesses a Leo, this heads the procession and is followed by the lesser banners. These in turn are followed by the Draco, behind which go the water-boy, the crucifers, the taperers and the thurifers. Behind these and before the subdeacon, two deacons[80] of the second form in copes advance, carrying between them the chest of relics. After the subdeacon goes the deacon, who carries a reliquary, if the church possesses one, in place of a Text. As

---

[66] P.117–121 supplemented by P.107–9.
[67] The instructions at P.118 and P.121 are less than clear, but it appears that a different litany should be sung on each of the four days. Presumably the first litany is reserved for St. Mark's Day because it makes special reference to evangelists.
[68] P.117; P.118; C.55.
[69] P.117. In the cathedral, the procession returned by the east door of the cloister and then the west door of the choir (P.117).
[70] P.118.
[71] *Quantum sufficit iter* (P.118).
[72] P.121.
[73] In some places, the three-dimensional Draco was carried with its tail inflated and erect on Monday and Tuesday but deflated and lowered on Wednesday (Frost, page 50; Chambers, page 212).
[74] P.121.
[75] P.145.
[76] Col 739.
[77] P.146. The route in the cathedral is given at Cons 93.
[78] P.121; Cons 99.
[79] Woodcut at P.122; F.357.
[80] P.121 merely says *duo de secunda forma*, but the equivalent clerks on Rogation Monday are called deacons (P.104).

on Easter Day,[81] the procession should go outside and walk round the church and churchyard in a clockwise direction before returning to the choir step.[82]

Before Mass on the following day, the Paschal Candle is removed.[83]

§5. WHITSUN

The function on Whitsun Eve is a simplified version of the Easter Vigil[84] and consists of three parts: (1) the lessons; (2) the litanies and ceremonies at the Font; and (3) Mass. For the Mass, the best vestments are worn.[85] The function begins after None.

The clergy who take part are: the celebrant; the principal deacon; the principal subdeacon; an acolyte, who will carry the processional cross; a server in a surplice to bear the candle used in blessing the font; two taperers; a thurifer; a server to take the place of Holy Saturday's water-boy and assist at the font; and a book-boy. The choir also attends. The lessons and the litanies are read, and the holy oils are carried, by clerks of the same station as on Holy Saturday. If catechumens are to be made during the lessons, a priest other than the celebrant will need to carry out this office. He may be one of the priests from the choir.

The following preparations are made.

In the vestry, everything is prepared as for Mass. The best vestments are worn.[86] If the neophytes are to communicate, hosts are prepared for them in the pyx. For the litanies and the blessing of the font, the celebrant will wear a red cope but, if there is no font, he may wear a chasuble throughout.[87] The deacon and subdeacon wear dalmatic and tunicle.[88] The acolyte[89] will wear an alb for the lessons and a tunicle for the blessing of the font.[90] The deacons of the oils wear amices, albs, cinctures, red stoles and humeral veils. Either in the vestry or near the font are prepared one white and two red copes for the priests who will sing the threefold litany. The four senior priests who will sing the lessons will wear surplices.[91] Surplices are prepared also for the server of the second candle, for the water-boy and the book-boy,[92] for the seven boys who will sing the sevenfold litany and for the five deacons who will sing the

---

[81] P.121: *ordinetur processio sicut in die Paschae.*
[82] In the cathedral, the procession left through the west door of the choir, out of the west door of the church, circumambulated the church and atrium (P.121, Cons 99) in a clockwise direction, entered the cloister by the canons' cemetery, walked round the cloister, went out through the canons' gate and entered the church again by the west door, advancing back to the choir.
[83] So C 59, presumably because, having been lit for Compline on the feast (C 62.2), it would be inconvenient to remove it before Matins. At Old Sarum, the arrangements were different (Cons 69.4).
[84] Col 418 and P.124 do little more than refer the reader to Holy Saturday. For an explanation of many of the directions given here, therefore, see there.
[85] Cons 69.
[86] *Crede Michi* [108]: *Precedant ministri in solemni apparatu.*
[87] F.350.
[88] Col 1.
[89] Cons 55.
[90] Since there is no triple candle, there seems no reason to insist on the surplice.
[91] Col 418.
[92] They wear surplices for the ordinary Sunday procession (P.2). P.84 also has the book-boy wear a surplice on the way to the font.

fivefold litany. If another priest will make the catechumens, he will do so in surplice and red stole. The choir attends in choir dress. Also prepared should be a candle for blessing the font, which suitably would be that blessed at Candlemas and used on Holy Saturday; the ordinary processional cross; the holy-water stoup and sprinkler; the book for the various blessings; and the chrism and the oil of the catechumens.

In the sanctuary, the altar is prepared as for Mass. The candles are not lit until the Mass.[93] The chasuble used for the Mass, if different from that worn during the lessons, lies on the altar. On the credence table, as well as those things ordinarily prepared for Mass, lies the book of lessons.[94] The lessons may be read from a lectern.

The font, which should have been emptied and cleaned, is prepared as on Holy Saturday.

The choir is presumed to be in its place. The clergy come from the vestry to the altar as on Holy Saturday. The ministers may carry the missal and Gospel-book,[95] or these may be on the altar in advance. The thurifer may omit the thurible: it will not be needed until much later. The celebrant wears the chasuble. At the altar, all bow. Standing on the top step between the ministers, the celebrant says *Pater noster*[96] silently. He goes up to the altar and kisses it in the middle. If they have brought the books with them, the deacon and subdeacon now go up and lay them on the altar. All three go at once to the sedilia for the lessons.[97] The taperers put down their tapers in their Mass places and take up their usual stations. The book-boy and water-boy retire to their places in the choir.

The lessons are read without titles at the choir step by senior clerks from the choir, in surplices. Everything is now done with the same ceremonies as on Holy Saturday, except that *Flectamus genua* is omitted.

As on Holy Saturday, during the tract, *Sicut cervus*, the acolyte goes to the vestry, whence he returns, vested in alb and red tunicle, carrying the cross, as the sevenfold litany is sung. With him go the two deacons who, having put on their vestments, bring the holy oils.

The three litanies, the ceremonies at the font and the Mass follow exactly as on Holy Saturday up to the offertory, except that *Habete osculum pacis* is not omitted and lights are carried at the Gospel.[98] Thereafter Mass continues as usual.[99] *Sanctus* and *Agnus Dei* are sung solemnly.[100] The Pax is given.[101] If the neophytes are ready to communicate, they should communicate and a general Communion may be held.

---

[93] F.350.
[94] Or this may be placed on the altar.
[95] OP.1523.
[96] Col 418.
[97] OP.1579.
[98] *Crede Michi* [108].
[99] In the Roman rite, the bells are rung at the *Gloria in excelsis* (F.352); among the Dominicans they are not (OP.1580). Col 423 makes no mention of them, even though Col 353 (Holy Saturday) does. Similarly, the Dominicans bear lights at the Gospel.
[100] Col 425.
[101] *Crede Michi* [108].

In case of necessity, this function may be simplified along the same lines as that on Holy Saturday. The Missal makes no provision for private Masses: the entire Vigil, except for the blessing of the font, must precede the Mass.

Whitsun and its octave have no special ceremonies beyond those clearly set out in the Missal and the Processional. The baptismal water may not be used at the *Vidi aquam* and the procession.[102] The procession leaves the church and walks round the churchyard in a clockwise direction as at Easter and Ascension.[103] The Ember Days in Whit Week are observed as in Advent. The ministers wear dalmatic and tunicle[104] and the acolyte his tunicle, according to the usual rule.[105] The prophecy on Wednesday is read from the pulpitum by a surpliced acolyte from the choir.[106] The order of reading the lessons on the Saturday is given in the Missal.[107] The chants[108] are sung in the usual manner but *Alleluya* is not repeated. The Alleluya after the last prophecy is sung by two surpliced deacons of the second form at the choir step.[109] The epistle and Gospel are sung from the pulpit, as is the Alleluya of the Mass, this by two clerks of the first form in copes.

The black *cappa choralis* is omitted at Mass throughout the octave.[110]

---

[102] M.31, M.41.
[103] P.124.
[104] Col 1; C 66.40.
[105] Cons 55.
[106] Col 435.
[107] Col 444.
[108] C 66.40; Col 450.
[109] Col 449.
[110] C 46.2.

XXXVII

SUMMER AND AUTUMN

§1. CORPUS CHRISTI

The feast of Corpus Christi, the focus of much pageantry and popular devotion, has surprisingly few liturgical peculiarities in the Sarum books.[1]

The procession[2] is modelled on that of the Ascension[3] and follows the same route, namely, going outside the church. Banners and relics are carried.[4] In addition, the Blessed Sacrament is carried by the celebrant in a vessel[5] through a humeral veil,[6] under a pallium of four poles,[7] borne by four clerks in albs and tunicles,[8] or by others according to local custom, and escorted by surpliced clerks carrying lit tapers.[9] The Sacrament may be carried hanging in a float[10] decorated as richly as possible and borne

---

[1] This feast, being of late introduction, brought considerable disorder to the calendar and was observed in widely differing ways across Western Christendom. It acquired considerable popular vigour, however, and was supported by many town guilds. For an example of how the civic element was combined with the clerical, see Durham.89–90.
[2] P.126–8, supplemented by Wells.46–7. For Dominican Sacrament processions, see OP.1739–50.
[3] Against OP.951, which omits the water-boy, P. 93 (after which this procession is marshalled) specifically requires him.
[4] P.12. There is no indication that incense was carried immediately before the Sacrament as at OP.970.
[5] P.126: *in tabernaculo*. This vessel will be a monstrance (Rock II.304) or pyx of some kind.
[6] Many, perhaps most, illuminations that shew this procession do not include a humeral veil, but practice probably varied. At the Communion of the sick, the Douay manuals of 1604–11 (following Roman and Mechlin practice) prescribe the humeral veil (M.97). OP.1741 prescribes the humeral veil for processions of the Blessed Sacrament.
[7] P.126; Bond, page 26.
[8] Wells.46, but it is worth bearing in mind that at the Wells Chrism Mass the taperers and thurifers also wore tunicles (Wells.105).
[9] The rubric of P.126 (*sub quodam pallio de serico, quod super quatuor hastas deferatur, cum cereis illuminatis a clericis in superpelliceis*) appears to leave open the possibility of the choir carrying the tapers, a special escort of surpliced clerks carrying tapers or a canopy adorned with lit tapers and carried by surpliced clerks. At Durham on Easter morning, the pallium held over the Sacrament was carried by 'four antient gentlemen belonginge to the prior' (Rock IV.290), by which we should possibly understand armigerous laymen of the prior's retinue (cf. a close parallel from 1463 in the OED s.v. 'Gentleman'). Such men are less difficult to find in England than is sometimes supposed. The Douay manuals of 1604–11 (after Roman and Mechlin customs) would have the canopy at the Communion of the sick borne by four *viri* (M.97). F.355 reports the *Caeremoniale Episcoporum* prescribing that on Corpus Christi the canopy should be borne outside the church by 'noble men or Barons and others'. Illuminations shew a variety of clerical and lay canopy-bearers. For details of decorated candles carried in this procession, see the example given in Rock II.342.
[10] *Processions*.163.

by priests in Mass vestments. In this case, the celebrant follows the float. The pallium should cover both the float and the celebrant. Three upper-step clergy in copes walk in the midst of the procession, that is to say, behind the celebrant, and sing the prose. The Sacrament is exposed at the altar, for which a corporal will be needed, and brought down to the choir step, from which the procession sets out as the verse *Rex sedet* is sung. As the procession returns from the west door to the Rood, *Respexit Elias* is sung. At the Cross, *O sacrum convivium* and its verse are sung by the cantors.[11] There is no collect. The Sacrament is reserved and Mass follows as usual.

§2. THE WEEKS AFTER TRINITY

The summer and autumn seasons contain many important feasts but, on the whole, few departures are made from the usual ceremonial.

In July is celebrated the feast of Relics. During the procession,[12] a station is made during which the relics are washed in the presence of the choir and the names of the relics are recited in the vernacular.[13] Once these things have been done, the procession continues to the choir as usual.

On the Ember Days and on vigils, the ministers wear neither chasubles nor dalmatic and tunicle.[14] The same ceremonial is observed as on the Ember Days in Advent.[15] On Ember Saturday, the tract before the Gospel is sung by two subdeacons of the second form in *cappae chorales* from the choir step.[16]

The black *cappa choralis* is omitted at Mass on all double feasts until Michaelmas.[17]

§3. ALL SOULS[18]

For the most part, the Mass *in commemoratione animarum* is said like an ordinary Requiem. The ministers wear dalmatic and tunicle.[19] The Missal supposes that the epistle and Gospel are read in the pulpit,[20] whence also the gradual is sung by three clerks of the second form in choir dress.[21] The tract, *De profundis*, is sung to a special tone by four clerks of the upper form at the choir step in choir dress, alternating as set

---

[11] This is presumed from the fact that the celebrant is carrying the Sacrament. This must be the reason for the absence of a collect.
[12] P.150.
[13] What is probably the text used at the cathedral is given and discussed in *Processions*.33–42.
[14] Coll 1 and also 676.
[15] Col 543.
[16] Col 548.
[17] C 46.2.
[18] Coll 957–9.
[19] Col 1.
[20] Coll 957–8; C 66.13.
[21] Coll 957 and 864*.

out in the Missal, while the choir sits.[22] The cross may be carried at the Gospel. In the Offertory, the verses *Hostias et preces* and *Requiem aeternam* are omitted.[23] The paten is handed to the acolyte as at ordinary Masses[24] but it is not held aloft by the deacon.[25]

---

[22] Coll 957–8, 864* and 865*.
[23] Coll 596, 958 and 868*; C 66.25.
[24] C 66.27.
[25] This detail is deduced from the fact that holding the paten aloft is a signal that a general Communion will be held. At Requiems, there is neither the Pax nor general Communion, so the rite should be omitted. It is an anomaly that the paten should be given to the acolyte today.

Appendix I

THE LAITY IN CHURCH

If the books say little about the clerk, they say little more about the laity. On occasion, laymen are supposed to be present in the presbytery,[1] though these may be references to greater personages only[2] or to the peculiar arrangement of the sanctuary in the cathedral itself. In principle, the congregation attends functions from the nave and should be divided by sex: the men on the south side; the women and young children on the north side.[3] At Low Mass in the sixteenth century, the laity probably knelt throughout,[4] except for the Gospel, during which they stood.[5] In modern churches, endowed as they are with seats, it is probable that laymen will wish to sit and stand for parts of the Mass. Although the rubrics are not concerned with this, and practice will vary from church to church, the following directions, taken from earlier mediæval practice,[6] may be taken into consideration.

---

[1] Cons 34; P.3; M.4; Frere, *Use of Sarum* II.230.
[2] The greatness of such personages should not be exaggerated. In 1776, the noble estate of the rural parish of La Espina in the diocese of Oviedo (Spain) embarked upon litigation in defence of its right to sit in the chancel. The Asturian noble is the equivalent of the Scot holden of his battered turret and inherited arms, and should not be confused with the puissant English peer. Yeoman and ordinary villagers sat in the nave, the nomadic cowherds ('vaqueiros de alzada') being relegated to the back of the church. See García-Rendueles, pages 59–60.
[3] This distinction was being lost rapidly in the sixteenth century (French, page 168). There seems no good reason to perpetuate a sixteenth-century abuse and departure from tradition merely because it is sixteenth century, but since the concept of segregation has become alien to our age, it may be impractical to insist upon it. The division by sex is ancient, but the precise location depends on local tradition: in the north of Spain, the women sometimes occupied the eastern part of the nave and the men the western (García-Rendueles, page 14).
[4] The people should probably kneel on both knees, though one knee may not have been unusual. See S.162.
[5] Rock I.59–60; S.140; Becon, page 119 ('Pope *Anastasius*, who lived in the yeare of our Lord 404. ordayned that the people should stand up when the Gospel is read, that they might heare and understand the Doctrine of the Gospell, and frame their lives according to the same. This use is observed at this day in the popish Masses, I meane the people stand up').
[6] For a general overview, see S.lxi–lxiii. It must be borne in mind that most of these directions come from Simmons's Text B, which is descended from a twelfth-century Norman treatise and so should be taken as no more than a rough guide to the practice of later English laymen. With these indications, the reader may wish to compare those given in 1502 by the Roman Burckard (*Tracts*.134).
  Tracts.238 has an extract from Richard Whitford's 1537 *A Dialogue or Comunication bytwene the Curate or Ghostly Father and the Parochiane or Ghostly Chyld for a Due Preparacion unto Howselynge*. In light of Whitford's steadfastness against the Supremacy, his treatise is likely to be free from innovation.

The congregants kneel for the preparation at the foot of the altar.[7] They stand from the Officium[8] to the end of the *Gloria in excelsis*. Then they kneel[9] and remain so until the Gospel, during which they stand.[10] At the end of the Gospel, as the celebrant kisses the book, they sign themselves.[11] Except for the prescribed parts of the bidding of the bedes,[12] they remain standing until the beginning of the secret,[13] for which they kneel.[14] They stand again at *Per omnia saecula saeculorum* until after the *Sanctus*.[15] They kneel for the Canon[16] but stand at *Per omnia saecula saeculorum*.[17] At the Pax, they kneel until after the ablutions, when they stand for the reading of the Communion.[18] They kneel for the postcommon and until the end.[19] If *In principio* is read at the altar, they stand for this,[20] but may kneel (or genuflect), kiss the ground and cross themselves at *Et Verbum caro factum est*.[21] If they wish to do so, they may sit for the epistle and the following chants, and during the offertory. They kneel to receive Communion and stand to drink the purification.[22]

Dialogue Masses, which survived on the Romance-speaking continent, died out in England some time before the sixteenth century.[23]

At High Mass, the congregation may stand, sit and kneel with the choir for the most part, though it would be peculiar for those in the nave not to kneel during the Canon.

---

[7] S.6 (B.10).
[8] S.10 (B.83–6); Whitford *apud Tracts*.238.
[9] S.16 (B.150–3).
[10] S.16 (B.153–4 and 177); Whitford *apud Tracts*.238.
[11] Becon, page 54, may be alluding to a laymen's custom of crossing the forehead with the thumbs and then kissing a cross made of thumb and index finger in a manner still seen in Europe today when he writes: 'and so a peece of the Gospell being once read, they stroke themselves on the head, and kisse the naile of their right thumbe, and sit down againe.' See S.19 and S.220.
[12] P.6–8.
[13] S.22 (B.245).
[14] S.26 (B.280–1).
[15] S.26 (B.302–3), 28 (B.328) and 272; Whitford *apud Tracts*.238.
[16] Col 839* of the spouses at the Nuptial Mass. See also Rock IV.181. S.38 (B.405) has the people hold up its hands at the elevation, while the Council of Exeter (1287), cap. IV has the laity kneel and not bow (Wilkins II.132).
[17] S.44 (B.481–2). Whitford *apud Tracts*.238 has the congregation stand for the *Pater noster* alone.
[18] S.48 (B.514–15) and 54 (B.576–7).
[19] S.66 (B.600).
[20] Whitford *apud Tracts*.238 presumes that this is said and is heard standing.
[21] For these popular devotions, once indulgenced, see S.146 and S.385.
[22] Gayton Thorpe font; Jerdan, page 22.
[23] S.181.

Appendix II

FORM OF BIDDING OF THE BEDES

Oremus pro ecclesia Romana …[1]

℣ We shall make our prayers to God, beseeching His mercy for all Holy Church, that God it keep in good estate.
℣ In especial, for the Church of Rome, this church and all others in Christendom; our holy father the Pope of Rome and all his cardinals.
℣ For archbishops and bishops, and in especial for my lord N. the Bishop of this see, that God him keep in his holy service.
℣ For my lord, the Dean, and my masters, the canons, vicars, priests and clerks, [*or* for the rector of this church][2] and all other ministers that this church serve.
℣ For the Holy Land, that God it deliver out of heathen hands.
℣ For our Sovereign Lord, the King; and the Queen and all her children; all other lords, dukes, marquises, earls, [viscounts] and barons, and all that have this land to govern.
℣ For the peace of these lands of England and France, that God make perpetual peace betwixt them.
℣ And for the good estate of N. that findeth continually light at the High Altar, and all this church's friends, our brethren and sistern, and all our parishioners, with all those that any good do to this church, and all true Christian people.

Oremus pro animabus …[3]

℣ We shall also pray and beseech God of His mercy for all true Christian souls.
℣ In especial, for all souls whose bodies rest in this holy place, for N. and N. And for all souls whose bones rest in this church and churchyard.
℣ And on the second part we shall pray for all souls, patrons of this church, and in especial for N. and N. And for all who have given rents, vestments, or any other goods,

---

[1] P.6. The form which we give here is a version of that in *Processions*.22–41, originally in use in Sarum church in the fifteenth century, adapted for modern use. It does not purport to be authoritative. Some elements may seem quaint: they have been retained as models after which churches may wish to compose their own forms. See also Rock II.286–98, Rock II.303 and Chapter VIII, note 26.
[2] P.6.
[3] P.7.

whereby God is more worshipped in this church and the ministers thereof better sustained.

¶ And for all souls, ministers of this church, and in especial for N. and N. And for the souls of all other ministers of this church which have served it or done any good thereto in their days.

¶ And for all our brethren's and sistern's souls; all our parishioners' souls; and for all the souls that have done any good to this church; and for all Christian souls.

Appendix III

ORDO MISSAE WITH SIMPLE RUBRICS

In this appendix, rubrics are printed in italics, text spoken quietly is in ordinary type and text spoken aloud appears in boldface.

Before Low Mass,[1] the priest washes his hands, dresses the chalice and vests. As he does so he says:

**Veni, creator Spiritus,
mentes tuorum visita,
imple superna gratia
quae tu creasti pectora.**

**Qui Paraclitus diceris,
donum Dei altissimi,
fons vivus, ignis, caritas
et spiritalis unctio.**

**Tu septiformis munere,
dextrae Dei tu digitus,
tu rite promissum Patris,
sermone ditans guttura.**

**Accende lumen sensibus,
infunde amorem cordibus,
infirma nostri corporis
virtute firmans perpetim.**

**Hostem repellas longius,
pacemque dones protinus,
ductore sic te praevio,
vitemus omne noxium.**

**Per te sciamus da Patrem,
noscamus atque Filium;
te utriusque Spiritum
credamus omni tempore.**

---

[1] This version of the ordinary of the Mass with simplified rubrics in English is designed to serve the novice celebrant as an *aide mémoire* and presupposes study of the main body of this work.

Sit laus Patri cum Filio,
Sancto simul Paraclito;
nobisque mittat Filius
carisma Sancti Spiritus. Amen.

P[riest]: **Emitte Spiritum tuum et creabuntur.**
M[inister]: **Et renovabis faciem terrae.**

P: **Oremus. Deus, cui omne cor patet et omnis voluntas loquitur, et quem nullum latet secretum, purifica per infusionem Sancti Spiritus cogitationes cordis nostri, ut te perfecte diligere et digne laudare mereamur. Per Dominum nostrum Jesum Christum, Filium tuum, qui tecum vivit et regnat in unitate ejusdem Spiritus Sancti, Deus, per omnia saecula saeculorum.**
M: **Amen.**

Once he has vested, the priest continues:
Introibo ad altare Dei.

Psalm 42.

Judica me Deus et discerne causam meam de gente non sancta: ab homine iniquo et doloso erue me.
Quia tu es Deus fortitudo mea: quare me reppulisti et quare tristis incedo dum affligit me inimicus.
Emitte lucem tuam et veritatem tuam: ipsa me deduxerunt et adduxerunt in montem sanctum tuum et in tabernacula tua.
Et introibo ad altare Dei ad Deum: qui laetificat juventutem meam.
Confitebor tibi in cithara Deus Deus meus: quare tristis es anima mea et quare conturbas me.
Spera in Deo: quoniam adhuc confitebor illi: salutare vultus mei et Deus meus.
Gloria Patri et Filio et Spiritui Sancto.
Sicut erat in principio, et nunc, et semper, et in saecula saeculorum. Amen.
Antiphon: **Introibo ad altare Dei, ad Deum qui laetificat juventutem meam.**

Kyrie eleyson. Christe eleyson. Kyrie eleyson. Pater noster *(he continues silently)* **qui es in coelis sanctificetur nomen tuum. Adveniat regnum tuum. Fiat voluntas tua sicut in coelo et in terra. Panem nostrum quotidianum da nobis hodie: et dimitte nobis debita nostra sicut et nos dimittimus debitoribus nostris. Et ne nos inducas in tentationem. Sed libera nos a malo. Amen. Ave Maria gratia plena Dominus tecum: benedicta tu in mulieribus: et benedictus fructus ventris tui Jesus. Amen.**

He takes the chalice and follows the clerk into the church. At the foot of the altar, he bows, goes up, puts the chalice on the unfolded corporal and takes it to the south corner to pour in wine and water.

He blesses the water quietly:
M: **Benedicite.**

P: Dominus. Ab eo sit benedicta, de cujus latere exivit sanguis et aqua. In nomine Patris ✠ et Filii et Spiritus Sancti. Amen.

He dresses the chalice, opens the missal at the Officium, comes down to the top step, bows and begins in the middle voice:

P: **Et ne nos inducas in tentationem.**
M: **Sed libera nos a malo.**
P: **✠ Confitemini Domino quoniam bonus.**
M: **Quoniam in saeculum misericordia ejus.**

Bowing, he continues:
Confiteor Deo, beatae Mariae, omnibus sanctis, et vobis; quia peccavi nimis cogitatione, locutione et opere: mea culpa: precor sanctam Mariam, omnes sanctos Dei, et vos, orare pro me.
M: **Misereatur tui ...**
P: **Amen.**
M: **Confiteor ... et tibi ... et te ...**
P: **Misereatur vestri omnipotens Deus, et dimittat vobis omnia peccata vestra; liberet vos ab omni malo; conservet et confirmet in bono; et ad vitam perducat aeternam.**
M: **Amen.**
P: **Absolutionem et remissionem omnium peccatorum vestrorum, spatium verae poenitentiae, et emendationem vitae, gratiam et consolationem Sancti Spiritus, tribuat vobis omnipotens et misericors Dominus.**
M: **Amen.**

He stands erect and continues:
P: **Adjutorium nostrum in nomine Domini.**
M: **Qui fecit coelum et terram.**
P: **Sit nomen Domini benedictum.**
M: **Ex hoc nunc et usque in saeculum.**
P: **Oremus.**

He bows and goes up to the altar. Bowing again in the middle, he continues silently:
Oremus. Aufer a nobis, quaesumus, Domine, cunctas iniquitates nostras, ut ad sancta sanctorum puris mereamur mentibus introire. Per Christum Dominum nostrum. Amen.

He kisses the altar, stands erect and signs himself, saying:
In nomine Patris ✠ et Filii et Spiritus Sancti. Amen.

He goes to the missal and reads the Officium aloud with joined hands.

Still at the missal, he alternates with the clerk:
Kyrie eleyson. Kyrie eleyson. Kyrie eleyson.
Christe eleyson. Christe eleyson. Christe eleyson.
Kyrie eleyson. Kyrie eleyson. Kyrie eleyson.

He uncovers his head.

He intones the Gloria *in the middle and continues it at the missal.*
Gloria in excelsis Deo. Et in terra pax hominibus bonae voluntatis. Laudamus te. Benedicimus te. Adoramus te. Glorificamus te. Gratias agimus tibi propter magnam gloriam tuam. Domine Deus, Rex coelestis, Deus Pater omnipotens. Domine Fili unigenite, Jesu Christe. Domine Deus, Agnus Dei, Filius Patris. Qui tollis peccata mundi, miserere nobis. Qui tollis peccata mundi, suscipe deprecationem nostram. Qui sedes ad dexteram Patris, miserere nobis. Quoniam tu solus sanctus. Tu solus Dominus. Tu solus altissimus, Jesu Christe. Cum Sancto Spiritu, in gloria Dei Patris. Amen.

Still at the missal, he signs himself, turns and says:
P: **Dominus vobiscum.**
M: **Et cum spiritu tuo.**
He turns back to the missal and reads the collects, followed by the epistle, gradual, Alleluya or tract and sequence.

(If there is no clerk he moves the missal to the north corner.)

He goes to the middle, peeps at the host, bows and says:
Jube, Domine, benedicere. Dominus sit in corde meo et in ore meo ad pronunciandum sanctum Evangelium Dei. In nomine Patris ✠ et Filii et Spiritus Sancti. Amen.

At the north corner, the celebrant says:
P: **Dominus vobiscum.**
M: **Et cum spiritu tuo.**
He crosses the book, his forehead and his breast as he says:
P: **Sequentia** (*or* **Initium**) **sancti evangelii secundum N.**
He turns to face the cross and signs himself as the clerk replies:
M: **Gloria tibi, Domine.**
He reads the Gospel. At the end, he kisses the book.

He goes to the middle (with the missal) and says the creed.
Credo in unum Deum, Patrem omnipotentem, factorem coeli et terrae, visibilium omnium et invisibilium. Et in unum Dominum Jesum Christum, Filium Dei unigenitum, Et ex Patre natum ante omnia saecula: Deum de Deo, Lumen de Lumine, Deum verum de Deo vero, Genitum non factum, consubstantialem Patri, per quem omnia facta sunt. Qui propter nos homines et propter nostram salutem descendit de coelis,
He bows and says:
Et incarnatus est de Spiritu Sancto ex Maria virgine,
He bows again and says:
Et homo factus est.
He bows a third time and says:
Crucifixus etiam pro nobis sub Pontio Pilato,
Standing erect, he continues:

passus et sepultus est. Et resurrexit tertia die secundum scripturas, et ascendit in coelum, sedet ad dexteram Patris, Et iterum venturus est cum gloria judicare vivos et mortuos, cujus regni non erit finis. Et in Spiritum Sanctum Dominum et vivificantem, Qui ex Patre Filioque procedit, Qui cum Patre et Filio simul adoratur et conglorificatur, qui locutus est per prophetas. Et unam sanctam Catholicam et Apostolicam Ecclesiam. Confiteor unum baptisma in remissionem peccatorum, et exspecto resurrectionem mortuorum,

He bows and says:
Et vitam venturi saeculi. Amen.

He stands erect, signs himself and turns.
P: **Dominus vobiscum.**
M: **Et cum spiritu tuo.**
Facing the altar, he says:
Oremus.
He reads the Offertory with joined hands.

He uncovers the chalice and offers it and the paten together:
Suscipe, Sancta Trinitas, hanc oblationem, quam ego indignus peccator offero in honore tuo, beatae Mariae et omnium sanctorum tuorum, pro peccatis et offensionibus meis: et pro salute vivorum et requie omnium fidelium defunctorum.

He places the chalice on the corporal, puts the paten down in front of it, tips the host onto the corporal, kisses the paten, half-hides it under the corporal, covers the chalice and signs the offerings, saying:
In nomine Patris ✠ et Filii et Spiritus Sancti acceptum sit omnipotenti Deo hoc sacrificium novum.

He goes to the south corner to wash his hands. As he does so, he says:
Munda me, Domine, ab omni inquinamento mentis et corporis; ut possim mundus implere opus sanctum Domini.

He bows in the middle with his joined hands on the altar and says:
In spiritu humilitatis et in animo contrito suscipiamur, Domine, a te: et sic fiat sacrificium nostrum in conspectu tuo, ut a te suscipiatur hodie, et placeat tibi, Domine Deus meus.

He kisses the altar to the right of the corporal, blesses the offerings and signs himself, saying:
In nomine Patris ✠ et Filii et Spiritus Sancti. Amen.

He turns and says in the middle voice:
Orate fratres.
He continues as he turns back to the altar:
Et sorores pro me, ut meum pariterque vestrum acceptum sit Domino Deo nostro sacrificium.
M: Spiritus Sancti gratia illuminet cor tuum et labia tua, et accipiat Dominus digne hoc sacrificium laudis de manibus tuis pro peccatis et offensionibus nostris.

With extended hands, he says Oremus *and reads the secrets. Then:*
P: **Per omnia saecula saeculorum.**
M: **Amen.**
P: **Dominus vobiscum.**
M: **Et cum spiritu tuo.**
P: **Sursum corda.**
M: **Habemus ad Dominum.**
P: **Gratias agamus Domino Deo nostro.**
M: **Dignum et justum est.**
He reads the preface aloud. At the end, standing erect throughout, he says the Sanctus. He raises his extended arms and joins his hands, beginning:
Sanctus, Sanctus, Sanctus, Dominus Deus Sabaoth; pleni sunt coeli et terra gloria tua; Osanna in excelsis; benedictus qui venit ✠ in nomine Domini; Osanna in excelsis.

He kisses the feet of the Crucifix in the missal. He raises his joined hands to the level of his face and lifts up his eyes as he begins the Canon.
Te igitur, clementissime Pater,
Immediately he lowers his hands and bows low.
per Jesum Christum Filium tuum Dominum nostrum, supplices rogamus ac petimus
He stands upright and kisses the corporal on the right as he continues:
uti accepta habeas et benedicas
Standing upright he blesses the offerings, saying:
haec ✠ dona, haec ✠ munera, haec san ✠ cta sacrificia illibata,
He stands erect and extends his hands, continuing:
Imprimis quae tibi offerimus pro Ecclesia tua sancta Catholica, quam pacificare, custodire, adunare, et regere digneris toto orbe terrarum, una cum famulo tuo Papa nostro N. et Antistite nostro N. et Rege nostro N. et omnibus orthodoxis atque catholicae et apostolicae fidei cultoribus.

Memento, Domine, famulorum famularumque tuarum N. et N.
He prays briefly with joined hands. Then he extends them and continues:
et omnium circumstantium quorum tibi fides cognita est et nota devotio: pro quibus tibi offerimus vel qui tibi offerunt hoc sacrificium laudis, pro se suisque omnibus, pro redemptione animarum suarum pro spe salutis et incolumitatis suae, tibique reddunt vota sua aeterno Deo vivo et vero.

Communicantes et memoriam venerantes, Inprimis gloriosae semperque virginis *(he bows his head)* Mariae, genetricis Dei et Domini nostri Jesu Christi *(he stands erect)*, Sed et beatorum apostolorum ac martyrum tuorum, Petri, et Pauli, Andreae, Jacobi, Johannis, Thomae, Jacobi, Philippi, Bartholomaei, Matthaei, Simonis et Thaddaei, Lini, Cleti, Clementis, Sixti, Cornelii, Cypriani, Laurentii, Chrysogoni, Johannis et Pauli, Cosmae et Damiani, et omnium sanctorum tuorum, quorum meritis precibusque concedas, ut in omnibus protectionis tuae muniamur auxilio. Per eundem Christum Dominum nostrum. Amen.

He lays his palms on either side of the corporal and, bowing slightly, looks at the host as he continues:
Hanc igitur oblationem servitutis nostrae, sed et cunctae familiae tuae, quaesumus, Domine,
He stands erect, extends his hands, as he lifts his eyes for a moment, and continues:
ut placatus accipias, diesque nostros in tua pace disponas, atque ab aeterna damnatione nos eripi, et in electorum tuorum jubeas grege numerari. Per Christum Dominum nostrum. Amen.

He looks at the host again and continues:
Quam oblationem tu, Deus omnipotens, in omnibus, quaesumus,
He makes the sign of the cross over the offerings, saying:
bene ✠ dictam, ascri ✠ ptam, ra ✠ tam, rationabilem, acceptabilemque facere digneris, ut nobis
(over the host only)
cor ✠ pus et
(over the chalice only)
san ✠ guis
He joins his hands and says:
fiat dilectissimi Filii tui Domini nostri Jesu Christi.

He extends, raises and joins his hands. He wipes his fingers, raises the host a little and holds it low over the corporal, saying:
Qui pridie quam pateretur, accepit panem in sanctas ac venerabiles manus suas, et, elevatis oculis in coelum
He raises his eyes briefly.
ad te Deum Patrem suum omnipotentem,
He bows slightly as he says:
tibi gratias agens,
He makes the sign of the cross over the host, saying:
bene ✠ dixit,
He touches the host with his fingertip, saying:
fregit,
Holding the host, he continues:
deditque discipulis suis, dicens,
Bowing, he says:

Accipite et manducate ex hoc omnes.
HOC EST ENIM CORPUS MEUM.

Still holding the Host, he stands erect, bows profoundly and elevates it. He makes the sign of the cross with the Host and places it on the corporal.

From now on until the second ablution, he keeps his thumbs and forefingers joined except when touching the Host or blessing.

He uncovers the chalice, rubs his fingers over it and holds it in both hands over the corporal, saying:
Simili modo postquam coenatum est, accipiens et hunc praeclarum calicem in sanctas ac venerabiles manus suas,
He bows as he says:
item tibi gratias agens,
He places the chalice on the corporal and makes the sign of the cross over it:
bene ✠ dixit,
Holding the chalice as before, he continues:
deditque discipulis suis, dicens,

> Accipite et bibite ex eo omnes.
> HIC EST ENIM CALIX SANGUINIS MEI,
> NOVI ET AETERNI TESTAMENTI,
> MYSTERIUM FIDEI,
> QUI PRO VOBIS ET PRO MULTIS EFFUNDETUR
> IN REMISSIONEM PECCATORUM.

He elevates the chalice as he says:
Haec quotiescumque feceritis, in mei memoriam facietis.

He sets the chalice on the corporal, rubs his fingers over it and covers it.

Extending his arms crosswise, he continues:

Unde et memores, Domine, nos tui servi sed et plebs tua sancta ejusdem Christi Filii tui Domini Dei nostri tam beatae passionis, necnon et ab inferis resurrectionis, sed et in coelos gloriosae ascensionis, offerimus praeclarae majestati tuae de tuis donis ac datis
He makes the sign of the cross over the offerings, saying:
hostiam pu ✠ ram, hostiam san ✠ ctam, hostiam immacu ✠ latam,
(over the Host only)
pa ✠ nem sanctum vitae aeternae,
(over the chalice only)
et cali ✠ cem salutis perpetuae.

He extends his hands as normal and says:
Supra quae propitio ac sereno vultu respicere digneris, et accepta habere sicut accepta habere dignatus es munera pueri tui justi Abel, et sacrificium patriarchae nostri Abrahae, et quod tibi obtulit summus sacerdos tuus Melchisedech, sanctum sacrificium, immaculatam hostiam.

With arms crossed on his breast and bowed low he continues:
Supplices te rogamus, omnipotens Deus, jube haec perferri per manus sancti angeli tui in sublime altare tuum, in conspectu divinae majestatis tuae, ut quotquot
He stands upright, kisses the right of the corporal and continues:
ex hac Altaris participatione sacrosanctum Filii tui
He makes the sign of the cross over the Host:

cor ✠ pus
and over the chalice:
et san ✠ guinem sumpserimus, omni
and on himself
bene ✠ dictione coelesti et gratia repleamur,
He joins his hands, continuing:
per eundem Christum Dominum nostrum. Amen.

Memento etiam, Domine, animarum famulorum famularumque tuarum N. et N.
He prays briefly. Then he extends his hands and continues:
qui nos praecesserunt cum signo fidei et dormiunt in somno pacis; ipsis, Domine, et omnibus in Christo quiescentibus locum refrigerii, lucis et pacis, ut indulgeas deprecamur.
He joins his hands, saying:
Per eundem Christum Dominum nostrum. Amen.

He beats his breast, saying in the middle voice:
Nobis quoque peccatoribus
and continues silently with extended hands:
famulis tuis de multitudine miserationum tuarum sperantibus, partem aliquam et societatem donare digneris, cum tuis sanctis apostolis et martyribus, cum Johanne, Stephano, Matthia, Barnaba, Ignatio, Alexandro, Marcellino, Petro, Felicitate, Perpetua, Agatha, Lucia, Agnete, Caecilia, Anastasia, et cum omnibus sanctis tuis, intra quorum nos consortium non aestimator meriti, sed veniae, quaesumus, largitor admitte. Per Christum Dominum nostrum.
Here Amen *is not said.*

He continues with extended hands:
Per quem haec omnia, Domine, semper bona creas,
He makes the sign of the cross over the offerings, saying:
sancti ✠ ficas, vivi ✠ ficas, bene ✠ dicis, et praestas nobis.
He uncovers the chalice, takes the Host in his right hand and makes five crosses with it as he says:
Per ip ✠ sum *(beyond the diameter of the cup)*
et cum ip ✠ so *(from lip to lip of the cup)*
et in ip ✠ so *(inside the cup)*
est tibi Deo Patri omni ✠ potenti *(beyond the diameter of the cup)*
in unitate Spiritus ✠ Sancti *(over the corporal in front of the chalice)*
Holding the Host over the bowl with his right, he elevates the chalice with his left.
He replaces the elements on the corporal, rubs his fingers over the bowl, covers the chalice and says:
omnis honor et gloria.
He lays his palms on the corporal and says aloud:
Per omnia saecula saeculorum.
M: **Amen.**

P: **Oremus. Praeceptis salutaribus moniti et divina institutione formati, audemus dicere:**
He raises and extends his hands as he begins:
Pater noster qui es in coelis sanctificetur nomen tuum. Adveniat regnum tuum. Fiat voluntas tua sicut in coelo et in terra. Panem nostrum quotidianum da nobis hodie: et dimitte nobis debita nostra sicut et nos dimittimus debitoribus nostris. Et ne nos inducas in tentationem.
M: **Sed libera nos a malo.**
P (silently): Amen.
Libera nos, quaesumus, Domine, ab omnibus malis, praeteritis, praesentibus, et futuris; et intercedente beata et gloriosa semperque virgine Dei genetrice *(here he bows slightly)* Maria et beatis apostolis tuis Petro et Paulo atque Andrea, cum omnibus sanctis,
He takes the paten, kisses it, puts it to his left and right eyes, makes the sign of the cross with it from above his head to his breast and from his left to his right shoulder and slips it under the Host, saying:
Da propitius pacem in diebus nostris, ut, ope misericordiae tuae adjuti, et a peccato simus semper liberi et ab omni perturbatione securi.
He uncovers the chalice, bows to the Host, takes it in his right hand and holds it with both hands over the bowl, breaking it in two halves, as he says:
Per eundem Dominum nostrum Jesum Christum Filium tuum,
He turns the right half of the Host and lays it on top of the left so that the break is uppermost. He breaks this in half as he continues:
Qui tecum vivit et regnat in unitate Spiritus Sancti Deus.
Holding the first two pieces in his left hand and the third, touching the other two, in his right, he says aloud:
Per omnia saecula saeculorum.
M: **Amen.**

He makes three signs of the cross in the bowl with the particle, saying:
Pax Domini sit semper vobiscum.
M: **Et cum spiritu tuo.**
Still holding the Host as before, he continues:
Agnus Dei, qui tollis peccata mundi: miserere nobis.
Agnus Dei, qui tollis peccata mundi: miserere nobis.
Agnus Dei, qui tollis peccata mundi: dona nobis pacem.

Keeping his left hand in place, he makes the sign of the cross in the bowl with the particle and drops this into the chalice, saying quietly:
Haec sacro ✠ sancta commixtio
He arranges the other two particles into a circle on the paten and rubs his fingers over the chalice as he continues:
corporis et sanguinis Domini nostri Jesu Christi, fiat mihi omnibusque sumentibus salus mentis et corporis, et ad vitam aeternam promerendam et capescendam praeparatio salutaris. Per eundem Christum Dominum nostrum. Amen.

He covers the chalice and with joined hands says secretly:

Domine, sancte Pater, omnipotens aeterne Deus, da mihi hoc sacrosanctum corpus et sanguinem Filii tui Domini nostri Jesu Christi ita digne sumere ut merear per hoc remissionem omnium peccatorum meorum accipere et tuo Sancto Spiritu repleri; et pacem tuam habere; quia tu es Deus solus et praeter te non est alius, cujus regnum et imperium gloriosum sine fine permanet in saecula saeculorum. Amen.

He uncovers the chalice, forms a circle with the Host and holds it in both hands cupped round the bowl of the chalice. Slightly bowed, he continues:
Deus Pater, fons et origo totius bonitatis, qui ductus misericordia Unigenitum tuum pro nobis ad infima mundi descendere et carnem sumere voluisti, quam ego indignus hic in manibus meis teneo, *(here he bows more deeply once)* Te adoro, *(and a second time)* te glorifico, *(and a third time)* te tota mentis ac cordis intentione laudo et precor; ut nos famulos tuos non deseras, sed peccata nostra dimittas, quatenus tibi soli vivo ac vero Deo, puro corde et casto corpore, servire valeamus. Per eundem Christum Dominum nostrum. Amen.

Domine Jesu Christe, Fili Dei vivi, qui ex voluntate Patris, cooperante Spiritu Sancto, per mortem tuam mundum vivificasti; libera me, quaeso, per hoc sacrosanctum corpus et hunc sanguinem tuum a cunctis iniquitatibus meis et ab universis malis; et fac me tuis semper obedire mandatis, et a te nunquam in perpetuum separari permittas, Salvator mundi. Qui cum Deo Patre et eodem Spiritu Sancto vivis et regnas Deus per omnia saecula saeculorum. Amen.

Corporis et sanguinis tui, Domine Jesu Christe, sacramentum, quod licet indignus accipio, non sit mihi judicio et condemnationi; sed tua prosit pietate corporis mei et animae saluti, Amen.

He bows low, hailing the Host as he says:
Ave in aeternum, sanctissima caro Christi, mihi ante omnia et super omnia summa dulcedo. Corpus Domini nostri Jesu Christi sit mihi peccatori via et vita.
Making the sign of the cross before his face with the Host, he says:
In no ✠ mine Patris et Filii et Spiritus Sancti, Amen.
So he consumes the Host and joins his hands.

He bows low again as he says:
Ave in aeternum, coelestis potus, mihi ante omnia et super omnia summa dulcedo. Corpus et sanguis Domini nostri Jesu Christi prosint mihi peccatori ad remedium sempiternum in vitam aeternam. Amen.
He makes the sign of the cross before his face with the chalice, saying:
In no ✠ mine Patris et Filii et Spiritus Sancti. Amen.
So he drains the chalice in two or three sips.

He covers the chalice and, bowing with joined hands, says secretly:
Gratias tibi ago, Domine, sancte Pater, omnipotens aeterne Deus, qui me refecisti de sacratissimo corpore et sanguine Filii tui Domini nostri Jesu Christi; et precor, ut hoc sacramentum salutis nostrae quod sumpsi indignus peccator, non veniat mihi ad judicium neque ad condemnationem pro meritis meis; sed ad profectum corporis mei et animae saluti in vitam aeternam. Amen.

He scrapes the crumbs from the corporal with the paten, uncovers the chalice, wipes the crumbs into the bowl, leaves the paten on the corporal and places the purificator on the altar towards the south end.

He takes the chalice round the bowl in both hands, keeping his fingers clear. He goes to the south corner. He receives wine and water into the chalice. He rubs his fingers over the bowl, faces the altar, revolves the chalice and drinks the first ablution. Then he says:

Quod ore sumpsimus, Domine, pura mente capiamus; et de munere temporali fiat nobis remedium sempiternum.

With his thumbs and forefingers over the bowl, he receives wine only over his fingers into the chalice. He turns to the altar, places the chalice on it, strikes his fingers on the rim and wipes them on the purificator. Holding this under the lip of the chalice, he drinks the second ablution. Replacing the chalice on the altar, he says:

Haec nos communio, Domine, purget a crimine, et coelestis remedii faciat esse consortes.

He receives water only into the chalice. Facing the altar, he drains the chalice thoroughly.

Going to the middle, he tips the chalice onto its side over the paten.

He raises his eyes to the cross and immediately bows, laying his joined hands on the altar. So he says:

Adoremus crucis signaculum: per quod salutis sumpsimus sacramentum.

He goes to the south corner and washes his hands as at the offertory, saying nothing.

He returns to the middle, drains the last drop, and wipes his lips and the inside of the chalice, which he dresses and replaces on the corporal.

If there is no clerk, he returns the missal to the south corner. At the missal there, he reads the Communion aloud.

He makes the sign of the cross and turns to say:
Dominus vobiscum.
M: **Et cum spiritu tuo.**
Turning back, he says **Oremus** *and the postcommons.*
M: **Amen.**

He signs himself again and turns.
P: **Dominus vobiscum.**
M: **Et cum spiritu tuo.**

When Gloria in excelsis *has been said (facing west):*
P: **Ite, missa est.**
M: **Deo gratias.**

When Gloria in excelsis *has not been said (facing the altar):*
P: **Benedicamus Domino.**
M: **Deo gratias.**

He turns to the altar, closes the book and goes to the middle.

Bowing with joined hands he says secretly:
Placeat tibi, Sancta Trinitas, obsequium servitutis meae, et praesta ut hoc sacrificium quod oculis tuae majestatis indignus obtuli, tibi sit acceptabile, mihique et omnibus pro quibus illud obtuli, sit, te miserante, propitiabile. Qui vivis et regnas Deus per omnia saecula saeculorum. Amen.

Standing erect, he kisses the altar and then signs himself, saying:
In nomine Patris et Filii et Spiritus Sancti. Amen.

He folds the corporal and inserts it in the burse, which he puts on top of the chalice.
He takes the chalice, comes down the steps, bows to the altar and returns to the vestry. As he goes, he says secretly the Gospel In principio.

If he wears the biretta, he receives this after bowing to the altar. If he will cover his head with the amice, he does this immediately before taking the chalice.

Bibliokaiallography

Books

Ahearne, P. and Lane, M. *Pontifical Ceremonies*. London, 1942.
Bailey, T. *The Processions of Sarum and the Western Church*. Toronto, 1971.
Becon, T. *The Displaying of the Popish Masse*. London, 1637.
Bishop, E. *Liturgica Historica*. Oxford, 1918.
Blunt, J. H. (ed.) *The Myroure of Oure Ladye*. London, 1873.
Bond, F. *The Chancel of English Churches*. Oxford, 1916.
Bonniwell, W. R. *A History of the Dominican Liturgy*. New York, 1945.
The Book of Common Prayer. London, 1857.
Burchfield, R. W. *The Compact Edition of the Oxford English Dictionary: Complete Text Reproduced Micrographically*. Oxford, 1971.
Burnet, G. *The History of the Reformation of the Church of England*, Vol. V. Oxford, 1865.
Caeremoniale Episcoporum. Rome, 1829.
Caeremoniale juxta Ritum S. Ordinis Praedicatorum. Mechlin, 1869. Retrieved from https://archive.org/details/cremonialejuxt00cath
Carrow Psalter, Walters Art Museum. Retrieved from http://www.thedigitalwalters.org/Data/WaltersManuscripts/html/W34/
Chambers, J. D. *Divine Worship in England in the Thirteenth and Fourteenth Centuries Contrasted with and Adapted to That in the Nineteenth*. London, 1877.
Cérémonial Romain-Lyonnais. Lyon, 1897.
Código de derecho canónico (edición bilingüe). Madrid, 1983.
Collins, A. J. (ed.) *Manuale ad Usum Percelebris Ecclesie Sarisburiensis from the Edition Printed at Rouen in 1543 Compared with Those of 1506 (London), 1516 (Rouen), 1523 (Antwerp), 1526 (Paris)*. Henry Bradshaw Society, Vol. XCI. Chichester, 1960.
Concilio Vaticano II. Constituciones. Decretos. Declaraciones. Legislación posconciliar. Madrid, 1967.
Concilium Tridentinum. Paris, 1676.
Cox, J. C. *Three Centuries of Derbyshire Annals*, Vol. I. London, 1890.
Cyril of Jerusalem (Migne, J. P. ed.) *Catecheses Mystagogicae Quinque. Patrologia Graeca*, Vol. XXXIII. Paris, 1857.
Dalton, J. N. (ed.) *The Collegiate Church of Ottery St. Mary*. Cambridge, 1917.
Daniel, H. A. *Codex liturgicus ecclesiae universae in epitomen redactus*, Vol. I. Lipsiae, 1847.
Dearmer, P. *The Parson's Handbook*. New York, 1931.
De Herdt, P. J. B. *Sacrae Liturgiae Praxis, juxta ritum Romanum*. Lovanii, 1855.
Dickinson, F. H. (ed.) *Missale ad Usum Insignis et Praeclarae Ecclesiae Sarum*. Burntisland, 1861–83.
Dix, G. *The Shape of the Liturgy*. London, 1978.
Du Cange, C. du Fresne, *Glossarium Mediae et Infimae Latinitatis*. Niort, 1883–7.
Duffy, E. *The Stripping of the Altars*. London, 1992.

Duffy, E. *The Voices of Morebath*. London, 2003.
Durandus, G. *Rationale Divinorum Officiorum*. Venice, 1609.
Feasey, H. J. *Ancient English Holy Week Ceremonial*. London, 1897.
Fortescue, A. H. T. K. *The Ceremonies of the Roman Rite Described*. London, 1920.
Fortescue, A. H. T. K. *The Mass: A Study of the Roman Liturgy*. London, 1955.
Fortescue, A., O'Connell, J. B. and Reid, A. *The Ceremonies of the Roman Rite Described*. Farnborough, 2003.
French, K. L. *The People of the Parish: Community Life in a Late Medieval Diocese*. Philadelphia, 2001.
Frere, W. H. (ed.) *Graduale Sarisburiense*. London, 1894.
Frere, W. H. (ed.) *The Use of Sarum. I. The Sarum Customs as Set Forth in the Consuetudinary and Customary. II. The Ordinal and Tonal*. Cambridge, 1898–1901.
Frost, C. *Time, Space and Order: The Making of Medieval Salisbury*. Bern, 2009.
García-Rendueles Gutiérrez, E. *Liturgia popular*. Oviedo, 1950.
Gibson, E. C. S. The Rt. Revd. and Ratcliff, E. C. (edd.) *The First and Second Prayer Books of Edward VI*. London, 1964.
Goude, G. vander (Dearmer, P. ed.) *Dat Boexken vander Missen*. London, 1903.
Henderson, W. G. (ed.) *Manuale et Processionale ad Usum Insignis Ecclesiae Eboracensis*. Durham, 1875.
Henderson, W. G. (ed.) *Missale ad Usum Percelebris Ecclesiae Herfordensis*. Leeds, 1874 (reprint of 1969).
Henderson, W. G. (ed.) *Processionale ad Usum Insignis ac Praeclarae Ecclesiae Sarum*. Leeds, 1882 (reprint of 1969).
Herbermann, C. G., Pace, E. A., Pallen, C. B., Shahan, T. J. and Wynne, J. J. (edd.), *The Catholic Encyclopedia*. New York, 1913.
Hope, W. H. St. J. *English Altars from Illuminated Manuscripts*. London, 1899.
Hope, Sir W. St. J. and Atchley, E. G. C. F. *English Liturgical Colours*. London, 1918.
Hours of the Umfray Family (Sloane 2468), British Library. Retrieved from http://www.bl.uk/catalogues/illuminatedmanuscripts/ILLUMIN.ASP?Size=mid&IllID=9270
Installation of the Most Reverend Vincent Gerard Nichols, Eleventh Archbishop of Westminster. Westminster, 2009.
Jerdan, W. (ed.) *Rutland Papers*. London, 1842.
John of Avranches (Joannes Abrincensis) (Migne, J. P. ed.) *Liber de Officiis Ecclesiasticis*. Patrologia Latina, Vol. CXLVII. Paris, 1853.
Jones, W. H. R. *Vetus Registrum Sarisberiense*, Vol. II. London, 1884.
Kempe, Margery (Meech, S. B. ed.) *The Book of Margery Kempe*. London, 1940.
King, A. A. *Liturgies of the Past*. London, 1959.
King, A. A. *Liturgies of the Religious Orders*. London, 1956.
King, A. A. *Liturgy of the Roman Church*. London, 1957.
Lefèvre, Pl. F. (ed.) *L' Ordinaire de Prémontré d'après des manuscrits du XIIe et du XIIIe siècle*. Louvain, 1941.
Lefèvre, Pl. F. (ed.) *Coutumieres liturgiques de Prémontré du XIIIe et du XIVe siècle*. Louvain, 1953.
Legg, J. W. *Ecclesiological Essays*. London, 1905.
Legg, J. W. (ed.) *The Sarum Missal Edited from Three Early Manuscripts*. Oxford, 1916.
Legg, J. W. (ed.) *Tracts on the Mass*. Henry Bradshaw Society, Vol. XXVII. London, 1904.
Liber Usuum Sacri Cisterciensis Ordinis. Paris, 1643. Retrieved from https://books.google.co.uk/books/about/Liber_usuum_Cisterciensis_ordinis.html?id=NS5FAAAAcAAJ&redir_esc=y

Littlehales, H. (ed.) *The Prymer*. London, 1891.
Livy, T. *Ab Urbe Condita* (Conway, R. S. and Walters, C. F. edd.). Oxford, 1914.
Manuale seu baptisterium secundum usum alme ecclesie Toletane. Seville, 1494.[1]
Martène, E. *De Antiquis Ecclesiae Ritibus*. Tomus Primus. Antuerpiae, 1763.
Maskell, W. *Ancient Liturgy of the Church of England: According to the Uses of Sarum, Bangor, York & Hereford, and the Modern Roman Liturgy; Arranged in Parallel Columns*. London, 1846.
Micrologus de Ecclesiasticis Observationibus. Patrologia Latina, Vol. CLI. Edited by J. P. Migne. Paris, 1853.
Missale candidissimi Ordinis Premonstratensis ad unguem recognitum et adauctum. Paris, 1530. Retrieved from https://books.google.co.uk/books?id=dW9FAAAAcAAJ& printsec=frontcover&dq=editions:8JQso3XLYhIC& hl=en&sa=X&ved=0ahUK EwjnzLvaqcDTAhWMC8AKHaXKAocQ6AEIFDAA#v=onepage&q&f=false
Missale Fratrum Carmelitarum Ordinis Beatae Dei Genitricis Mariae. Venice, 1621. Retrieved from https://books.google.co.uk/books/about/Missale_fratrum_ Carmelitarum_Ordinis_bea.html?id=PUEgJFAvalgC&redir_esc=y
Missale Romanum. Edited by H. Dessain. Mechlin, 1889.
Missale secundum Ordinem Fratrum Praedicatorum. Paris, 1586. Retrieved from https://books.google.co.uk/books?id=VxQ2cNwAkyUC&printsec= frontcover#v=onepage&q&f=false
Morison, S. *English Prayer Books: An Introduction to the Literature of Christian Public Worship*. Cambridge, 1949.
Morse, H. G. *Notes on Ceremonial*. London, 1911.
MS. Auct. D. Inf. 2. 11 (Bodleian Library). Retrieved from http://bodley30.bodley.ox.ac. uk:8180/luna/servlet/view/
Olalla Aragón, F. B. *Ceremonias de las missas solemnes cantadas con diaconos ò sin ellos, segun las Rubricas del Missal Romano*. Madrid, 1707. Retrieved from https://books. google.co.uk/books?id=Ah-MwIpycS8C&printsec=frontcover&dq=olalla+ceremonial +de+las+missas+solemnes&hl=en&sa=X&ved=0ahUKEwjD2peu783WAhWmJsAKH YhiB58Q6AEIMjAF#v=onepage&q=olalla%20ceremonial%20de%20las%20missas%20 solemnes&f=false
Ordinarius sive Liber Caeremoniarum ad Usum Canonici Ordinis Praemonstratensis in Capitulo Generali an. 1738 Renovatus. Verdun, 1739. Retrieved from https:// books.google.co.uk/books/about/Ordinarius_sive_liber_caeremoniarum_ad_u. html?id=vEw17I7wuK8C&redir_esc=y
Ordo Romanus XIV. Patrologia Latina, Vol. LXXVIII. Edited by J. P. Migne. Paris, 1849.
Orme, N. *Medieval Schools: From Roman Britain to Renaissance England*. London, 2006.
O'Connell, J. B. *Church Building and Furnishing: the Church's Way*. London, 1955.
O'Connell, J. B. *The Celebration of Mass*, Vol. III. London, 1945.
Pagden, F. A. *A History of Alfriston*. No date.
Pastoureau, M. *Blue: The History of a Colour*. Princeton, 2001.
Pearson, A. H. (ed.) *The Sarum Missal Done into English*. London, 1868.
Pfaff, R. W. *The Liturgy in Medieval England: A History*. Cambridge, 2012.

---

[1] Data retrieved from USUARIUM: A Digital Library and Database for the Study of Latin Liturgical History in the Middle Ages and Early Modern Period (http://usuarium.elte.hu) builded by Miklós István Földváry et al. at Eötvös Loránd University (Budapest, Hungary), Research Group of Liturgical History – from 2015 onwards.

Procter, F. and Wordsworth, Chr. (edd.) *Breviarium ad usum insignis ecclesiae Sarum.* Cambridge, 1879–86 (reprint of 1970).
Raine, J. (ed.) *A Description or Breife Declaration of all the Ancient Monuments, Rites, and Customs Belonginge or Beinge within the Monastical Church of Durham before the Suppression.* London, 1844.
Ranworth Antiphoner (manuscript, no number). Located in Ranworth parish church. ca. 1478.
Reichert, B. M. (ed.) *Acta Capitulorum Generalium Ordinis Praedicatorum.* Rome, 1898–1904.
Reid, A. *The Organic Development of the Liturgy.* Farnborough, 2004.
Reynolds, H. E. *Wells Cathedral: Its Foundation, Constitutional History and Statutes.* Wells, 1881.
Rituale Romanum cum Appendice Toletano. Toledo, 1950.
Rock, D. (Hart, G. W. and Frere, W. H. edd.) *The Church of Our Fathers.* London, 1905.
Rose-Troup, F. *The Western Rebellion of 1549: An Account of the Insurrections in Devonshire and Cornwall against Religious Innovations in the Reign of Edward VI.* London, 1913.
Rowse, A. L. (ed.) *A Man of Singular Virtue, being A Life of Sir Thomas More by His Son-in-Law William Roper and a Selection of More's Letters.* London, 1980.
Sacerdotale juxta S. Romanae Ecclesiae ... Venice, 1559. Retrieved from https://books.google.co.uk/books?id=sFIftm8PlfkC&printsec=frontcover&dq=sacerdotale+iuxta&hl=en&sa=X&ved=0ahUKEwiP_7mWzc3WAhWIB8AKHQvFABsQ6AEIIDAC#v=onepage&q&f=false
Sacerdotale Romanum. Venice, 1585. Retrieved from https://books.google.co.uk/books?id=JfGgQgXL_u0C&pg=PP14&dq=sacerdotale+romanum&hl=en&sa=X&ved=0ahUKEwi4vdb4yc3WAhUKDMAKHXwhC_sQ6AEIHzAD#v=onepage&q&f=false
Simmons, T. F. (ed.) *The Lay Folks Mass Book.* Oxford, 1879 (reprint of 1968).
Thomas Aquinas, St. *Summa Theologiae.* Coloniae Agrippinae, 1604.
Thurston, H., S.J. (trans. and ed.), *The Life of Saint Hugh of Lincoln.* London, 1898.
Walsingham, T. (Riley, H. T. ed.) *Historia Anglicana,* Vol. I. London, 1863 (reprint of 1965).
Warner, Sir G. F. (ed.) *The Stowe Missal.* Henry Bradshaw Society, Vol. XXXII. London, 1915.
Wilkins, D. *Concilia Magnae Britanniae et Hiberniae,* Vol. I. London, 1737.
Wilkins, D. *Concilia Magnae Britanniae et Hiberniae,* Vol. II. London, 1737.
Wood-Legh, K. L. *Perpetual Chantries in Britain.* Cambridge, 1965.
Wordsworth, Chr. (ed.) *Ordinale Sarum sive Directorium Sacerdotum (Liber, quem* Pica Sarum *vulgo vocitat clerus) auctore Clemente Maydeston, sacerdote.* Henry Bradshaw Society, Voll. XX and XXII. London, 1901 and 1902.
Wordsworth, Chr. (ed.) *Statutes of Lincoln Cathedral.* Cambridge, 1892–7.
Wordsworth, Chr. *Salisbury Processions and Ceremonies.* Cambridge, 1901.
Wordsworth, C. (ed.) *The Tracts of Clement Maydeston with the Remains of Caxton's Ordinale.* Henry Bradshaw Society, Vol. VII. London, 1894.
Zimmerman, B. (ed.) *Ordinaire de l'Ordre de Notre-Dame du Mont-Carmel par Sibert de Beka vers 1312.* Paris, 1910.

Articles and journals

Acta Apostolicae Sedis, Vol. XCIX, N.9. Vatican City State, 2007.
Acta Apostolicae Sedis, Vol. CIII, N.6. Vatican City State, 2011.
Anon. 'An Archbishop's Enthronement', *The Tablet*, 20 July 1957, pages 66–7.
Blum, P. Z. 'Liturgical Influences on the Design of the West Front at Wells and Salisbury', *Gesta*, Vol. XXV, No. 1 (1986).
Davison, N. 'So Which Way Round Did They Go? The Palm Sunday Procession at Salisbury', *Music & Letters*, Vol. 61, No. 1 (1980).
García Alonso, I. 'El manual toledano para la administración de sacramentos a través de los siglos XIV-XVI', *Salmanticensis*, Vol. V (1958).
Haines, W. (ed.), 'Stanford Churchwardens' Accounts 1552–1602', *The Antiquary*, Vol. XVII (1888).
Pérès, M. 'The Choirmaster and his Liturgical Role', *Ministerial and Common Priesthood in the Eucharistic Celebration: The Proceedings of the Fourth International Colloquium of Historical, Canonical and Theological Studies on the Roman Catholic Liturgy.* London, 1999.
Sweeney, T. C. 'From Canterbury to Westminster: The Rites Used for the Enthronement of the Archbishop of Westminster', *The Tablet*, 28 September 1963, pages 1032–3.
Thompson, A. 'Incense and Thuribles in the Dominican Rite'. Retrieved from http://dominican-liturgy.blogspot.com/2015/09/incense-and-thuribles-in-dominican-rite.html
Thurston, H. H. C. 'The *Sanctus* Bell', *The Tablet*, 15 October 1938, page 20.

Websites (other than eBooks and articles)

Ceremonia y rúbrica de la iglesia española: 'La palia y la hijuela'. Retrieved from http://liturgia.mforos.com/1699127/8380846-la-palia-y-la-hijuela/ (accessed 25 March 2017).
Peter Wimberley (poster) *Carmelite Rite 1960 Aylesford Priory*. Retrieved from https://www.youtube.com/playlist?list=PL701297BE44543D9C (accessed 21 November 2015).
Sloper, B. *Salisbury – A Divined Cathedral*: 'Right Dimension'. Retrieved from https://salisburycathedral.wordpress.com/the-right-dimension/ (accessed 22 November 2017).

Index

ablutions 67 nn.84, 85, 86, 71–2,
    75 n.1, 137
Absolutionem 45, 45 n.6, 91 n.5
acolyte 4 n.11, 18, 88, 88 nn.14, 16, 99 n.1,
    103–4, 103 n.5, 125, 132,
    135 n.51, 191
Advent 88 n.14, 151, 197
alb 18 n.11
Alfriston 4 n.11, 26 n.31
All Hallows 52 n.26
All Souls 270–1
Alleluya 148, 151, 259
almuce 6 n.29
altar 2 (Fig. I), 4–5, 4 n.16, 5 n.23, 216 n.20
    incensation of. *See* incensation of
        the altar
    movement about 33, 34, 34 nn.11, 12,
        43, 88–9, 147
    stripping and washing of 228–30
    turning from and to 43 n.25, 47, 47 n.23,
        53, 112
altar-cards 9
amice. *See* headcovering
Annunciation. *See* Lady Day
apparels 17 n.2
arrhae 164, 165 n.27
Ascension 260, 265–6
Ash Wednesday 211–14
Asperges 87 n.1, 187–9, 256, 259, 268
assistant priests and deacons. *See the days
    of Holy Week*
aumbry. *See* credence
Ave Maria 42 n.18

Badingham font 13 n.26
banners 191, 211, 215, 218, 218 n.40, 269
    in Eastertide 262–5, 262 n.42, 263 n.47,
        265 n.73
baptism 247, 253, 255–6, 255 n.103,
    257 n.127
bede roll 5, 52 n.26

bedes. *See* bidding of the bedes
bell, church 82 n.24, 127, 133, 133 n.28,
    225, 257, 261
bell, hand 12 n.25, 13 n.26, 82, 82 n.23,
    127, 225, 257, 263
bidding of the bedes 51 n.18, 52, 52 n.26,
    81, 124, 190, 275–6
bination 72, 72 n.23
biretta. *See* headcovering
blessing at Mass 71 n.22, 72 n.34
blessings 140, 193, 107 n.2, 193 n.1
    at weddings 165 n.27, 168–70
book-boy 188 n.9
books 9
bow 34, 43, 89, 92 n.13, 108 n.9, 147.
    See also under obeisance
bread, blessing of 73 n.37, 193, 193 n.1
breast, striking of 45, 62, 91 n.3

Candlemas 201–5
candles 5 n.22, 16 n.40, 247 n.33, 269 n.9
Canon of the Mass 54–5, 57–62, 129–32
canonical status xiv–xviii
canons, cathedral 6, 29 n.57, 145 n.5,
    152–3, 154, 217 n.29
canopy over the Sacrament 215, 215
    n.4, 219, 219 n.45, 228 n.45, 269,
    269 n.9
canopy, wedding. *See* care-cloth
cantors 150–2, 171, 174, 191
care-cloth 164, 168
cassock 79 n.3
catechumens, oil of. *See* oils
chalice
    at High Mass 4 n.11, 117 n.1, 118 n.9,
        121 n.11, 129 n.1, 139. *See also*
        entrance, great
    at Low Mass 42, 48, 53 n.38, 71, 72 n.34
    making of 43, 43 n.21, 103–6, 160,
        172, 174
    non-sacramental 12

chancel 2 (Fig. I), 3, 3 n.4, 124 n.32
chasuble on altar or seat 204 n.36, 247 n.29
   ministers', at High Mass 17, 99, 105, 105 n.29, 106, 106 n.32, 138, 138 n.12
   days when worn 197, 209
   raised 12 n.25, 82 n.28, 94, 96, 96 n.53, 126
choir 89 n.30, 114–15, 114 n.55, 142–3, 145–55, 171, 189–90, 191, 225 n.2
choir dress 6 n.29, 18, 18 n.13, 145
   cappa choralis 145 n.5, 150, 256, 257, 268, 270
choir stalls 2 (Fig. I), 6–7, 6 n.29, 114–15, 135 n.48
choir step. *See* gradus chori
choir, rulers of 2 (Fig. I), 7, 15 n.33, 146, 152–5, 190
chrism. *See* oils
Christmas 198–9
church (building) 2 (Fig. I), 3–7, 3 n.3, 4 n.11
clerk 79–84, 79 n.1, 135 n.51
colours, liturgical 5 n.17, 21–9, 21 n.1, 247 n.29
Communion, celebrant's 67
Communion, general, occasions of 75 n.1, 162 n.46, 227, 246, 256, 257, 257 n.127, 267
   purification after 69 n.6, 77, 83, 141, 141 n.2, 142
   ritual of 75–8, 75 n.1, 76 n.9, 77 nn.19, 20, 83, 150 n.57, 171–3, 273. *See also* Gayton Thorpe
confessio 91, 238, 238 n.87, 256
confirmation 256 n.110, 257 n.127
Confiteor 45, 76–7, 76 n.9, 91 n.3. *See also* confessio
consecration. *See* sacring
cope 18, 18 nn.14, 16, 145, 150, 152, 201, 145 n.1
corporal 11–12, 11 nn.20, 21, 59, 104, 106, 131 n.15
Corpus Christi 26 n.31, 269
credence 2 (Fig. I), 6, 6 n.25
Credo in unum Deum 46 n.16, 49, 112–16
cross, altar 5, 5 n.21
cross, processional 5 n.21, 16, 88, 88 n.12, 108, 191, 201
   in Eastertide 260, 263, 267
   in Lent 208, 209, 215, 218, 221, 222, 232, 246
cross, sign of the 34, 34 n.6, 47, 47 n.23, 59, 274 n.11
Cross, veneration of the 234–7, 261
crucifer. *See* acolyte
cushion 13, 87 n.7, 88

deacon 91, 94, 113 n.53, 121–3, 126, 129 n.5, 131–2, 135 n.46
deacon's step 2 (Fig. I)
double rite 87–9, 87 n.7, 108, 148, 150, 153, 191
Draco *and* Leo. *See* banners in Eastertide

eagle. *See* lectern, Gospel
Easter 26 n.30, 149 n.49, 259–68, 261 n.25
elevation 12 n.25, 13 n.26, 59, 60, 60 n.27, 82, 82 n.28
Ember Days 197–8
entrance, great 4 n.11, 95, 95 n.40, 103, 103 n.1
Epiphany 199
epistle 99–100, 100 n.17, 172
evensong 226–8, 240, 241 n.124, 257

fan. *See* flabellum
farsing 147, 168, 199, 226, 256
fast, Eucharistic 41 n.3
feretrum 218, 218 n.43, 221, 263, 265
feria 149, 207, 21 n.1
figures xxvi, 2, 110, 111, 180, 220, 249, 250, 254
flabellum 15 n.34
Flectamus genua 35 n.21, 198
flitting the book
   at High Mass 108, 108 n.6, 138
   at Low Mass 48, 72 n.27, 81, 81 n.17, 83
   at Sung Mass 172
font 247–8, 253–6, 254 (Fig. VIII), 260, 267. *See also* Gayton Thorpe, Great Glemham, Great Witchingham, Westhall
font, candle for blessing 202, 202 n.13, 203, 249, 251 n.64, 255, 267
fraction 63–4, 65 n.68
frontal *and* frontlet 4
funerals 28 n.56, 159 n.2, 260 n.12

garland 17 n.1
Gayton Thorpe 12 n.23, 17 n.3, 42 n.16, 75
    n.1, 76 n.2, 77 nn.12, 14, 15, 16, 21,
    141 nn.1, 2, 274 n.22
genuflection 35, 35 nn.20, 21, 22, 59 n.17,
    60 n.27, 96 n.53
Gloria in excelsis 46–7, 46 n.16, 95–6
Good Friday 231–44
Gospel 49, 101 n.21, 107–12, 109 n.12,
    110 (Fig. II), 110 n.20, 111 (Fig.
    III), 173, 180 (Fig. IV)
Gospel-book 87–8, 89. *See also* Text *and
    under* kissing
Gospel lectern. *See* lectern, Gospel
Gospel, Last. *See* In principio
Goude 136 n.53
gradual 48, 100, 148, 150–1
gradus chori 2 (Fig. I), 3, 99, 100, 124 n.32,
    151–2, 188, 193
gradus presbyterii 2 (Fig. I), 3
Great Glemham 12 n.23, 17 n.3, 42 n.16,
    75 n.1, 76 n.2, 141 n.1, 165 n.16
Great Witchingham 5 n.23, 29 n.58,
    246 n.21
gremial. *See* mappula

hands 33, 33 nn.2, 4, 46 n.12, 133 n.33
headcovering 19, 19 n.19, 42, 73,
    89, 140
history of the rite. *See* canonical status
Holy Saturday 245–58, 249 (Fig. VI), 250
    (Fig. VII), 254 (Fig. VIII)
holy water 35, 43, 87 n.1, 187–90, 256,
    263, 268
Holy Week 209. *See also individual days*
hour of functions 41, 87, 87 n.1, 207,
    209 n.27
    processions 87 n.1, 187, 191, 191 n.46
    on certain days 201, 211, 233, 266
houseling cloth 76, 142
humiliatio 34–5, 35 n.20, 66, 92 n.13,
    108 n.9

In principio 73, 73 n.37, 140, 193
incense *and* incensation 35, 36–7, 36 n.28,
    107–15, 107 n.2, 125
    incensation of the altar 92–3, 93 n.20,
        108, 108 n.8, 118 n.10, 121–3,
        123 n.30

incensation of the celebrant 93–4, 113,
    118 n.10
incensation of other people 113–14, 125,
    114 n.55, 118 n.10
incensation of the sacrifice 118–22, 118
    n.10, 127 n.62, 130, 130 n.8
incensation on particular days 160–1,
    168, 239, 242
inclinatio 34, 59, 64, 66 n.77, 223 n.82
introit. *See* Officium
inventories, Sarum cathedral
    1214–1222 4 n.14, 5 nn.21, 24, 11 n.19,
        14 n.27, 15 n.34, 21 n.1
    1219–1225 5 n.22
    1389 10 n.10, 14 n.28, 26 n.37
    1536 9 n.3, 15 n.33, 17 n.1, 28 n.56

Jesus, name of 34, 34 n.15, 58, 72

kissing
    of the altar 46, 46 n.12, 72, 104, 132
    of the celebrant 51, 80 n.11, 92, 117, 117
        n.6, 132, 133
    of the corporal 53, 61, 65 n.68
    of the cross 54 n.50, 80, 236, 261
    of the floor or form 61, 198, 208, 212,
        221, 222, 235, 264
    of the missal 49, 54, 54 n.50
    omitted 161 (book), 226 (ministers), 238
        (ministers), 239, 249, 257
    of other people 65 n.68, 91, 134–6,
        274 n.11
    of the Text or Gospel-book 14 n.28, 91
        n.8, 94, 112, 112 n.39, 114 n.55,
        115, 122
    of vessels 50, 63, 65 n.68, 134
Kyrie 64, 147. *See also* farsing

Lady Day 207 n.1, 209, 260
laity 12 n.25, 52, 77, 77 n.15, 125, 135,
    142, 273–4
lavabo. *See* lavatory
lavatory
    after Communion 69 n.1, 71,
        71 n.17, 138
    ministers' 104, 106, 130, 130 n.13
    at the offertory 10, 52–3, 124–5
lectern 2 (Fig. I), 3, 3 n.7, 88, 107, 107 n.1,
    153 n.99. *See also* cantors

lector 172, 198
Lent 207-9
Liber vitæ. *See* bede roll
litanies 208, 208 n.17, 252, 256, 263, 265.
　　See also Rogation Days
locus (ad)ministrationis. *See* credence

maniple 51, 17 n.4
mantellum. *See* veil, humeral
mappula 94 n.38
Mark, St. 262, 265. *See also* Rogation Days
Mary, name of 34, 34 n.15, 58, 63 n.54
Mass
　　High 87-155, 88 n.14, 139 n.24
　　Low 41-84, 139 n.24, 150
　　private 224, 268
　　Sung 171-83, 171 nn.1, 2, 174 n.17
Mass book. *See* missal
Maundy Thursday 225-30
Missa Cantata. *See* Mass, Sung
missal 9 n.1, 72, 87, 87 n.7, 89, 93, 122, 174
　　transferring of. *See* flitting
monstrance. *See* pyx

nave 2 (Fig. I), 3
notices 43, 52, 191

obeisance 34-5. *See also* bow, genuflection, humiliatio, inclinatio, prostration
oblation of the people 51-2, 51 nn.18, 23, 81, 123-4, 161, 193
offertorium. *See* veil, chalice
offertory 50, 117-18, 149 n.44
Officium 46, 89, 139 n.24, 147, 153, 209
oils, holy 245, 255, 258, 266
Ordo Missae 277-89
organ 160
orientation 4

pall, chalice 10 n.17, 11 n.20
pall, funeral 159
Palm Sunday 215-24
palms 216, 216 n.9, 217
Paschal Candle 107 n.2, 247, 247 n.32, 250-1, 260, 260 n.12
Passion (Gospels) 209, 223, 233-4
Passiontide 147, 209
paten 48, 63, 117, 126, 132, 161, 271

pax
　　on certain days 162, 169, 226, 226 n.14, 257
　　at High Mass 14 n.28, 133-6, 135 n.46, 149, 154
　　at Low Mass 65, 65 nn.68, 72, 83
pax-brede 14 n.28, 65 n.72, 135 n.46
penitents 211, 225
Pentecost. *See* Whitsun
Per Ipsum 62, 131, 131 n.15
piscina 2 (Fig. I), 6, 53 n.34, 69 n.1, 71 n.18, 124 n.38, 130 n.13
pontifical rites
　　at High Mass 12 n.24, 63 n.59, 89 nn.17, 20, 112 n.39, 113 n.51, 114 n.59, 153 n.105
　　in Holy Week 89 n.20, 135 n.50, 155 n.112, 226 n.14, 228 n.45, 246 n.17, 251 n.58, 253 n.87, 256 n.110, 262 n.43
　　on other occasions 5 n.22, 199 n.31, 203 n.33, 213 n.22, 261 n.25, 263 n.51
prayer over the people 72, 139
prayers, requested 52-3, 124-5, 133, 133 n.28
preces in prostratione 64, 133, 133 n.28, 149
preparatory prayers. *See* confessio
presbyterium 2 (Fig. I), 3-4, 168
presbytery step. *See* gradus presbyterii
processional (book) 9 n.6, 187 n.1
processions 187-92
　　in Eastertide 260-6, 261 n.25, 264 n.59
　　in Holy Week 217-22, 250, 253
　　throughout the year 187 n.2, 188 n.9, 208, 269-70
　　at Mass 109
　　occasional 192
prophecy 99 n.1, 101 n.219, 199
prostration 35, 35 nn.22, 24, 167, 168
　　penitential 208, 211-12, 223, 223 n.82, 236
　　before the Sacrament 76 n.9, 142, 149, 149 n.52, 168, 239
pulpit 52
pulpitum 2 (Fig. I), 3, 3 n.7, 15 n.30, 100, 109, 150, 150 n.64
purification after Communion
　　See Communion, general, purification after

purificator 10 n.16
pyx 10, 232, 238–9, 269

reception of dignitaries 192
relics 93, 122, 191, 269, 270. *See also* feretrum
Requiem Mass 29 n.57, 83, 159–62, 162 n.46, 270–1
reservation, Eucharistic
   in Holy Week 225, 228, 240–2, 257
   place of 5, 5 n.24, 47 n.24, 142 n.13
   renewal of species 67, 67 n.85, 75 n.1
rochet. *See* surplice
Rogation Days 262–5, 263 n.51
rood, screen and loft 2 (Fig. I), 3, 3 n.7, 190, 222

Sacrament 89 n.29, 93 n.23, 228. *See also* canopy *and* reservation
sacring 58–60, 58 n.13, 82 n.27, 129 n.4, 130
   ceremonial additaments 12 n.25, 13 n.26, 127 n.62
   obeisance at the 59 n.17, 60 n.27, 129 n.5, 149 n.52
sacristan 3 n.1, 6, 201, 245, 261
Salisbury, St. Edmund's 6 n.25
Sanctus 54 n.46, 129 n.4, 174 n.20
Sandwich, St. Mary's 4 n.12, 5 n.21
seats 2 (Fig. I), 3, 6, 6 n.27, 88, 94, 101 n.21, 273
Septuagesima 208
Sepulchre, Easter 233, 233 n.22, 240–2, 247, 260, 260–2
sequence 48, 48 n.31, 148, 160
   on certain days 160, 204, 209
sermon 51 n.18, 52, 124, 211, 225 n.2, 264
server. *See* clerk
serving Low Mass 79–84
Sovereign 35 n.24, 57, 57 n.3, 192, 192 nn.56, 57, 251
stations
   in Holy Week 218, 221–2, 250–1, 253–4. *See also* figures
   in processions 190, 264, 264 n.59
subdeacon 91, 96, 113 n.53, 116, 122, 129 n.5
subdeacon's step 2 (Fig. I)
Summe sacerdos et vere pontifex 94

superaltar 4 n.14
surplice 17 n.1, 18 n.17, 79 n.3

taperers 88, 92, 127, 131, 257, 91 n.1
Textus 9 n.3, 87, 87 n.7, 110 n.25. *See also under* kissing
   at the Gospel 108, 110 n.25
   in processions 188, 191
thanksgiving. *See* Trium puerorum
thuribles and thurifers 12 n.24, 88, 89 n.17, 191. *See also under* incense and incensation
tones
   in Holy Week 217, 233, 248, 255 n.98
   in Masses for the Dead 161 nn.30, 42, 270
   official 9, 147
   on other occasions 169, 199, 212 n.15
torches and torchbearers 12 n.25, 82, 89, 126
tract 148, 151, 198, 209
Trium puerorum 74
tunicle 17, 18 n.12, 269 n.8

veil, chalice (offertorium) 10 n.18, 18 n.9, 22, 117, 117 n.1
veil, Gospel lectern 4 n.11, 88, 172
veil, humeral (mantellum):
   colour of 22, 22 n.3
   at Mass 103, 138 n.13, 142
   nature and purpose of 10 n.18, 18 n.9, 177 n.30
veil, nuptial 164
veils in Lent 4, 207, 207 n.1, 261
   in Holy Week 209, 222, 232, 246
vergers 88 n.15, 140, 188, 263
vernacular 52, 163
vessels 10–12
vesting 42, 42 n.13
vestments 17–19, 21–2, 21 n.1
vestry 4, 42 n.13, 191 n.45, 225
   during functions 191 n.41, 204 n.36, 208, 213 n.27, 222, 256 n.117
vigils 197, 199
voice
   on certain days 161, 217, 239, 240
   at High Mass 94, 101, 108, 133
   at Low Mass 42, 43, 45, 53, 53 n.54 n.46, 62 n.42, 72 n.34

weddings 163–70, 165 n.27, 166 n.29, 193 n.2
Westhall 17 n.2
Westminster Abbey 5 n.23, 6 n.25, 110 n.23
Whitsun 266–8
wine 10 n.16

www.ingramcontent.com/pod-product-compliance
Lightning Source LLC
Chambersburg PA
CBHW072121290426
44111CB00012B/1741